CHILDREN OF THE WHALES

Story and Art by Abi Umeda

Volume

4

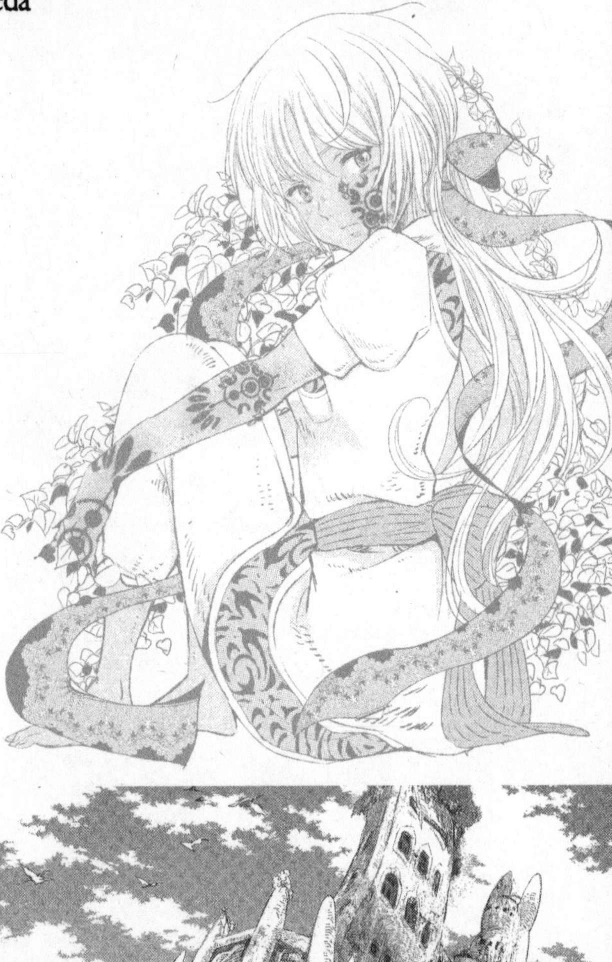

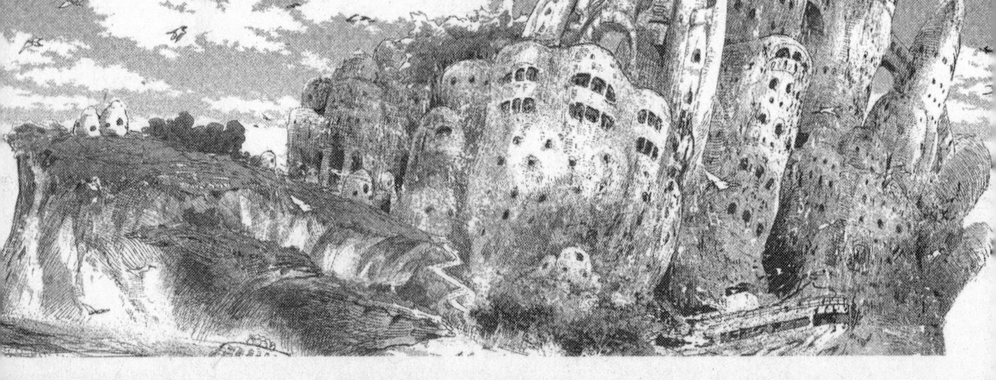

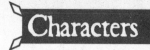

On the Mud Whale

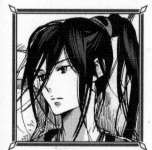

Ouni
(Marked, 16 years old)

A very powerful thymia user and the leader of the Moles, a group of delinquents on the Mud Whale.

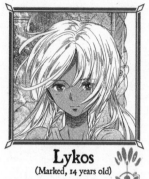

Lykos
(Marked, 14 years old)

A girl from the Allied Empire who comes aboard the Mud Whale. She has a connection with Chakuro.

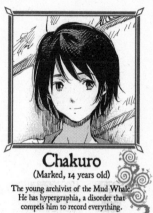

Chakuro
(Marked, 14 years old)

The young archivist of the Mud Whale. He has hypergraphia, a disorder that compels him to record everything.

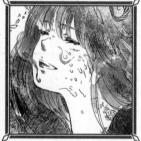

Aima
(???)

She appears to Chakuro after Neri disappears. She calls herself Neri's twin, but...

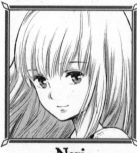

Neri
(???)

Caretaker of the tower where the Committee of Elders lives. She reveals her mysterious, boundless powers to Chakuro.

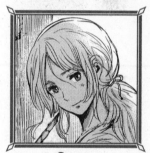

Suou
(Unmarked, 17 years old)

The new mayor of the Mud Whale. He is the leader of the opposition to the imperial attack.

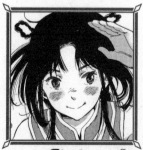

Ginshu
(Marked, 16 years old)

Serves in the Vigilante Corps.

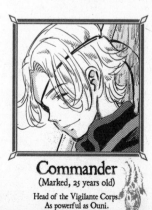

Commander
(Marked, 25 years old)

Head of the Vigilante Corps. As powerful as Ouni.

From the Allied Empire

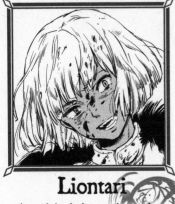

Liontari

An apátheia who has excessive emotions.
He grew up with Lykos.

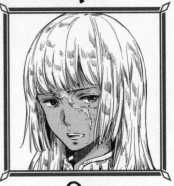

Orca

Commander of the apátheia forces that
attacked the Mud Whale. Lykos's
older brother.

A Record of the Mud Whale and the Sea of Sand

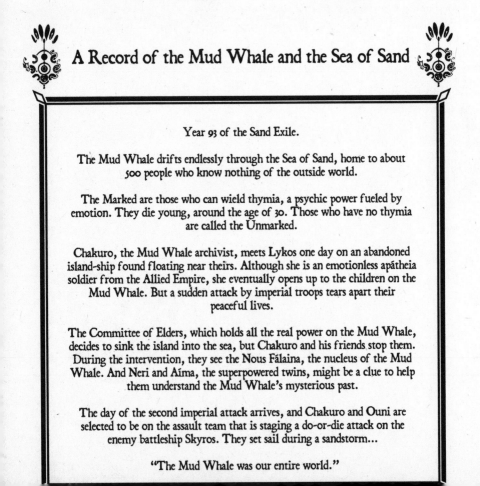

Year 93 of the Sand Exile.

The Mud Whale drifts endlessly through the Sea of Sand, home to about
500 people who know nothing of the outside world.

The Marked are those who can wield thymia, a psychic power fueled by
emotion. They die young, around the age of 30. Those who have no thymia
are called the Unmarked.

Chakuro, the Mud Whale archivist, meets Lykos one day on an abandoned
island-ship found floating near theirs. Although she is an emotionless apátheia
soldier from the Allied Empire, she eventually opens up to the children on the
Mud Whale. But a sudden attack by imperial troops tears apart their
peaceful lives.

The Committee of Elders, which holds all the real power on the Mud Whale,
decides to sink the island into the sea, but Chakuro and his friends stop them.
During the intervention, they see the Nous Fálaina, the nucleus of the Mud
Whale. And Neri and Aíma, the superpowered twins, might be a clue to help
them understand the Mud Whale's mysterious past.

The day of the second imperial attack arrives, and Chakuro and Ouni are
selected to be on the assault team that is staging a do-or-die attack on the
enemy battleship Skyros. They set sail during a sandstorm...

"The Mud Whale was our entire world."

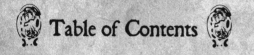 # Table of Contents

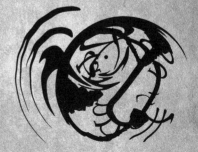

Chapter 13
Sins of the Flower

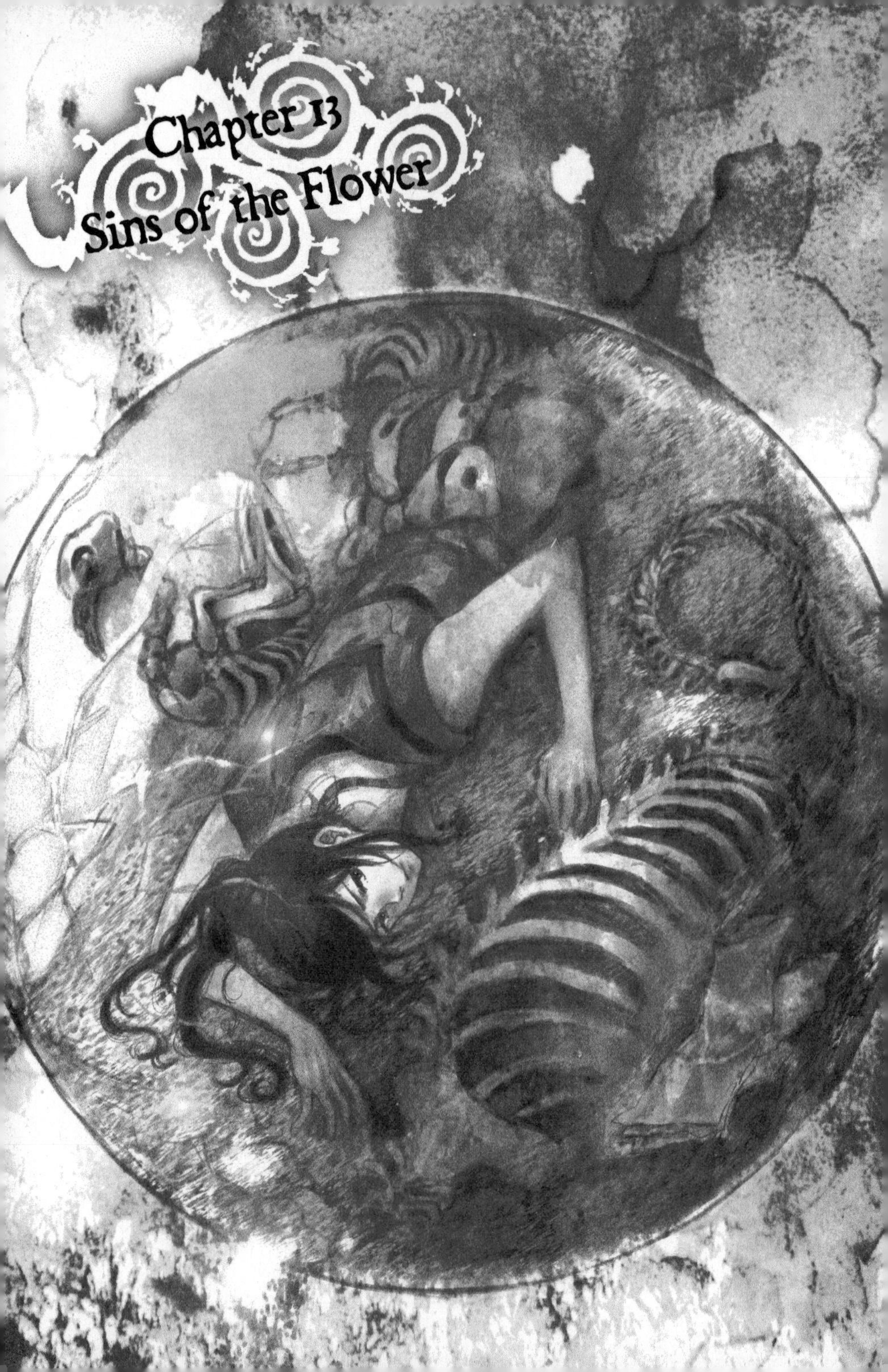

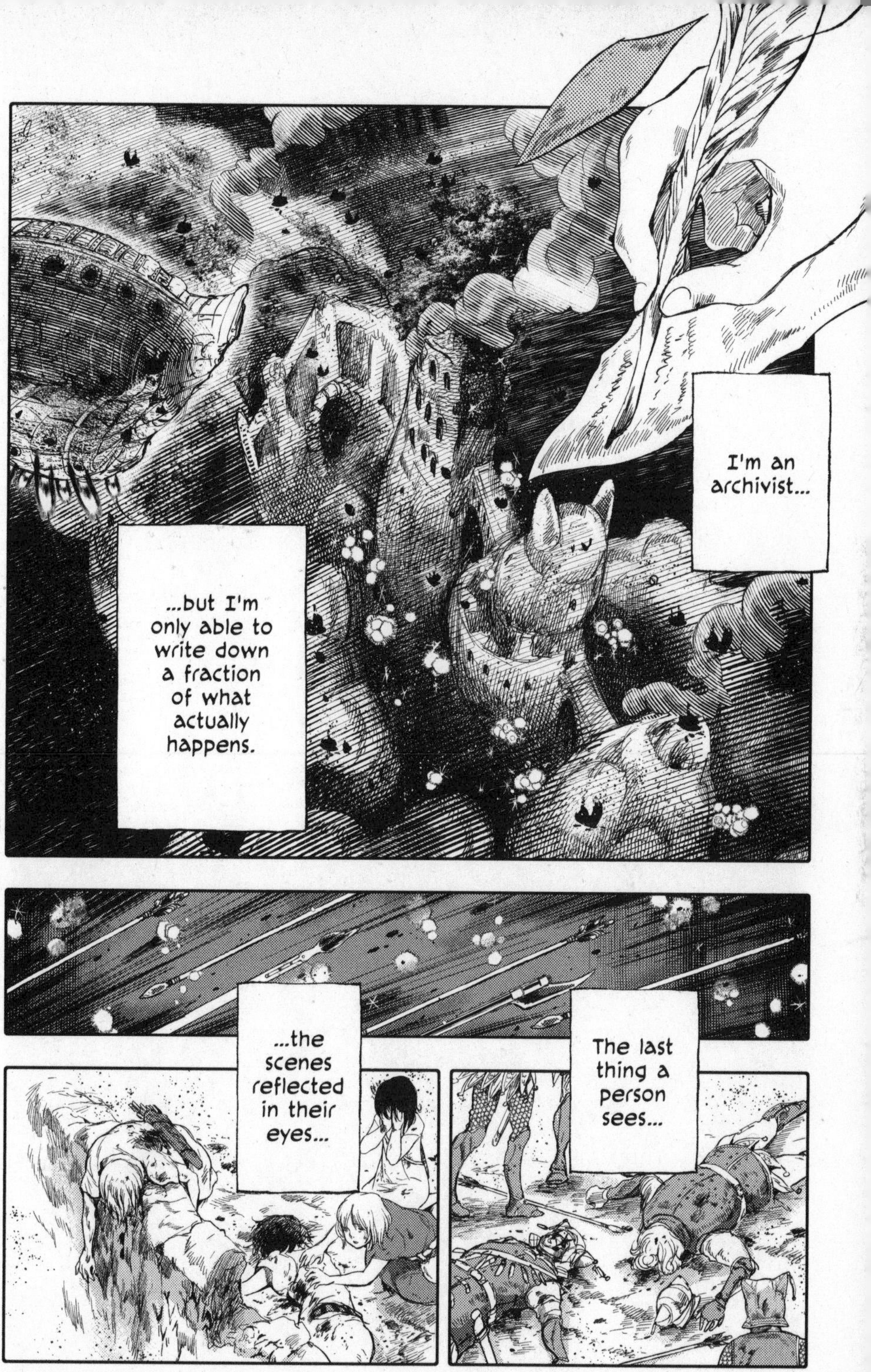
I'm an archivist...
...but I'm only able to write down a fraction of what actually happens.
The last thing a person sees...
...the scenes reflected in their eyes...

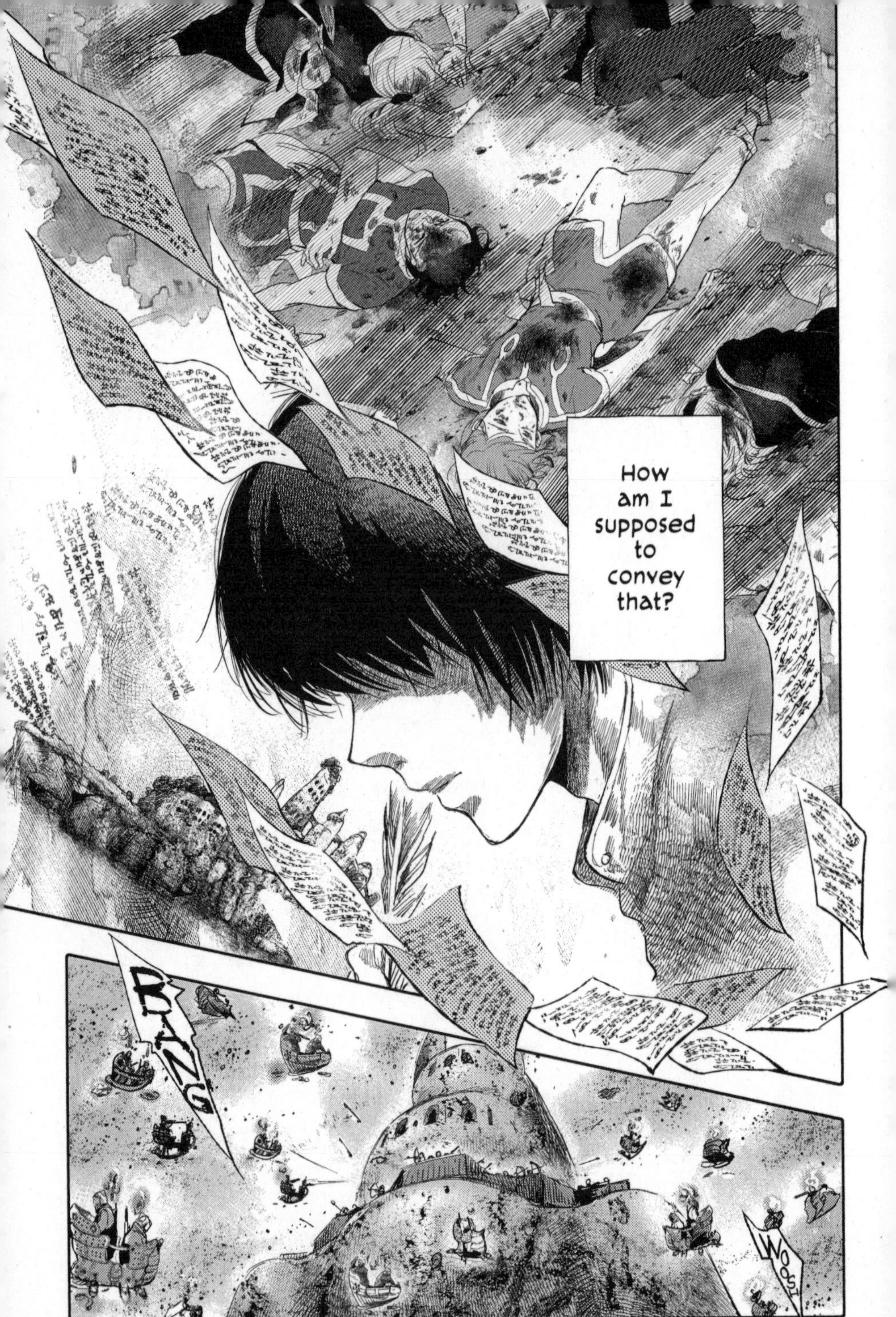
How am I supposed to convey that?
BANG
WOOSH

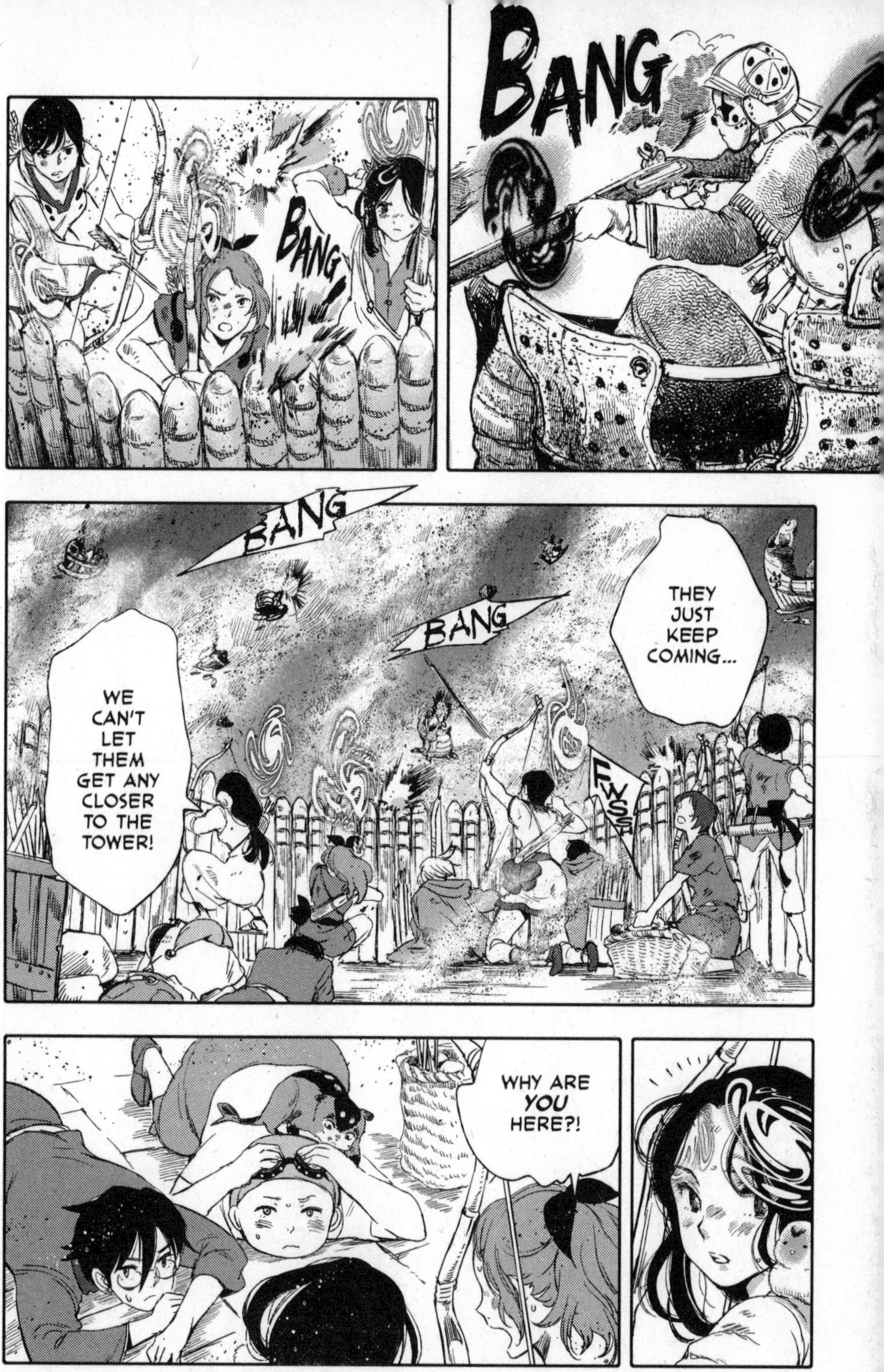
BANG
BANG
BANG
THEY JUST KEEP COMING...
BANG
FWSSH
WE CAN'T LET THEM GET ANY CLOSER TO THE TOWER!
WHY ARE *YOU* HERE?!

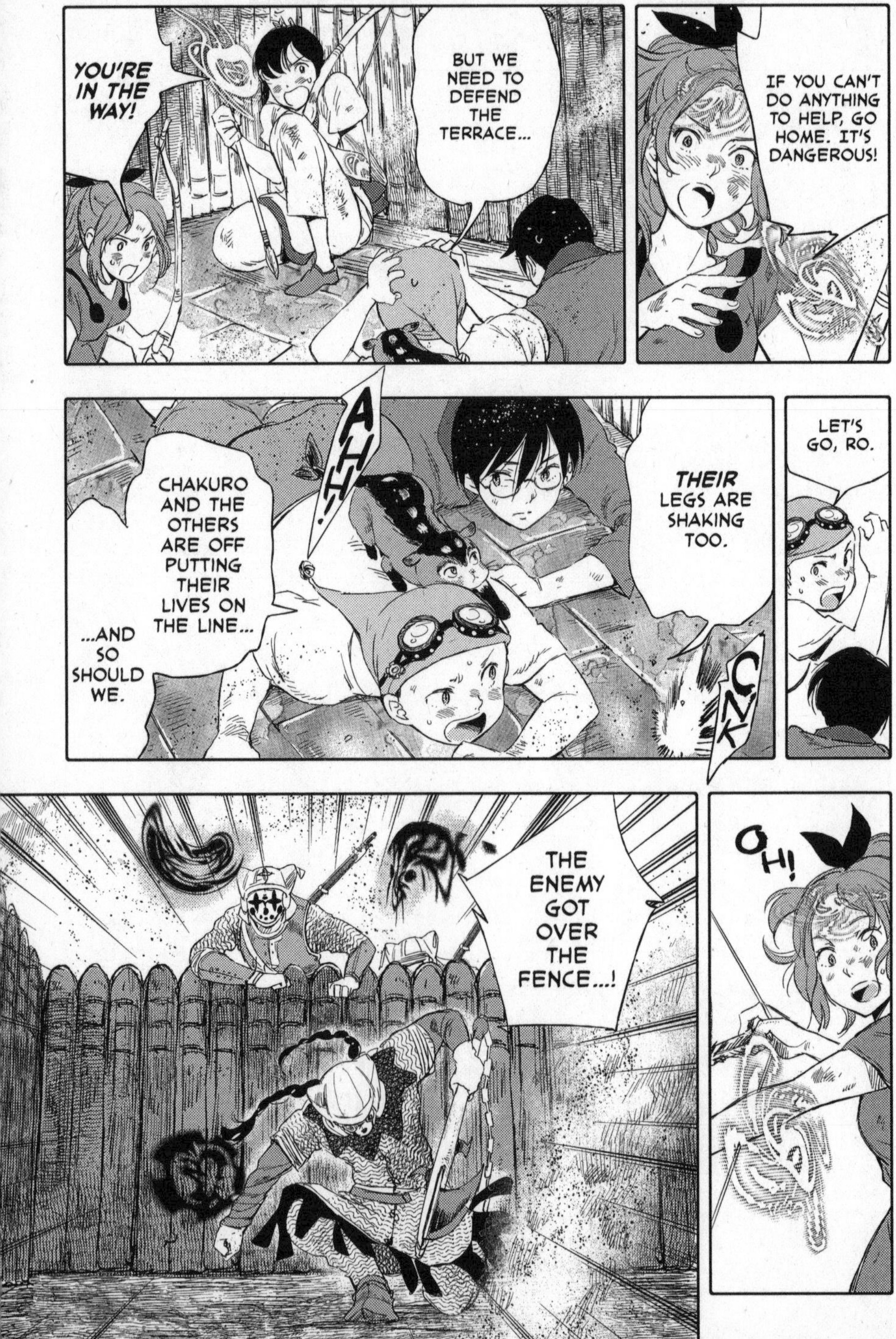
IF YOU CAN'T DO ANYTHING TO HELP, GO HOME. IT'S DANGEROUS!
BUT WE NEED TO DEFEND THE TERRACE...
YOU'RE IN THE WAY!
LET'S GO, RO.
THEIR LEGS ARE SHAKING TOO.
AHH!
CNK
CHAKURO AND THE OTHERS ARE OFF PUTTING THEIR LIVES ON THE LINE...
...AND SO SHOULD WE.
OH!
THE ENEMY GOT OVER THE FENCE...!

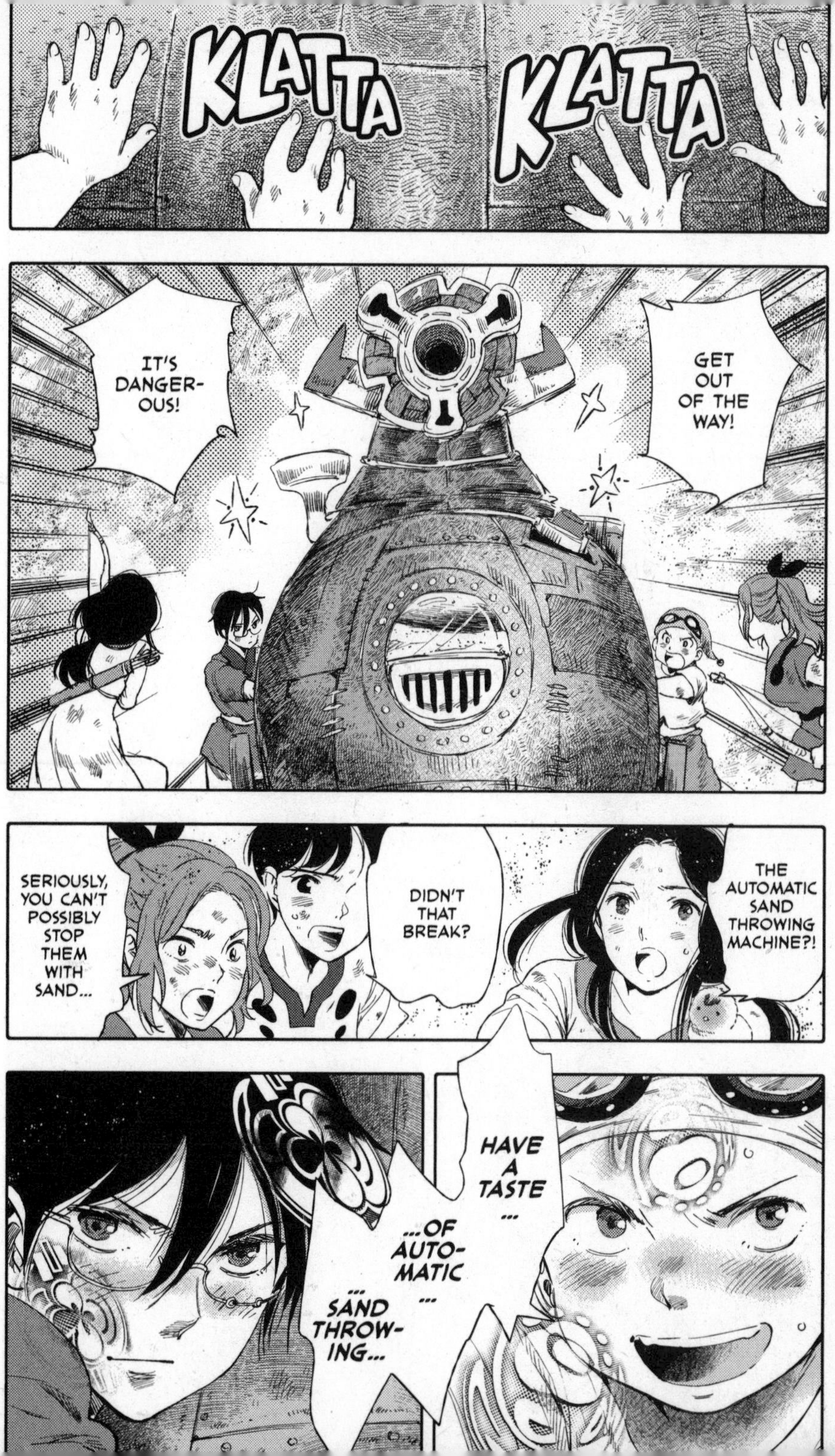
KLATTA
KLATTA
GET OUT OF THE WAY!
IT'S DANGER-OUS!
THE AUTOMATIC SAND THROWING MACHINE?!
DIDN'T THAT BREAK?
SERIOUSLY, YOU CAN'T POSSIBLY STOP THEM WITH SAND...
HAVE A TASTE...
...OF AUTO-MATIC...
...SAND THROW-ING...

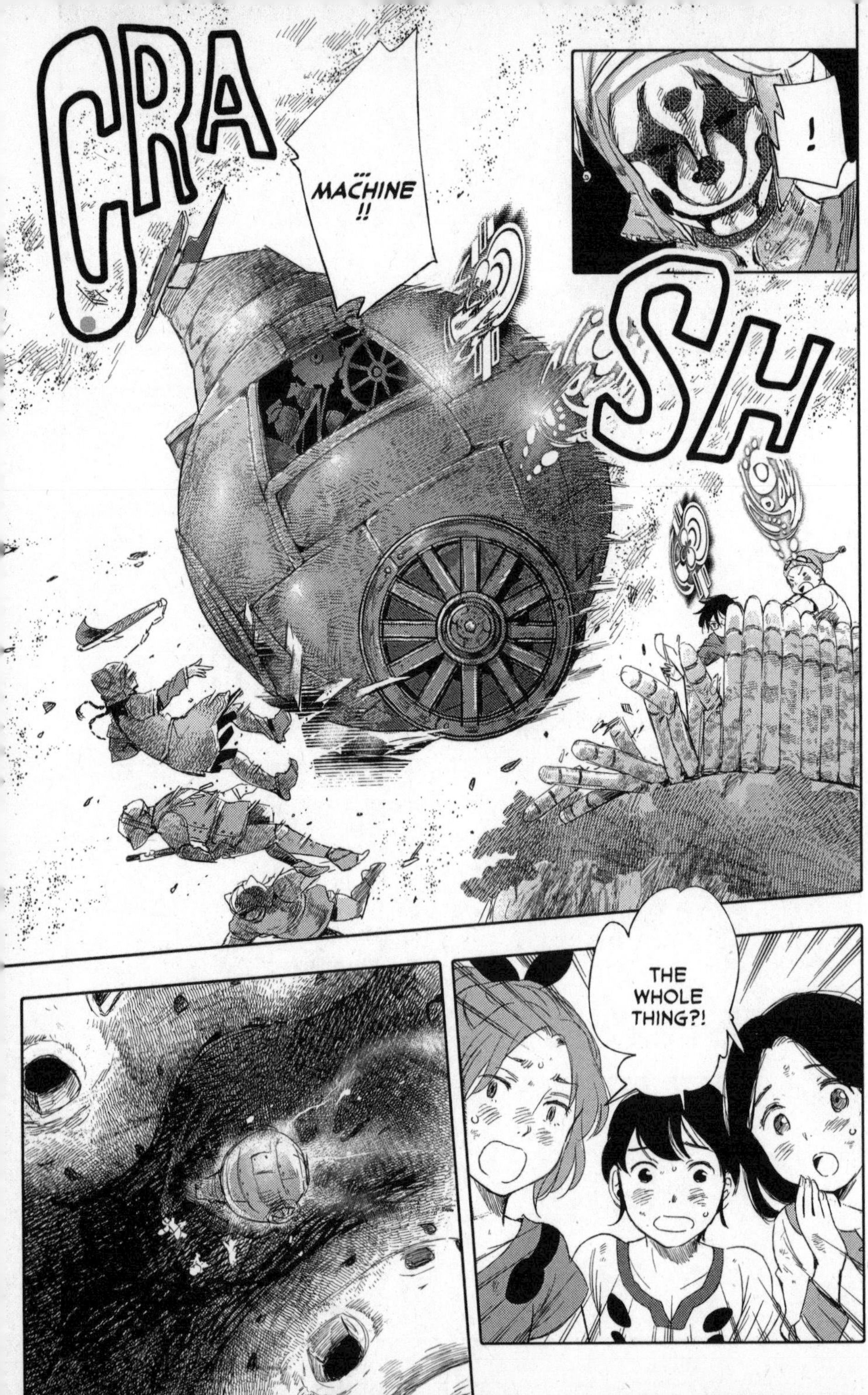
!
...MACHINE!!
CRASH
THE WHOLE THING?!

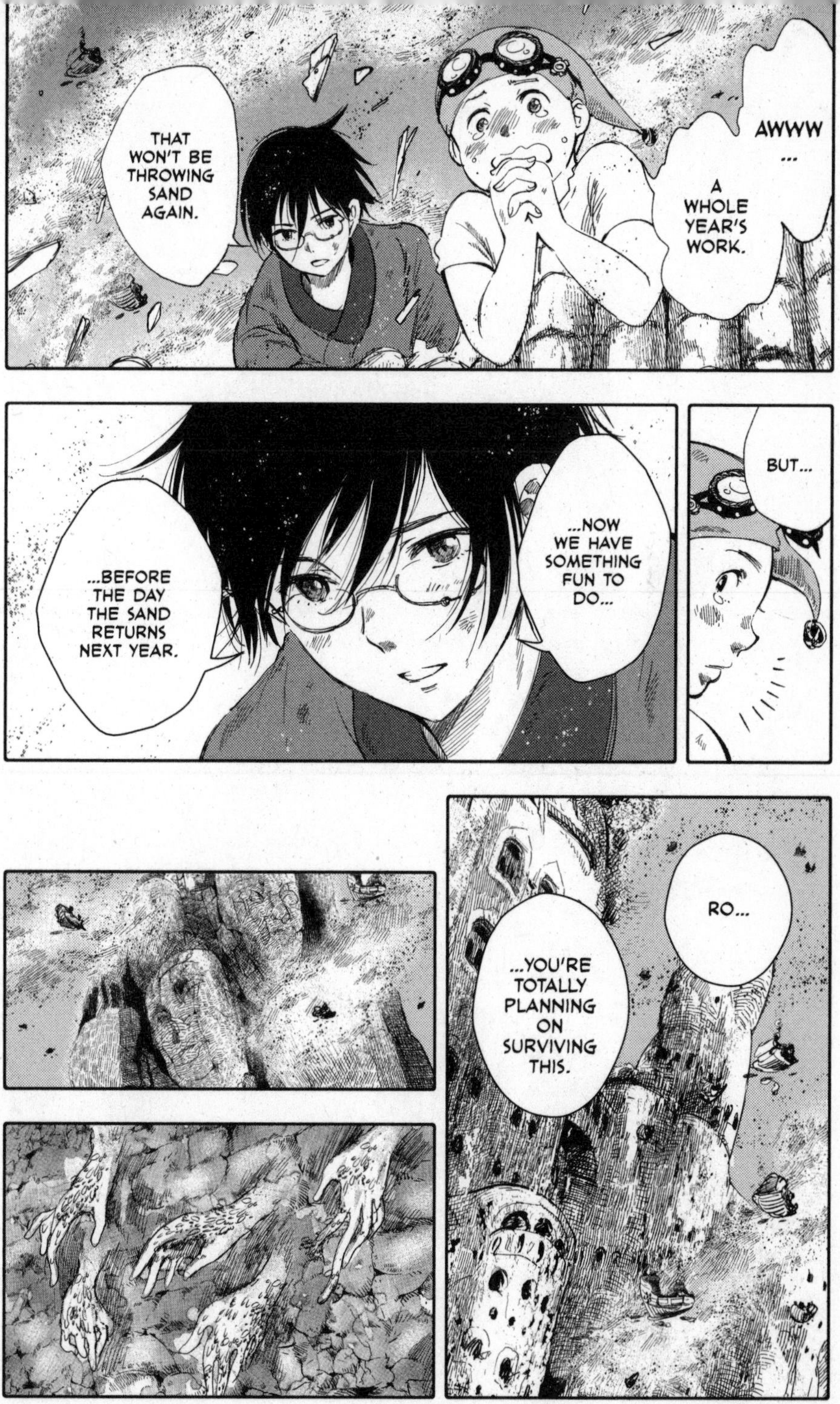
AWWW...
A WHOLE YEAR'S WORK.
THAT WON'T BE THROWING SAND AGAIN.
BUT...
...NOW WE HAVE SOMETHING FUN TO DO...
...BEFORE THE DAY THE SAND RETURNS NEXT YEAR.
RO...
...YOU'RE TOTALLY PLANNING ON SURVIVING THIS.

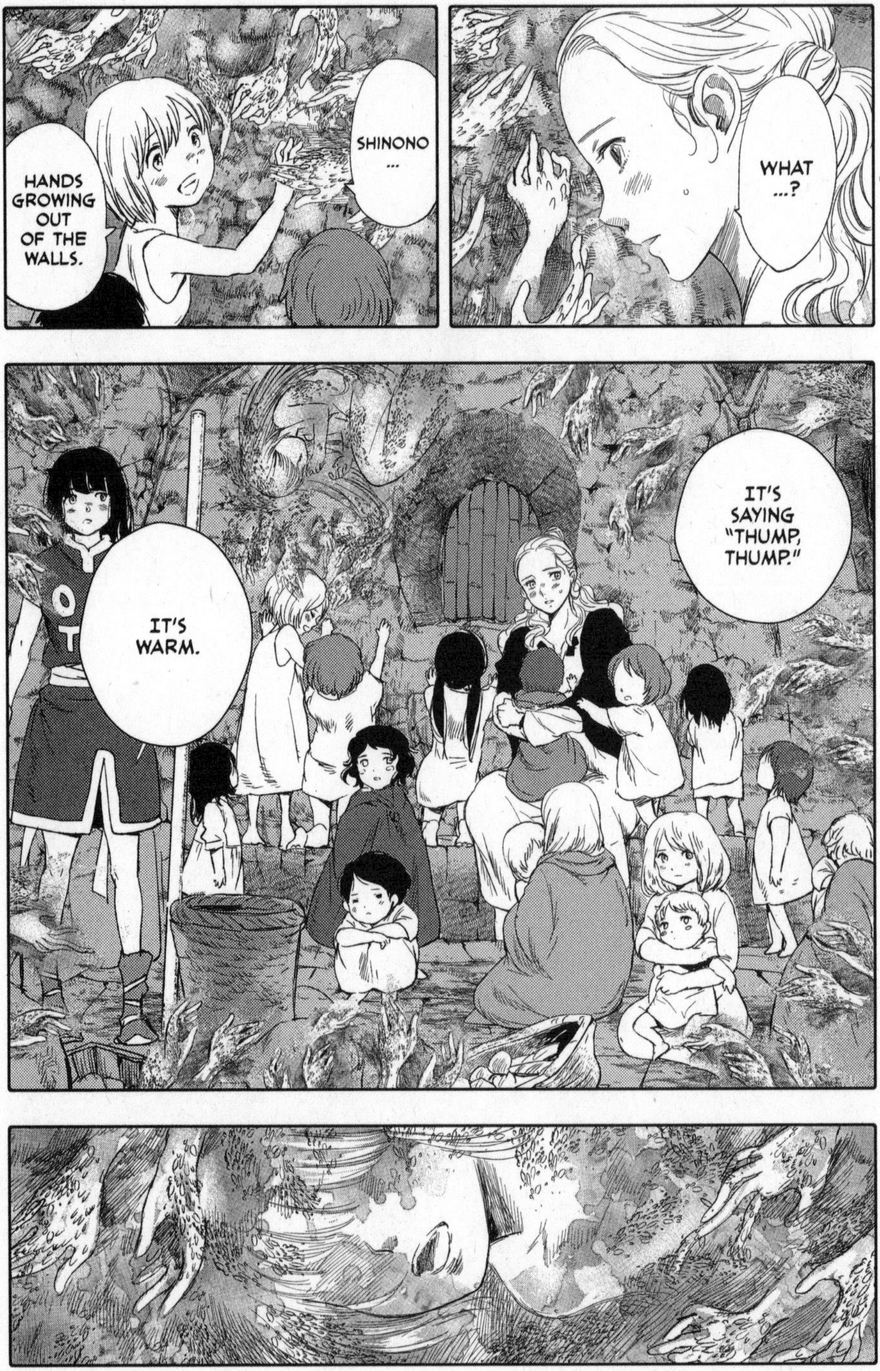
WHAT ...?
SHINONO ...
HANDS GROWING OUT OF THE WALLS.
IT'S SAYING "THUMP, THUMP."
IT'S WARM.

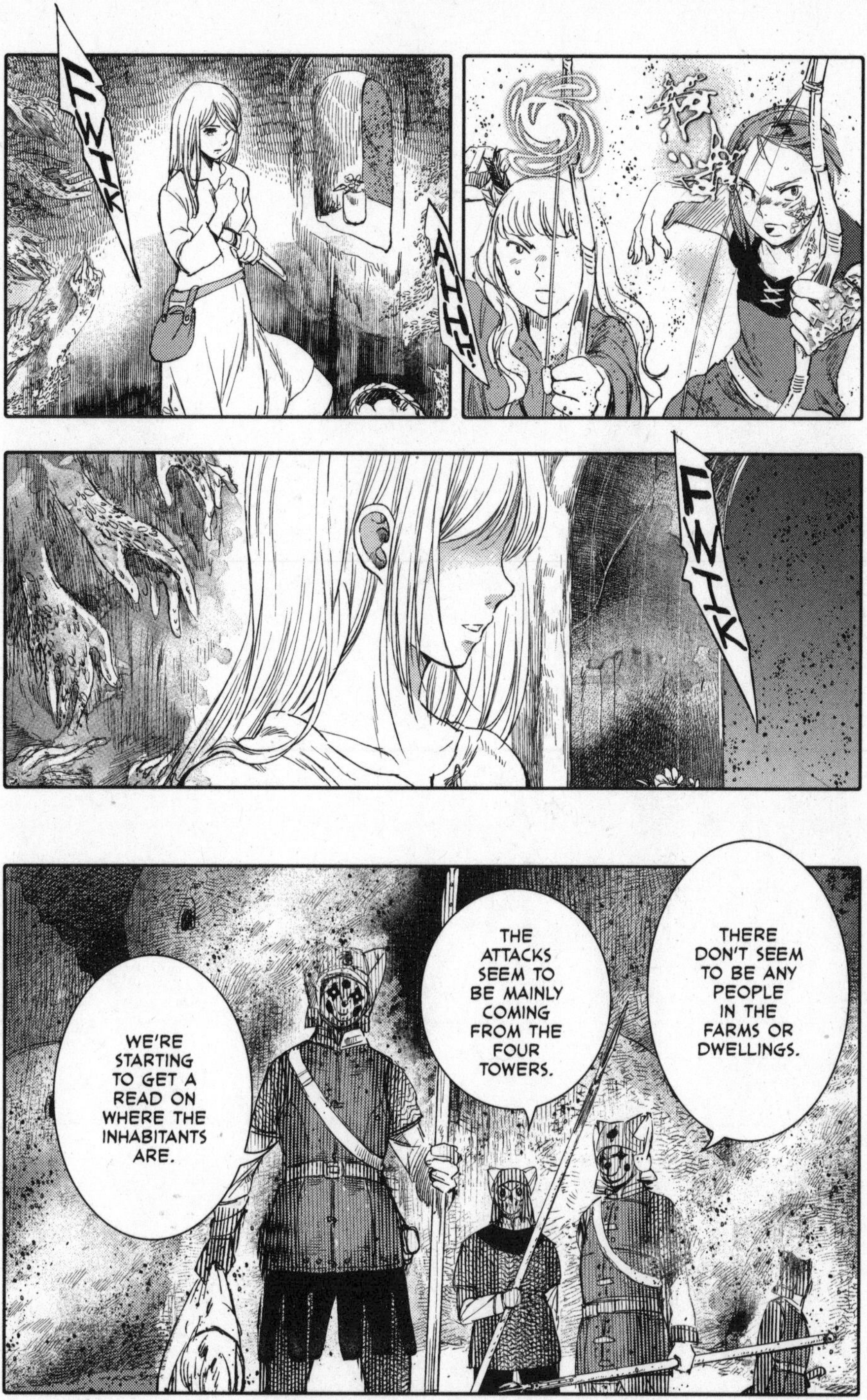
AHHH!!
FWIK
FWIK
THERE DON'T SEEM TO BE ANY PEOPLE IN THE FARMS OR DWELLINGS.
THE ATTACKS SEEM TO BE MAINLY COMING FROM THE FOUR TOWERS.
WE'RE STARTING TO GET A READ ON WHERE THE INHABITANTS ARE.

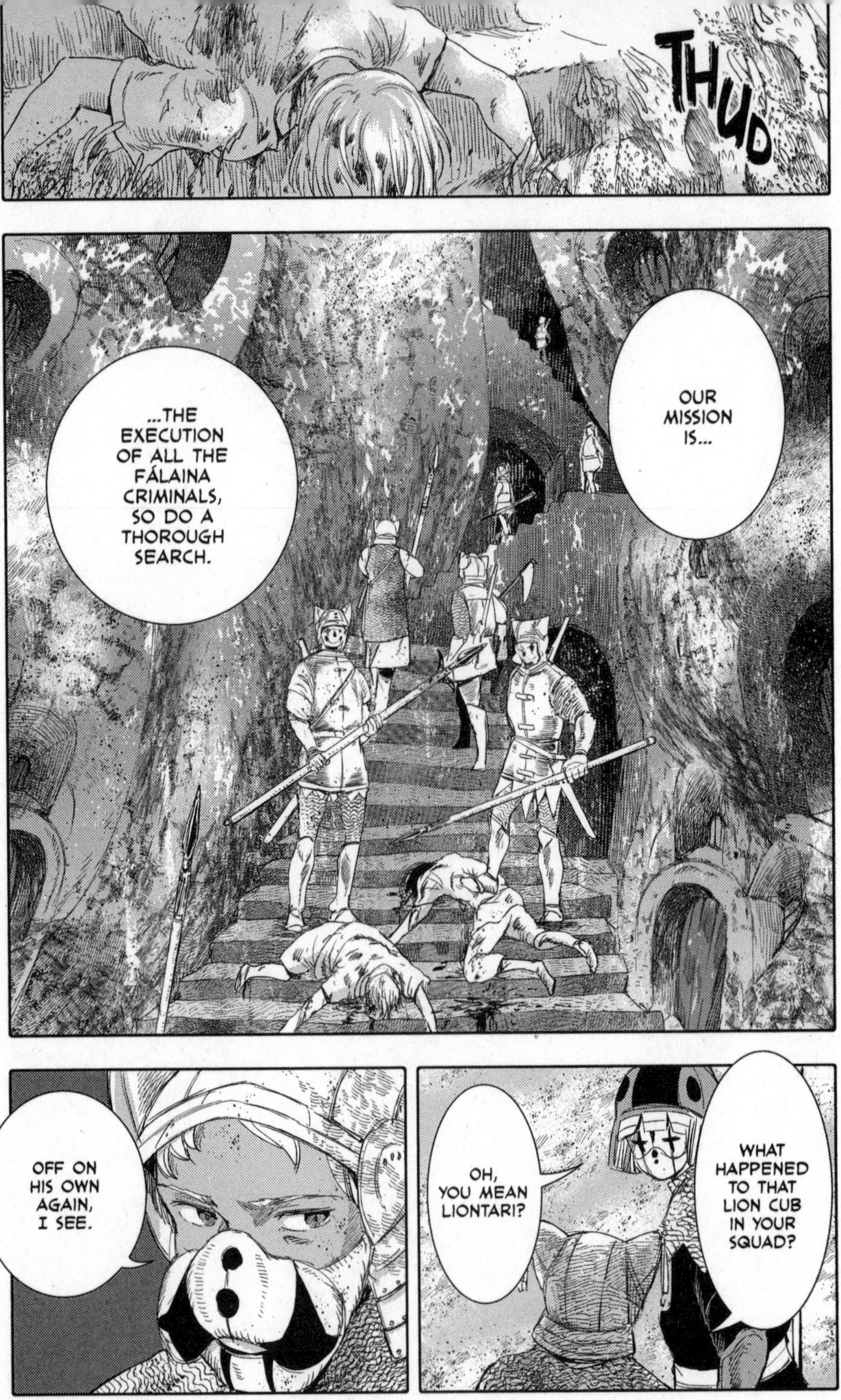
THUD
OUR MISSION IS...
...THE EXECUTION OF ALL THE FÁLAINA CRIMINALS, SO DO A THOROUGH SEARCH.
WHAT HAPPENED TO THAT LION CUB IN YOUR SQUAD?
OH, YOU MEAN LIONTARI?
OFF ON HIS OWN AGAIN, I SEE.

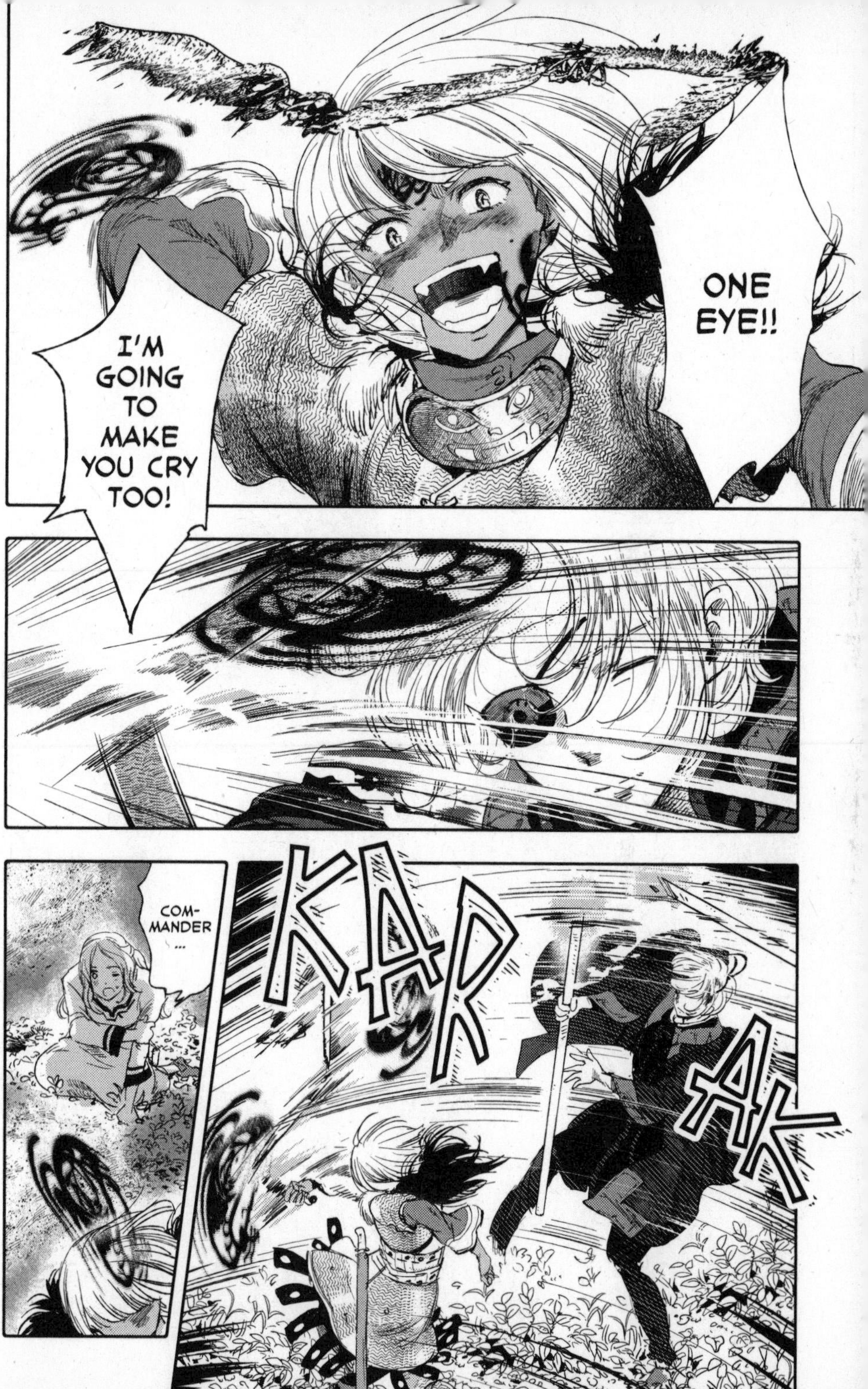
ONE EYE!!
I'M GOING TO MAKE YOU CRY TOO!
KARAK
COM-MANDER ...

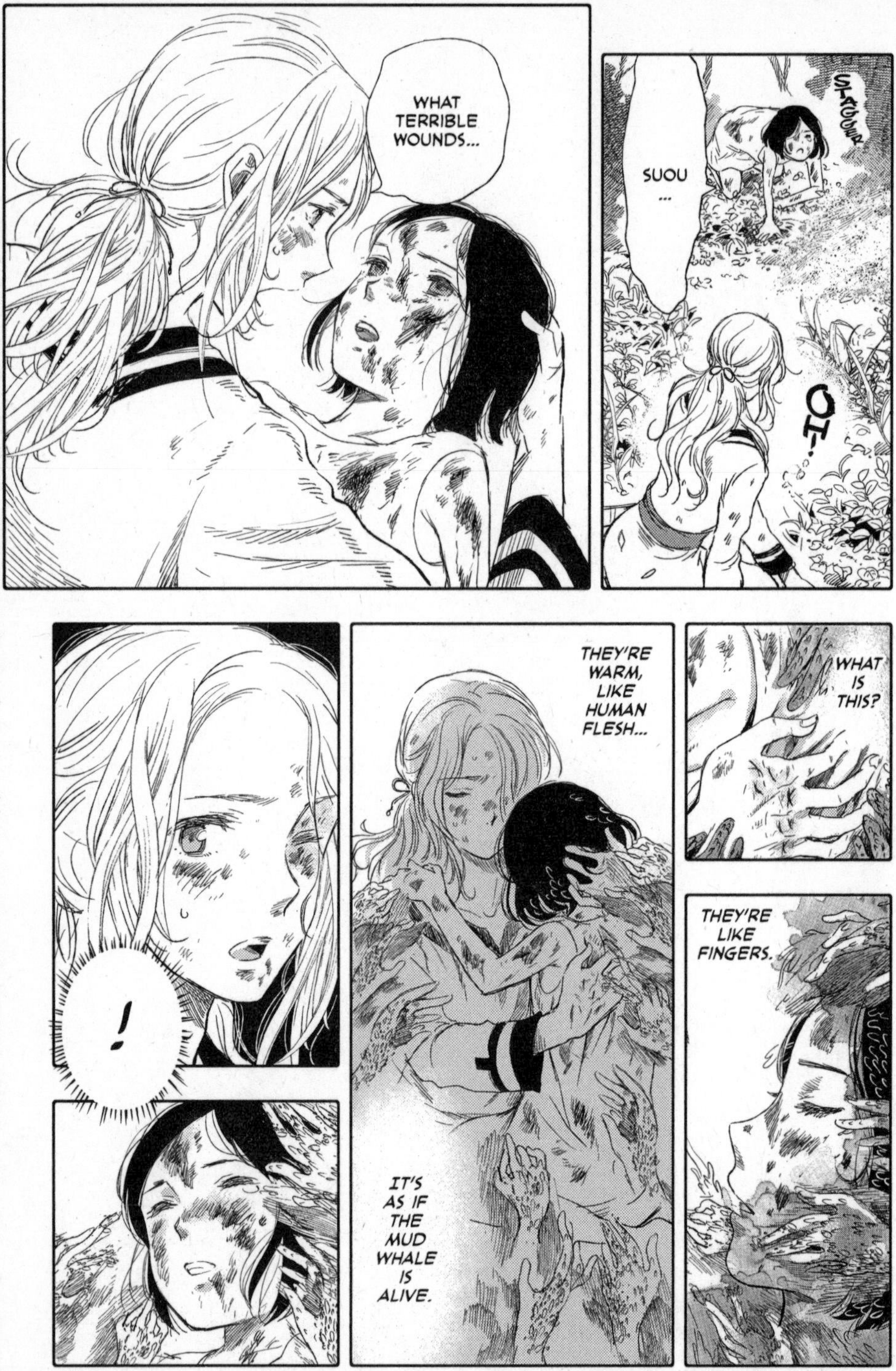
STAGGER
SUOU ...
OH!
WHAT TERRIBLE WOUNDS...
WHAT IS THIS?
THEY'RE LIKE FINGERS.
THEY'RE WARM, LIKE HUMAN FLESH...
IT'S AS IF THE MUD WHALE IS ALIVE.
!

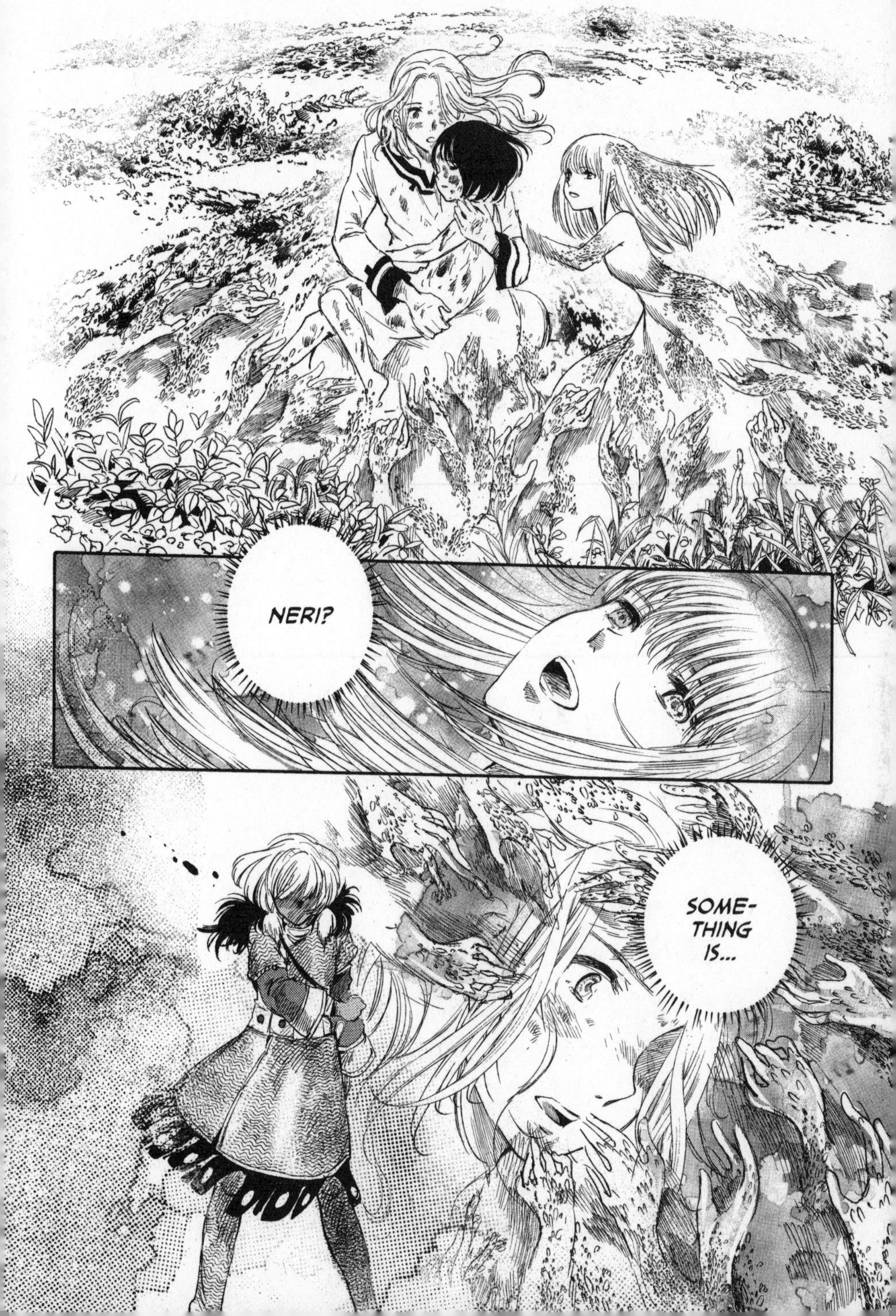
NERI?
SOME-THING IS...

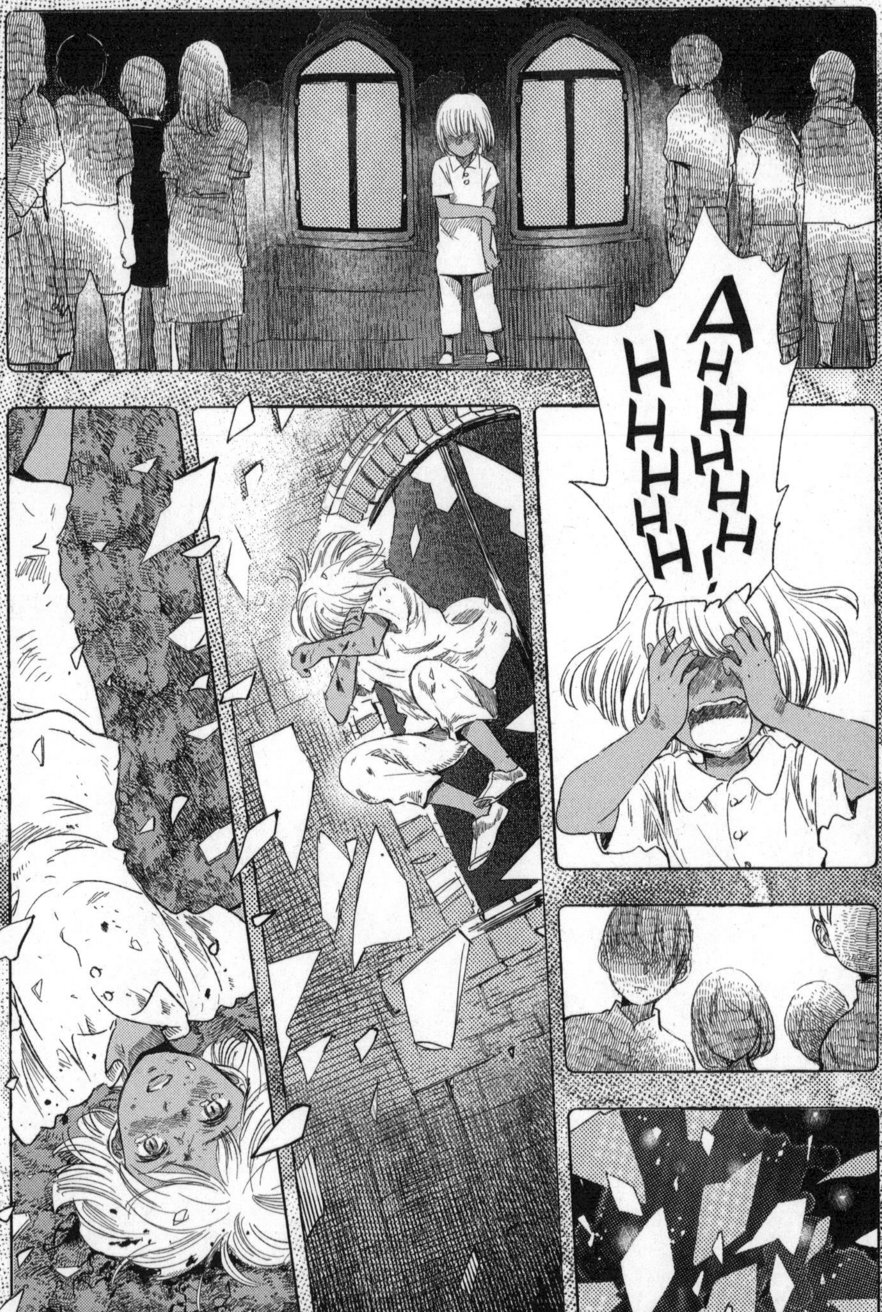
AHHHHHHHHHHH!

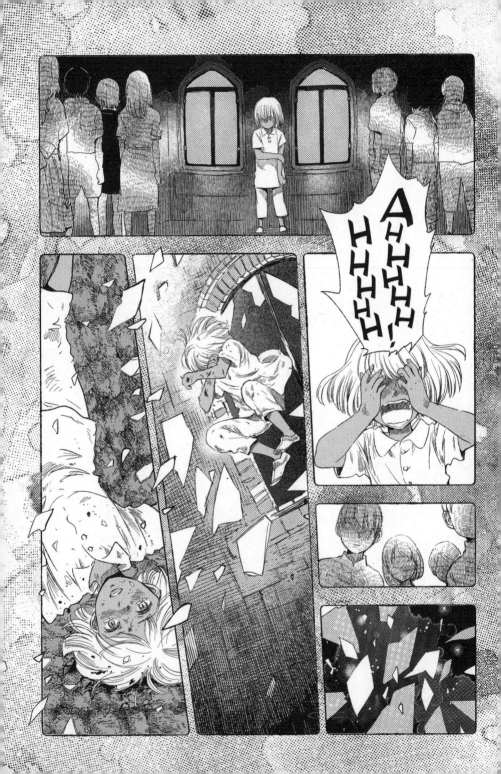

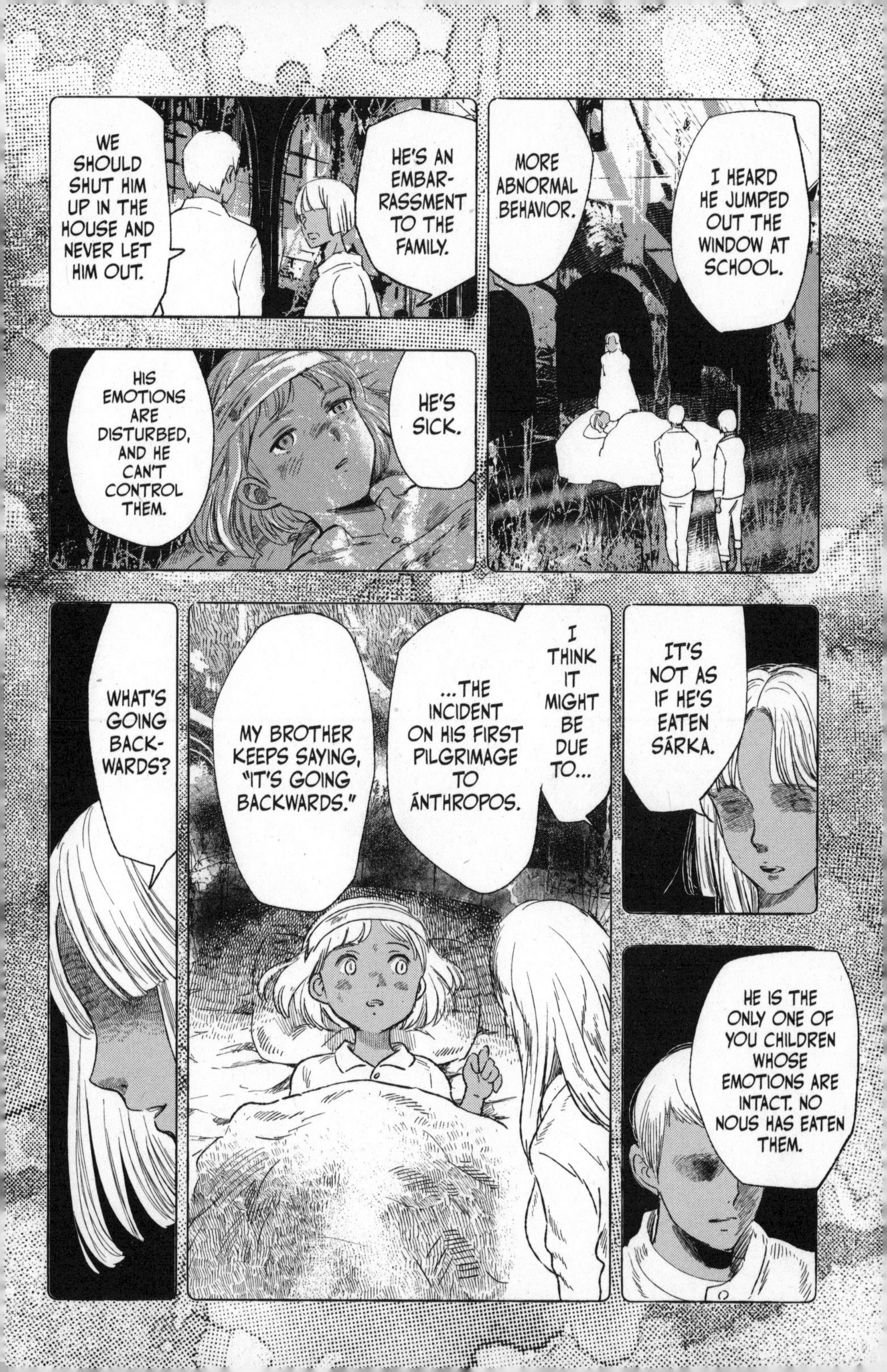
I HEARD HE JUMPED OUT THE WINDOW AT SCHOOL.
MORE ABNORMAL BEHAVIOR.
HE'S AN EMBAR-RASSMENT TO THE FAMILY.
WE SHOULD SHUT HIM UP IN THE HOUSE AND NEVER LET HIM OUT.
HE'S SICK.
HIS EMOTIONS ARE DISTURBED, AND HE CAN'T CONTROL THEM.
IT'S NOT AS IF HE'S EATEN SÁRKA.
HE IS THE ONLY ONE OF YOU CHILDREN WHOSE EMOTIONS ARE INTACT. NO NOUS HAS EATEN THEM.
I THINK IT MIGHT BE DUE TO...
...THE INCIDENT ON HIS FIRST PILGRIMAGE TO ÁNTHROPOS.
MY BROTHER KEEPS SAYING, "IT'S GOING BACKWARDS."
WHAT'S GOING BACKWARDS?

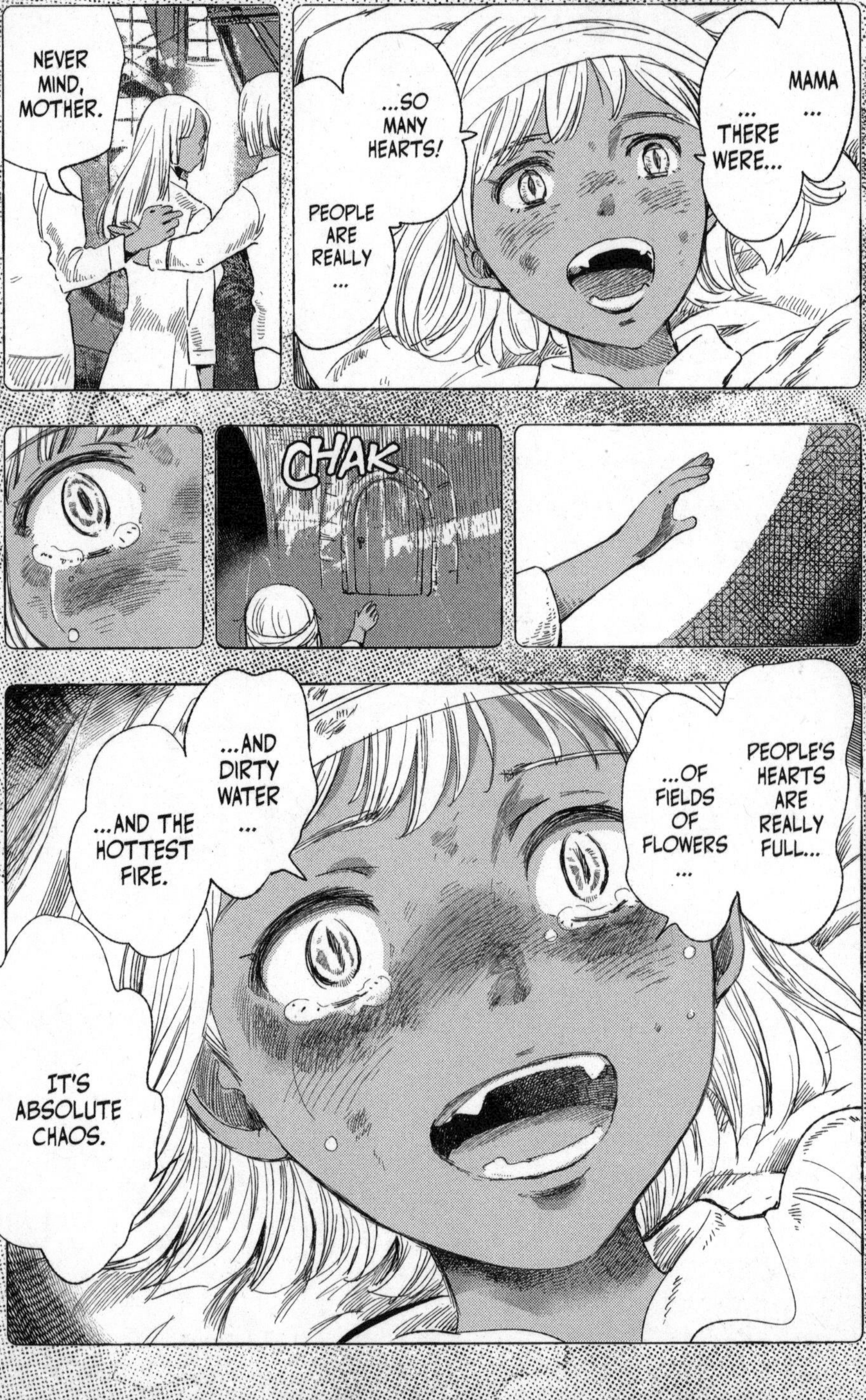
MAMA... THERE WERE...
...SO MANY HEARTS!
PEOPLE ARE REALLY...
NEVER MIND, MOTHER.
CHAK
PEOPLE'S HEARTS ARE REALLY FULL...
...OF FIELDS OF FLOWERS...
...AND DIRTY WATER...
...AND THE HOTTEST FIRE.
IT'S ABSOLUTE CHAOS.

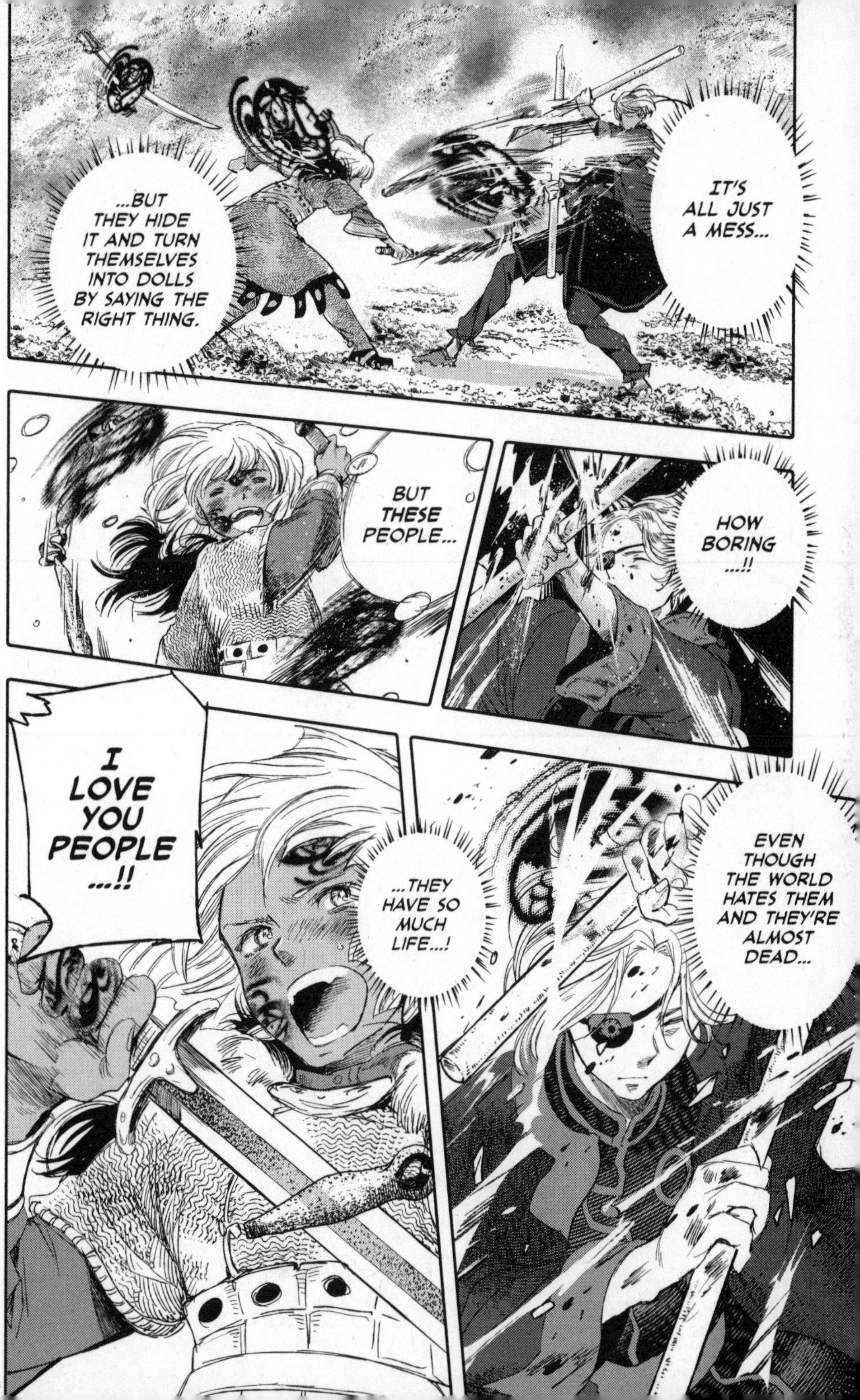
IT'S ALL JUST A MESS...
...BUT THEY HIDE IT AND TURN THEMSELVES INTO DOLLS BY SAYING THE RIGHT THING.
HOW BORING ...!!
BUT THESE PEOPLE...
EVEN THOUGH THE WORLD HATES THEM AND THEY'RE ALMOST DEAD...
...THEY HAVE SO MUCH LIFE...!
I LOVE YOU PEOPLE ...!!

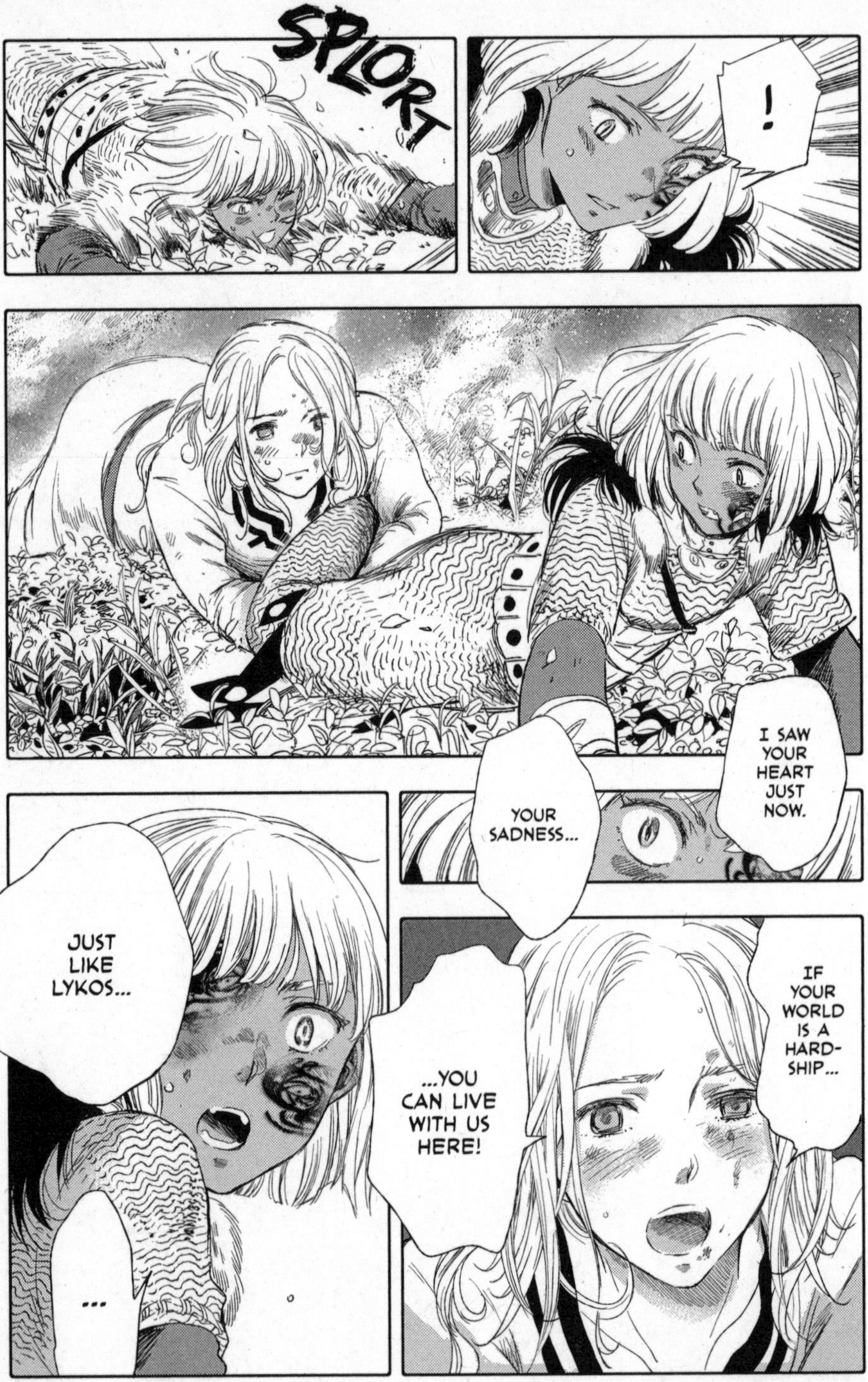
!
SPLORT
I SAW YOUR HEART JUST NOW.
YOUR SADNESS...
IF YOUR WORLD IS A HARDSHIP...
...YOU CAN LIVE WITH US HERE!
JUST LIKE LYKOS...
...

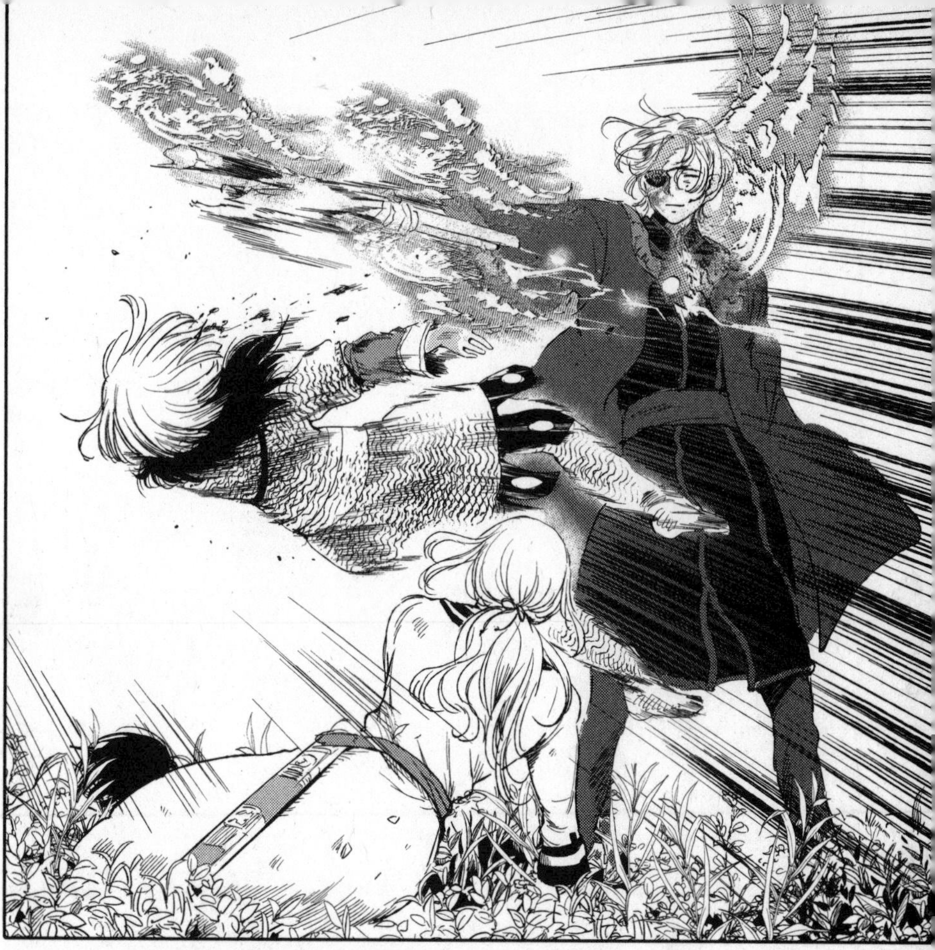

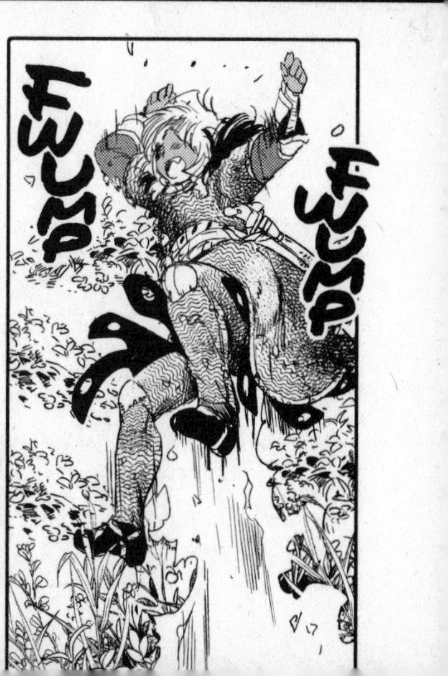
FWUMP
FWUMP

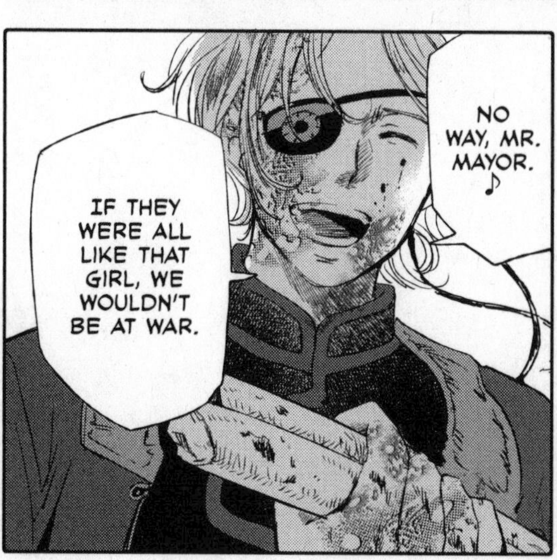
NO WAY, MR. MAYOR. ♪
IF THEY WERE ALL LIKE THAT GIRL, WE WOULDN'T BE AT WAR.

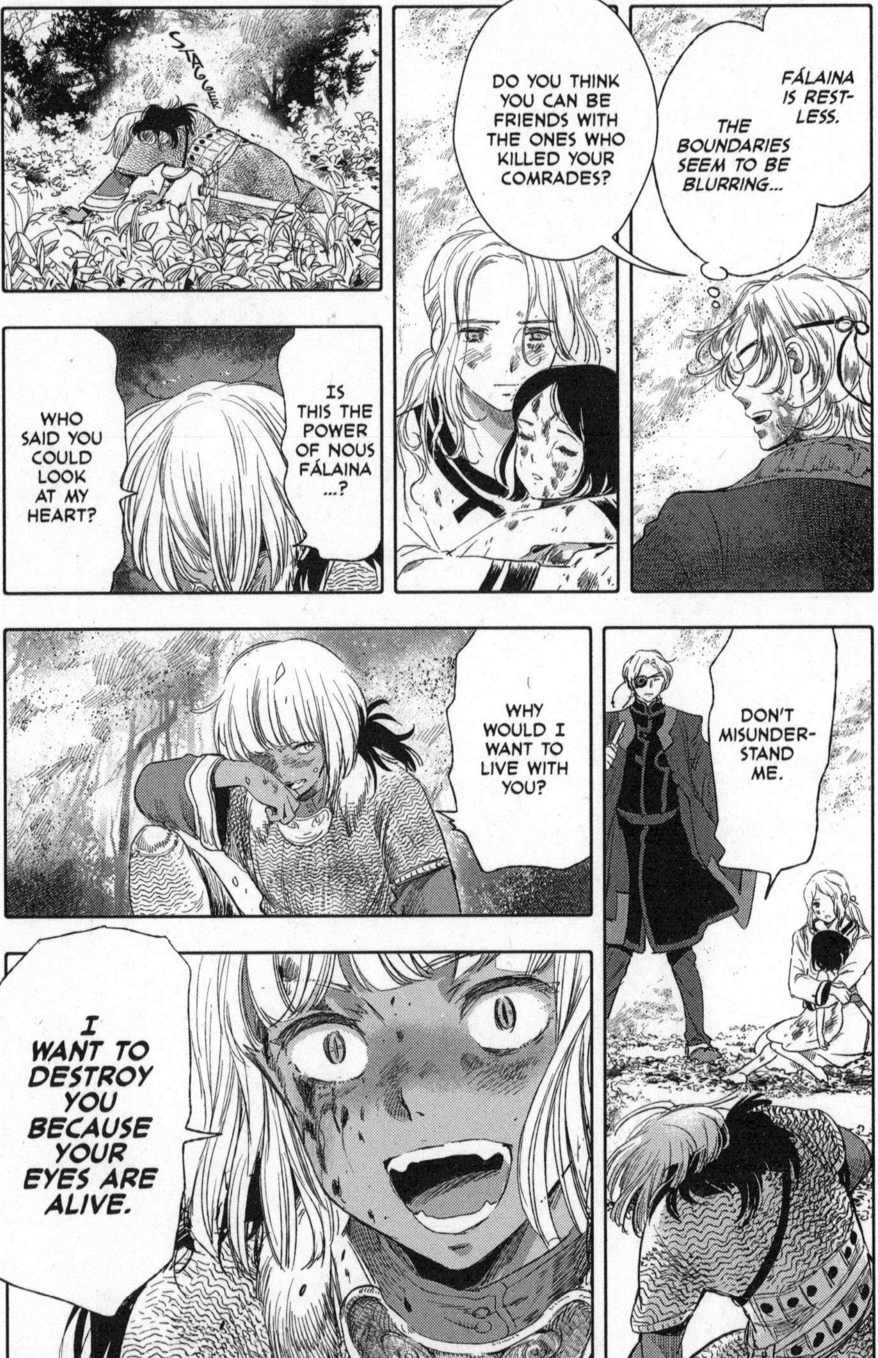
FÁLAINA IS REST-LESS.
THE BOUNDARIES SEEM TO BE BLURRING...
DO YOU THINK YOU CAN BE FRIENDS WITH THE ONES WHO KILLED YOUR COMRADES?
IS THIS THE POWER OF NOUS FÁLAINA ...?
WHO SAID YOU COULD LOOK AT MY HEART?
DON'T MISUNDER-STAND ME.
WHY WOULD I WANT TO LIVE WITH YOU?
I WANT TO DESTROY YOU BECAUSE YOUR EYES ARE ALIVE.

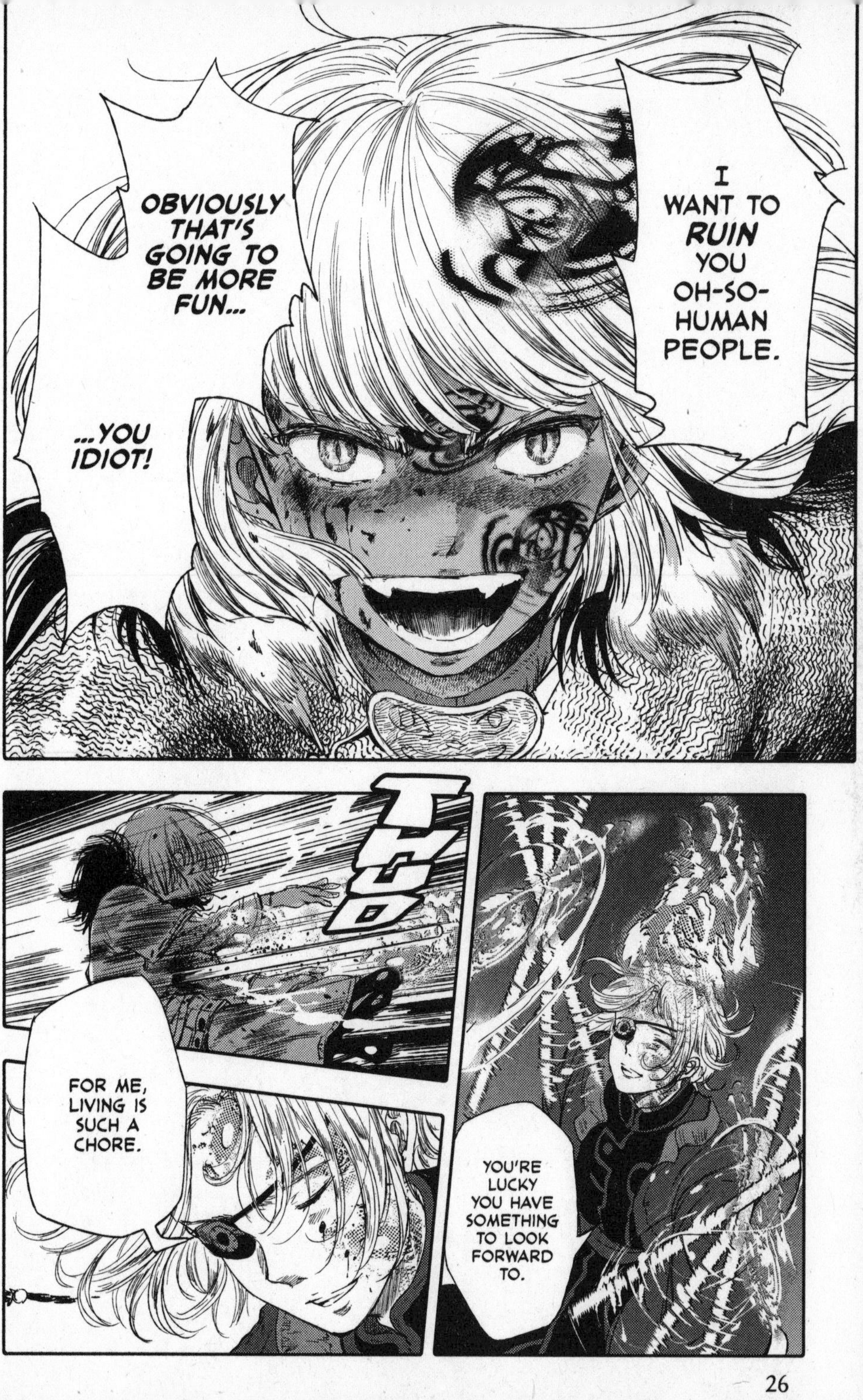
I WANT TO RUIN YOU OH-SO-HUMAN PEOPLE.
OBVIOUSLY THAT'S GOING TO BE MORE FUN...
...YOU IDIOT!
YOU'RE LUCKY YOU HAVE SOMETHING TO LOOK FORWARD TO.
THUD
FOR ME, LIVING IS SUCH A CHORE.

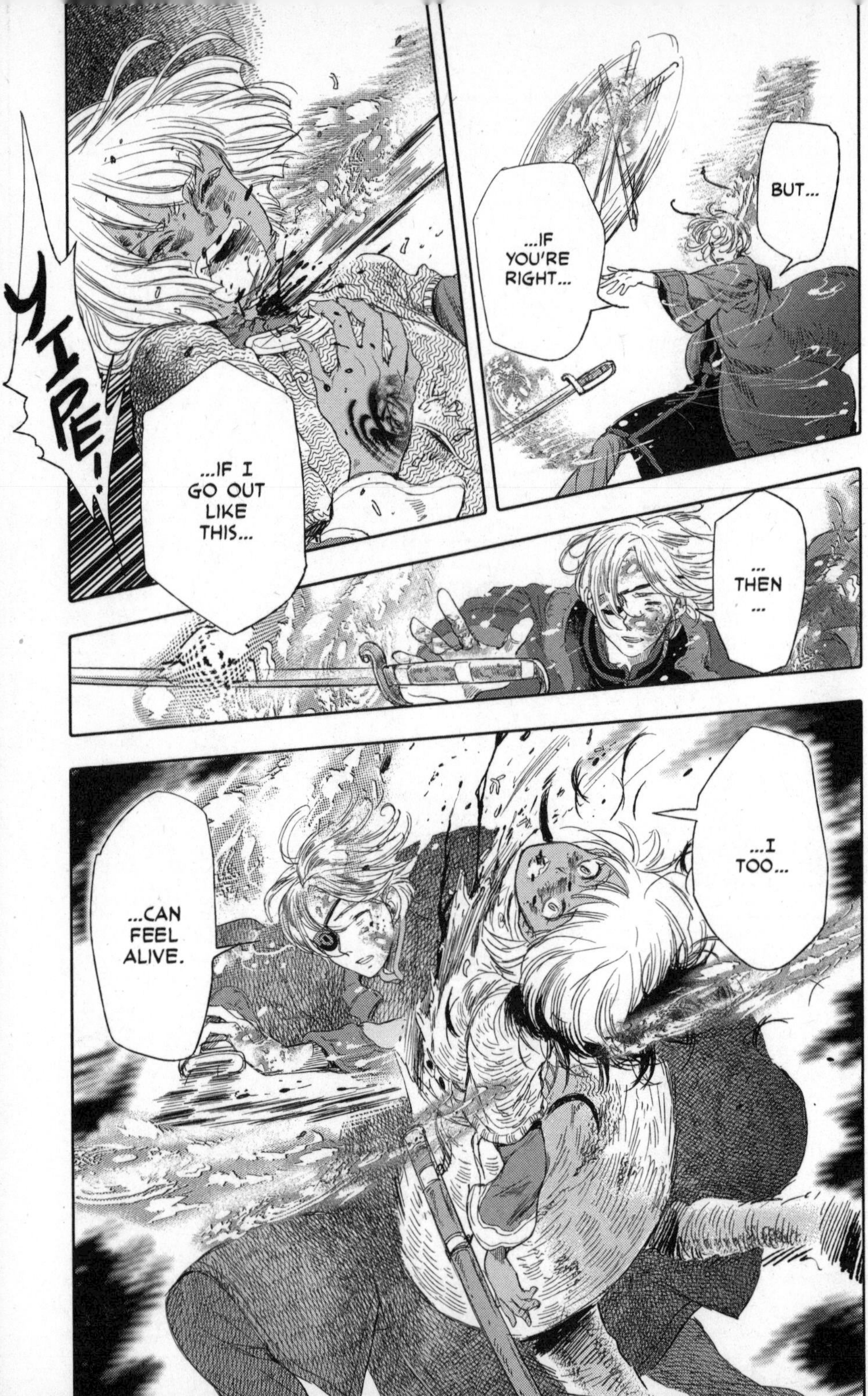
BUT...
...IF YOU'RE RIGHT...
YIPE!
...IF I GO OUT LIKE THIS...
...THEN...
...I TOO...
...CAN FEEL ALIVE.

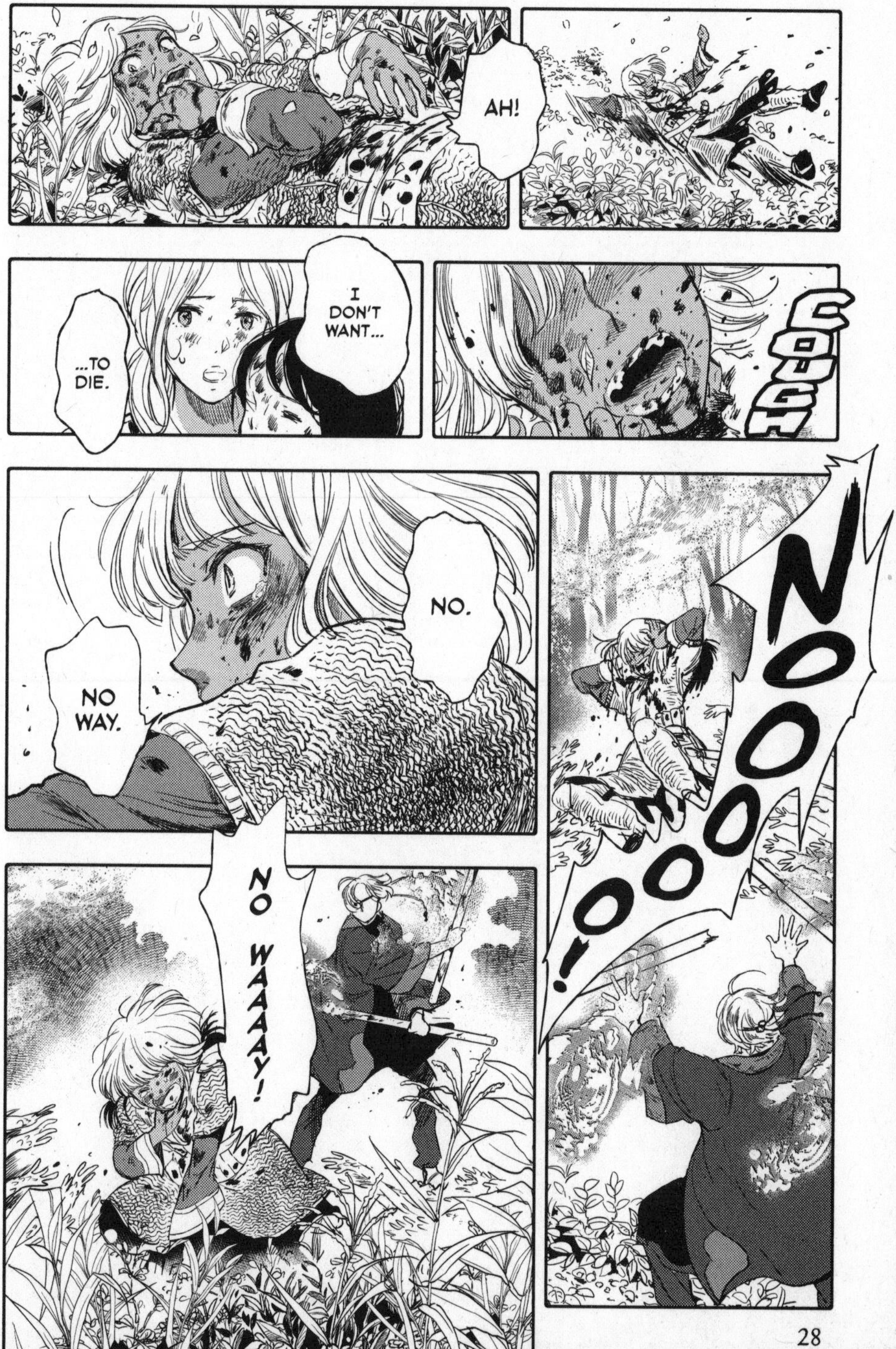
AH!
COUGH
I DON'T WANT...
...TO DIE.
NOOOOOO!
NO.
NO WAY.
NO WAAAAY!

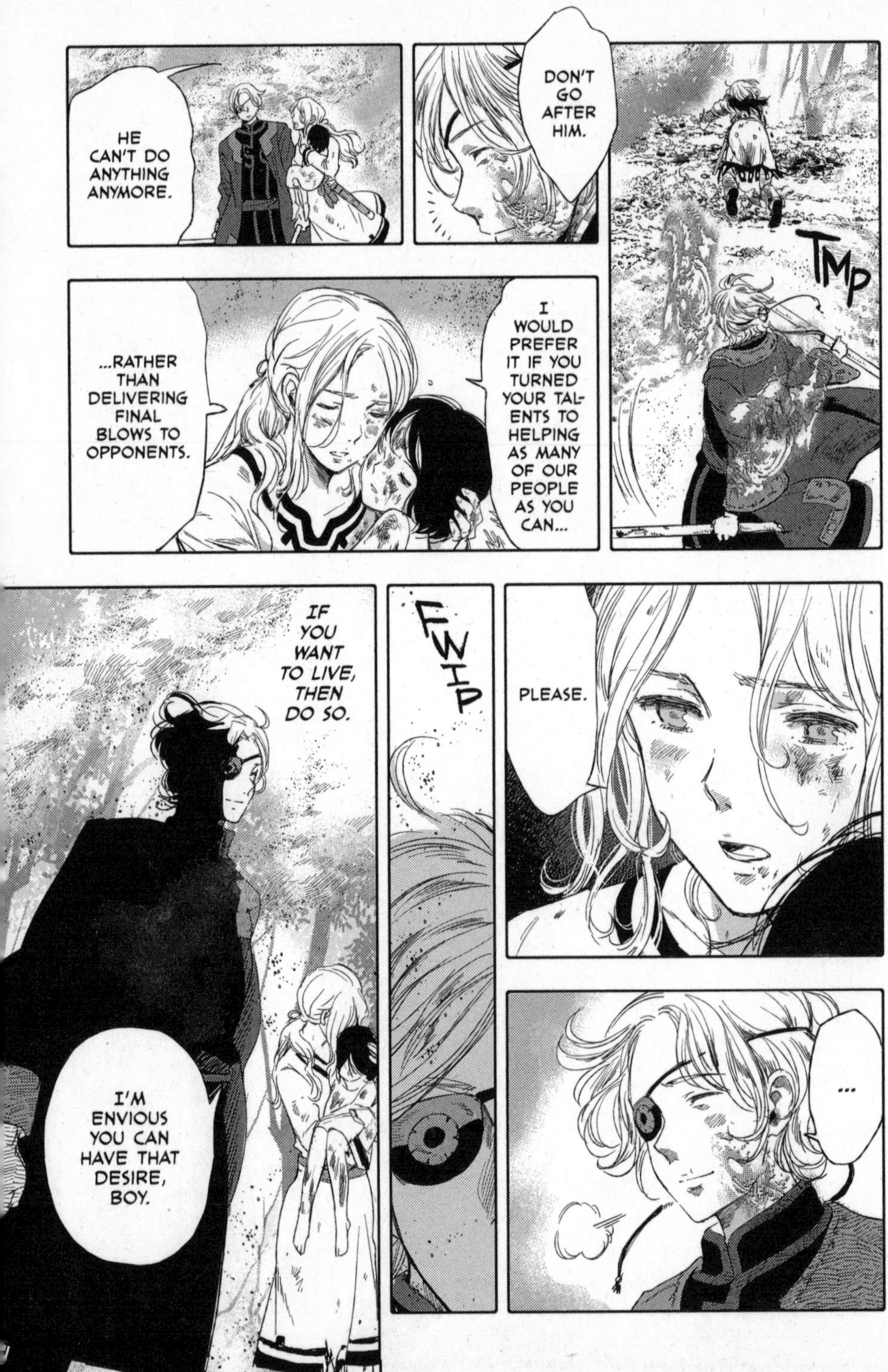
TMP
DON'T GO AFTER HIM.
HE CAN'T DO ANYTHING ANYMORE.
I WOULD PREFER IT IF YOU TURNED YOUR TALENTS TO HELPING AS MANY OF OUR PEOPLE AS YOU CAN...
...RATHER THAN DELIVERING FINAL BLOWS TO OPPONENTS.
PLEASE.
...
FWIP
IF YOU WANT TO LIVE, THEN DO SO.
I'M ENVIOUS YOU CAN HAVE THAT DESIRE, BOY.

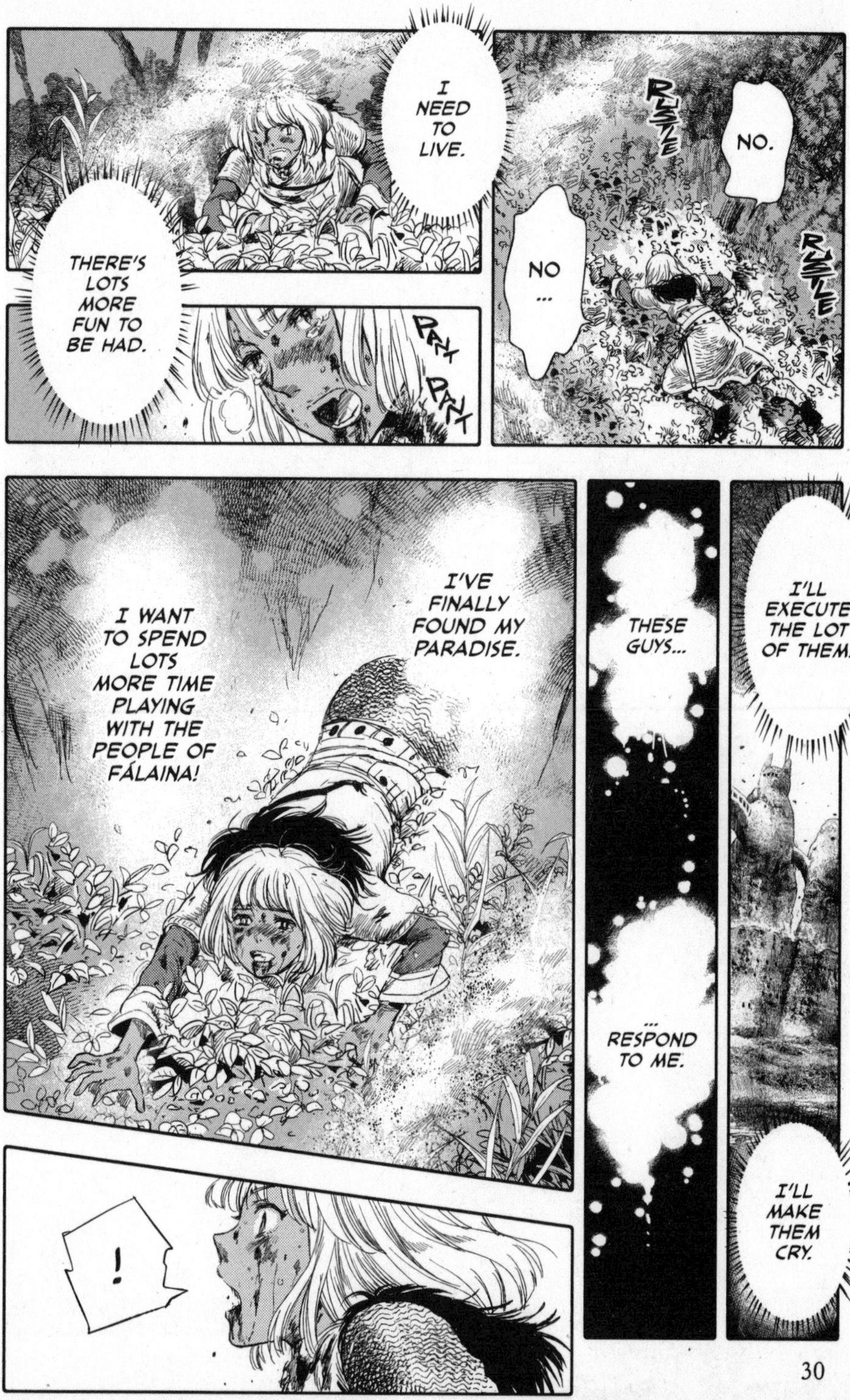
RUSTLE
NO.
NO ...
RUSTLE
I NEED TO LIVE.
THERE'S LOTS MORE FUN TO BE HAD.
PANT PANT
I'LL EXECUTE THE LOT OF THEM.
I'LL MAKE THEM CRY.
THESE GUYS...
... RESPOND TO ME.
I'VE FINALLY FOUND MY PARADISE.
I WANT TO SPEND LOTS MORE TIME PLAYING WITH THE PEOPLE OF FÁLAINA!
!

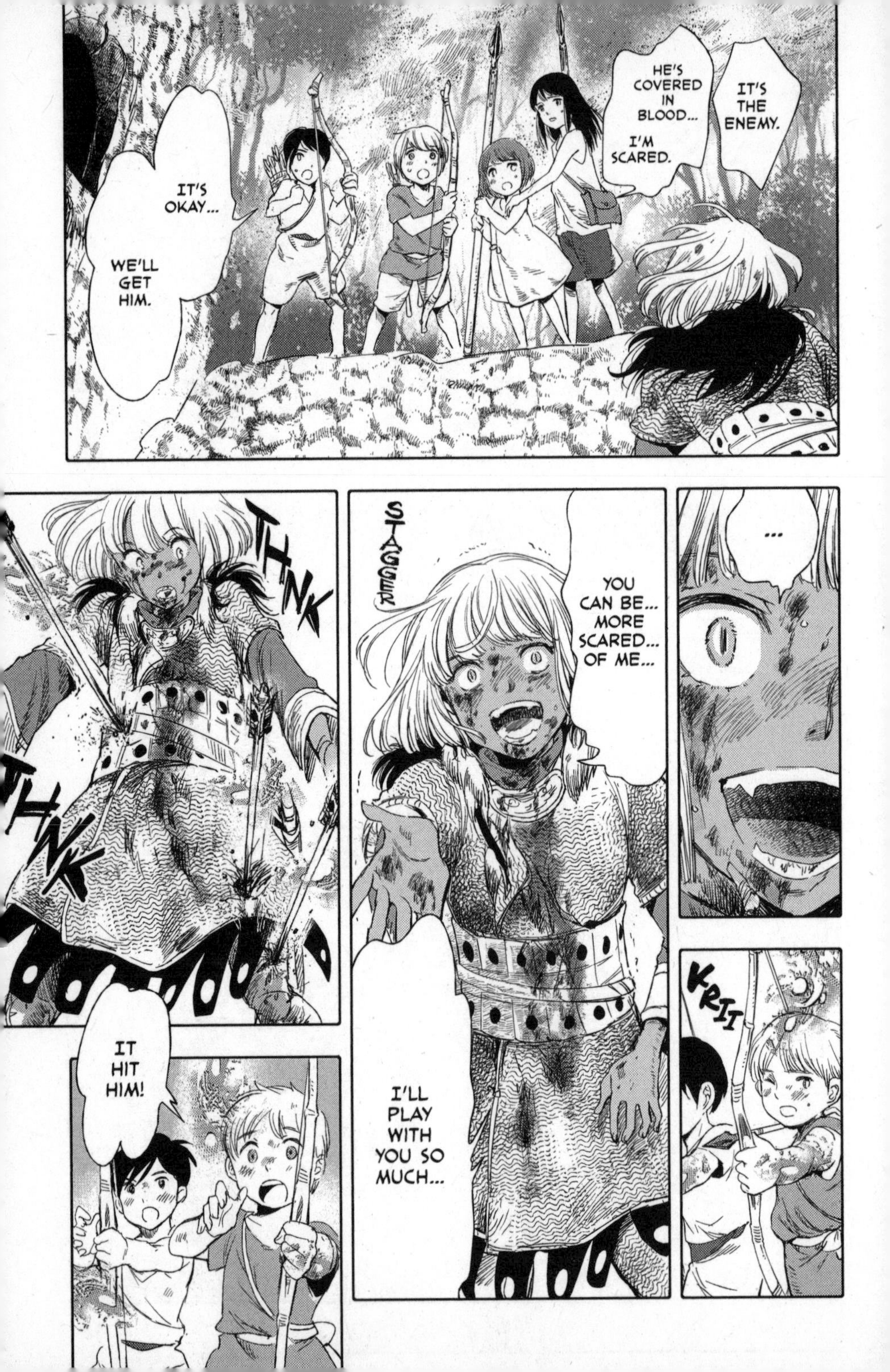
IT'S THE ENEMY.
HE'S COVERED IN BLOOD...
I'M SCARED.
IT'S OKAY...
WE'LL GET HIM.
...
KRIIT
STAGGER
YOU CAN BE... MORE SCARED... OF ME...
I'LL PLAY WITH YOU SO MUCH...
THNK
THNK
IT HIT HIM!

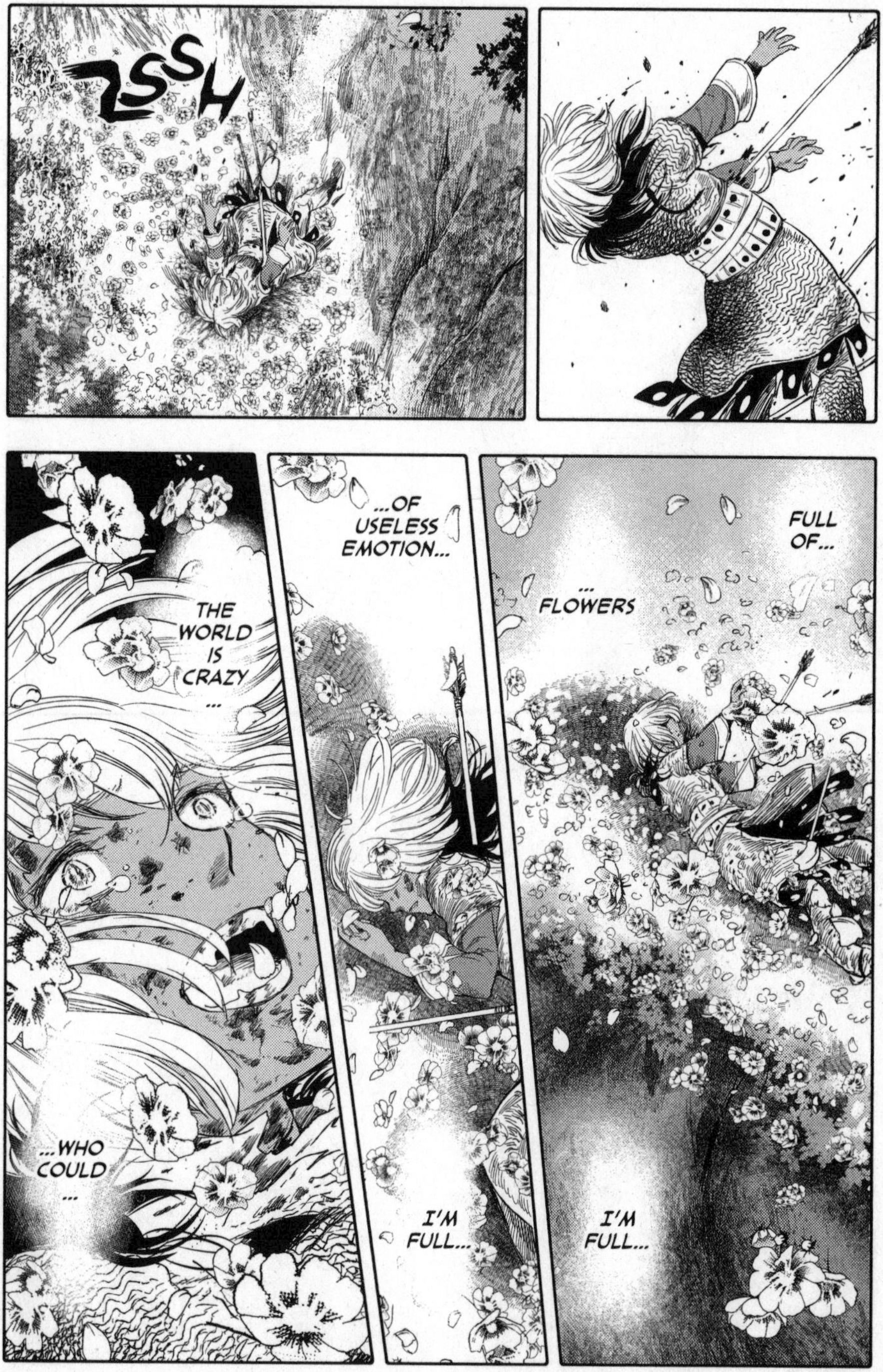
ZSSH
FULL OF...
... FLOWERS
I'M FULL...
...OF USELESS EMOTION...
I'M FULL...
THE WORLD IS CRAZY ...
...WHO COULD ...

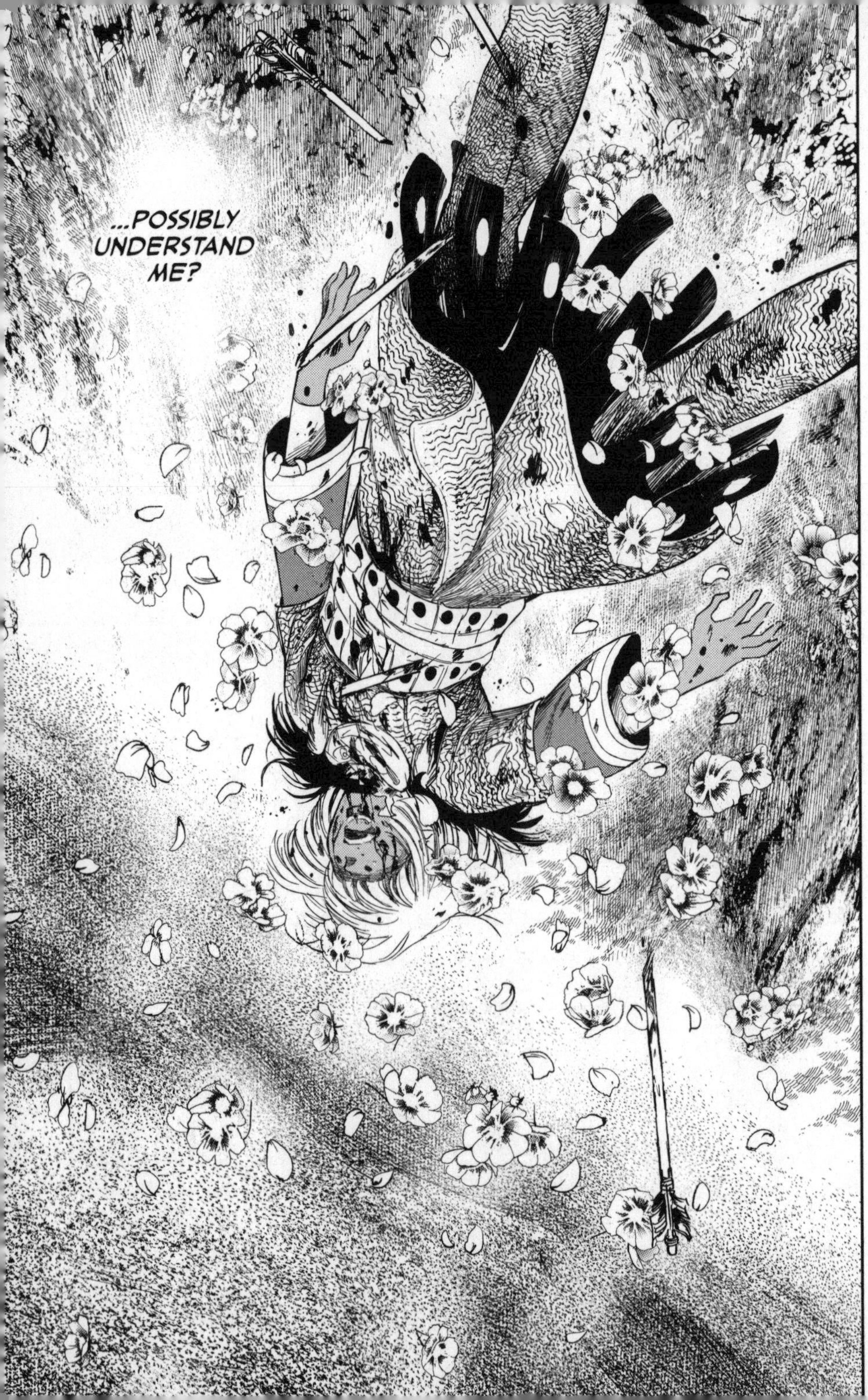
...POSSIBLY UNDERSTAND ME?

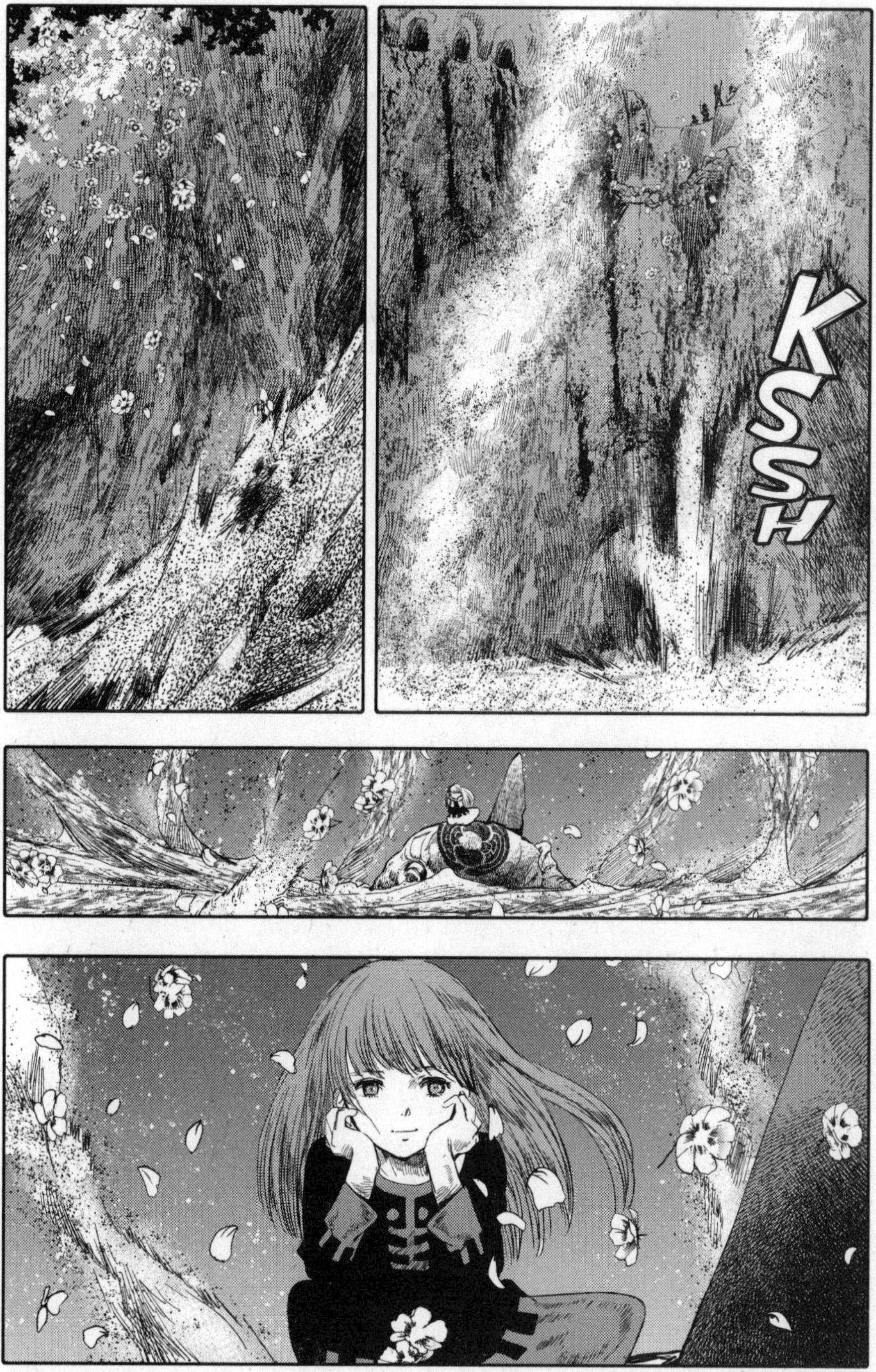
KSSH

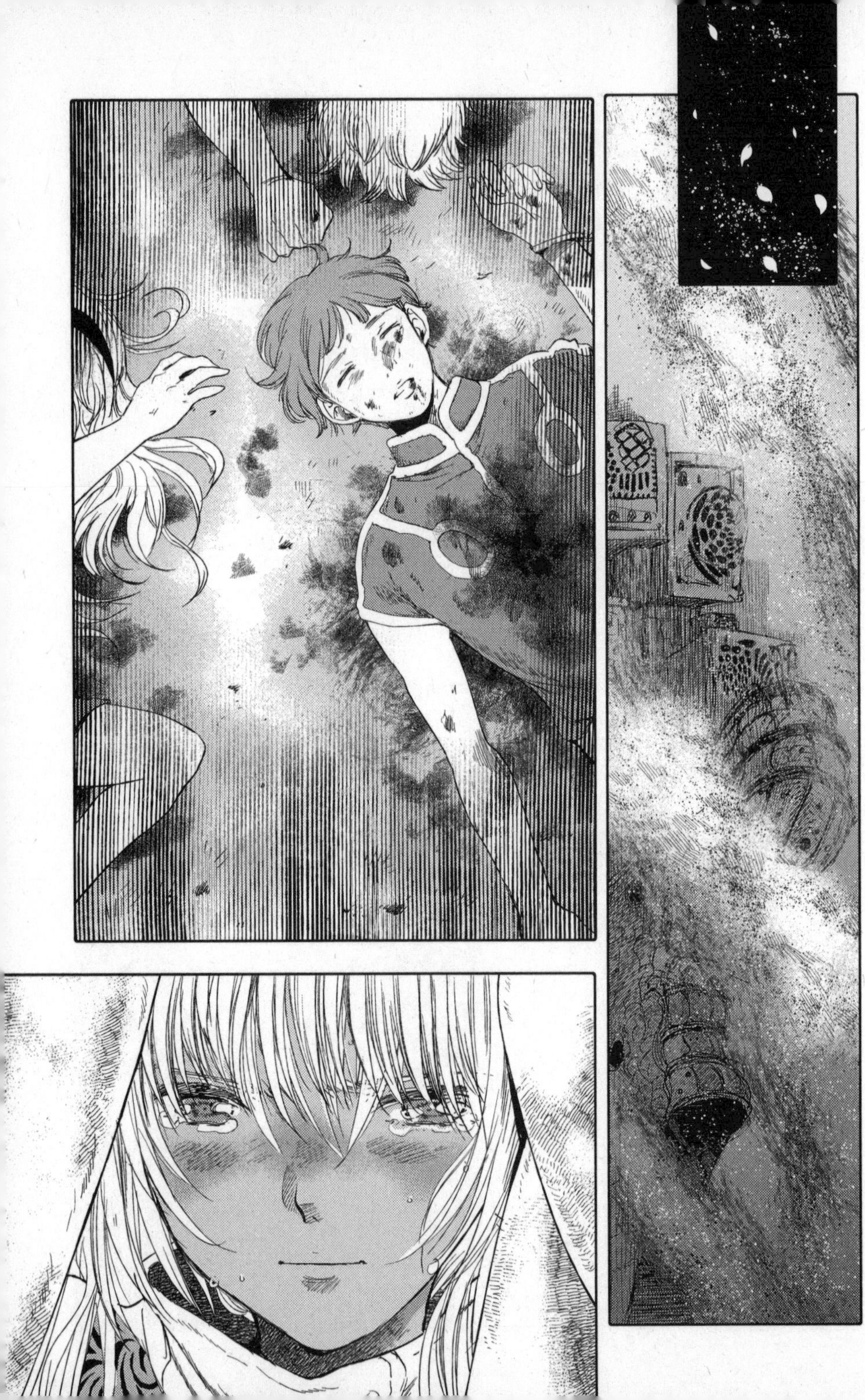

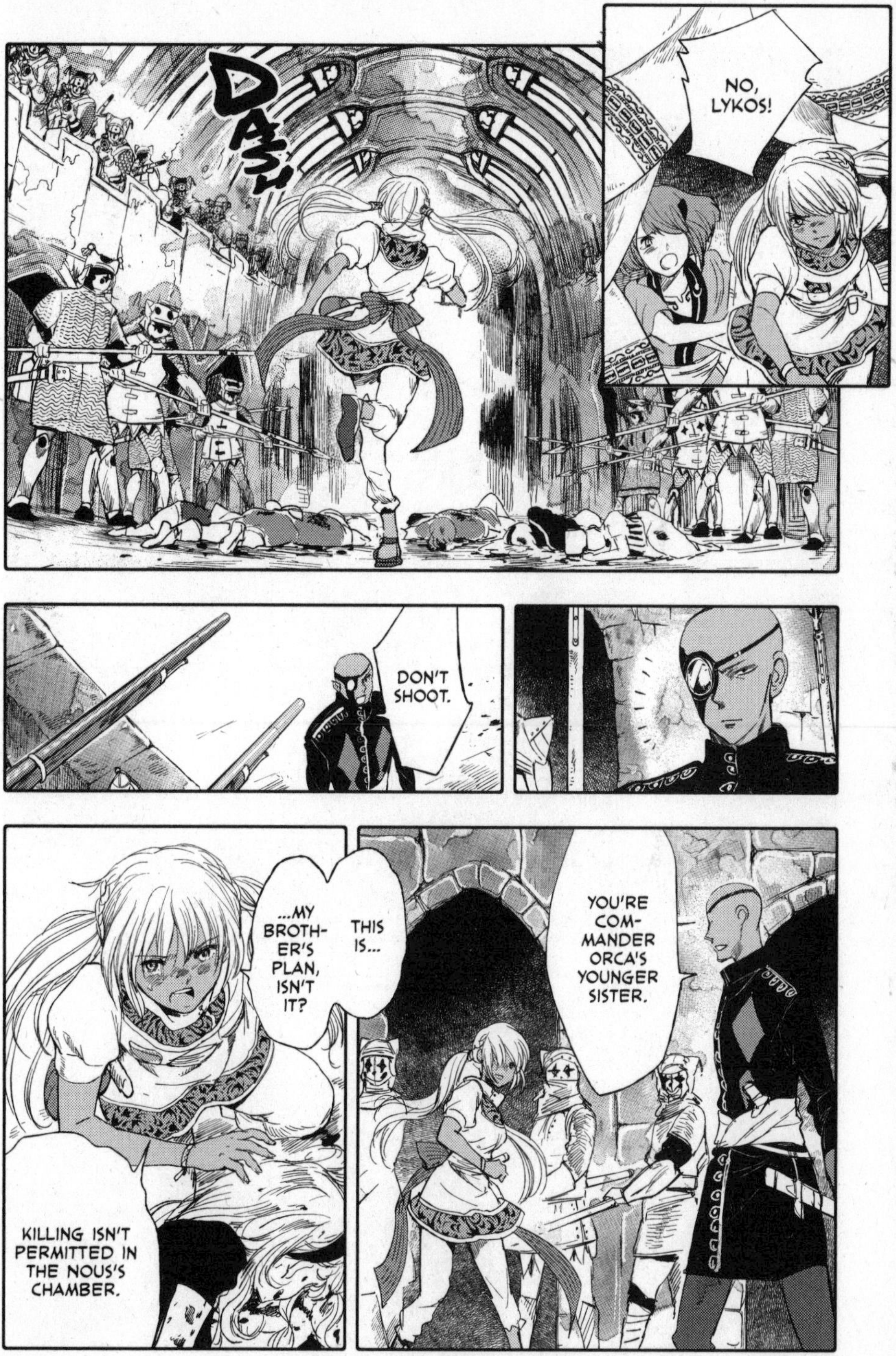
NO, LYKOS!
DASH
DON'T SHOOT.
YOU'RE COM-MANDER ORCA'S YOUNGER SISTER.
THIS IS...
...MY BROTH-ER'S PLAN, ISN'T IT?
KILLING ISN'T PERMITTED IN THE NOUS'S CHAMBER.

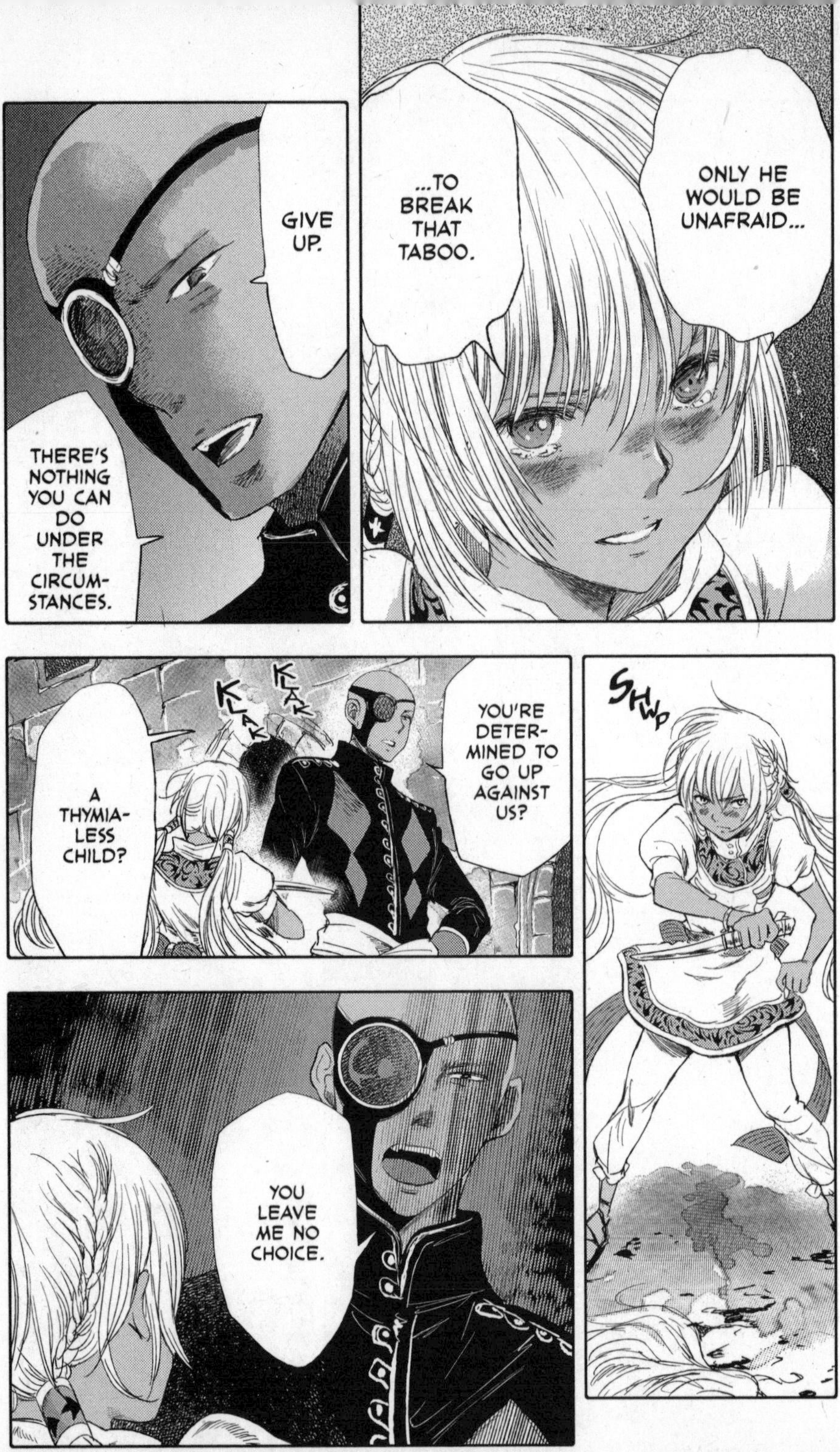
ONLY HE WOULD BE UNAFRAID...
...TO BREAK THAT TABOO.
GIVE UP.
THERE'S NOTHING YOU CAN DO UNDER THE CIRCUMSTANCES.
SHWP
YOU'RE DETERMINED TO GO UP AGAINST US?
KLAK
KLAK
A THYMIA-LESS CHILD?
YOU LEAVE ME NO CHOICE.

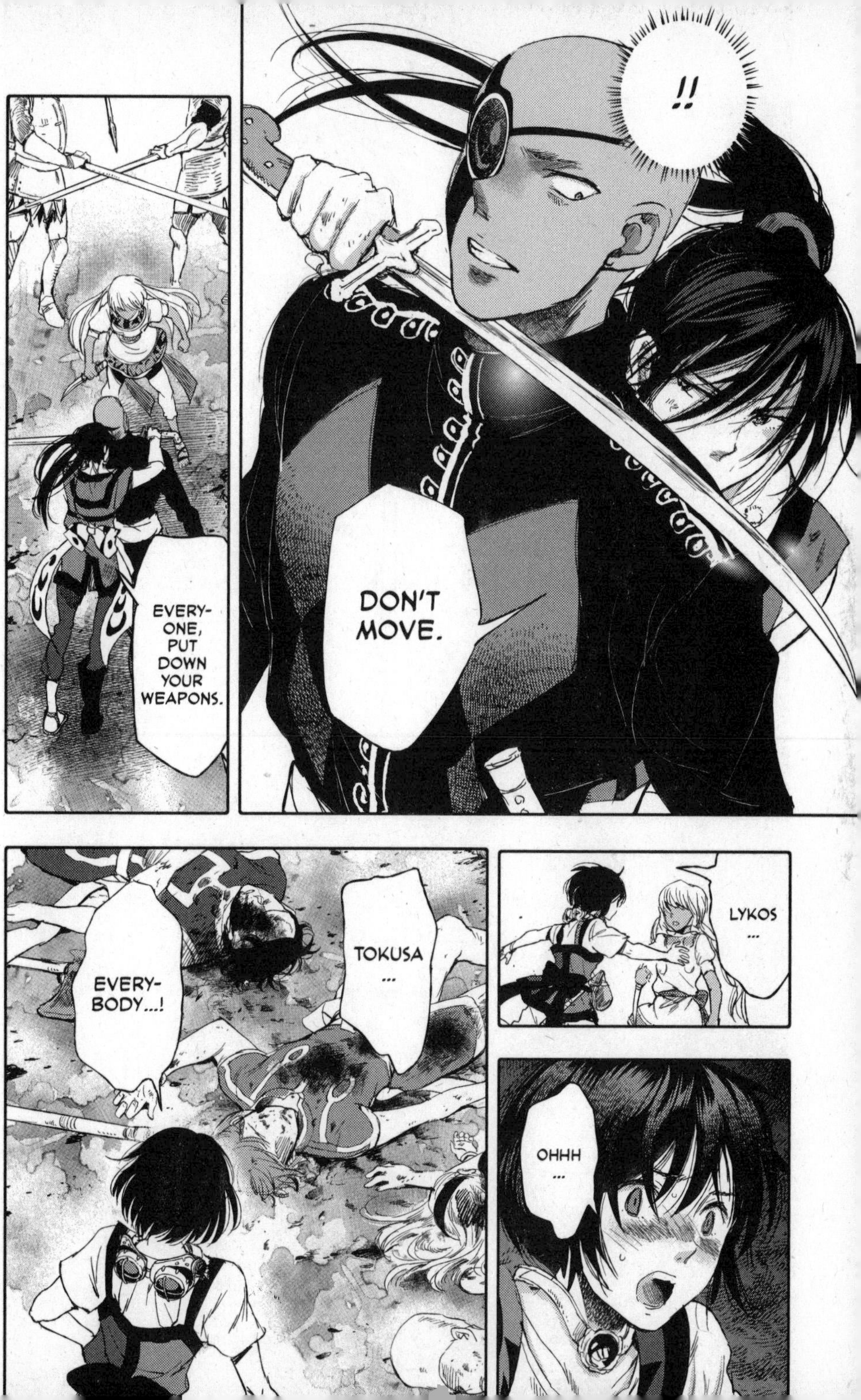
!!
DON'T MOVE.
EVERY-ONE, PUT DOWN YOUR WEAPONS.
LYKOS ...
OHHH ...
TOKUSA ...
EVERY-BODY...!

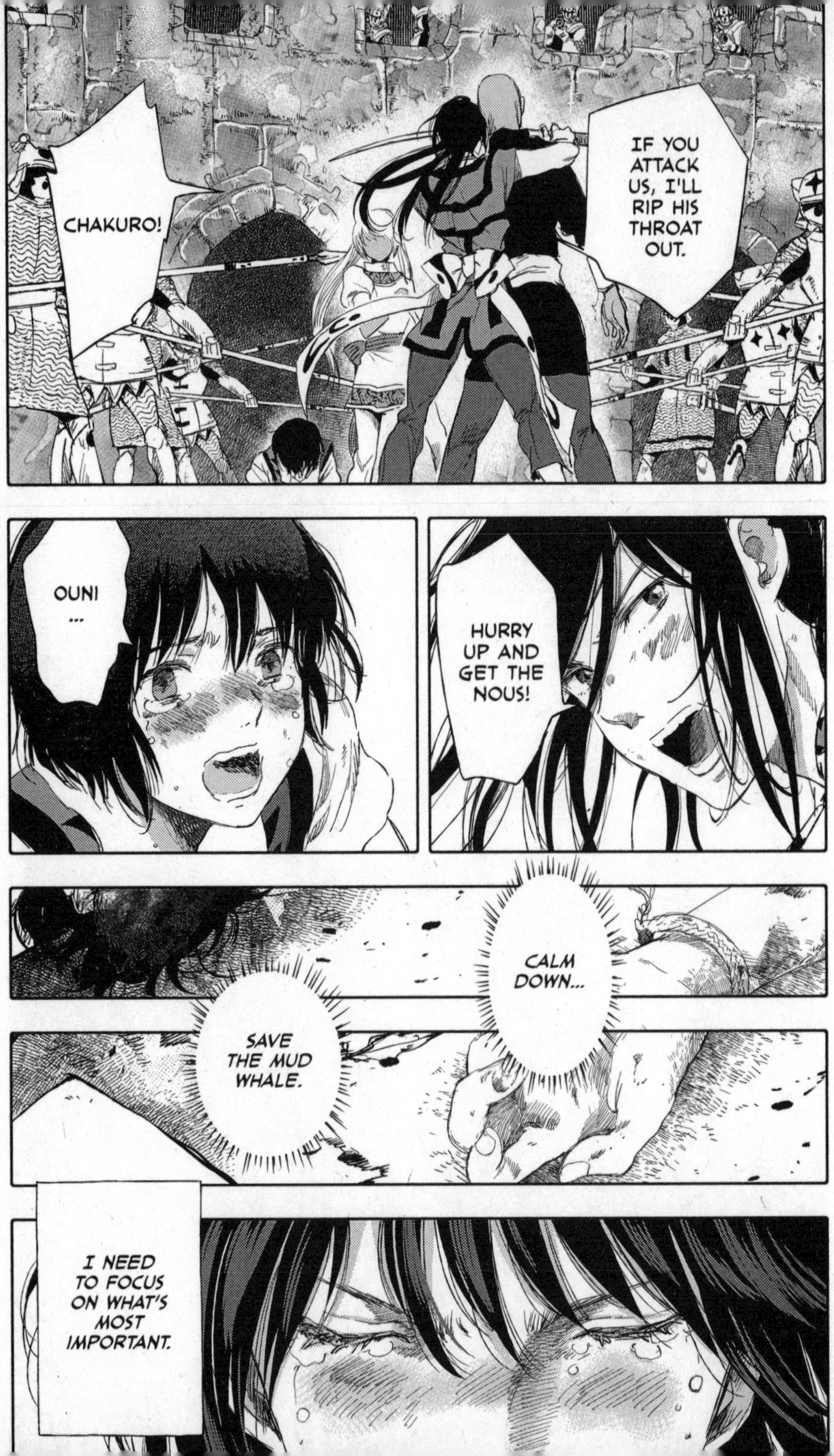
IF YOU ATTACK US, I'LL RIP HIS THROAT OUT.
CHAKURO!
HURRY UP AND GET THE NOUS!
OUNI ...
CALM DOWN...
SAVE THE MUD WHALE.
I NEED TO FOCUS ON WHAT'S MOST IMPORTANT.

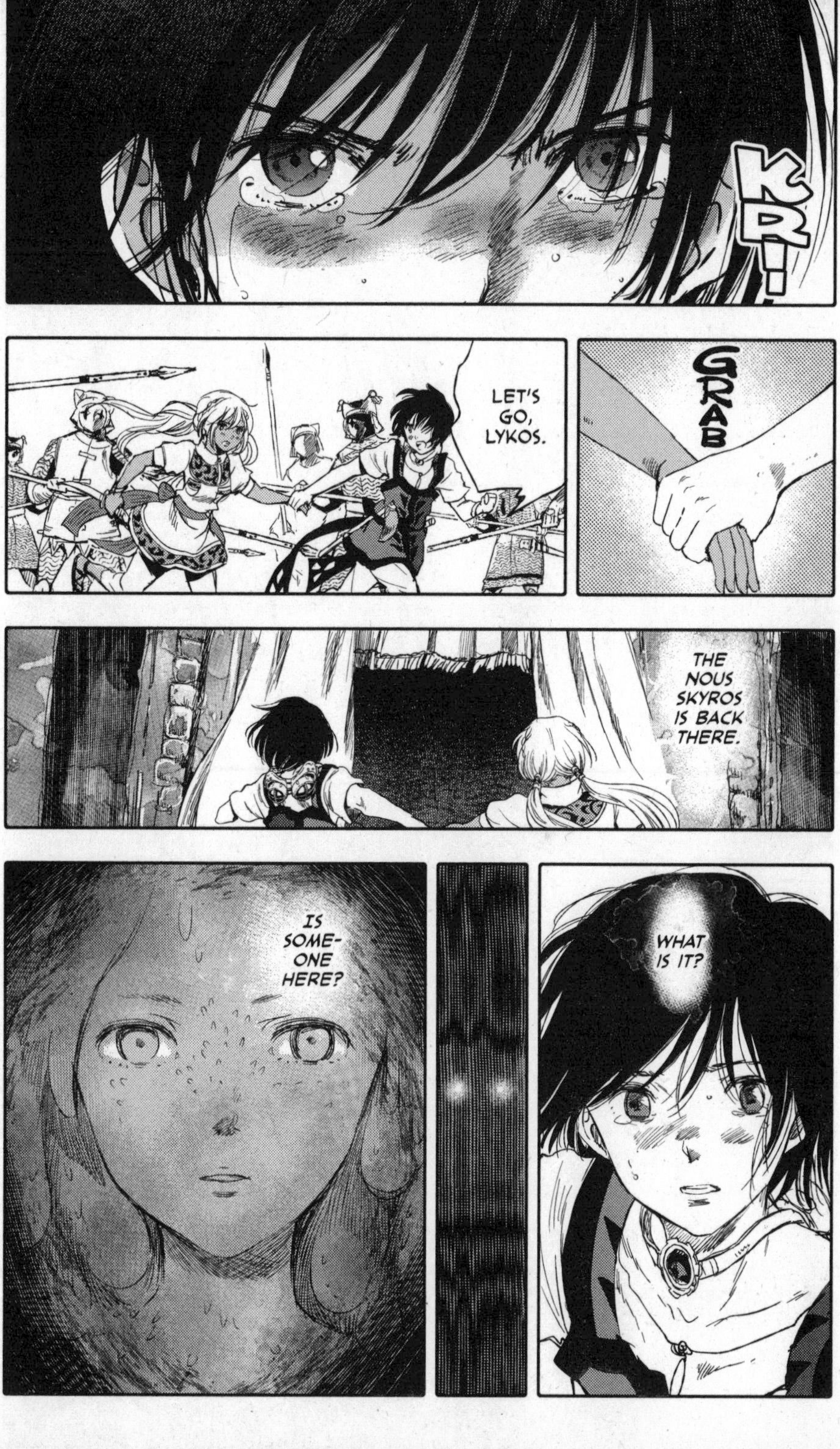
KRI!
GRAB
LET'S GO, LYKOS.
THE NOUS SKYROS IS BACK THERE.
WHAT IS IT?
IS SOME-ONE HERE?

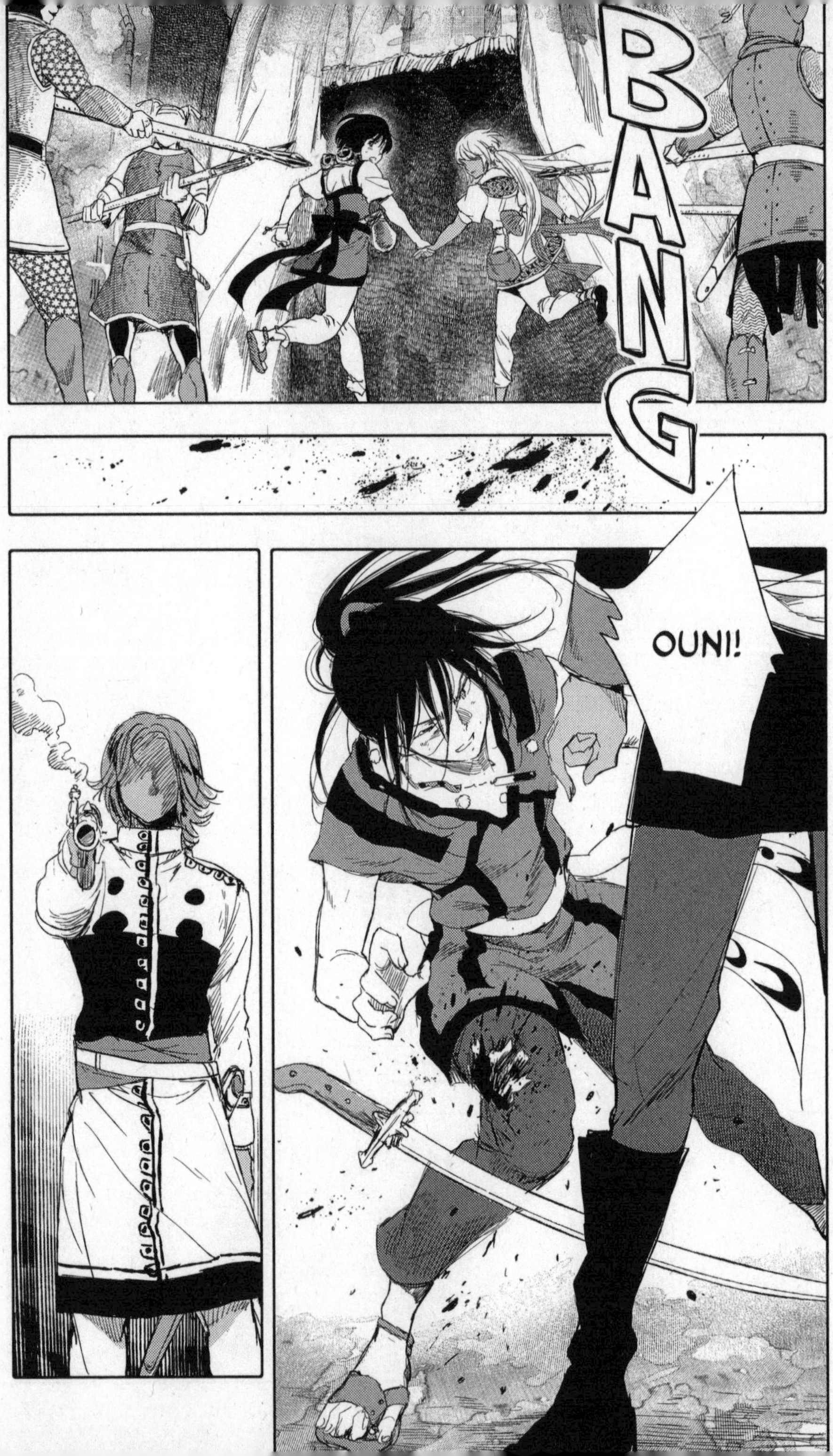
BANG
OUNI!

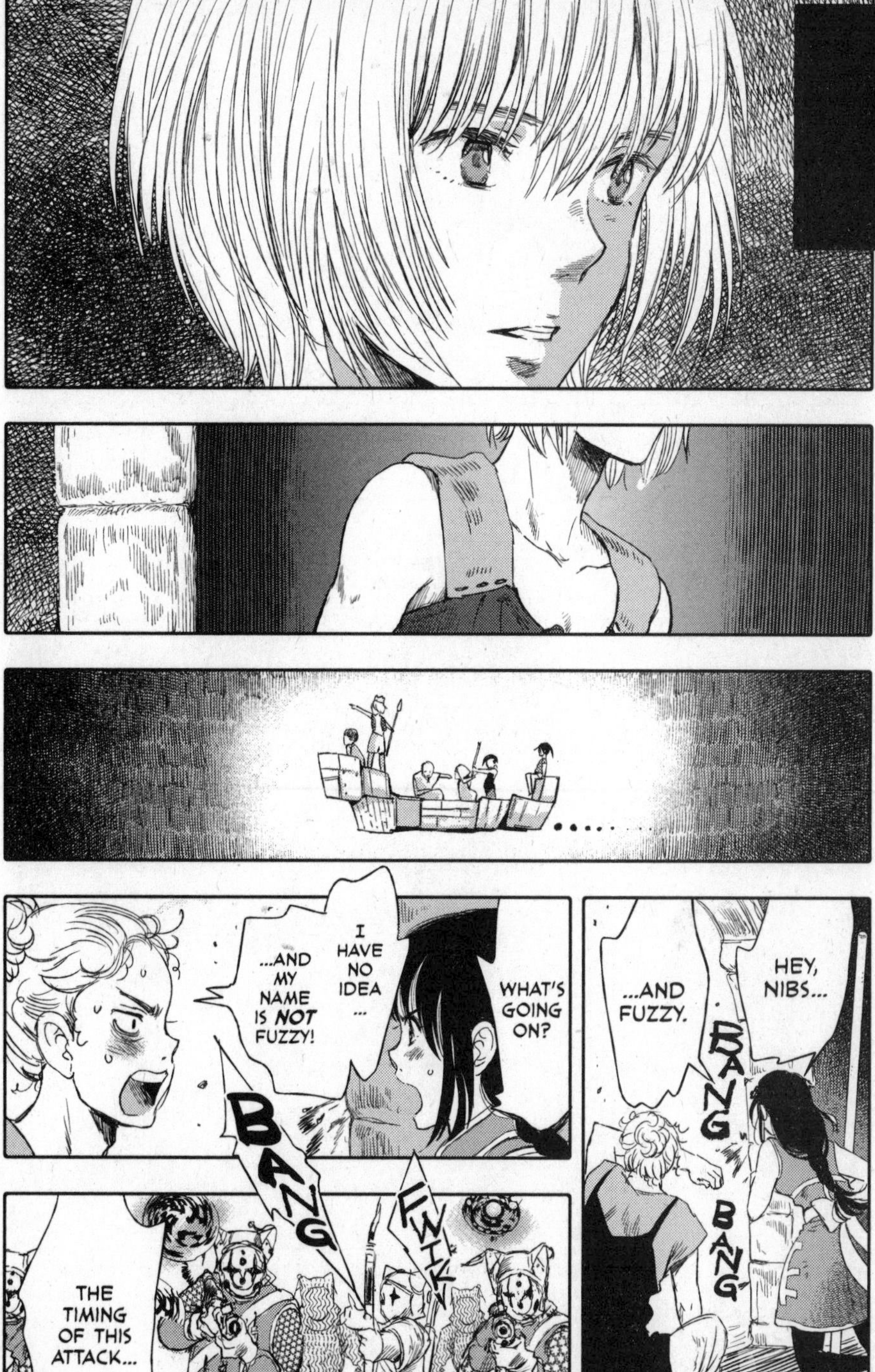
HEY, NIBS...
...AND FUZZY.
BANG
BANG
BANG
WHAT'S GOING ON?
I HAVE NO IDEA ...
...AND MY NAME IS NOT FUZZY!
BANG
FWIK
THE TIMING OF THIS ATTACK...

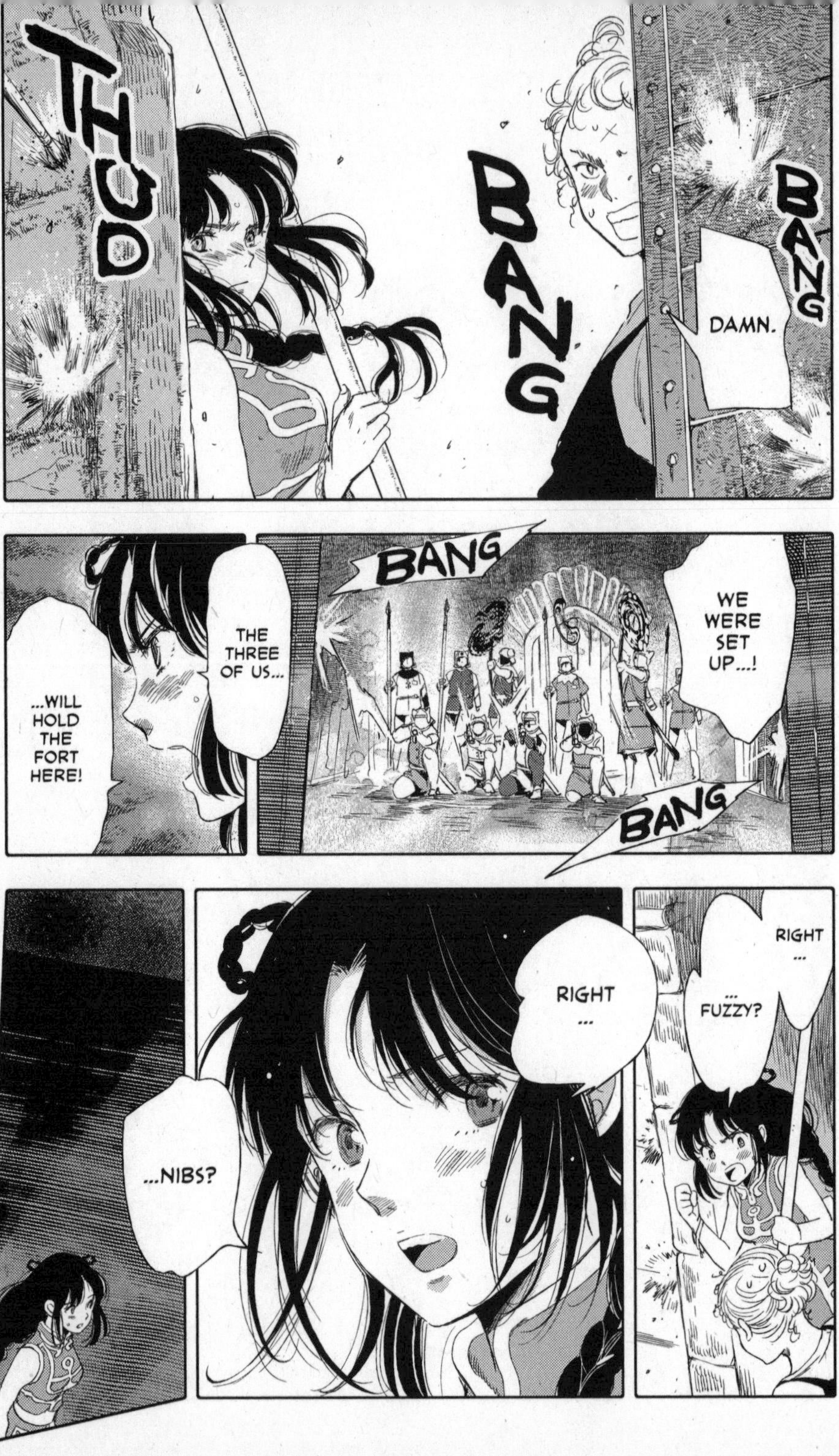
BANG
DAMN.
BANG
THUD
WE WERE SET UP...!
BANG
BANG
THE THREE OF US...
...WILL HOLD THE FORT HERE!
RIGHT ...
... FUZZY?
RIGHT ...
...NIBS?

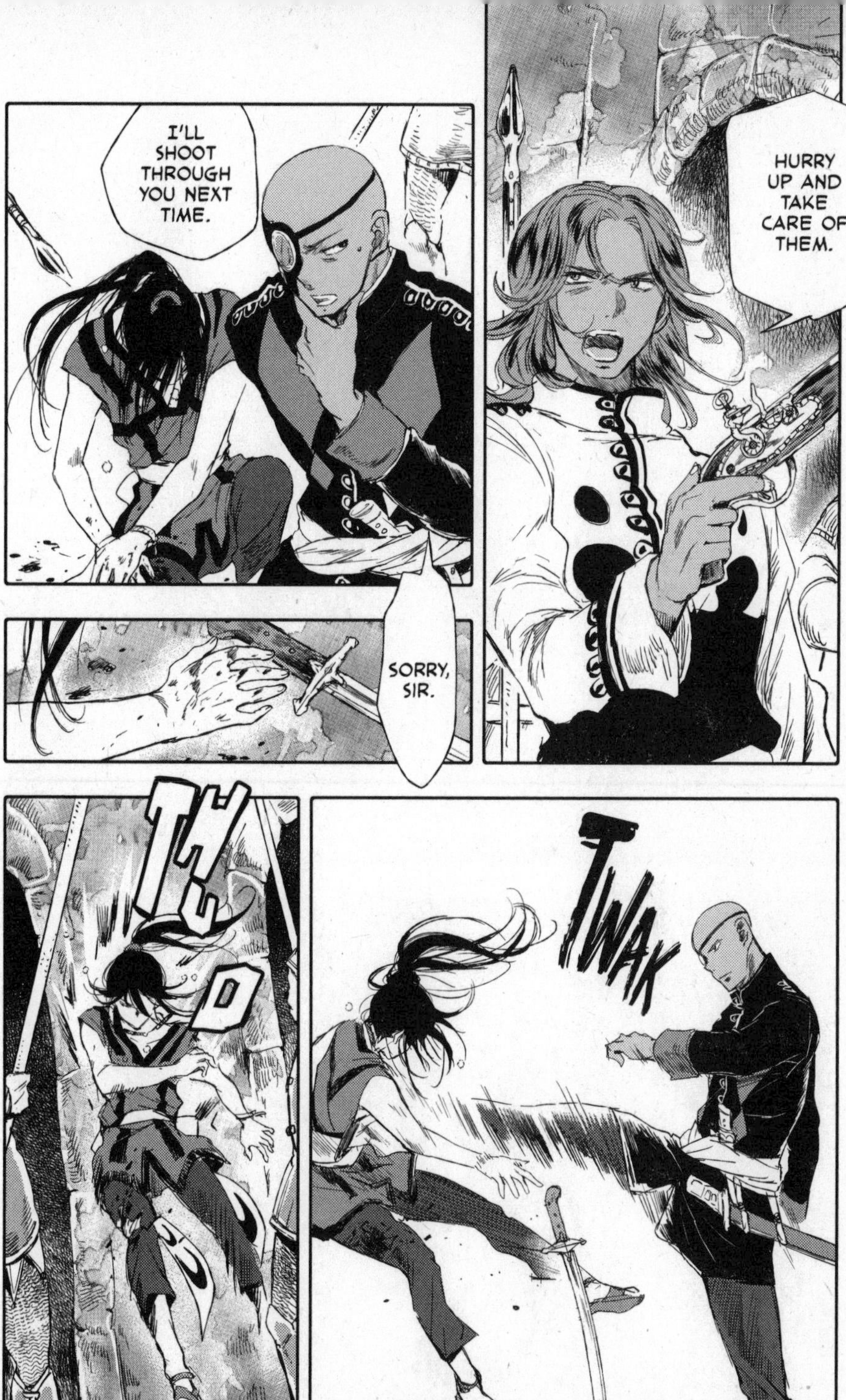
HURRY UP AND TAKE CARE OF THEM.
I'LL SHOOT THROUGH YOU NEXT TIME.
SORRY, SIR.
TWAK
THUD

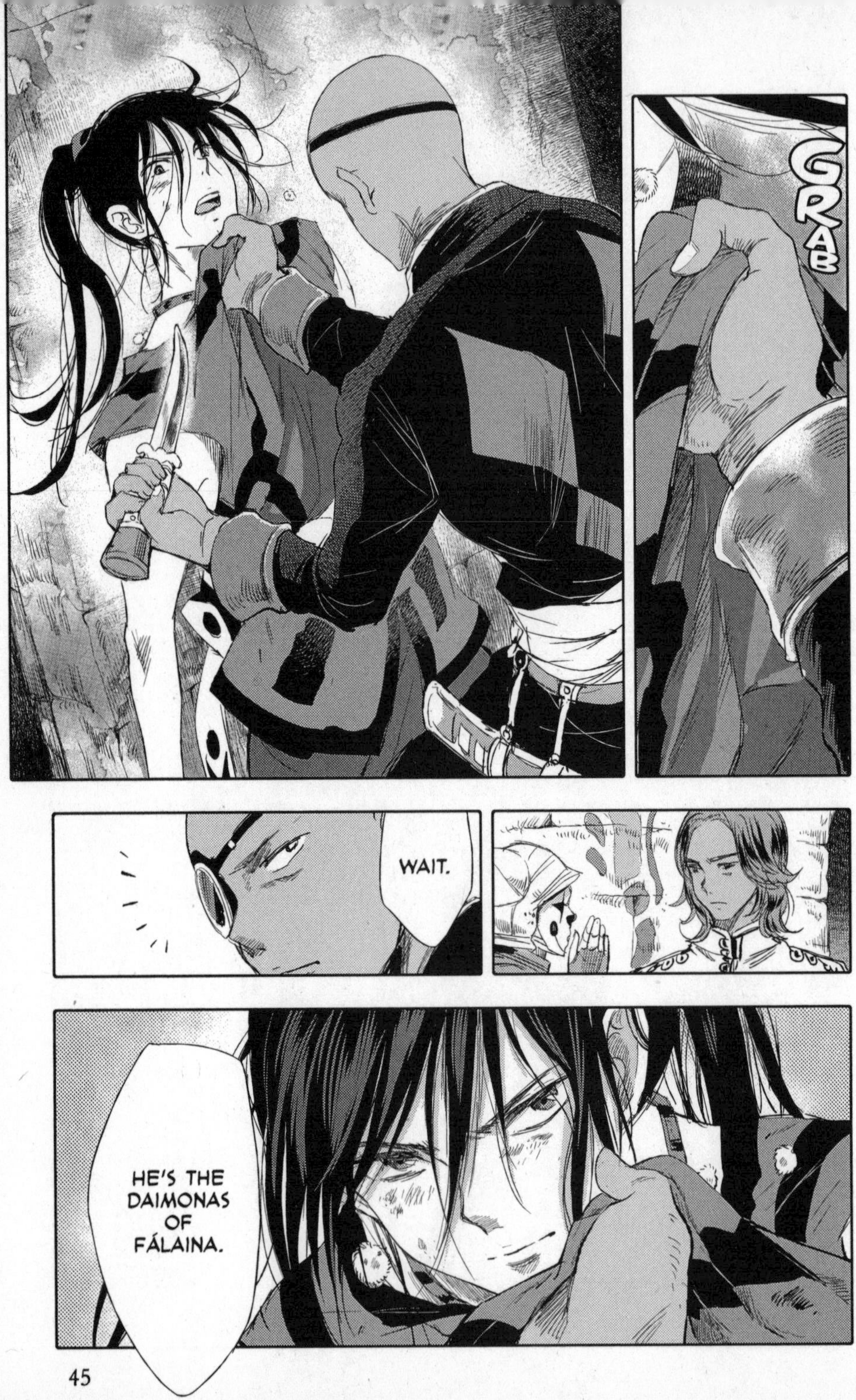
GRAB
WAIT.
HE'S THE DAIMONAS OF FÁLAINA.

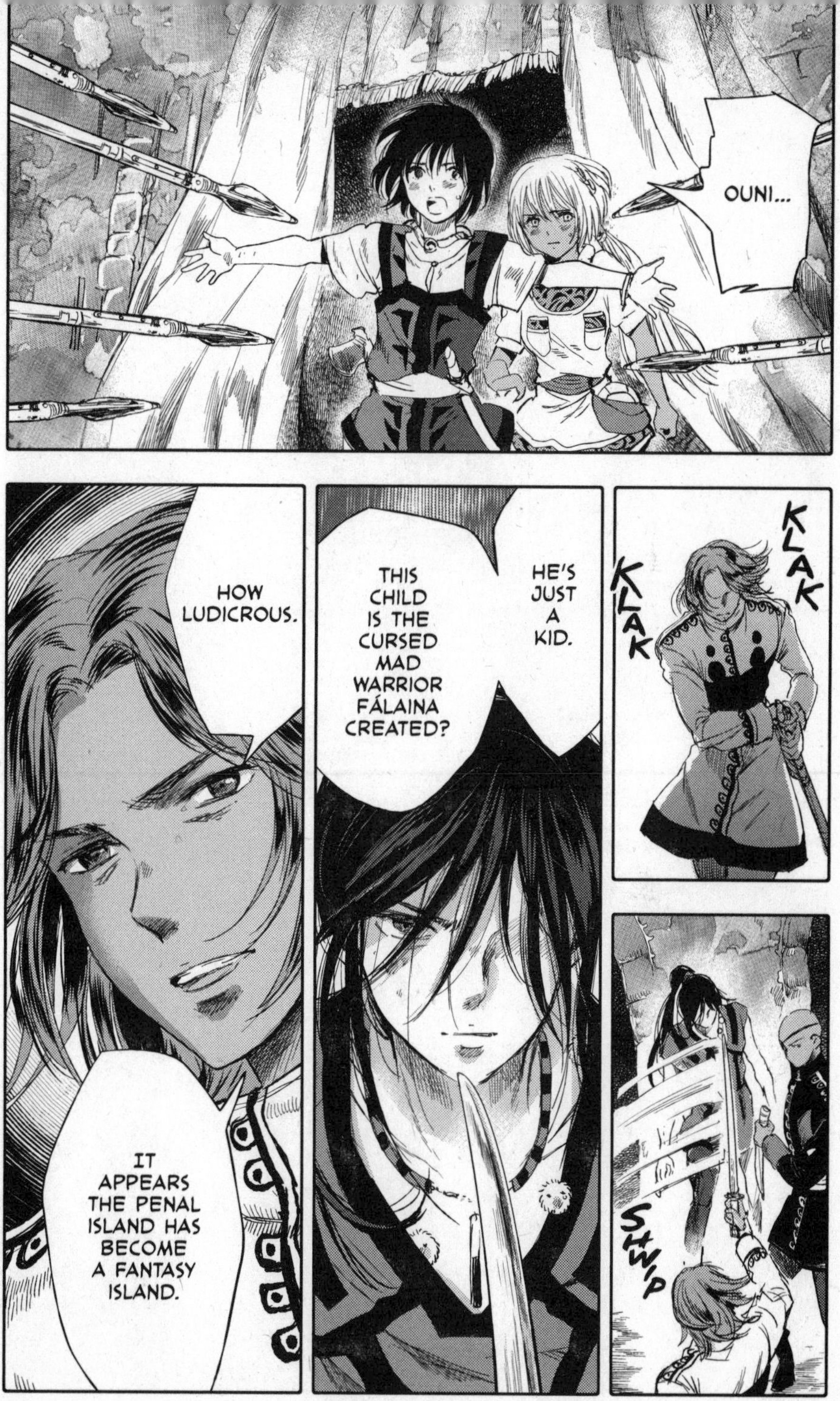
OUNI...
KLAK KLAK
SHWIP
HE'S JUST A KID.
THIS CHILD IS THE CURSED MAD WARRIOR FÁLAINA CREATED?
HOW LUDICROUS.
IT APPEARS THE PENAL ISLAND HAS BECOME A FANTASY ISLAND.

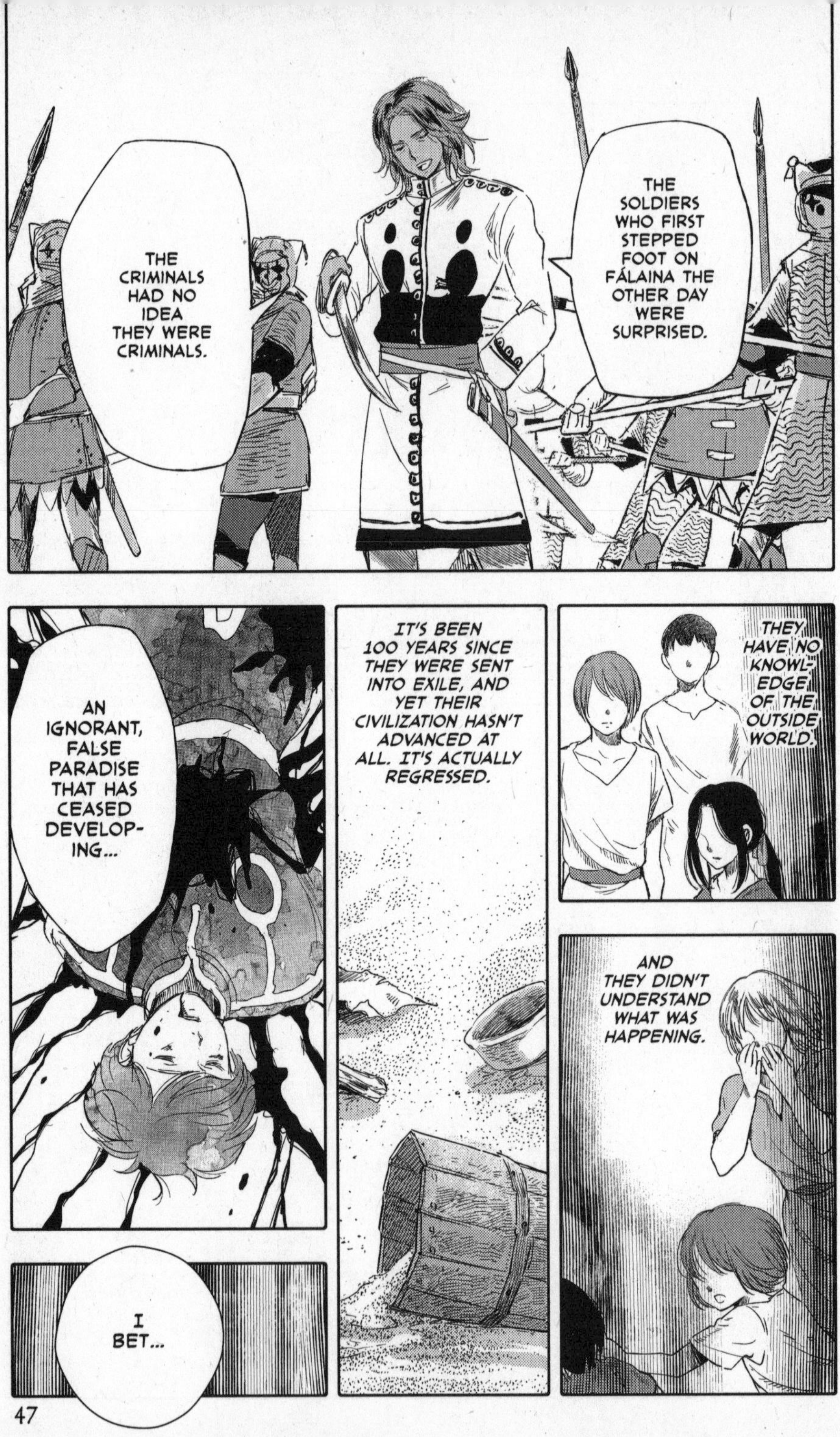
THE SOLDIERS WHO FIRST STEPPED FOOT ON FÁLAINA THE OTHER DAY WERE SURPRISED.
THE CRIMINALS HAD NO IDEA THEY WERE CRIMINALS.
THEY HAVE NO KNOWL-EDGE OF THE OUTSIDE WORLD.
AND THEY DIDN'T UNDERSTAND WHAT WAS HAPPENING.
IT'S BEEN 100 YEARS SINCE THEY WERE SENT INTO EXILE, AND YET THEIR CIVILIZATION HASN'T ADVANCED AT ALL. IT'S ACTUALLY REGRESSED.
AN IGNORANT, FALSE PARADISE THAT HAS CEASED DEVELOP-ING...
I BET...

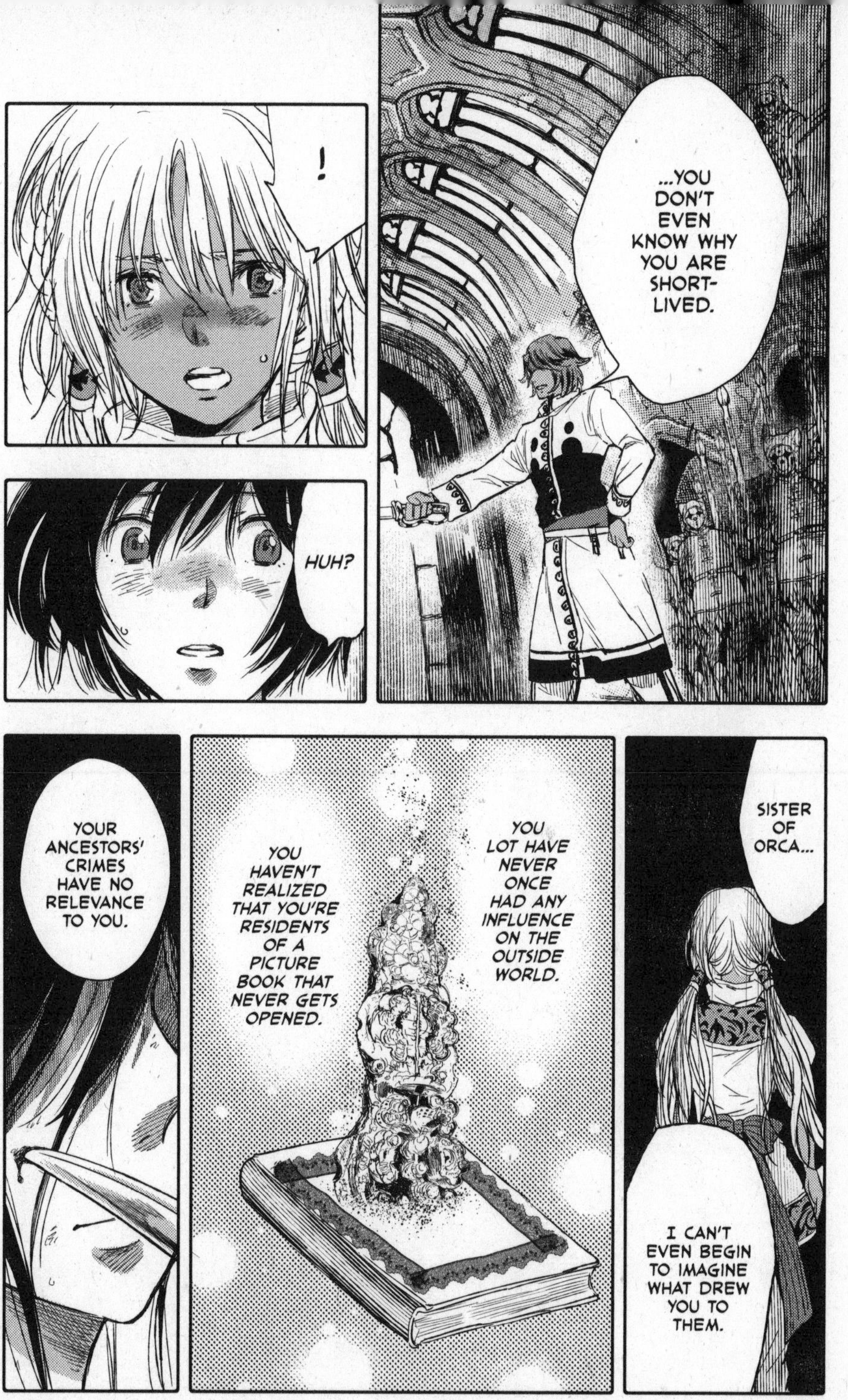
...YOU DON'T EVEN KNOW WHY YOU ARE SHORT-LIVED.
!
HUH?
SISTER OF ORCA...
I CAN'T EVEN BEGIN TO IMAGINE WHAT DREW YOU TO THEM.
YOU LOT HAVE NEVER ONCE HAD ANY INFLUENCE ON THE OUTSIDE WORLD.
YOU HAVEN'T REALIZED THAT YOU'RE RESIDENTS OF A PICTURE BOOK THAT NEVER GETS OPENED.
YOUR ANCESTORS' CRIMES HAVE NO RELEVANCE TO YOU.

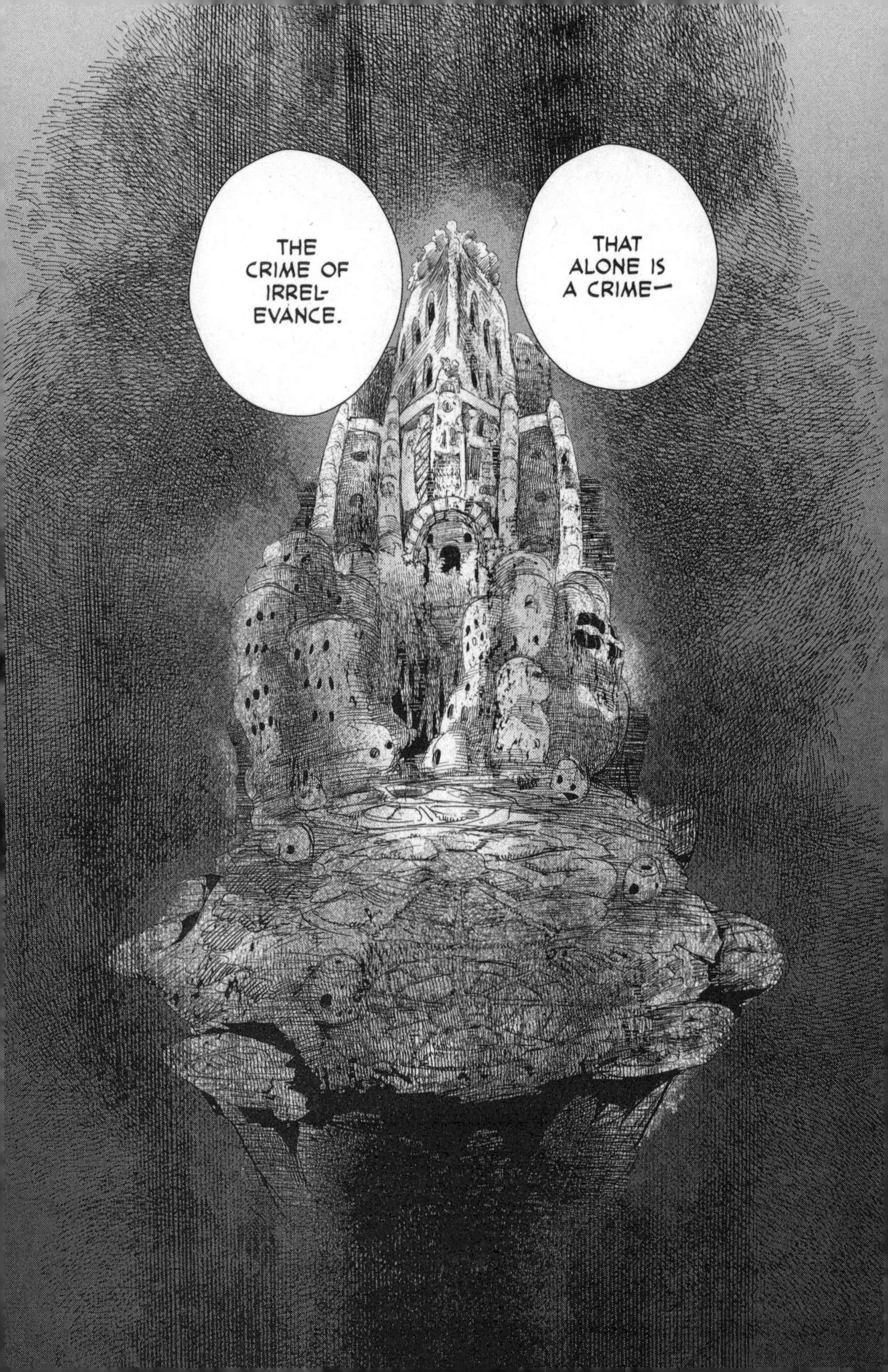
THAT ALONE IS A CRIME—
THE CRIME OF IRREL-EVANCE.

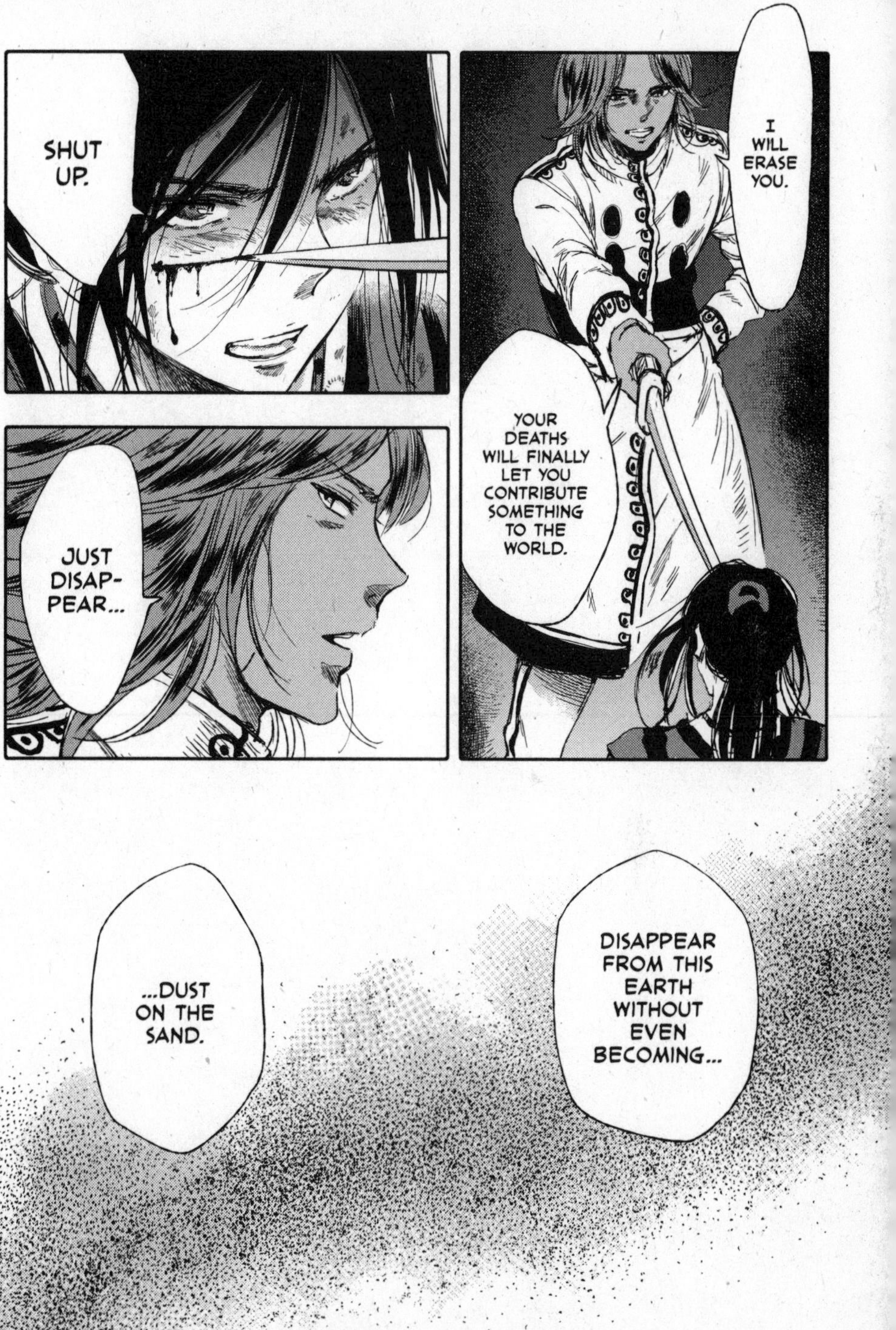
I WILL ERASE YOU.
YOUR DEATHS WILL FINALLY LET YOU CONTRIBUTE SOMETHING TO THE WORLD.
SHUT UP.
JUST DISAP-PEAR...
DISAPPEAR FROM THIS EARTH WITHOUT EVEN BECOMING...
...DUST ON THE SAND.

Sins of the Flower -The End-

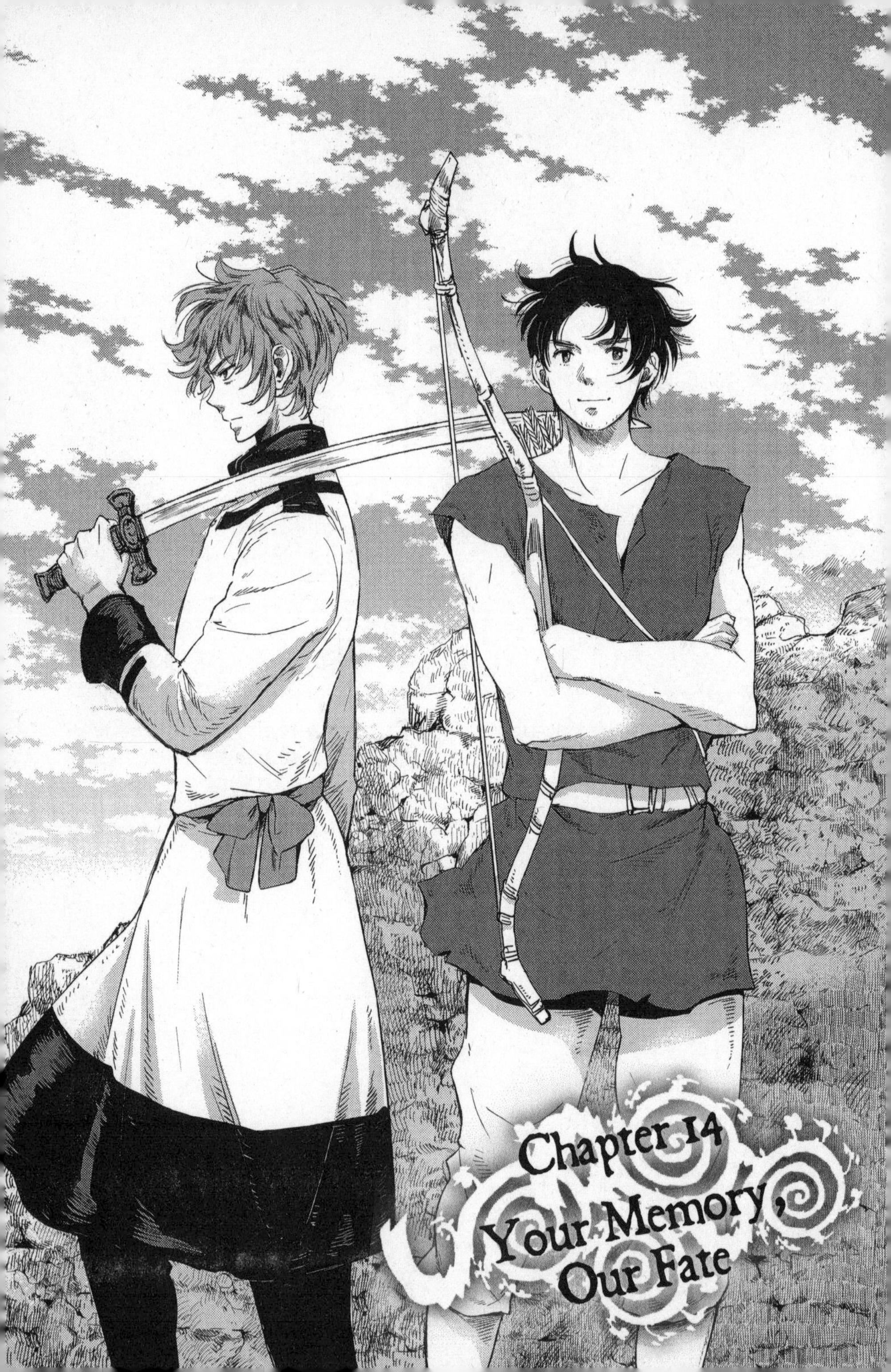
Chapter 14
Your Memory,
Our Fate

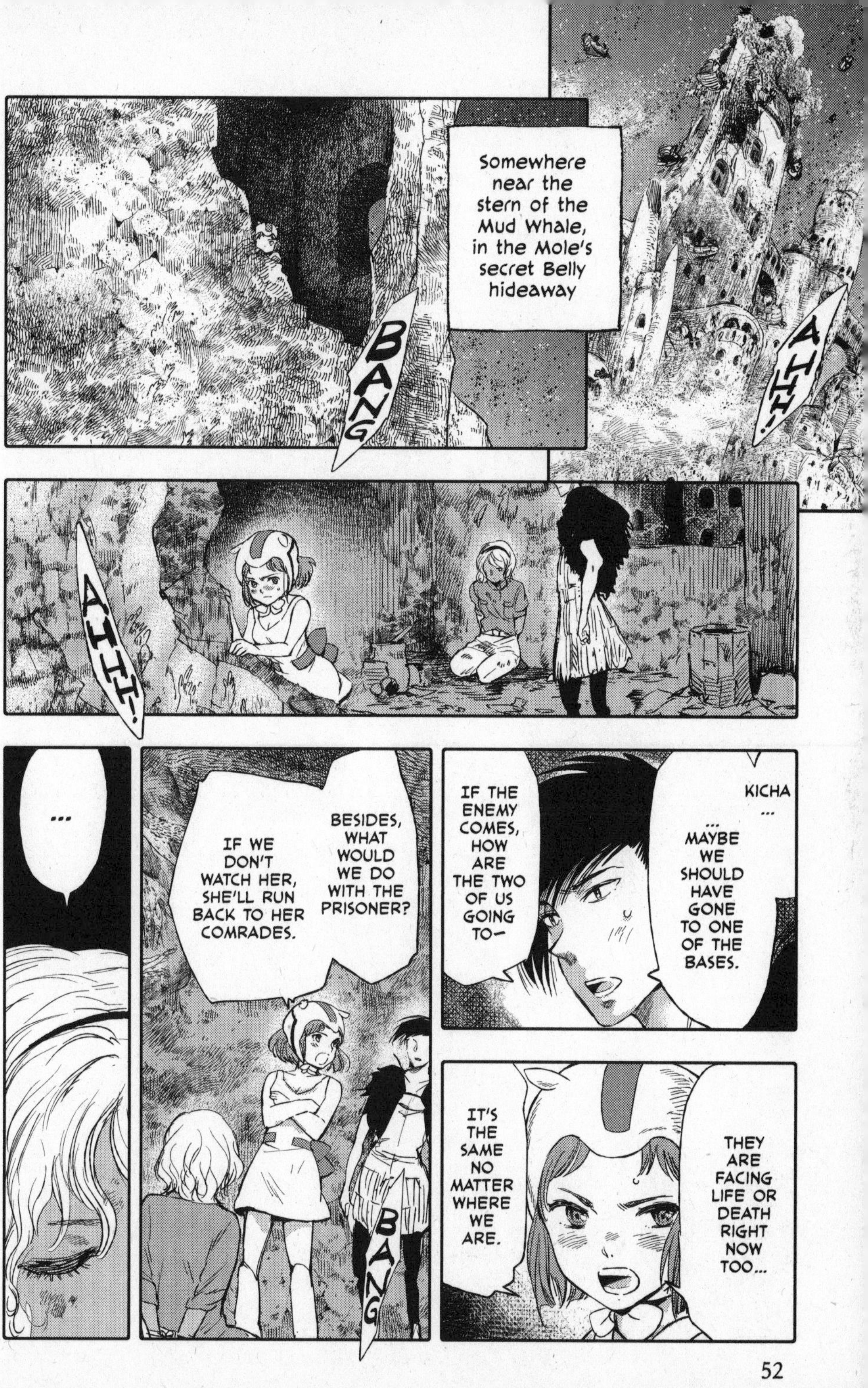
AHHH!
Somewhere near the stern of the Mud Whale, in the Mole's secret Belly hideaway
BANG
AHHH!
KICHA... ...MAYBE WE SHOULD HAVE GONE TO ONE OF THE BASES.
IF THE ENEMY COMES, HOW ARE THE TWO OF US GOING TO—
THEY ARE FACING LIFE OR DEATH RIGHT NOW TOO...
IT'S THE SAME NO MATTER WHERE WE ARE.
BESIDES, WHAT WOULD WE DO WITH THE PRISONER?
IF WE DON'T WATCH HER, SHE'LL RUN BACK TO HER COMRADES.
BANG
...

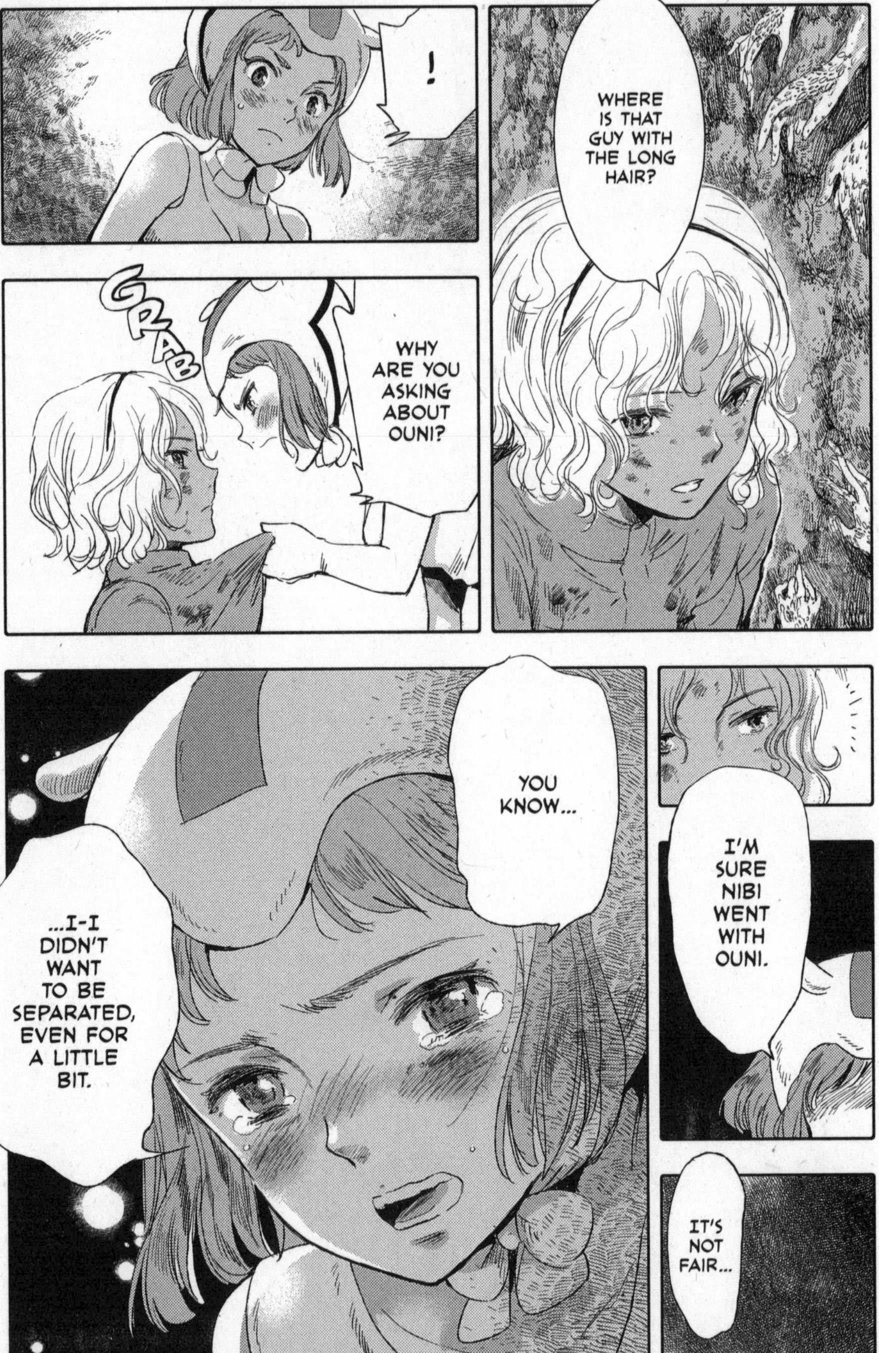
WHERE IS THAT GUY WITH THE LONG HAIR?
!
GRAB
WHY ARE YOU ASKING ABOUT OUNI?
I'M SURE NIBI WENT WITH OUNI.
IT'S NOT FAIR...
YOU KNOW...
...I-I DIDN'T WANT TO BE SEPARATED, EVEN FOR A LITTLE BIT.

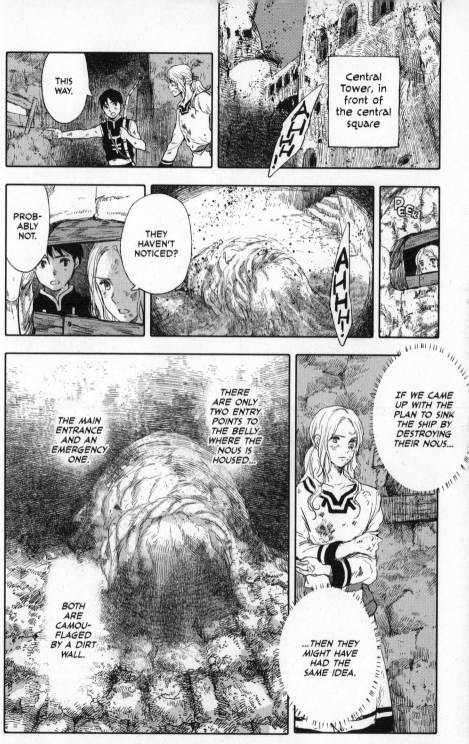

Central Tower, in front of the central square
AHHH!
THIS WAY.
PEEK
AHHH!
THEY HAVEN'T NOTICED?
PROB-ABLY NOT.
IF WE CAME UP WITH THE PLAN TO SINK THE SHIP BY DESTROYING THEIR NOUS...
...THEN THEY MIGHT HAVE HAD THE SAME IDEA.
THERE ARE ONLY TWO ENTRY POINTS TO THE BELLY WHERE THE NOUS IS HOUSED...
THE MAIN ENTRANCE AND AN EMERGENCY ONE.
BOTH ARE CAMOU-FLAGED BY A DIRT WALL.

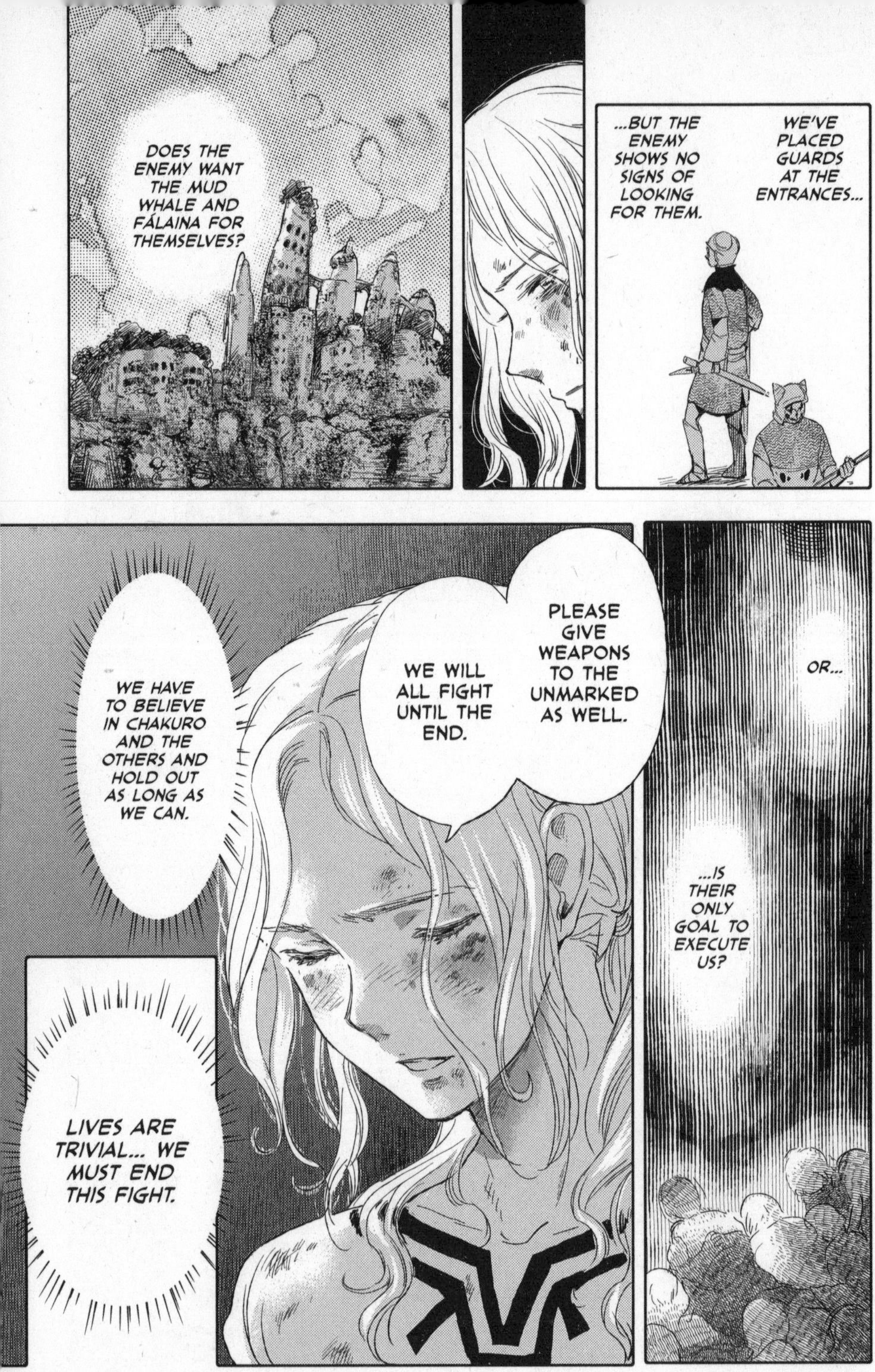
WE'VE PLACED GUARDS AT THE ENTRANCES...
...BUT THE ENEMY SHOWS NO SIGNS OF LOOKING FOR THEM.
DOES THE ENEMY WANT THE MUD WHALE AND FÁLAINA FOR THEMSELVES?
OR...
...IS THEIR ONLY GOAL TO EXECUTE US?
PLEASE GIVE WEAPONS TO THE UNMARKED AS WELL.
WE WILL ALL FIGHT UNTIL THE END.
WE HAVE TO BELIEVE IN CHAKURO AND THE OTHERS AND HOLD OUT AS LONG AS WE CAN.
LIVES ARE TRIVIAL... WE MUST END THIS FIGHT.

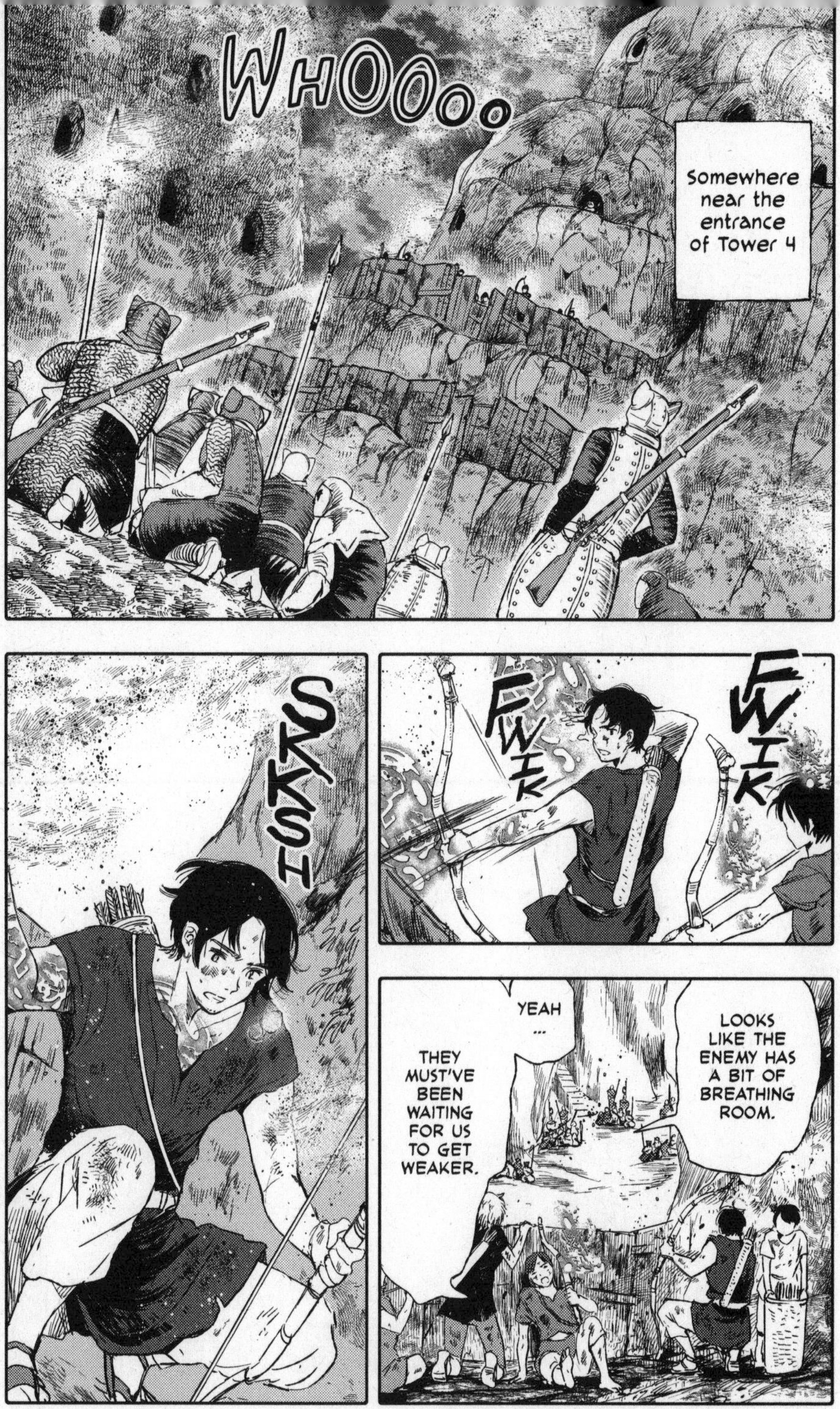
WHOOOOO
Somewhere near the entrance of Tower 4
FWIK
FWIK
LOOKS LIKE THE ENEMY HAS A BIT OF BREATHING ROOM.
YEAH ...
THEY MUST'VE BEEN WAITING FOR US TO GET WEAKER.
SRKSH

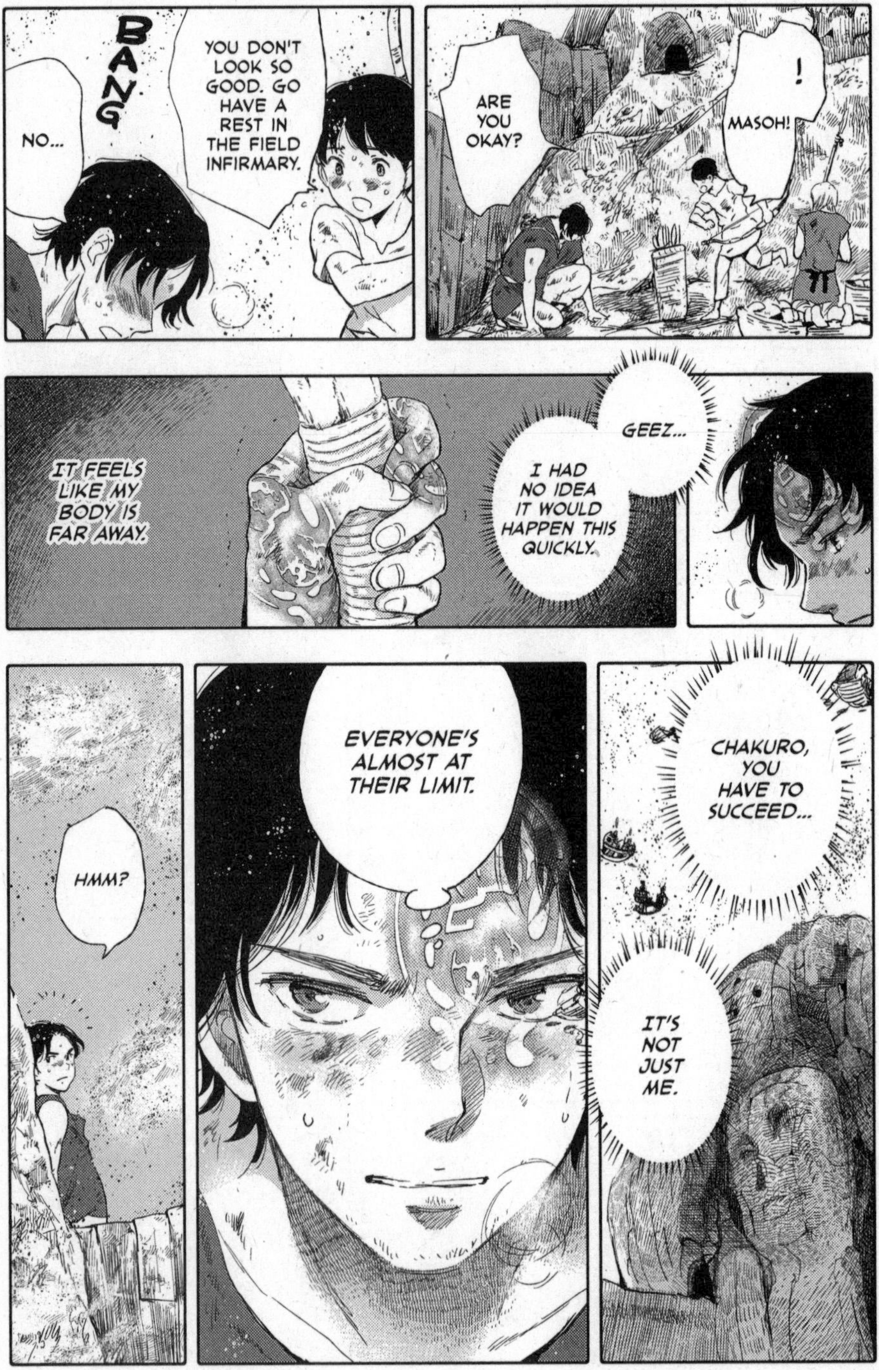
!
MASOH!
ARE YOU OKAY?
YOU DON'T LOOK SO GOOD. GO HAVE A REST IN THE FIELD INFIRMARY.
BANG
NO...
GEEZ...
I HAD NO IDEA IT WOULD HAPPEN THIS QUICKLY.
IT FEELS LIKE MY BODY IS FAR AWAY.
CHAKURO, YOU HAVE TO SUCCEED...
IT'S NOT JUST ME.
EVERYONE'S ALMOST AT THEIR LIMIT.
HMM?

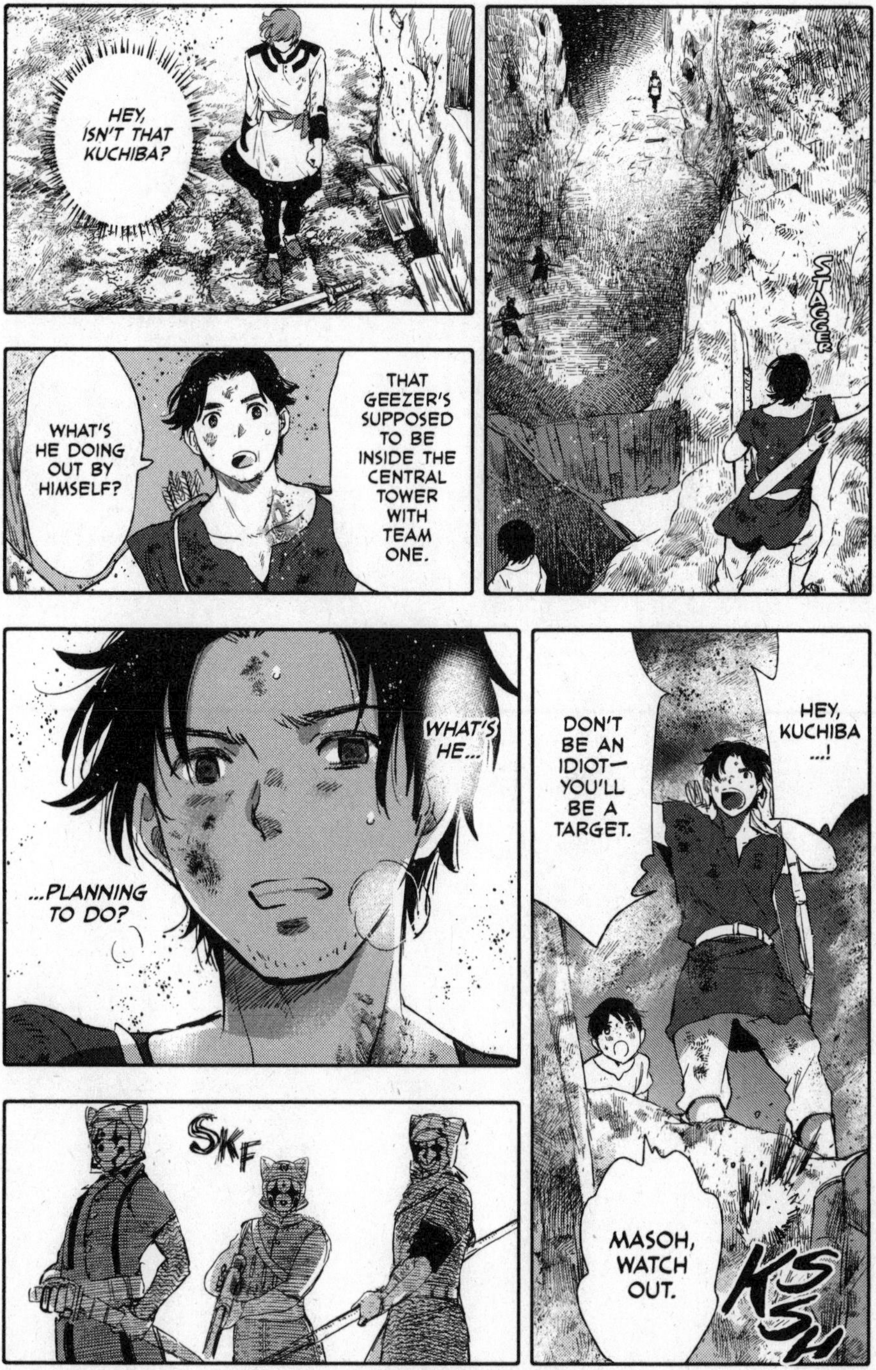
STAGGER
HEY, ISN'T THAT KUCHIBA?
THAT GEEZER'S SUPPOSED TO BE INSIDE THE CENTRAL TOWER WITH TEAM ONE.
WHAT'S HE DOING OUT BY HIMSELF?
HEY, KUCHIBA ...!
DON'T BE AN IDIOT— YOU'LL BE A TARGET.
MASOH, WATCH OUT.
KSH
WHAT'S HE...
...PLANNING TO DO?
SKF

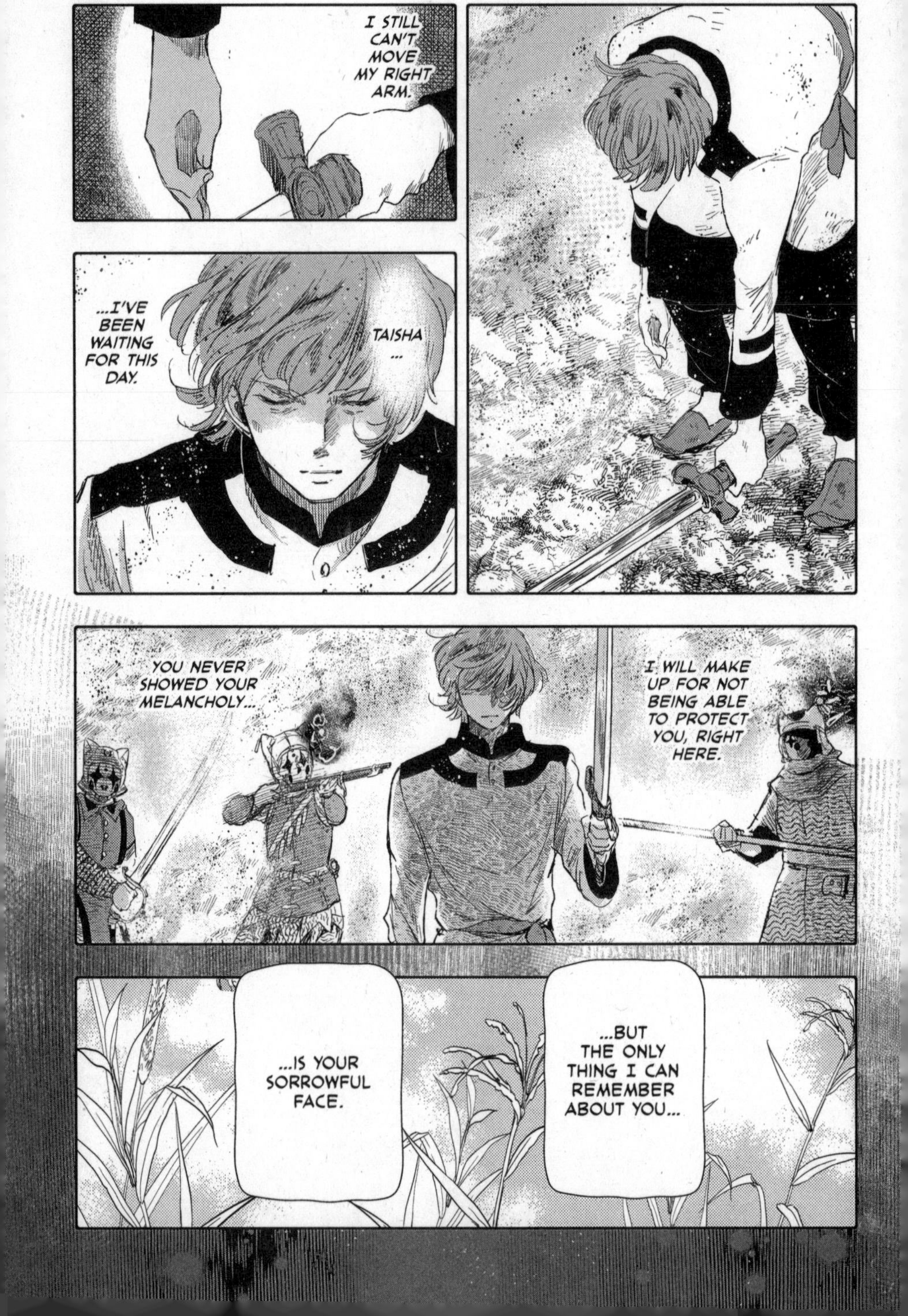
I STILL CAN'T MOVE MY RIGHT ARM.
TAISHA ...
...I'VE BEEN WAITING FOR THIS DAY.
I WILL MAKE UP FOR NOT BEING ABLE TO PROTECT YOU, RIGHT HERE.
YOU NEVER SHOWED YOUR MELANCHOLY...
...BUT THE ONLY THING I CAN REMEMBER ABOUT YOU...
...IS YOUR SORROWFUL FACE.

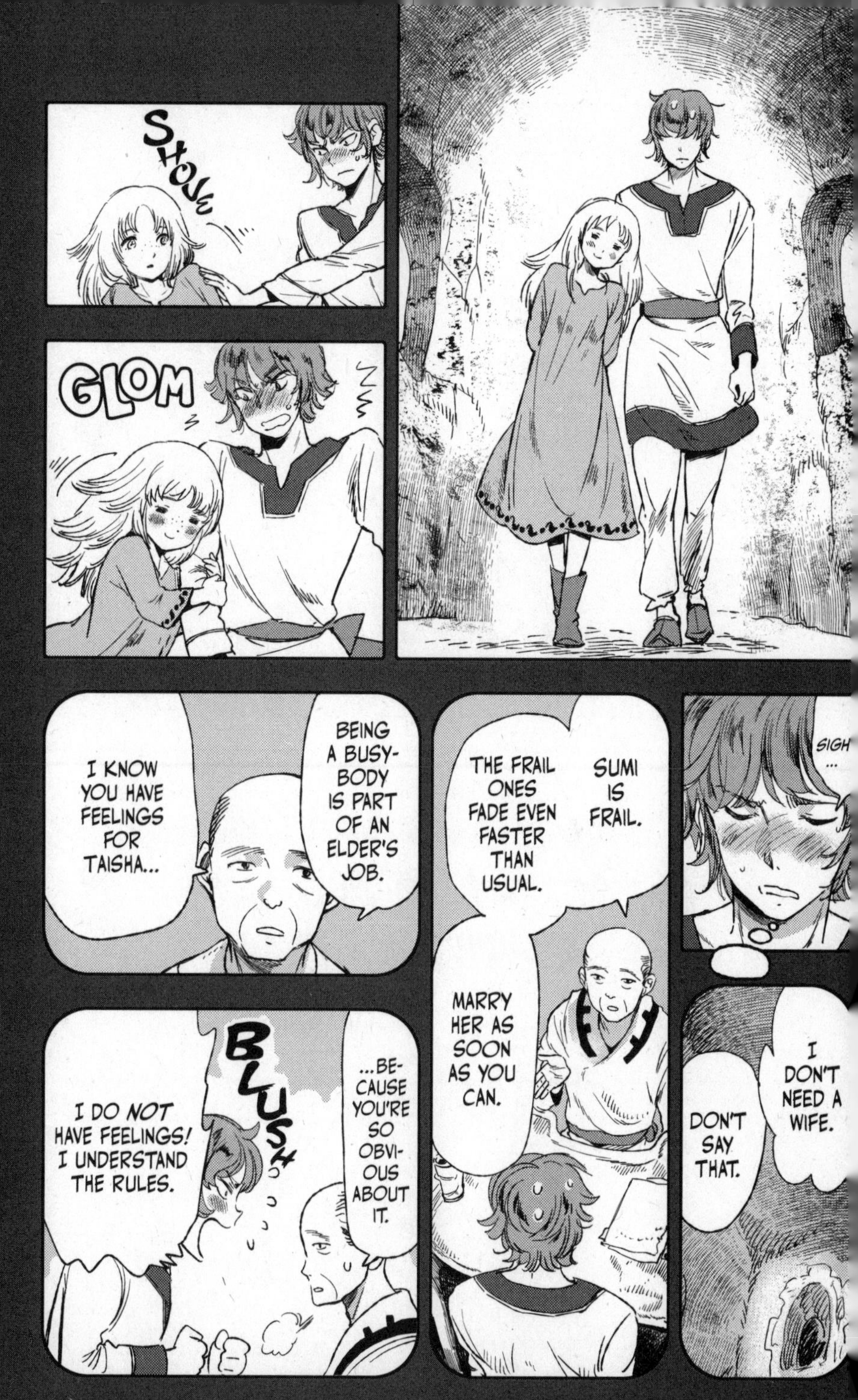
SHOVE
GLOM
SIGH...
I DON'T NEED A WIFE.
DON'T SAY THAT.
SUMI IS FRAIL.
THE FRAIL ONES FADE EVEN FASTER THAN USUAL.
MARRY HER AS SOON AS YOU CAN.
BEING A BUSY-BODY IS PART OF AN ELDER'S JOB.
I KNOW YOU HAVE FEELINGS FOR TAISHA...
...BE-CAUSE YOU'RE SO OBVI-OUS ABOUT IT.
BLUSH
I DO *NOT* HAVE FEELINGS! I UNDERSTAND THE RULES.

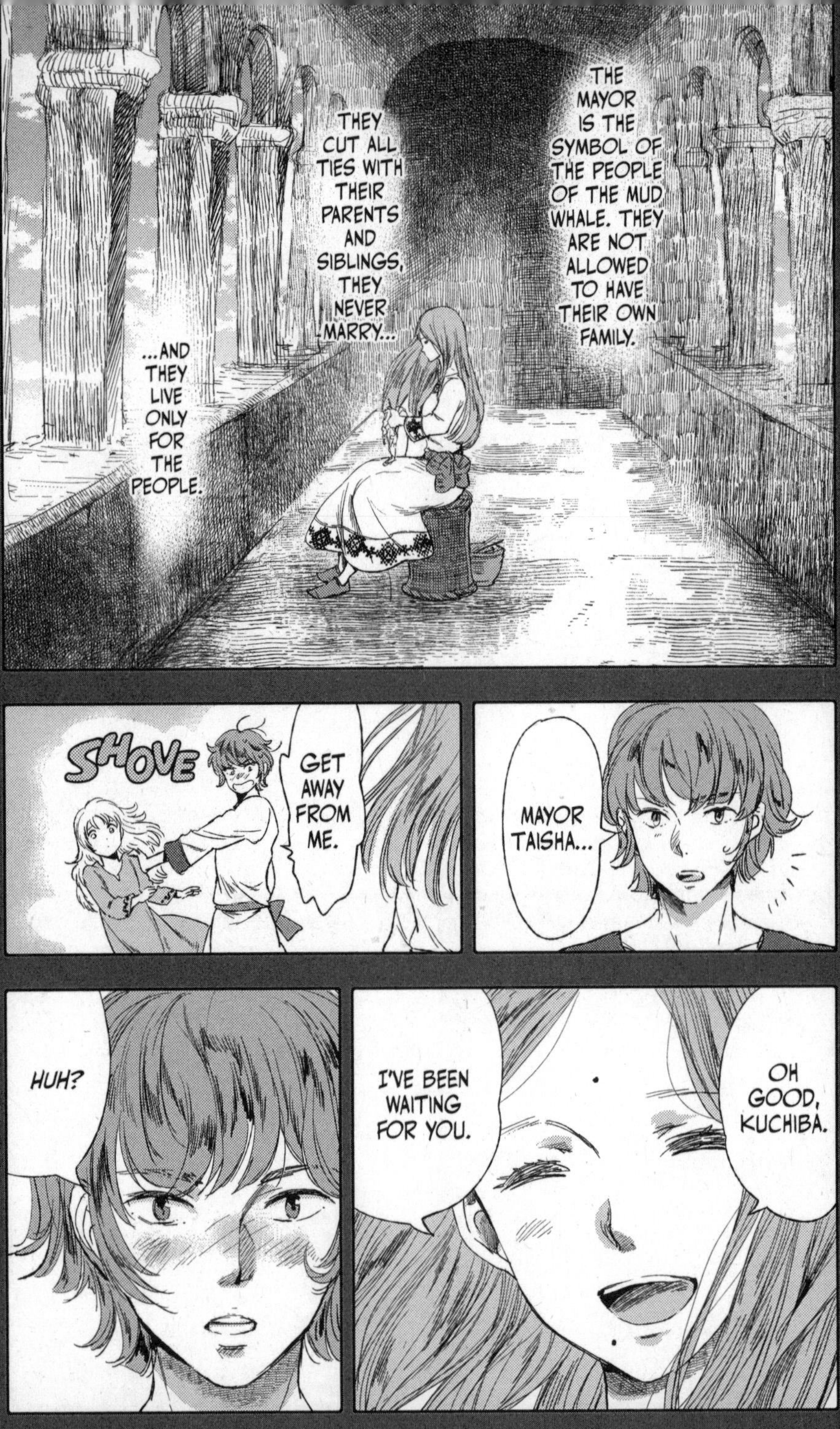
THE MAYOR IS THE SYMBOL OF THE PEOPLE OF THE MUD WHALE. THEY ARE NOT ALLOWED TO HAVE THEIR OWN FAMILY.
THEY CUT ALL TIES WITH THEIR PARENTS AND SIBLINGS, THEY NEVER MARRY...
...AND THEY LIVE ONLY FOR THE PEOPLE.
MAYOR TAISHA...
SHOVE
GET AWAY FROM ME.
OH GOOD, KUCHIBA.
I'VE BEEN WAITING FOR YOU.
HUH?

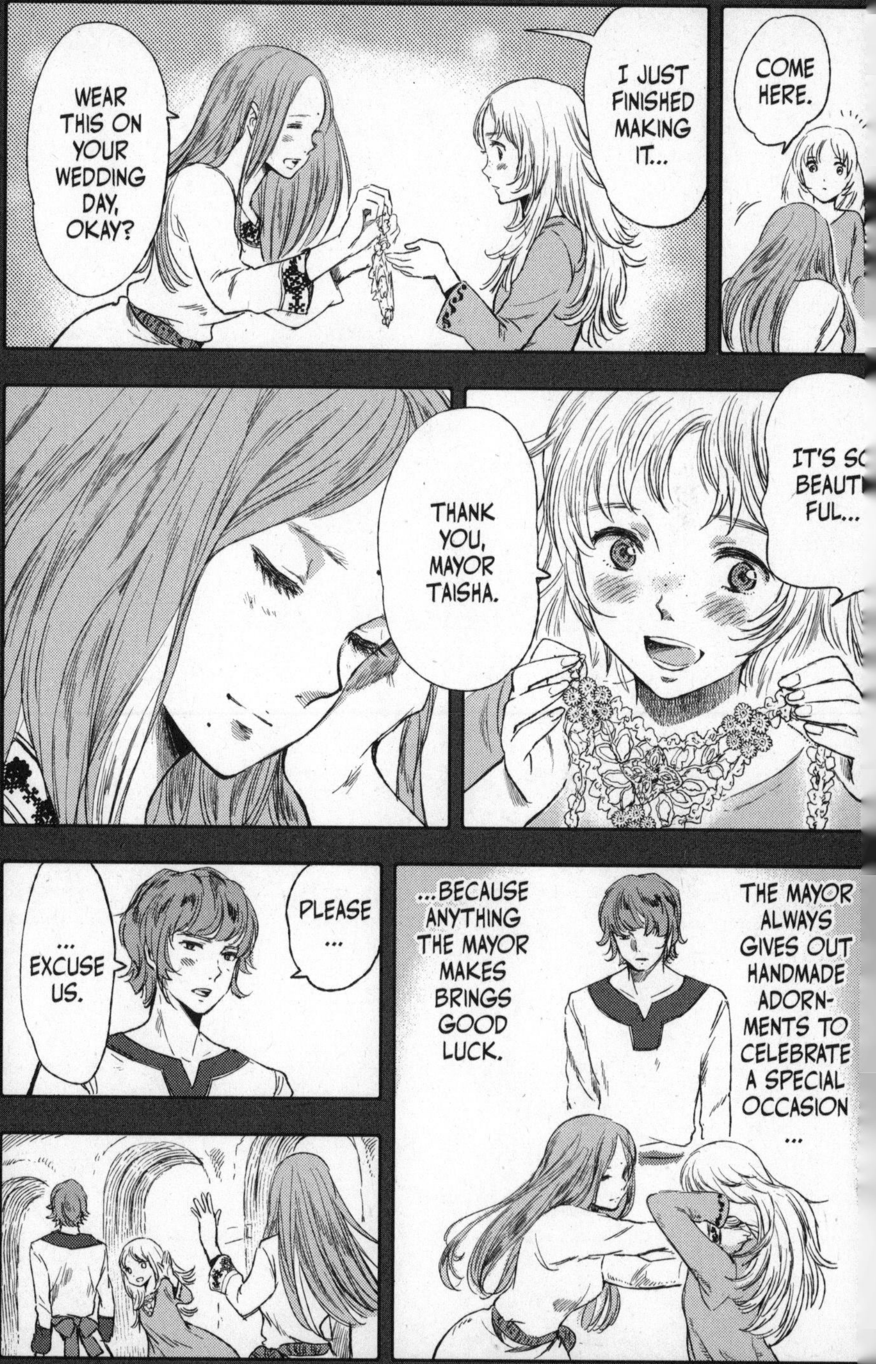
COME HERE.
I JUST FINISHED MAKING IT...
WEAR THIS ON YOUR WEDDING DAY, OKAY?
IT'S SO BEAUTIFUL...
THANK YOU, MAYOR TAISHA.
THE MAYOR ALWAYS GIVES OUT HANDMADE ADORNMENTS TO CELEBRATE A SPECIAL OCCASION...
...BECAUSE ANYTHING THE MAYOR MAKES BRINGS GOOD LUCK.
PLEASE...
...EXCUSE US.

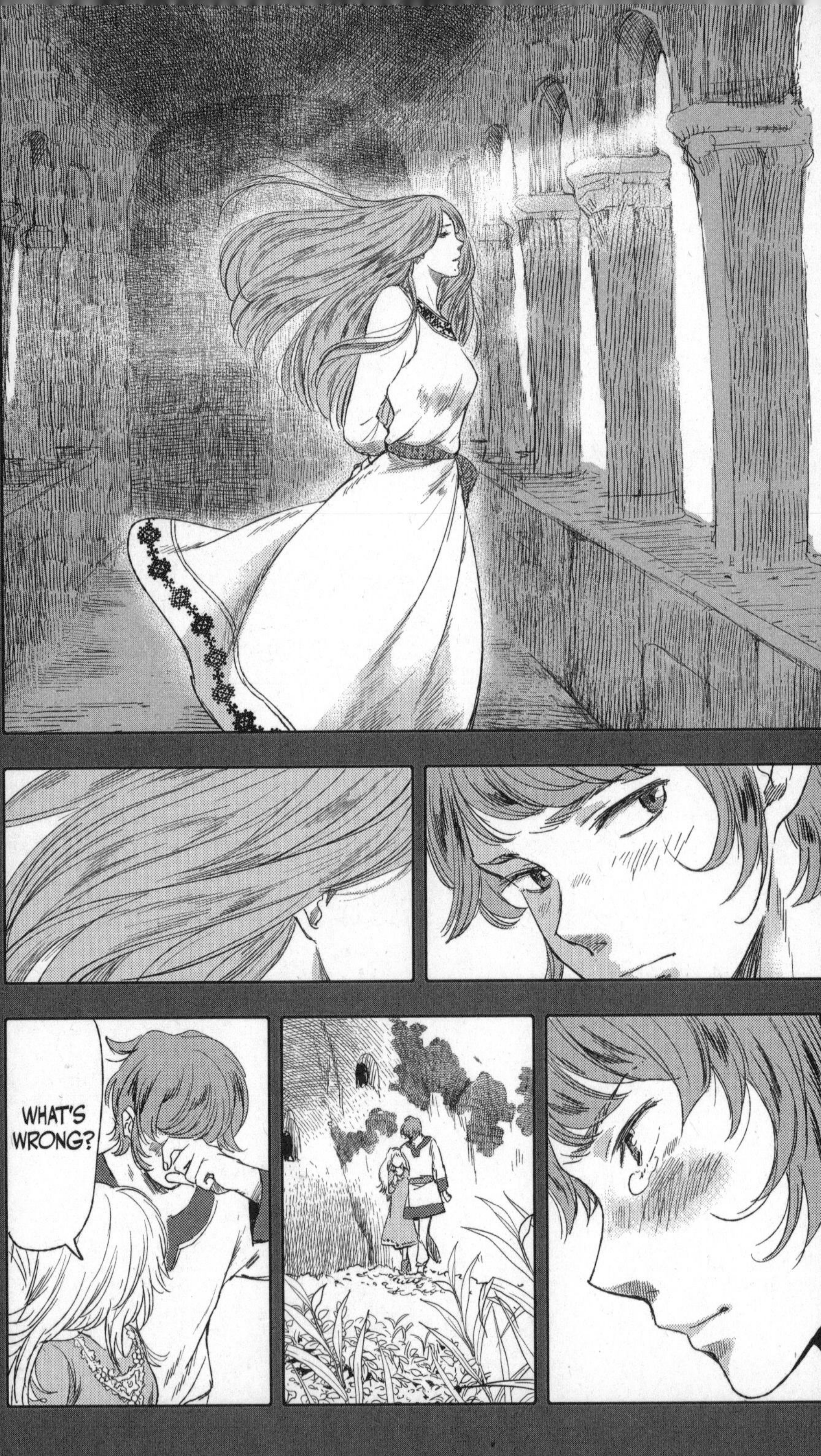
WHAT'S WRONG?

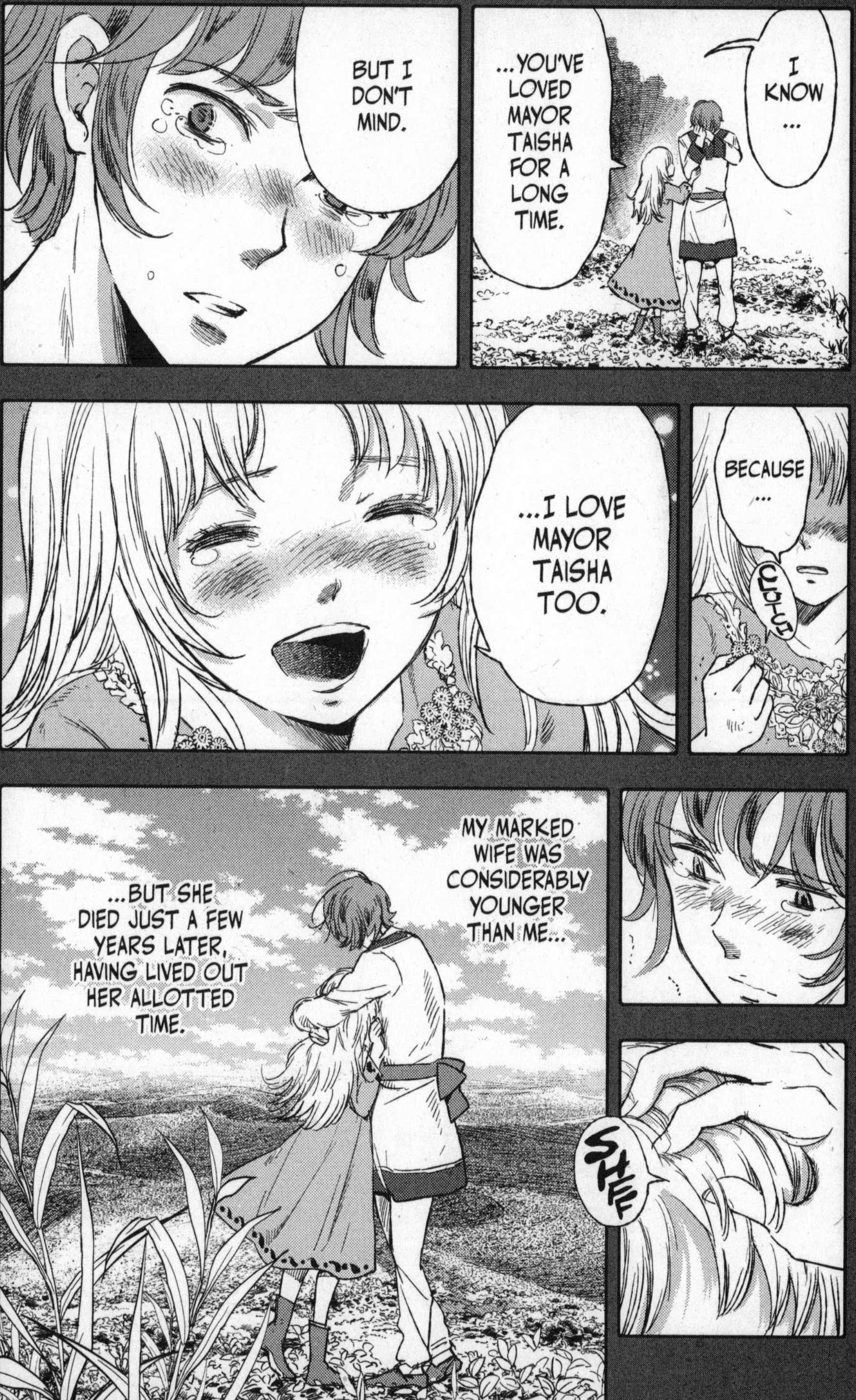
I KNOW ...
...YOU'VE LOVED MAYOR TAISHA FOR A LONG TIME.
BUT I DON'T MIND.
BECAUSE ...
CLUTCH
...I LOVE MAYOR TAISHA TOO.
SHFF
MY MARKED WIFE WAS CONSIDERABLY YOUNGER THAN ME...
...BUT SHE DIED JUST A FEW YEARS LATER, HAVING LIVED OUT HER ALLOTTED TIME.

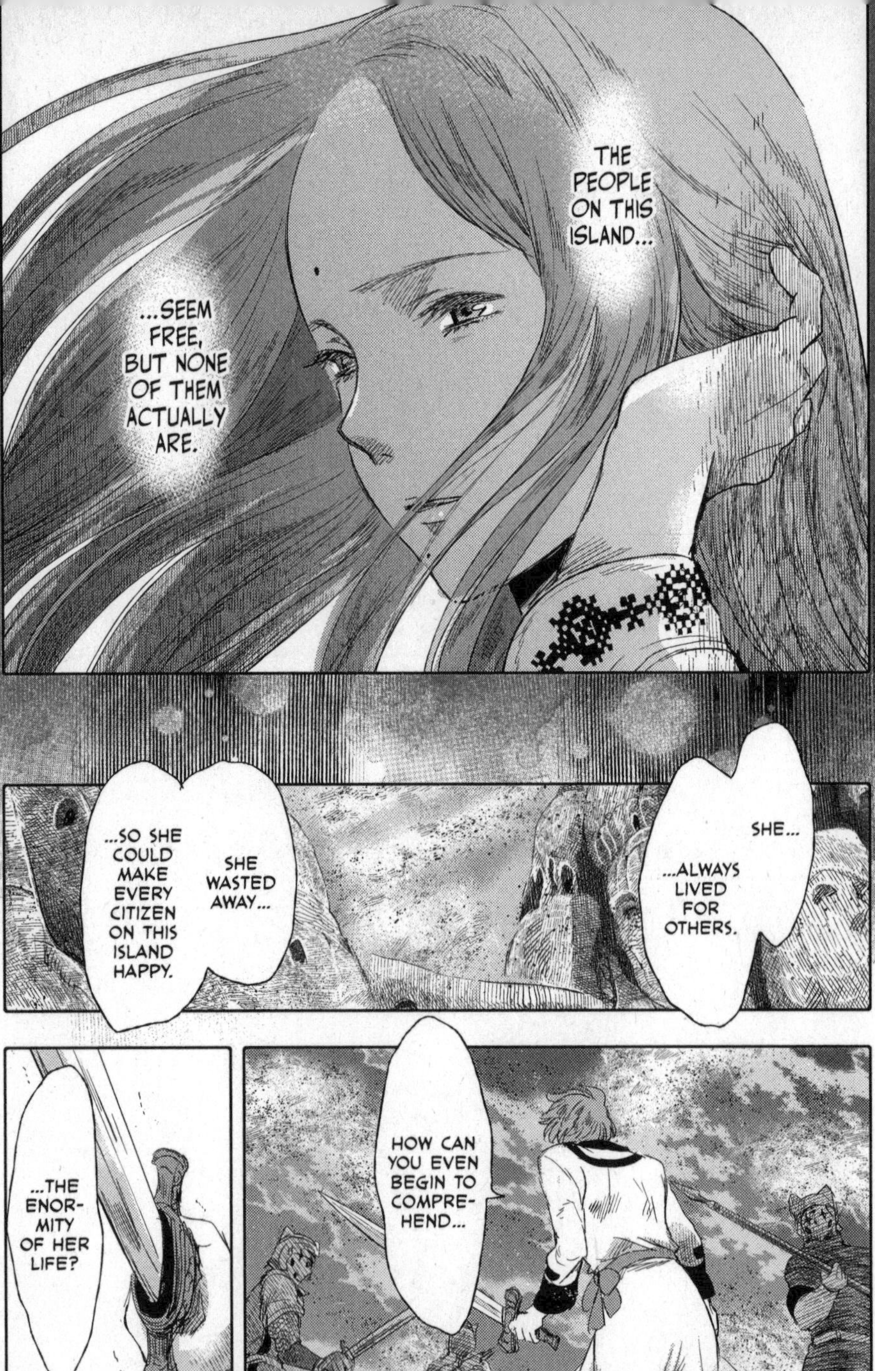
THE PEOPLE ON THIS ISLAND...
...SEEM FREE, BUT NONE OF THEM ACTUALLY ARE.
SHE...
...ALWAYS LIVED FOR OTHERS.
SHE WASTED AWAY...
...SO SHE COULD MAKE EVERY CITIZEN ON THIS ISLAND HAPPY.
HOW CAN YOU EVEN BEGIN TO COMPRE-HEND...
...THE ENOR-MITY OF HER LIFE?

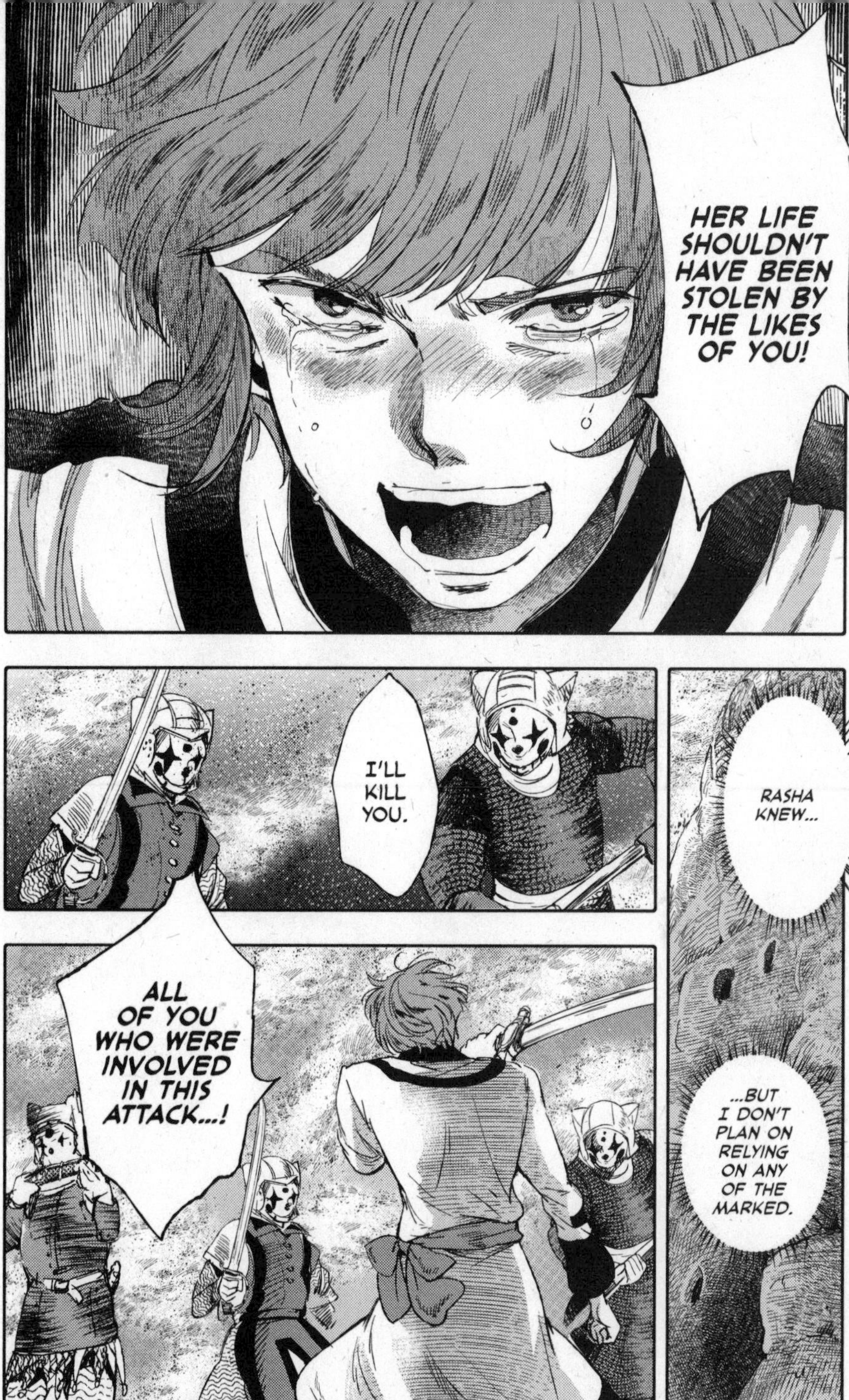
HER LIFE SHOULDN'T HAVE BEEN STOLEN BY THE LIKES OF YOU!
RASHA KNEW...
...BUT I DON'T PLAN ON RELYING ON ANY OF THE MARKED.
I'LL KILL YOU.
ALL OF YOU WHO WERE INVOLVED IN THIS ATTACK...!

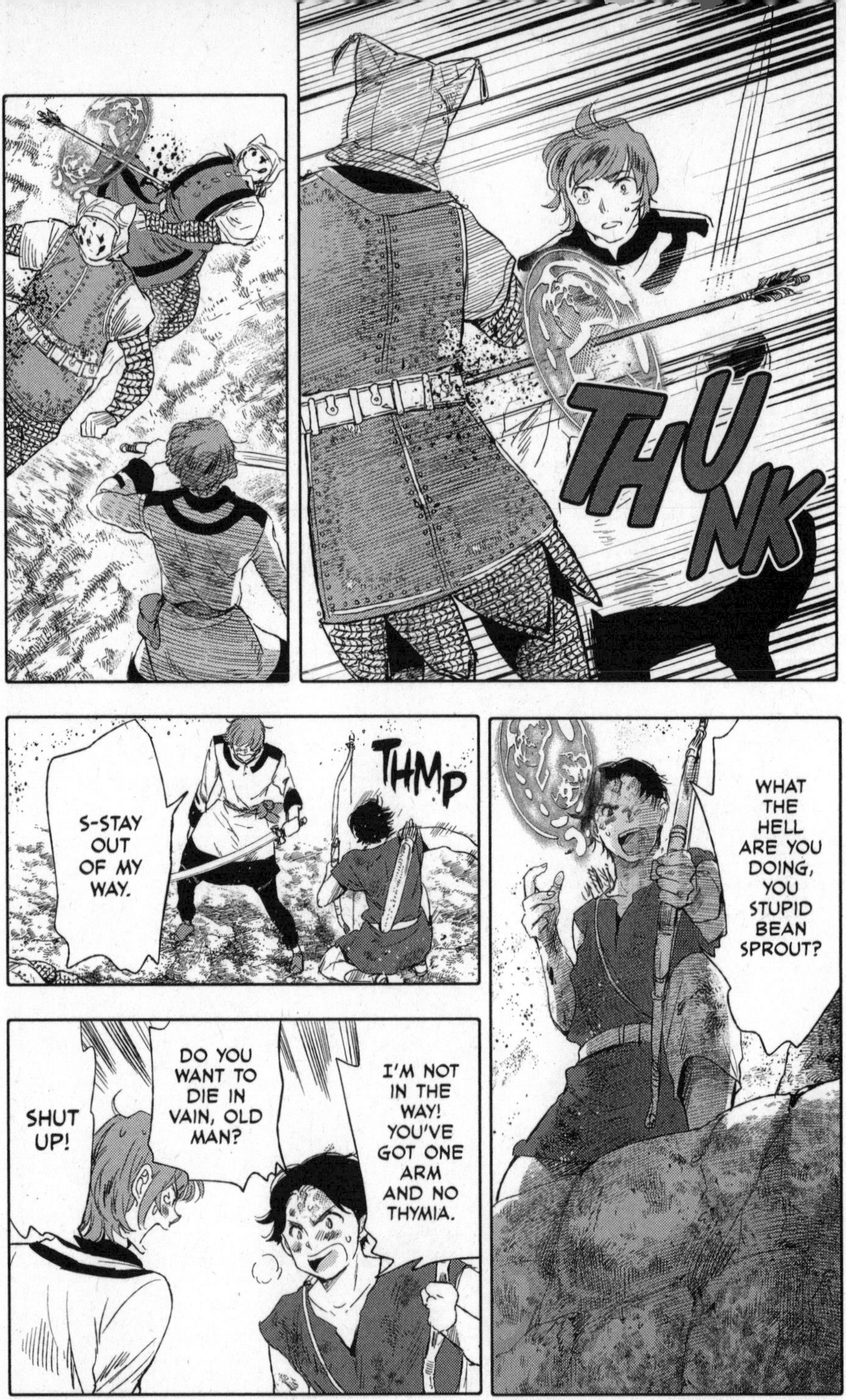
THUNK
WHAT THE HELL ARE YOU DOING, YOU STUPID BEAN SPROUT?
THMP
S-STAY OUT OF MY WAY.
I'M NOT IN THE WAY! YOU'VE GOT ONE ARM AND NO THYMIA.
DO YOU WANT TO DIE IN VAIN, OLD MAN?
SHUT UP!

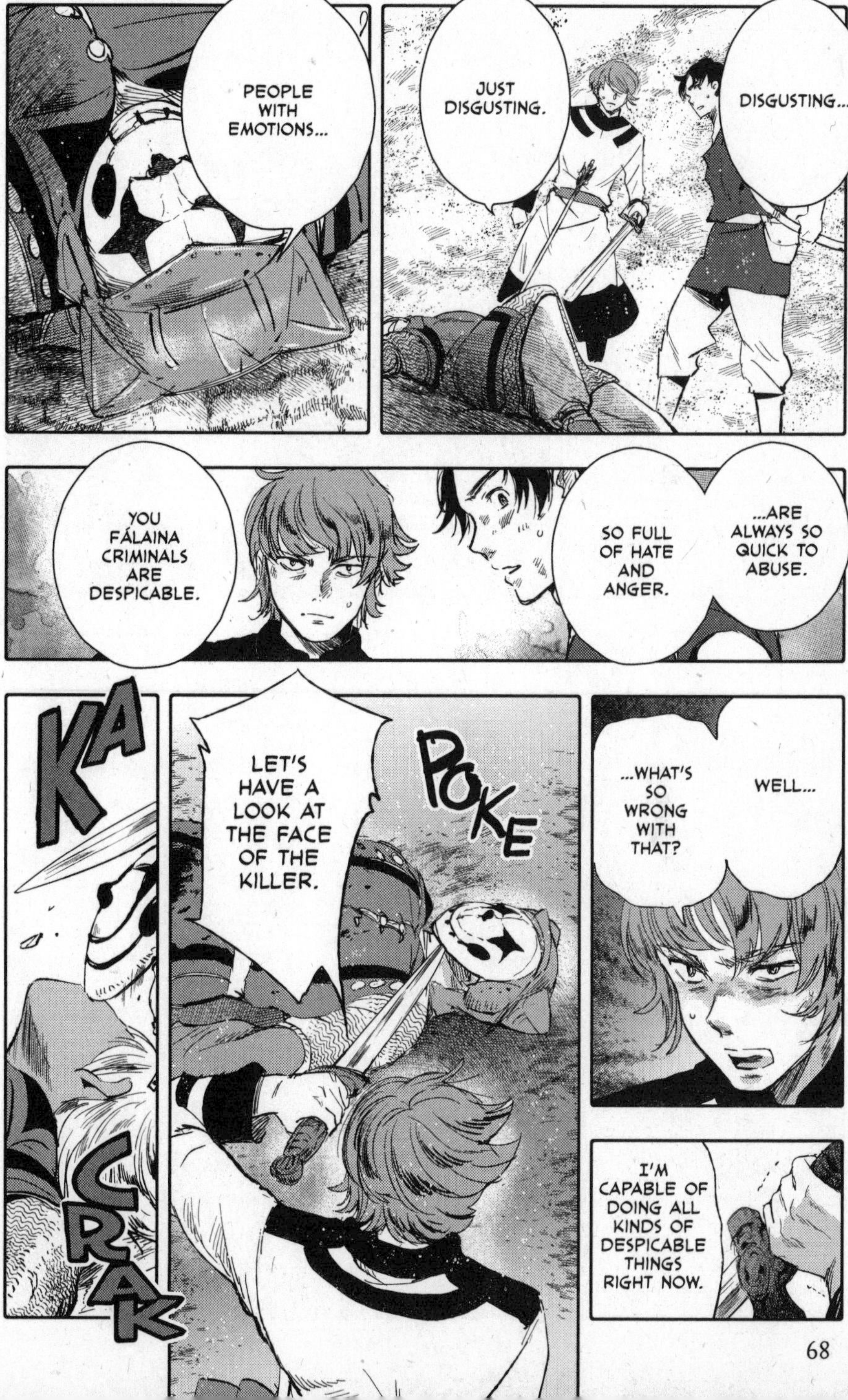
DISGUSTING...
JUST DISGUSTING.
PEOPLE WITH EMOTIONS...
...ARE ALWAYS SO QUICK TO ABUSE.
SO FULL OF HATE AND ANGER.
YOU FÁLAINA CRIMINALS ARE DESPICABLE.
WELL...
...WHAT'S SO WRONG WITH THAT?
I'M CAPABLE OF DOING ALL KINDS OF DESPICABLE THINGS RIGHT NOW.
POKE
LET'S HAVE A LOOK AT THE FACE OF THE KILLER.
KA
CRAK

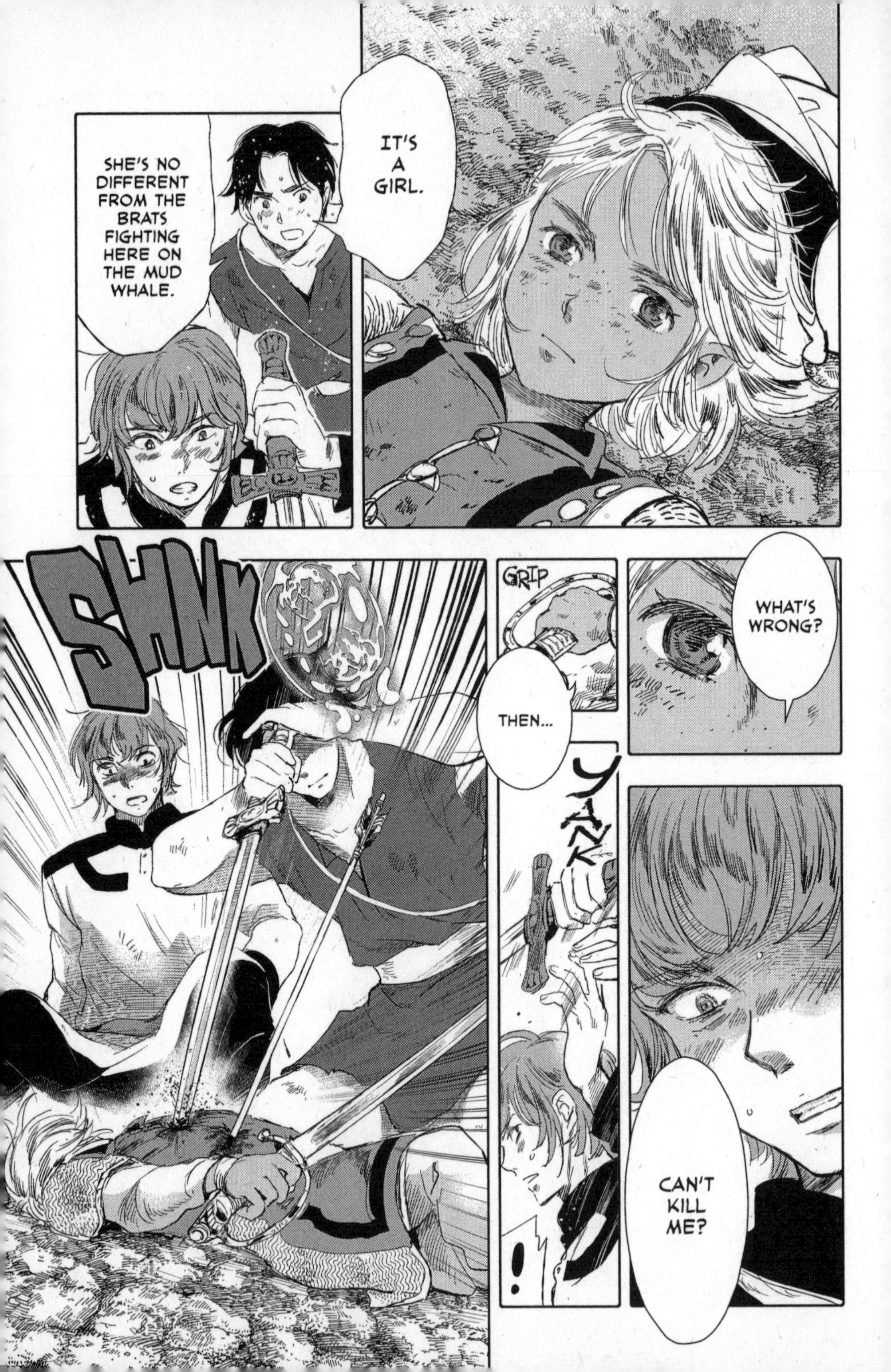
IT'S A GIRL.
SHE'S NO DIFFERENT FROM THE BRATS FIGHTING HERE ON THE MUD WHALE.
WHAT'S WRONG?
GRIP
THEN...
YANK
!
CAN'T KILL ME?
SHNK

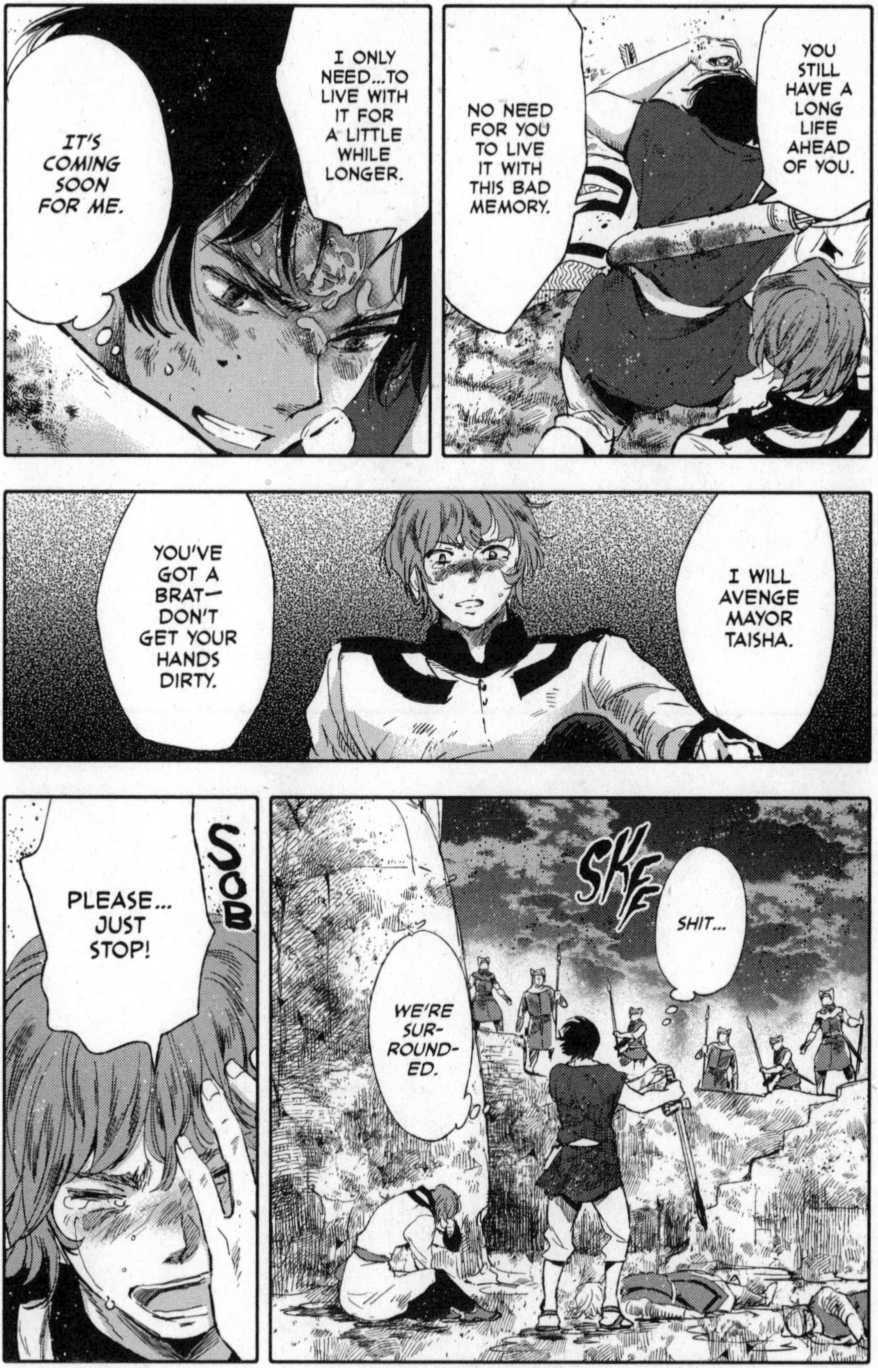
YOU STILL HAVE A LONG LIFE AHEAD OF YOU.
NO NEED FOR YOU TO LIVE IT WITH THIS BAD MEMORY.
I ONLY NEED...TO LIVE WITH IT FOR A LITTLE WHILE LONGER.
IT'S COMING SOON FOR ME.
I WILL AVENGE MAYOR TAISHA.
YOU'VE GOT A BRAT—DON'T GET YOUR HANDS DIRTY.
SKF
SHIT...
WE'RE SUR-ROUND-ED.
SOB
PLEASE... JUST STOP!

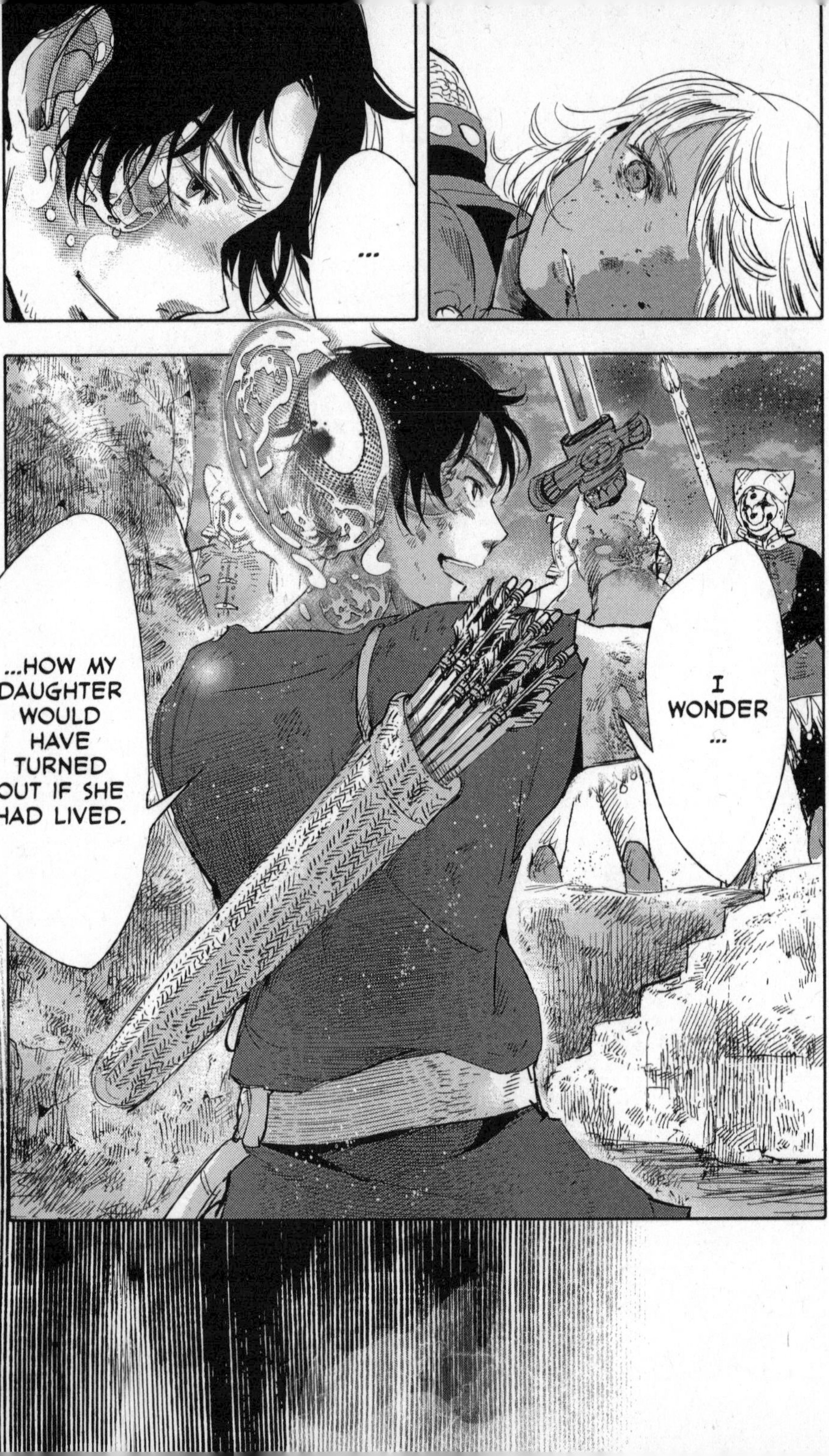
...
I WONDER ...
...HOW MY DAUGHTER WOULD HAVE TURNED OUT IF SHE HAD LIVED.

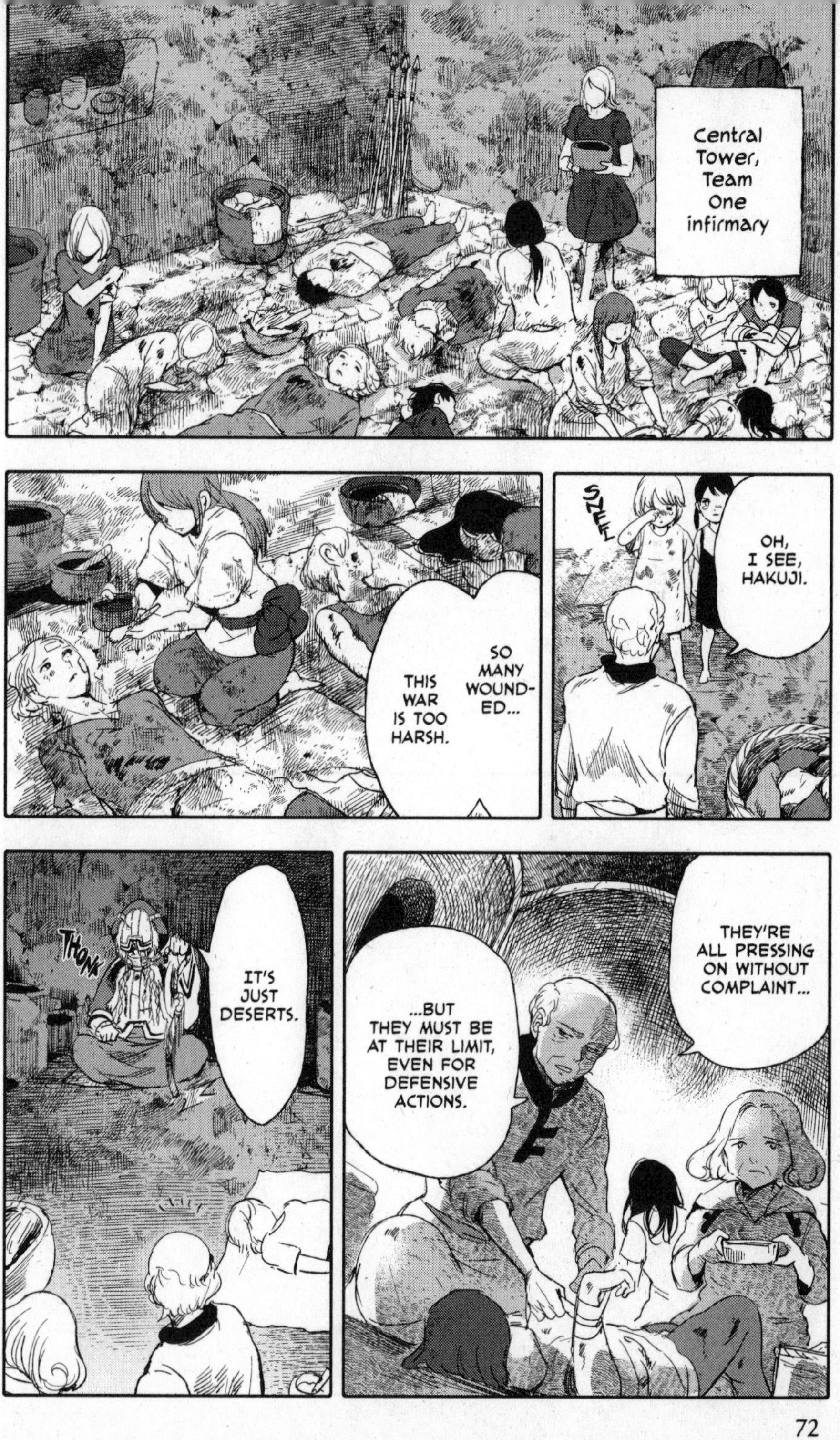
Central Tower, Team One infirmary
OH, I SEE, HAKUJI.
SO MANY WOUNDED...
THIS WAR IS TOO HARSH.
THEY'RE ALL PRESSING ON WITHOUT COMPLAINT...
...BUT THEY MUST BE AT THEIR LIMIT, EVEN FOR DEFENSIVE ACTIONS.
THONK
IT'S JUST DESERTS.

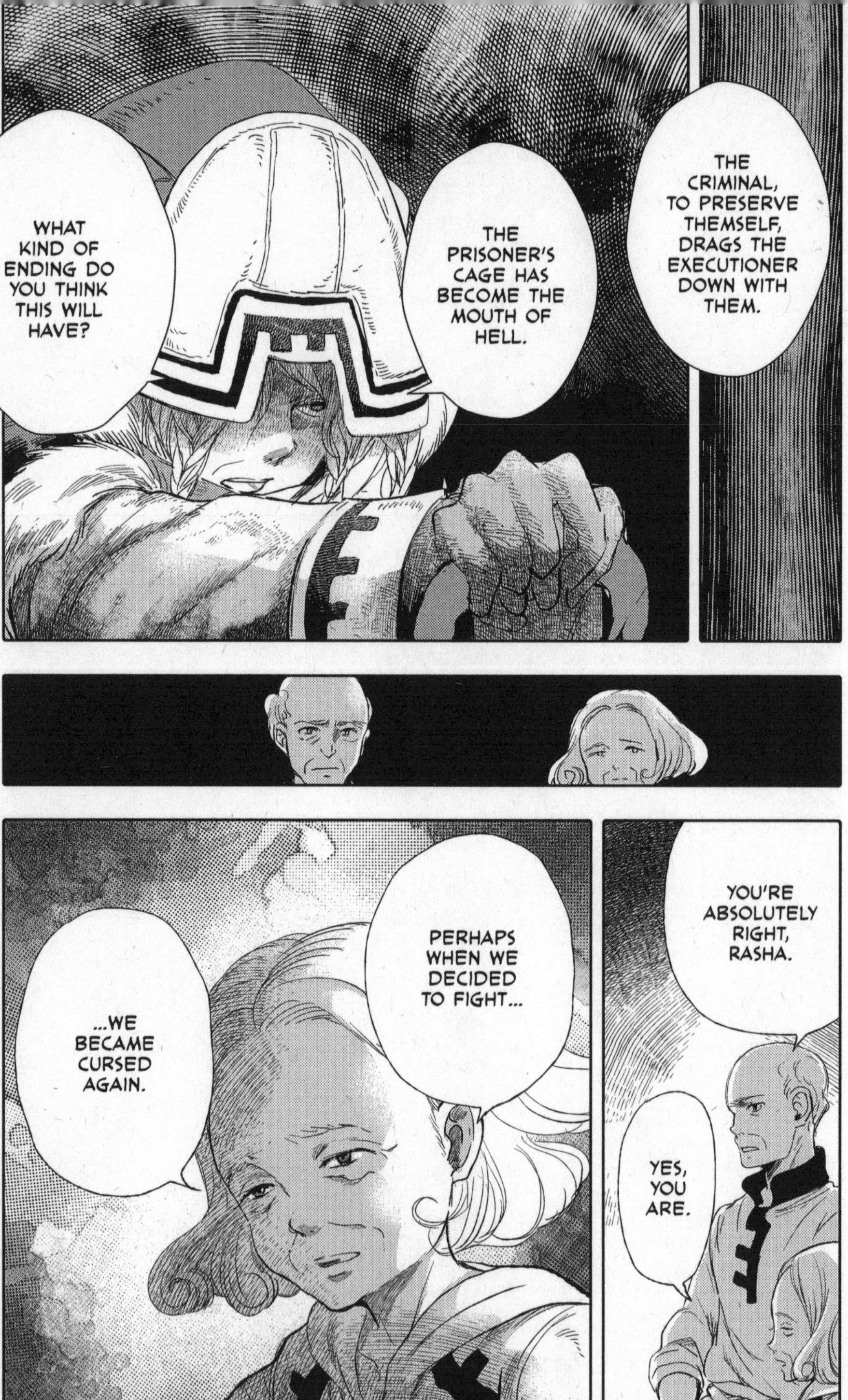
THE CRIMINAL, TO PRESERVE THEMSELF, DRAGS THE EXECUTIONER DOWN WITH THEM.
THE PRISONER'S CAGE HAS BECOME THE MOUTH OF HELL.
WHAT KIND OF ENDING DO YOU THINK THIS WILL HAVE?
YOU'RE ABSOLUTELY RIGHT, RASHA.
YES, YOU ARE.
PERHAPS WHEN WE DECIDED TO FIGHT...
...WE BECAME CURSED AGAIN.

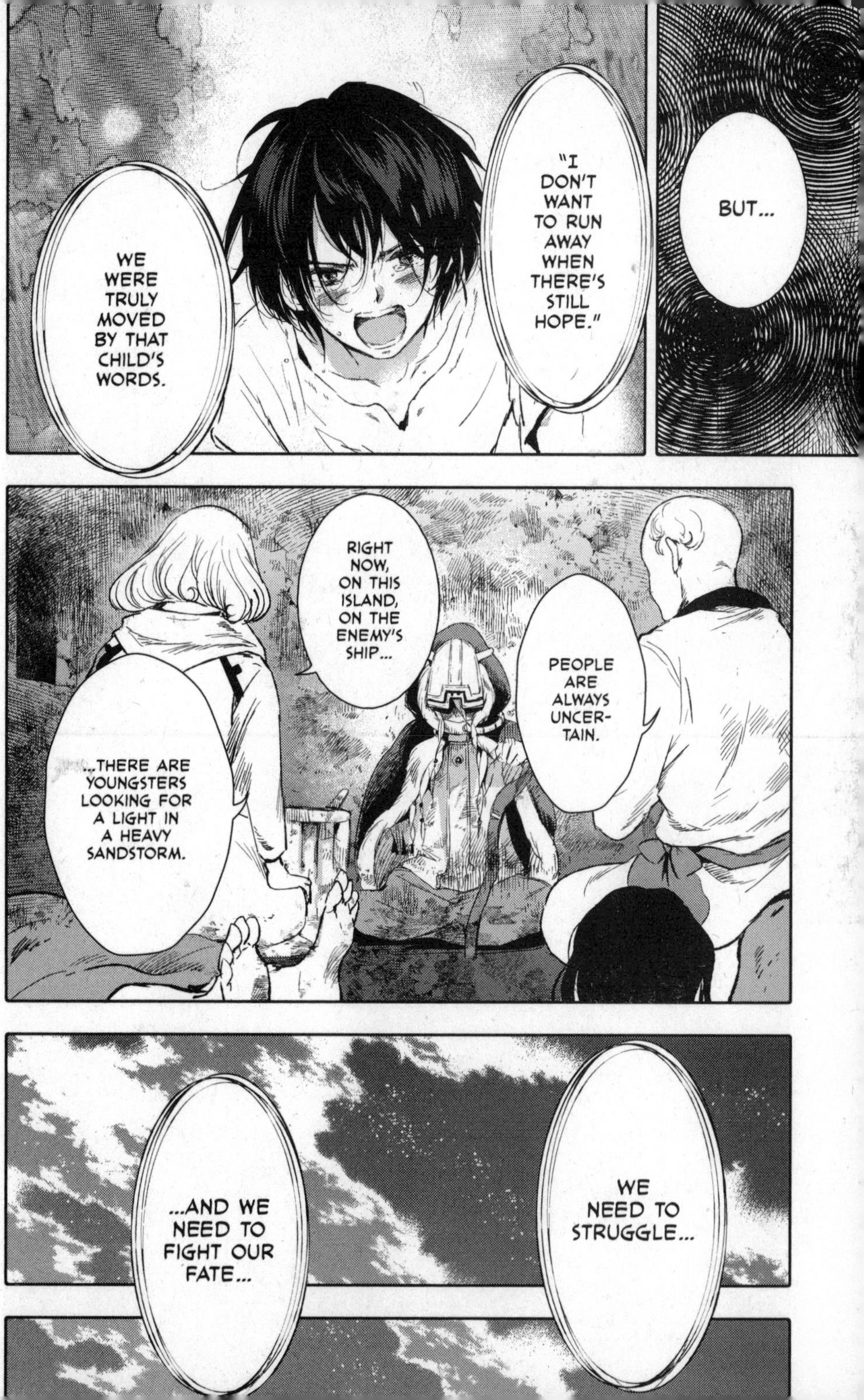
BUT...
"I DON'T WANT TO RUN AWAY WHEN THERE'S STILL HOPE."
WE WERE TRULY MOVED BY THAT CHILD'S WORDS.
PEOPLE ARE ALWAYS UNCER-TAIN.
RIGHT NOW, ON THIS ISLAND, ON THE ENEMY'S SHIP...
...THERE ARE YOUNGSTERS LOOKING FOR A LIGHT IN A HEAVY SANDSTORM.
WE NEED TO STRUGGLE...
...AND WE NEED TO FIGHT OUR FATE...

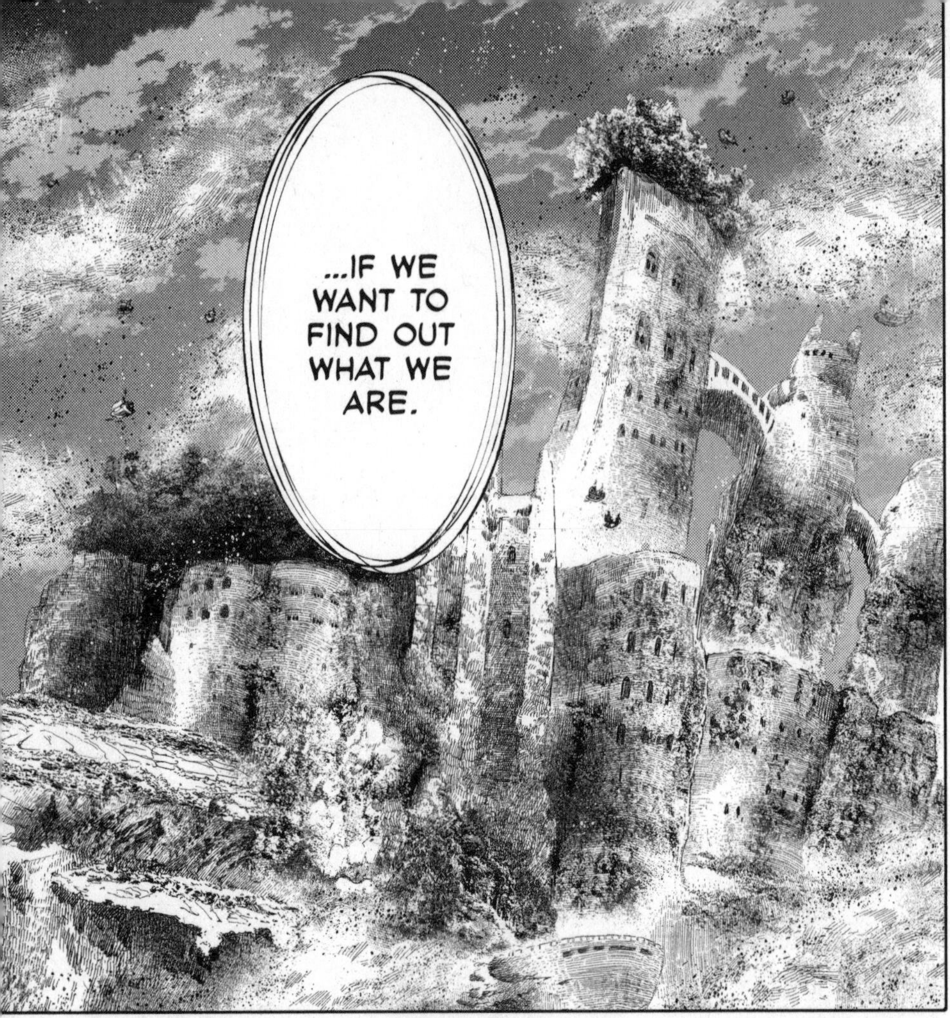
...IF WE WANT TO FIND OUT WHAT WE ARE.

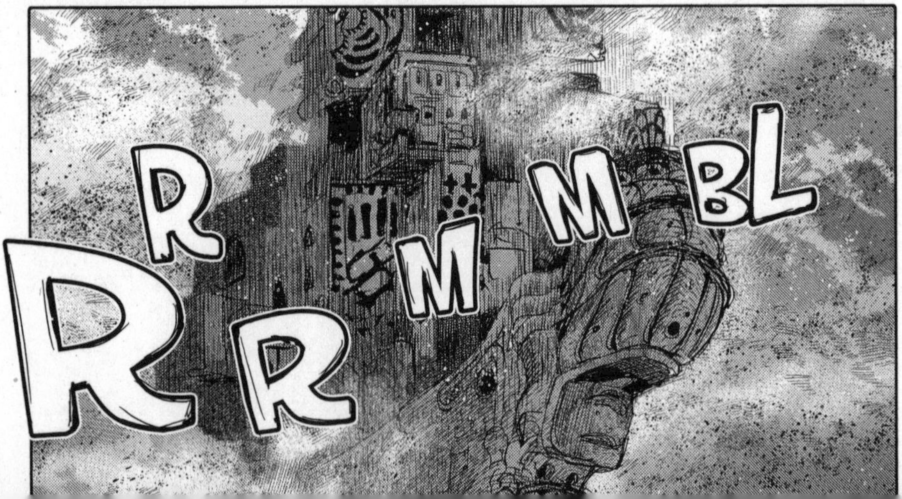
RRRMMBL

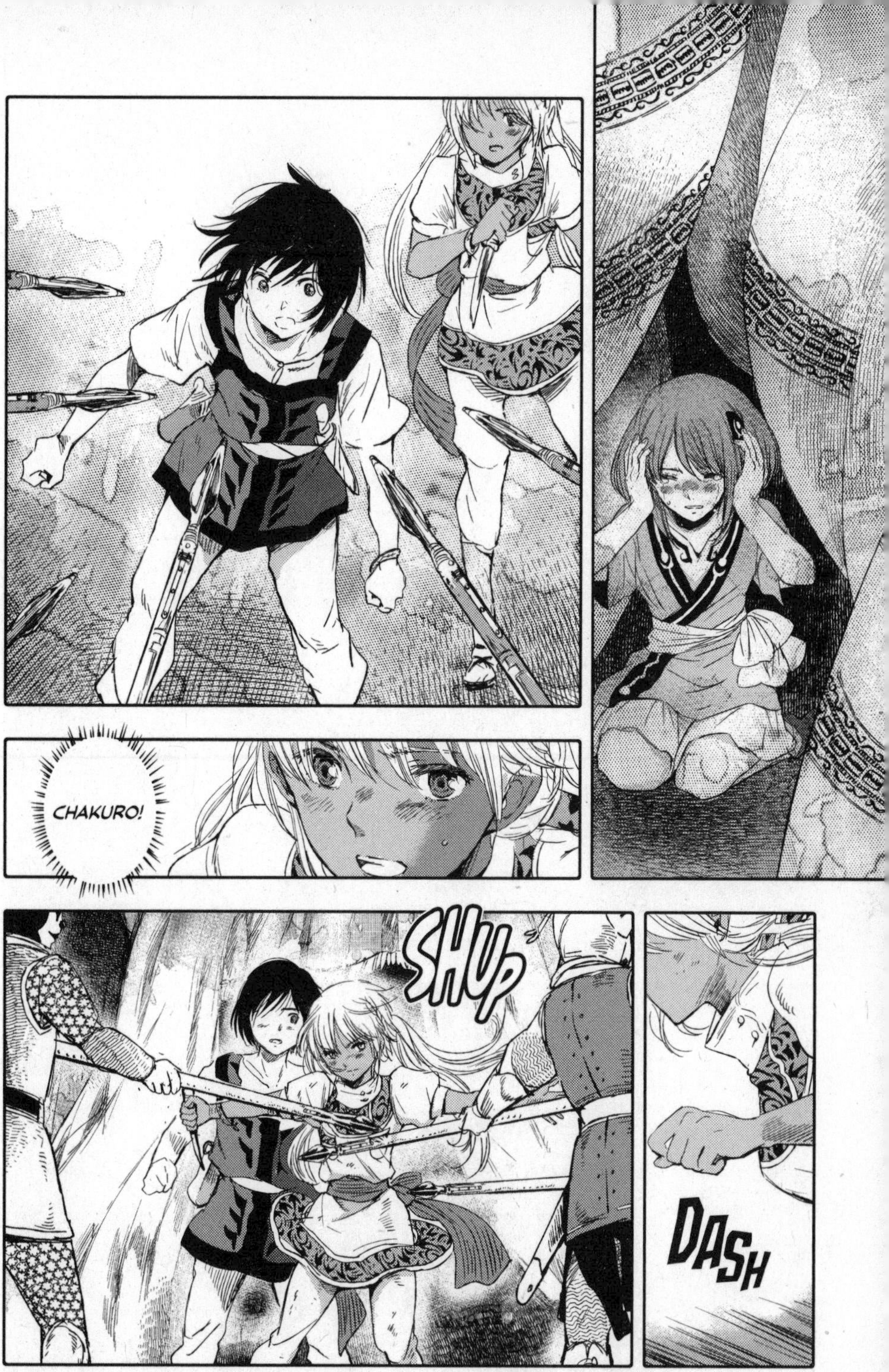
CHAKURO!
DASH
SHUP

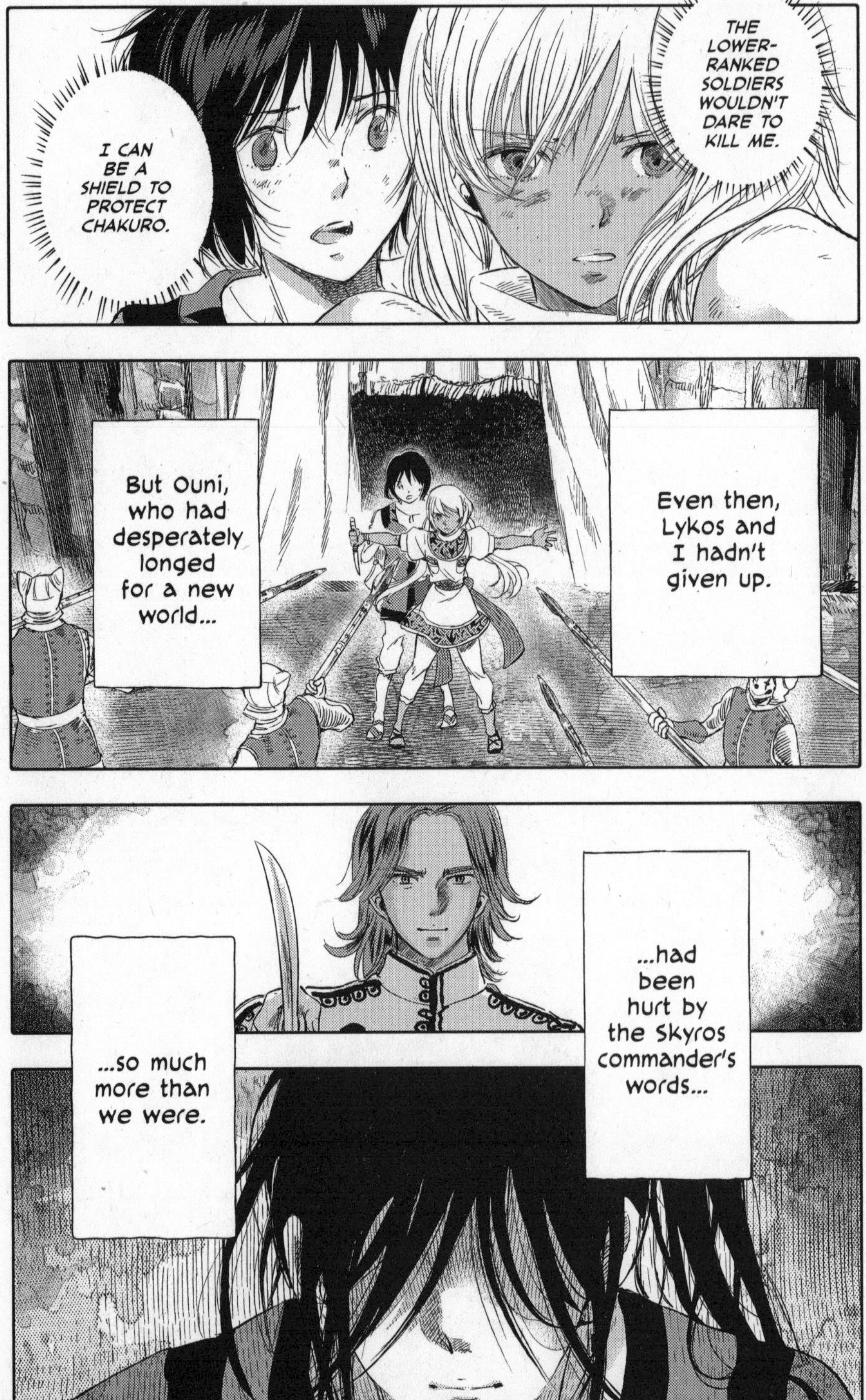
THE LOWER-RANKED SOLDIERS WOULDN'T DARE TO KILL ME.
I CAN BE A SHIELD TO PROTECT CHAKURO.
Even then, Lykos and I hadn't given up.
But Ouni, who had desperately longed for a new world...
...had been hurt by the Skyros commander's words...
...so much more than we were.

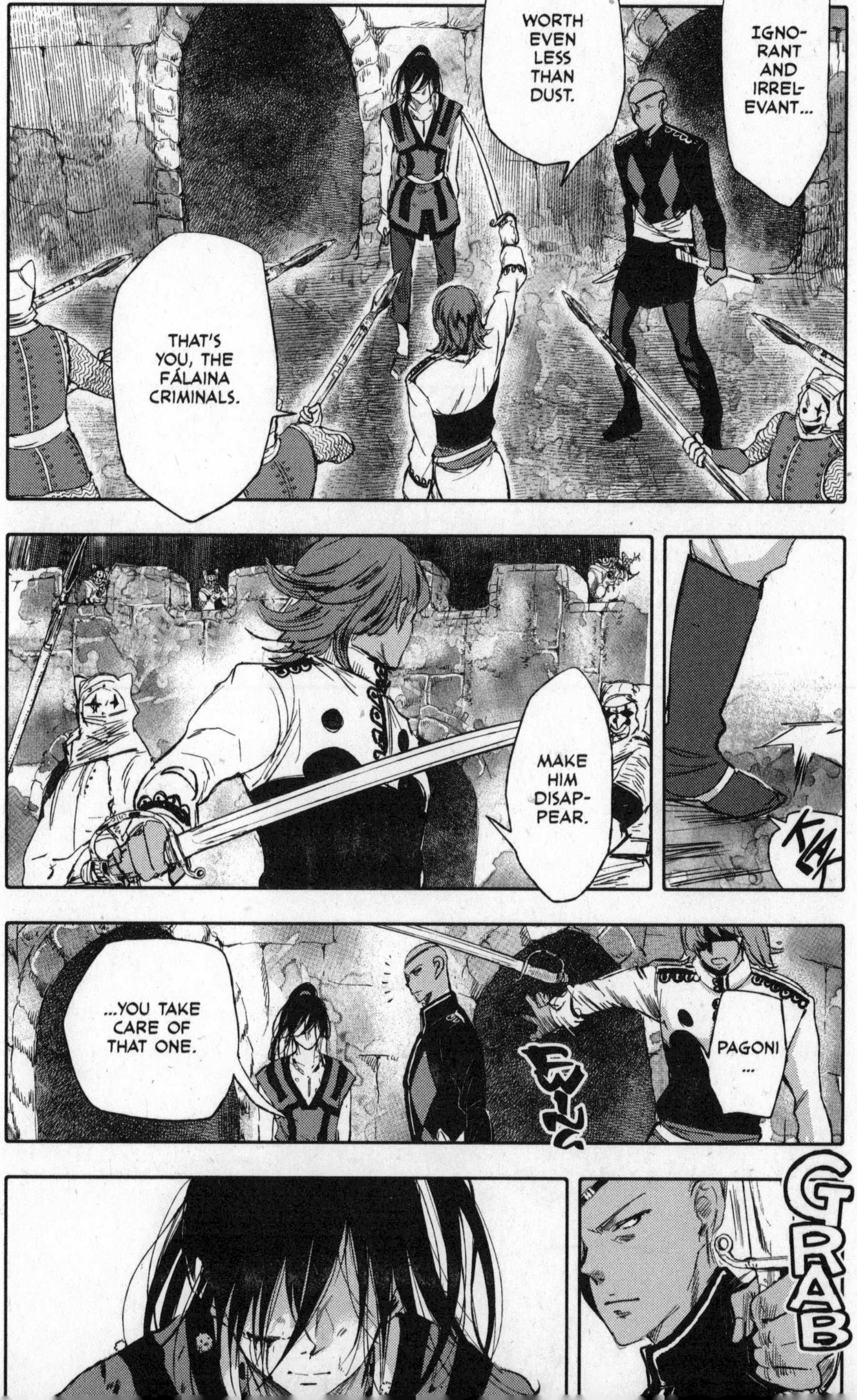
IGNORANT AND IRRELEVANT...
WORTH EVEN LESS THAN DUST.
THAT'S YOU, THE FÁLAINA CRIMINALS.
KLAK
MAKE HIM DISAPPEAR.
PAGONI...
FWING
...YOU TAKE CARE OF THAT ONE.
GRAB

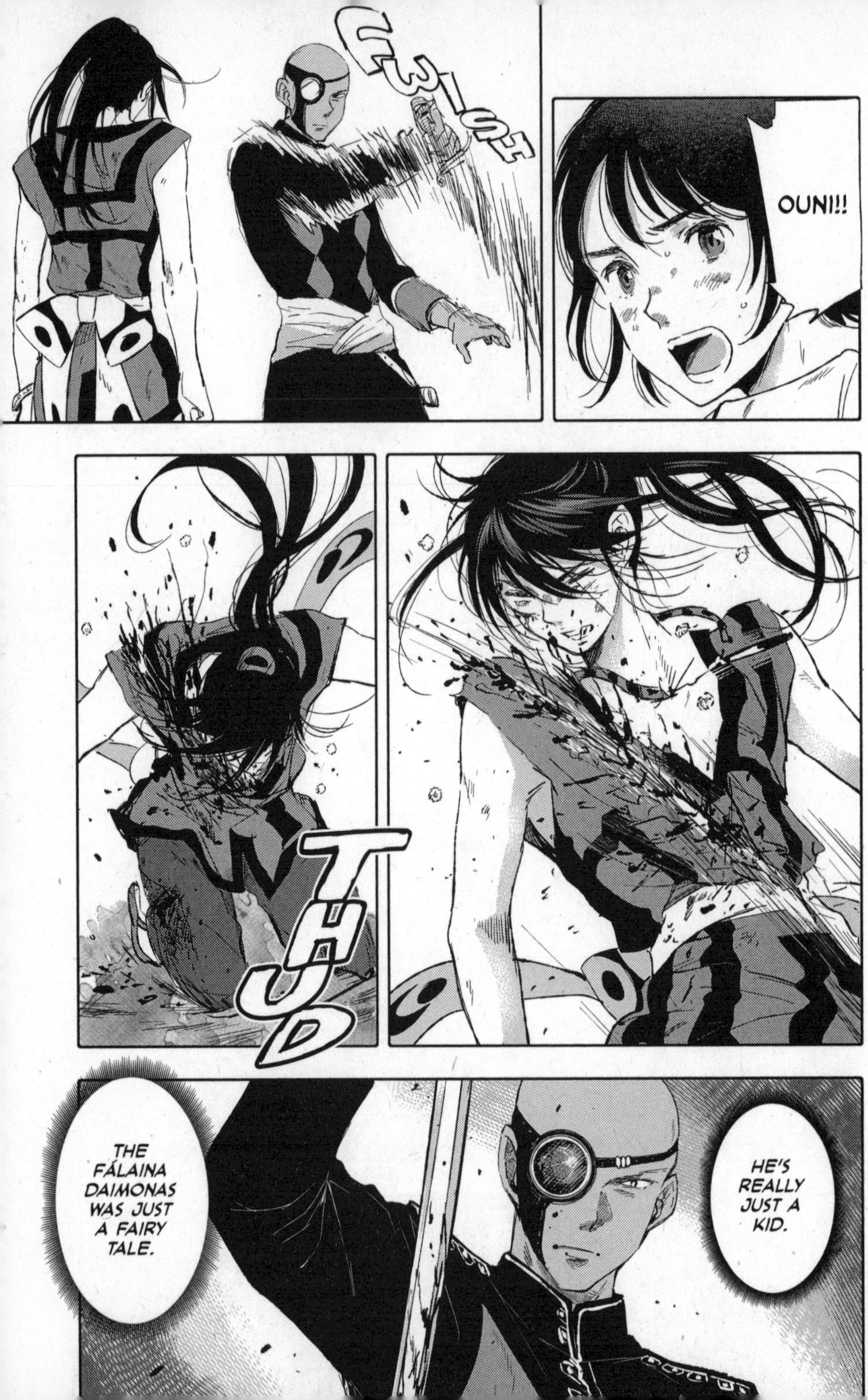
OUNI!!
SWISH
THUD
HE'S REALLY JUST A KID.
THE FÁLAINA DAIMONAS WAS JUST A FAIRY TALE.

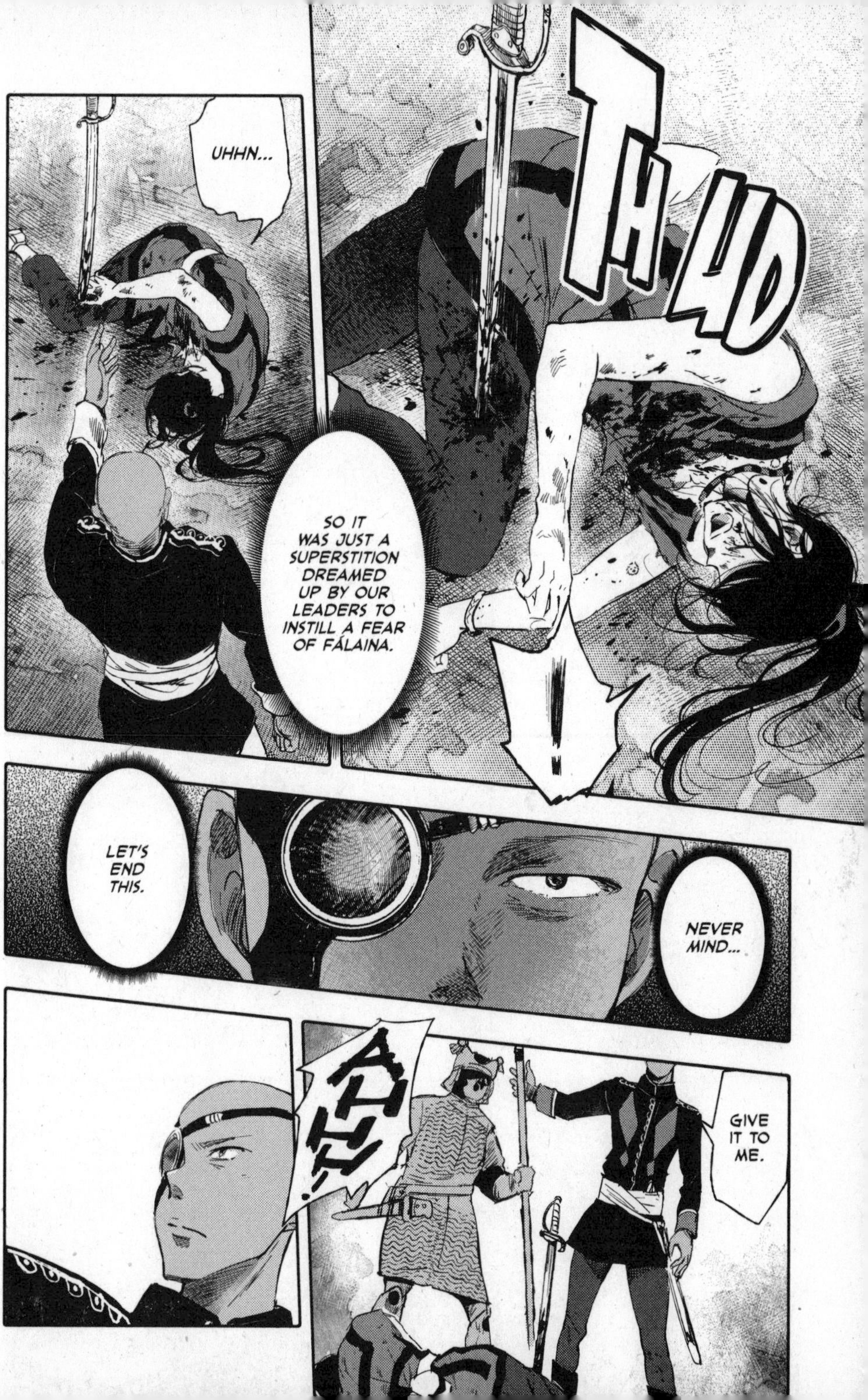
THUD
SO IT WAS JUST A SUPERSTITION DREAMED UP BY OUR LEADERS TO INSTILL A FEAR OF FÁLAINA.
!
UHHN...
NEVER MIND...
LET'S END THIS.
GIVE IT TO ME.
AHH!

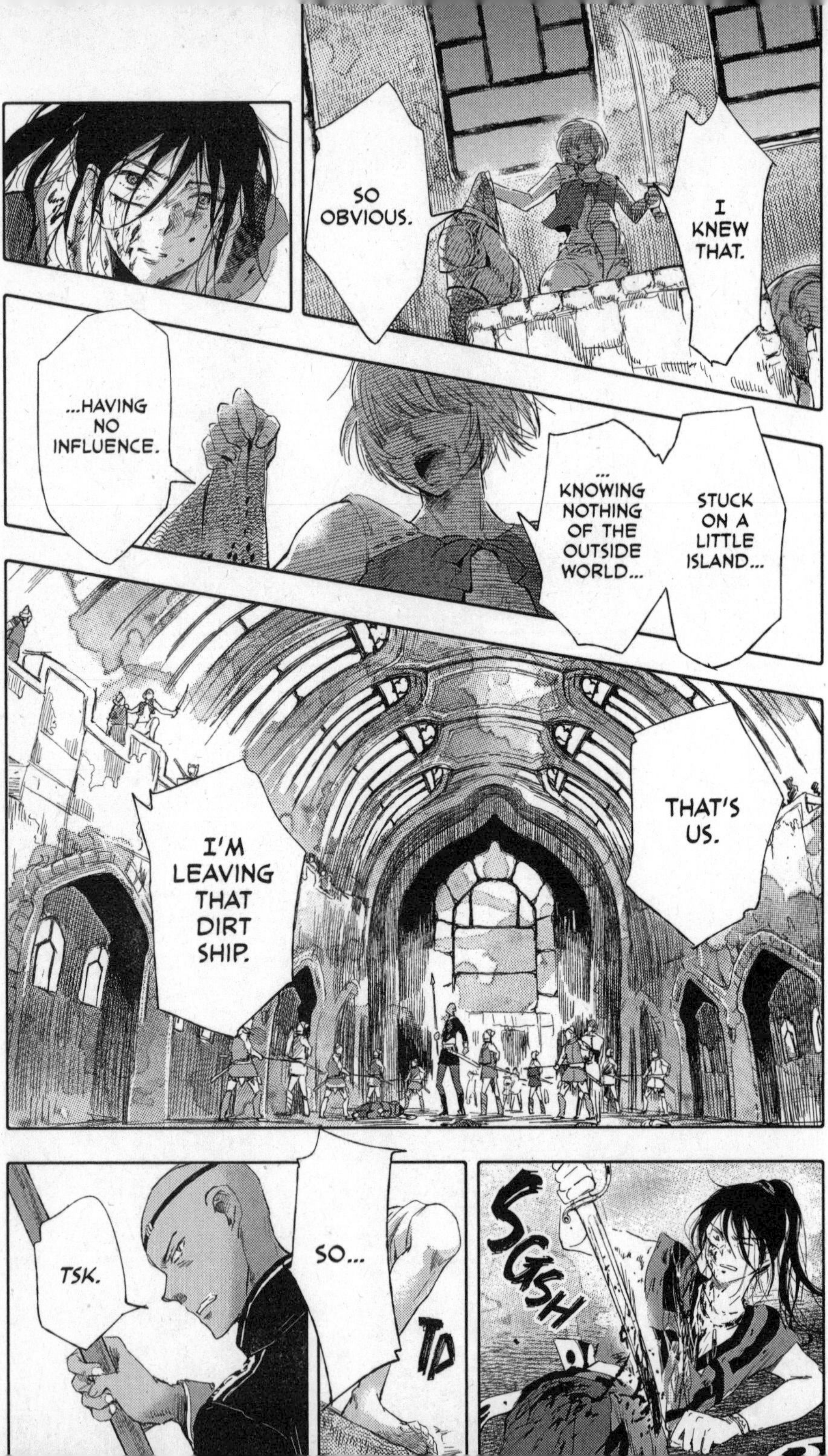

I KNEW THAT.
SO OBVIOUS.
STUCK ON A LITTLE ISLAND...
...KNOWING NOTHING OF THE OUTSIDE WORLD...
...HAVING NO INFLUENCE.
THAT'S US.
I'M LEAVING THAT DIRT SHIP.
SO...
SGSH
TD
TSK.

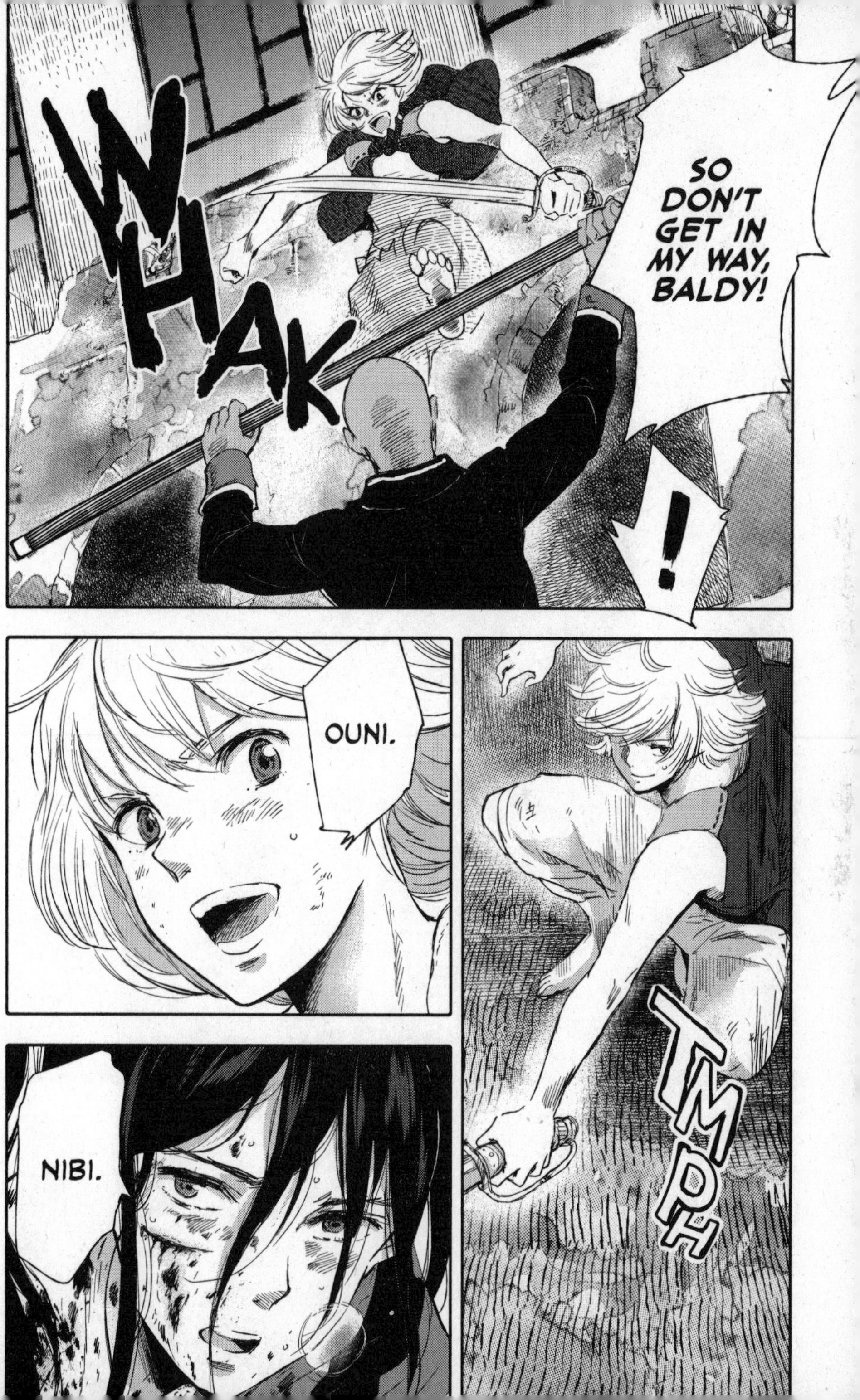
SO DON'T GET IN MY WAY, BALDY!
!
WHAK
TMPH
OUNI.
NIBI.

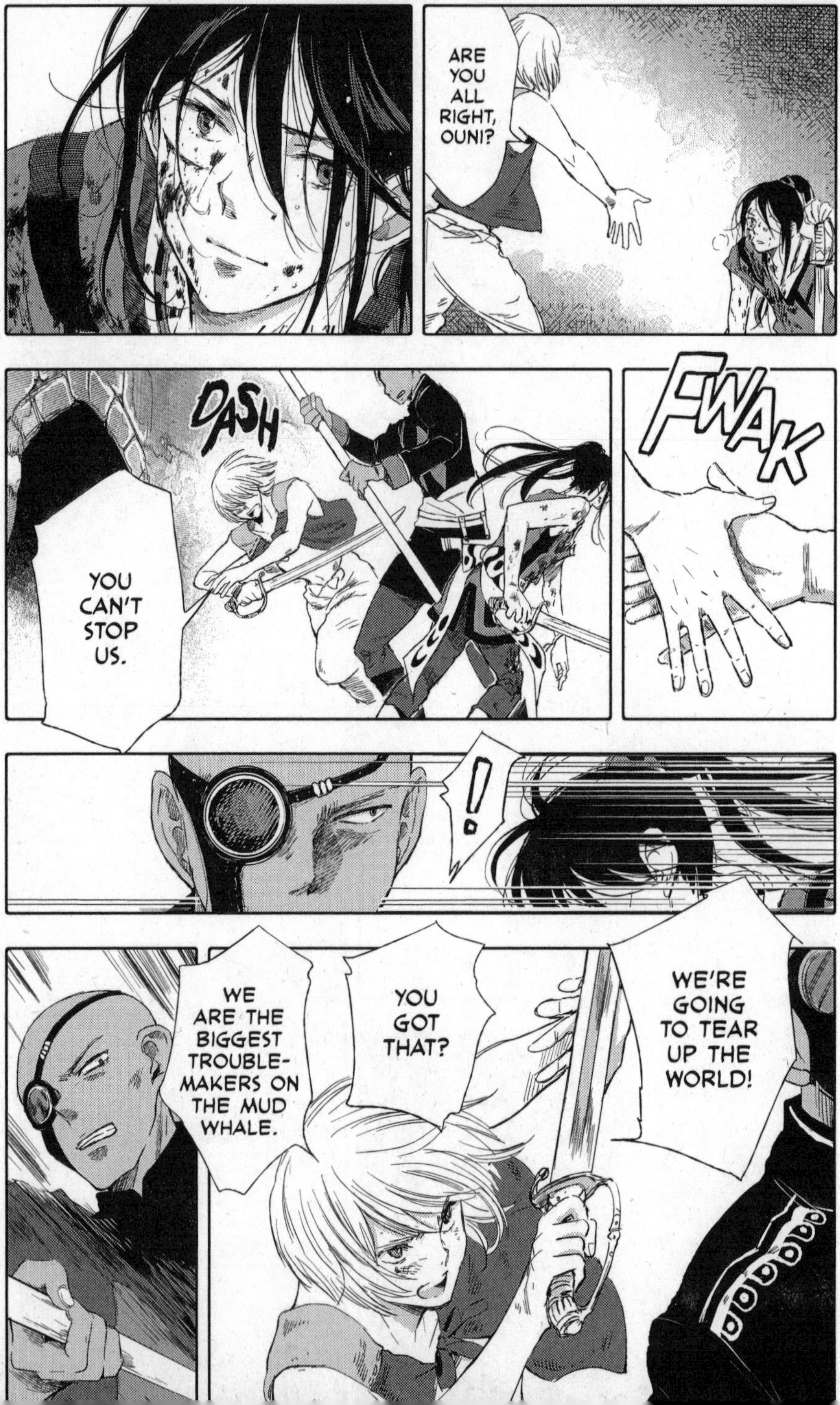
ARE YOU ALL RIGHT, OUNI?
FWAK
DASH
YOU CAN'T STOP US.
!
WE'RE GOING TO TEAR UP THE WORLD!
YOU GOT THAT?
WE ARE THE BIGGEST TROUBLE-MAKERS ON THE MUD WHALE.

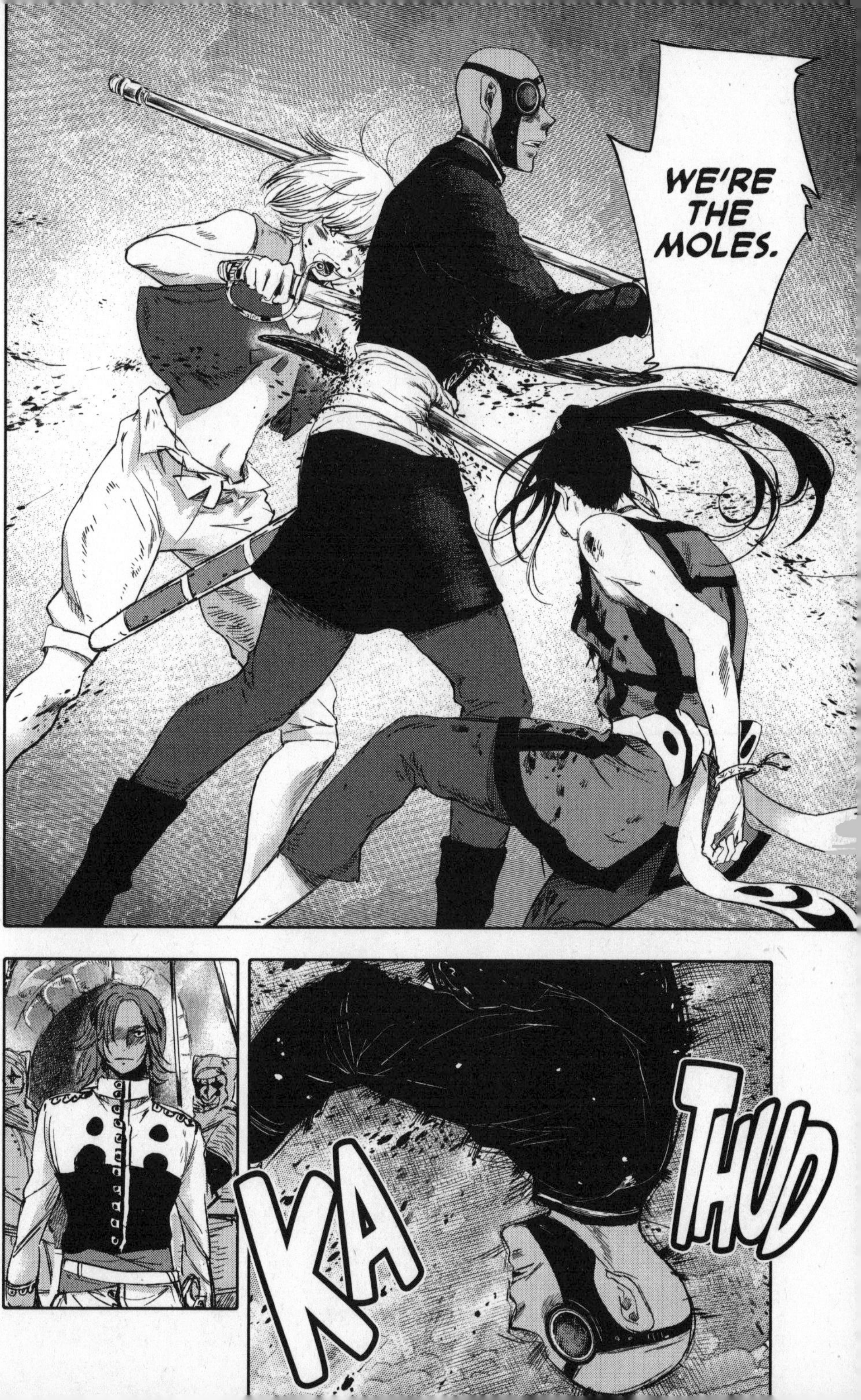
WE'RE THE MOLES.
KA
THUD

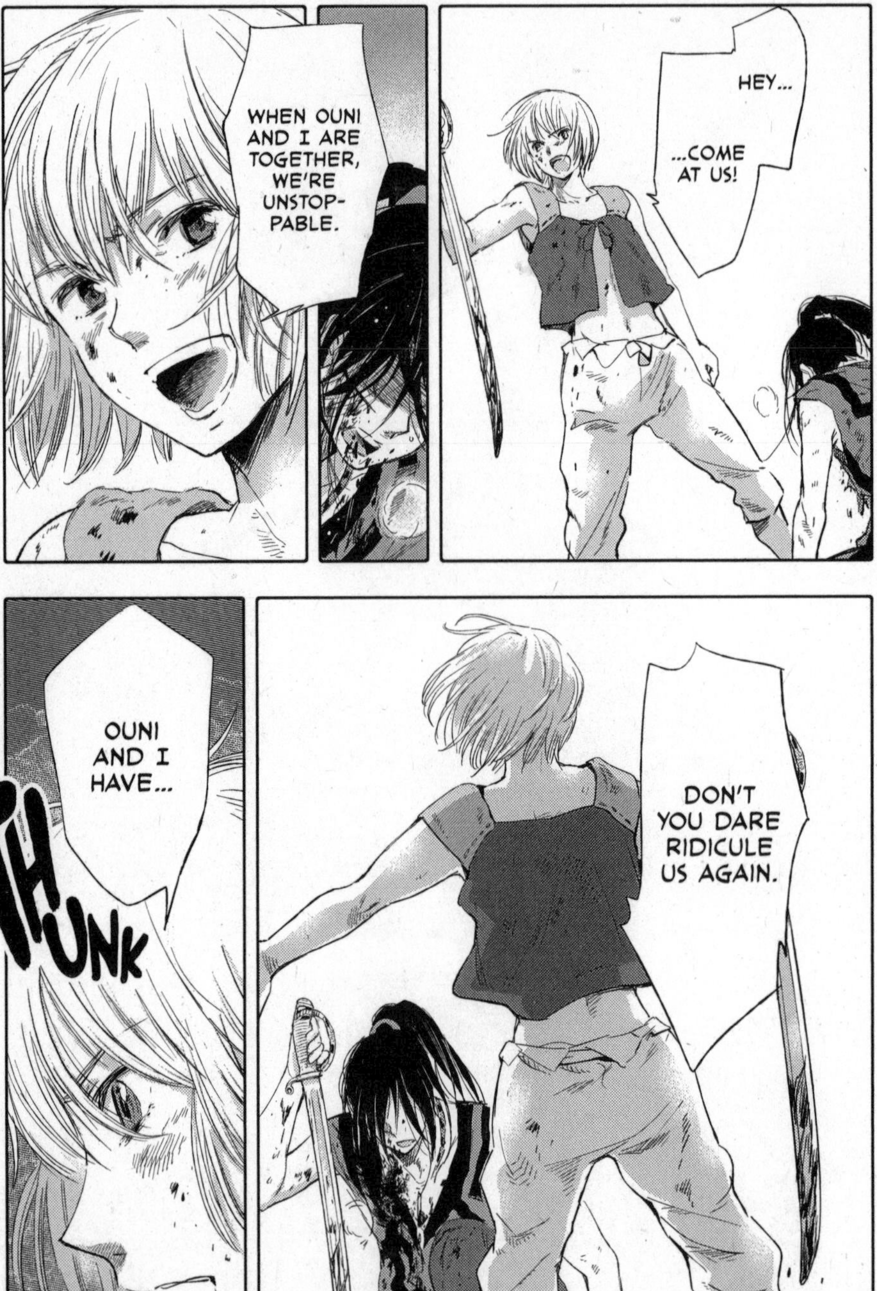
HEY...
...COME AT US!
WHEN OUNI AND I ARE TOGETHER, WE'RE UNSTOP-PABLE.
DON'T YOU DARE RIDICULE US AGAIN.
OUNI AND I HAVE...
THUNK

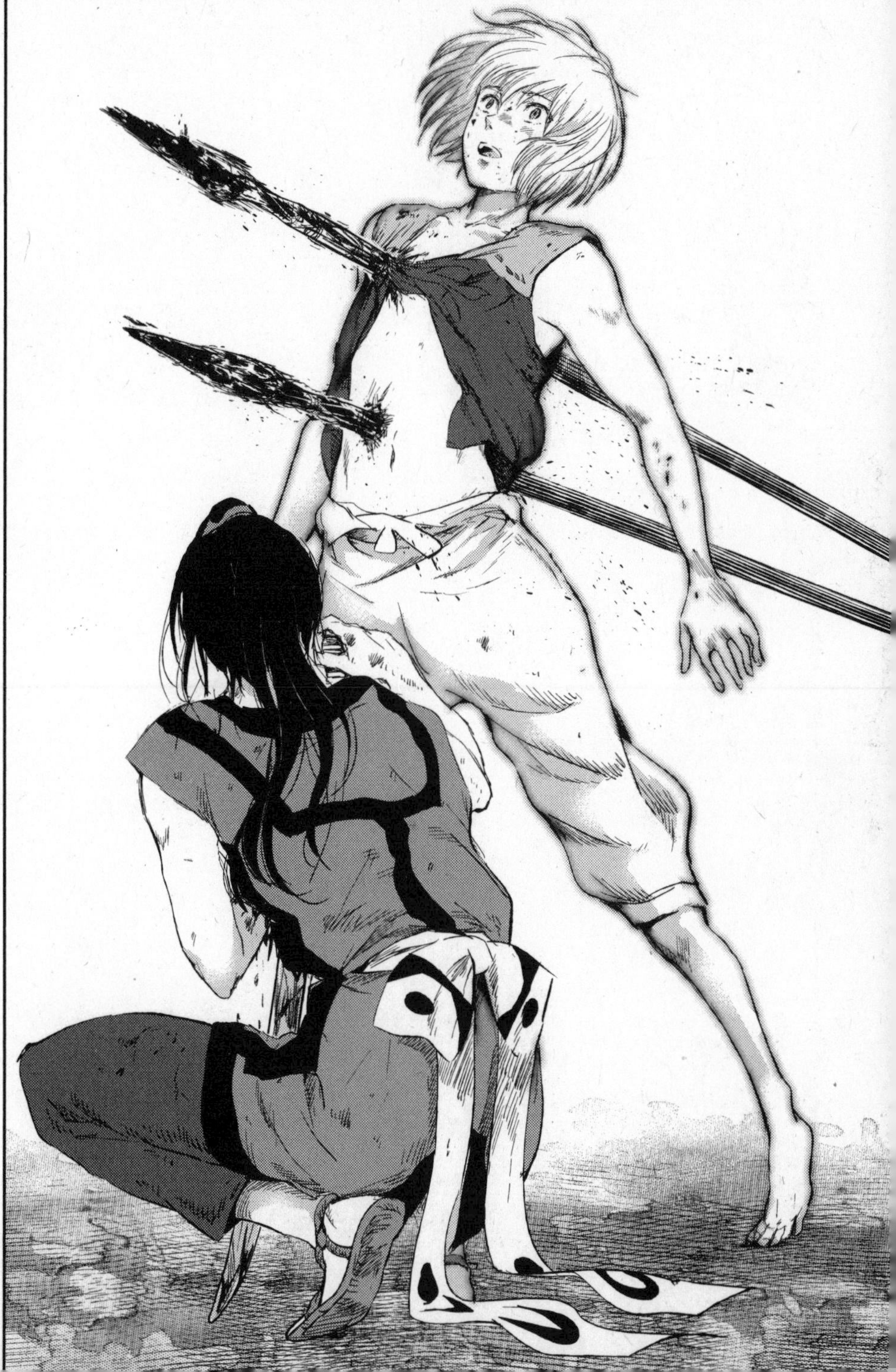

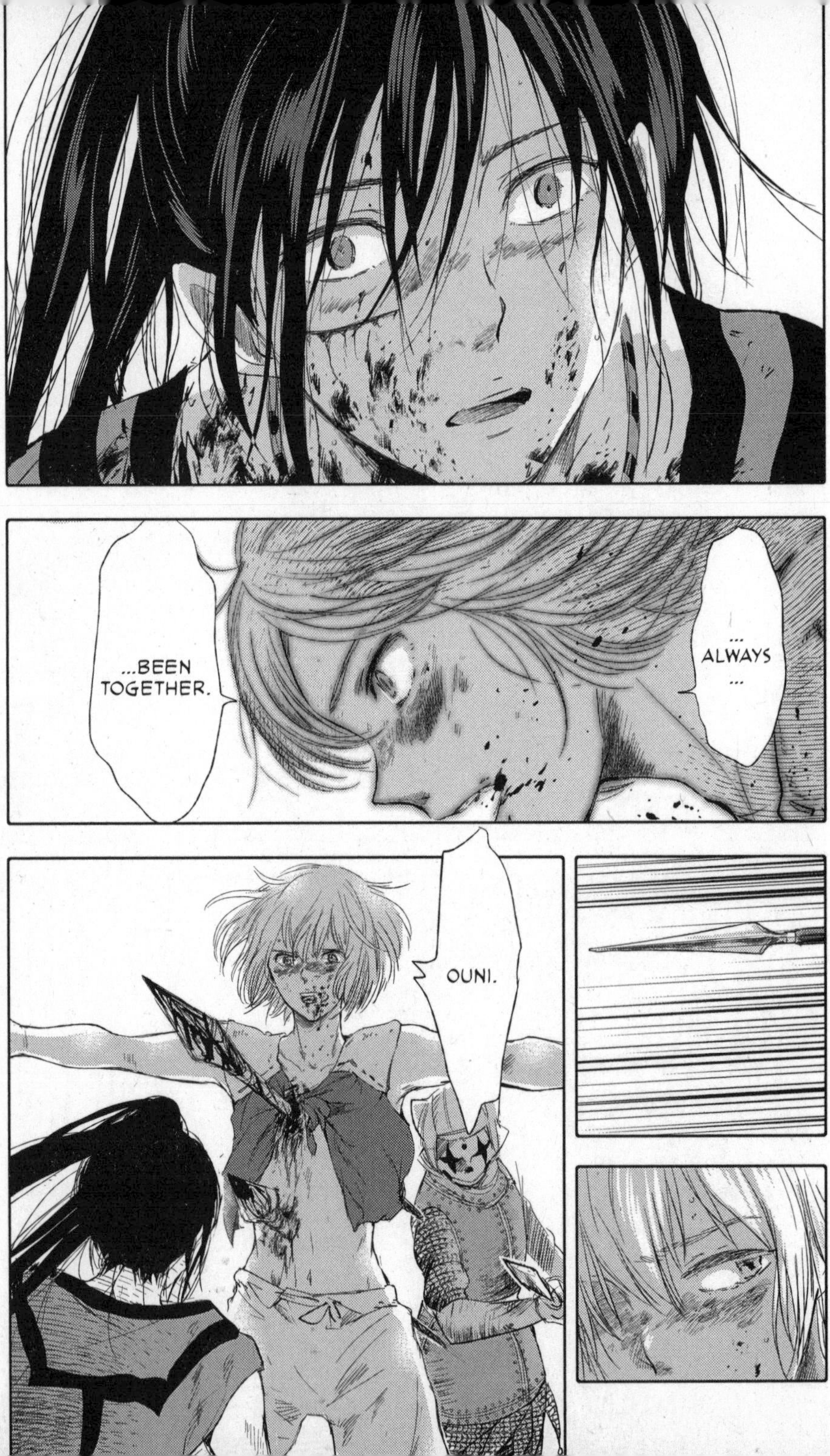
... ALWAYS ...
...BEEN TOGETHER.
OUNI.

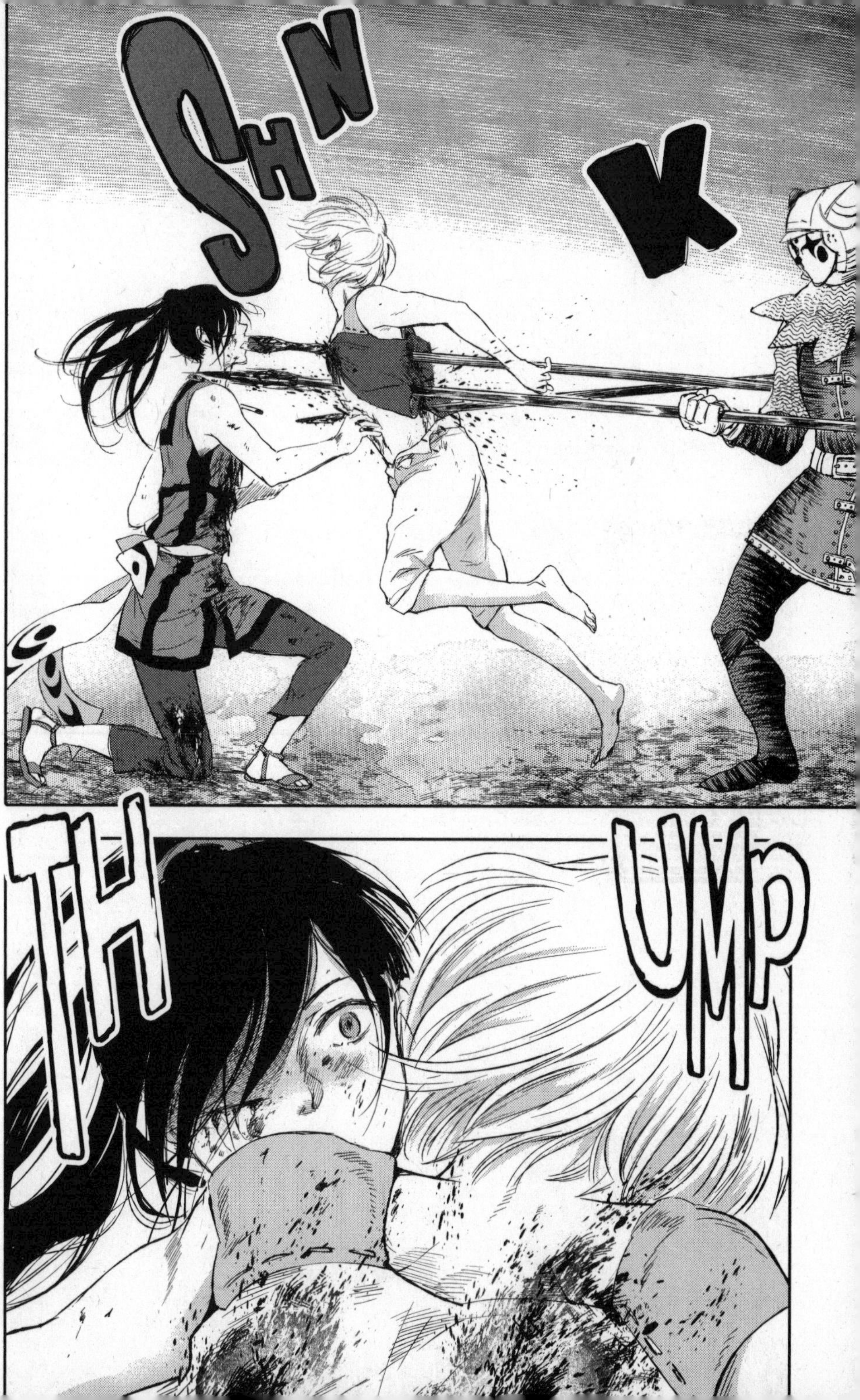
SHNK
THUMP

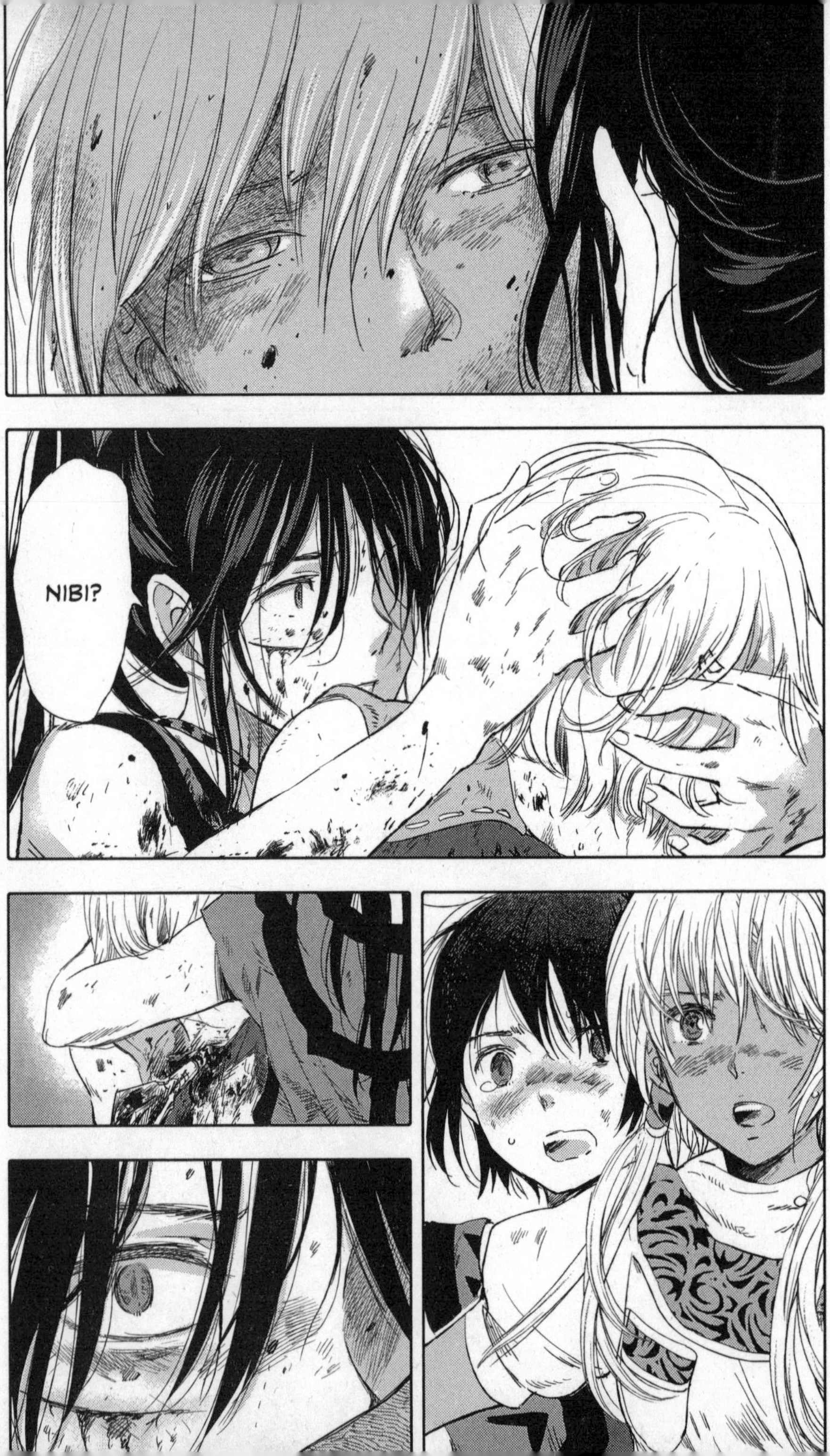
NIBI?

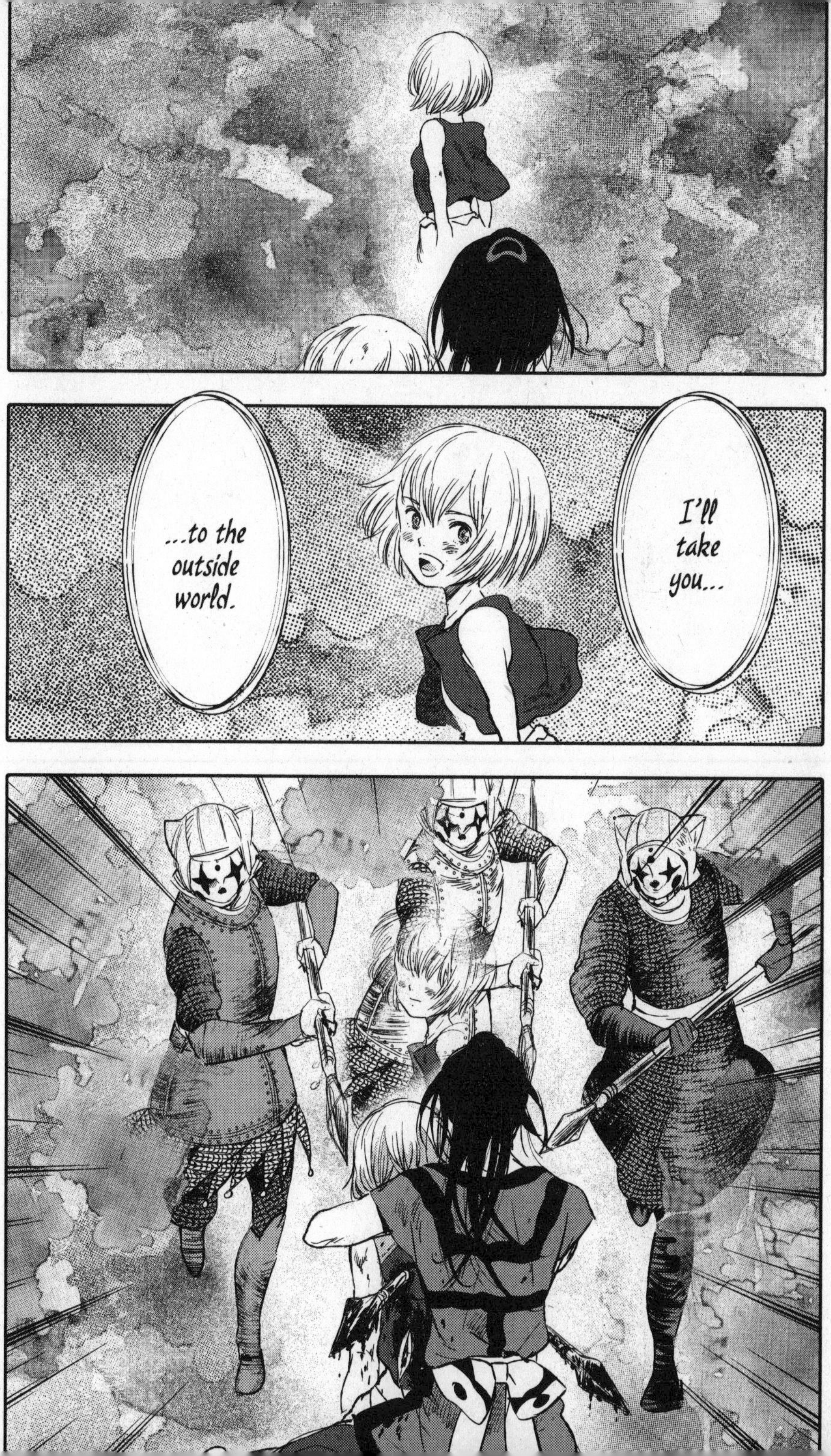
I'll take you...
...to the outside world.

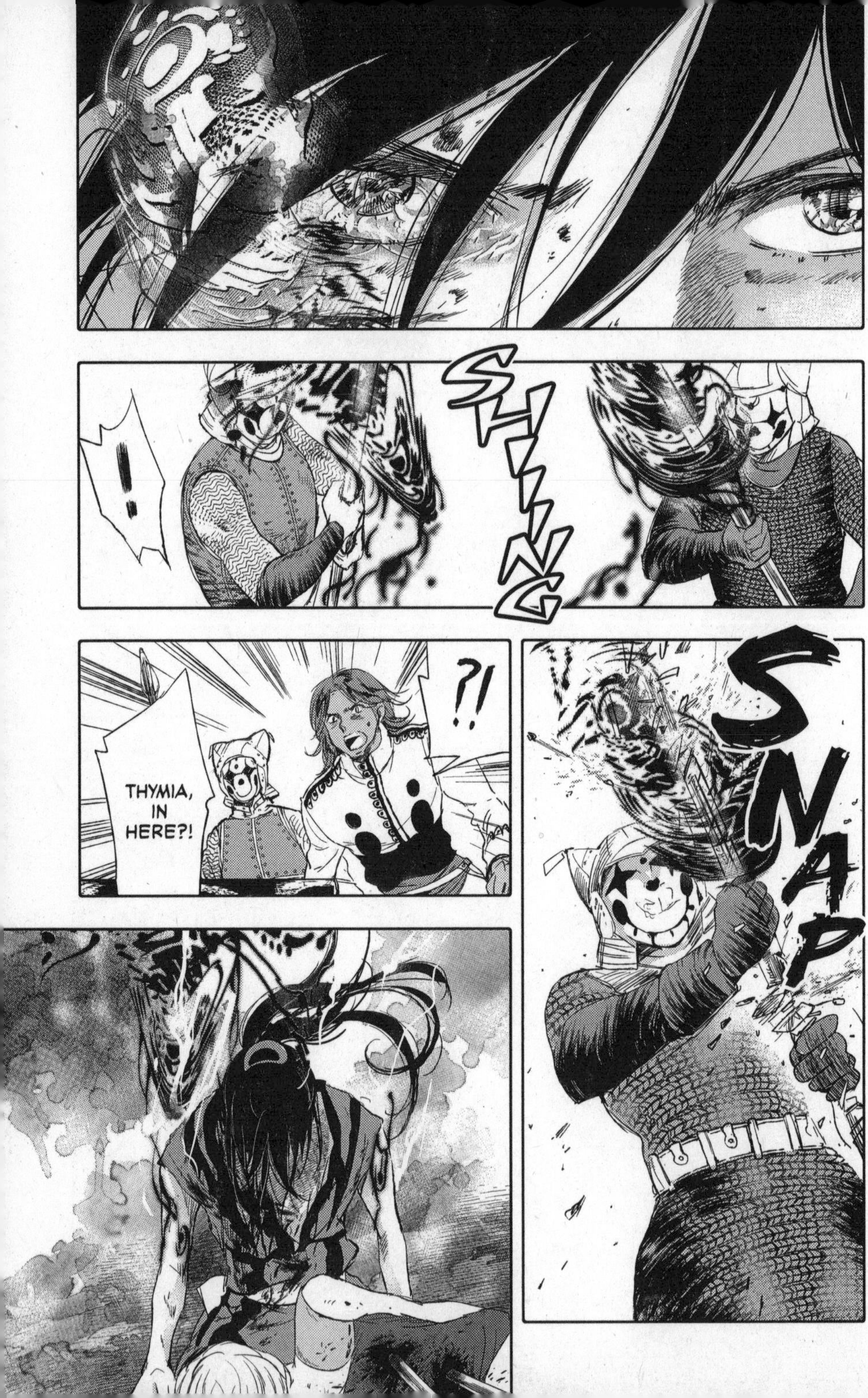
SHING
!
SNAP
?!
THYMIA, IN HERE?!

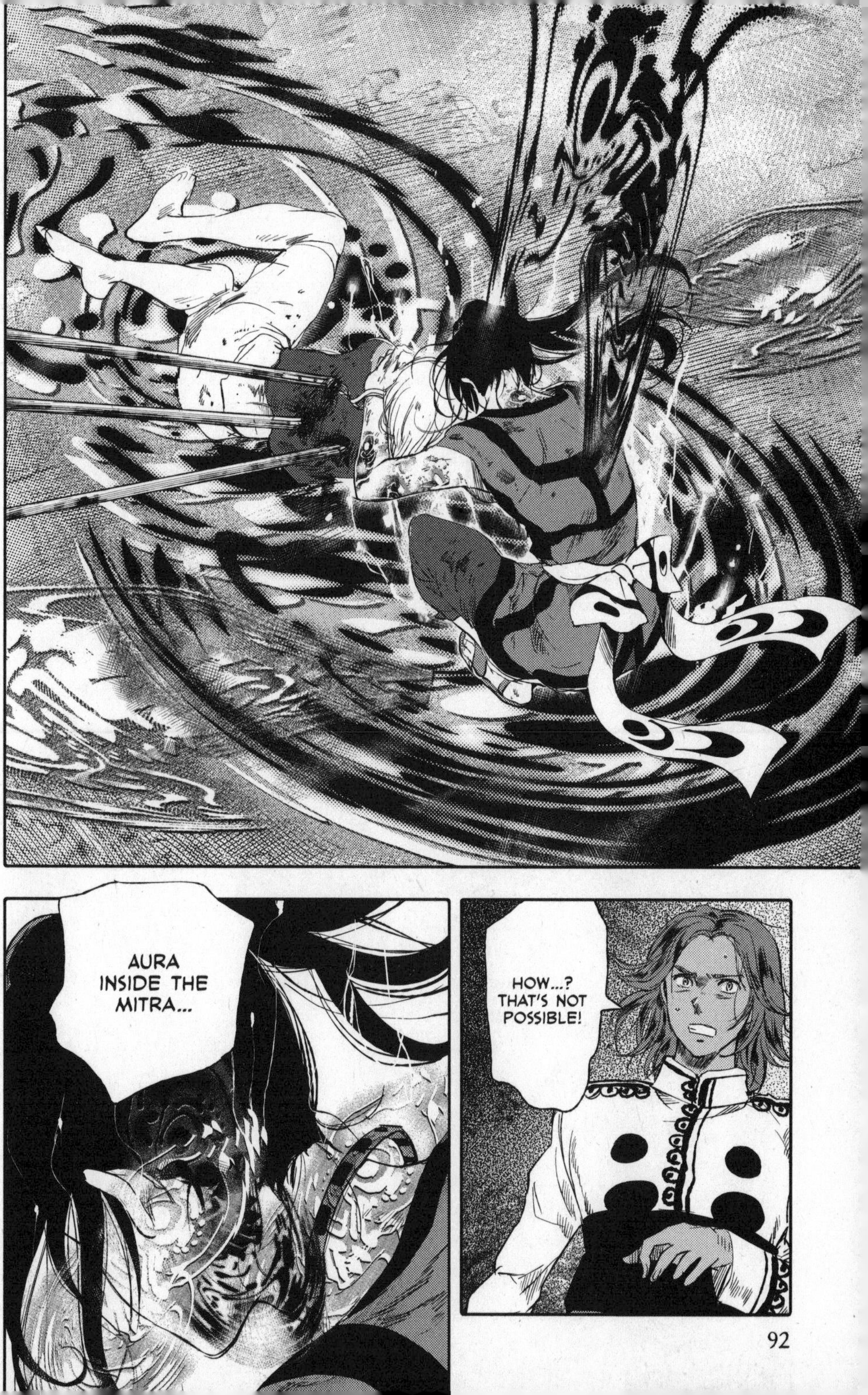
HOW...? THAT'S NOT POSSIBLE!
AURA INSIDE THE MITRA...

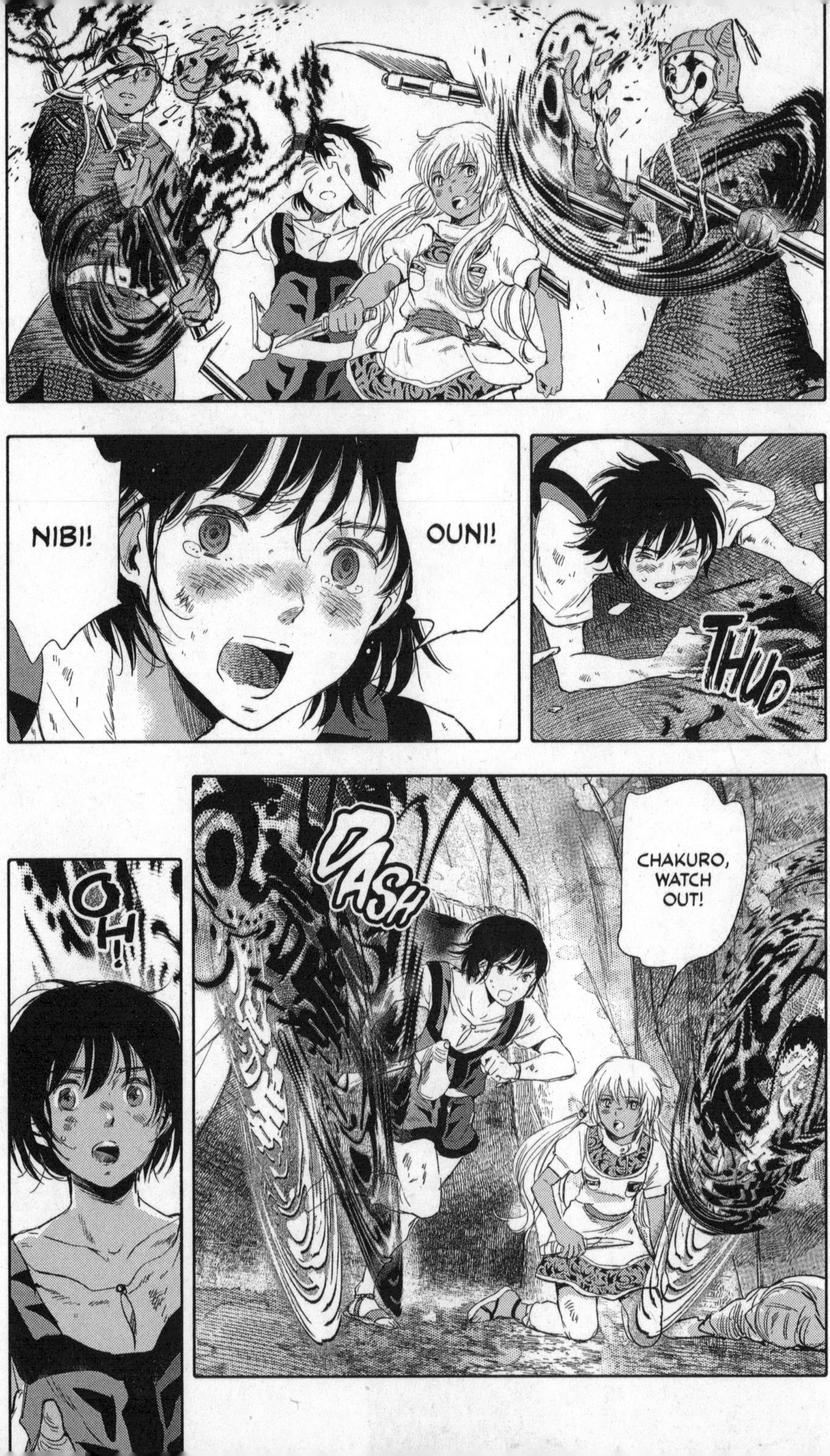
THUD
OUNI!
NIBI!
CHAKURO, WATCH OUT!
DASH
OH!

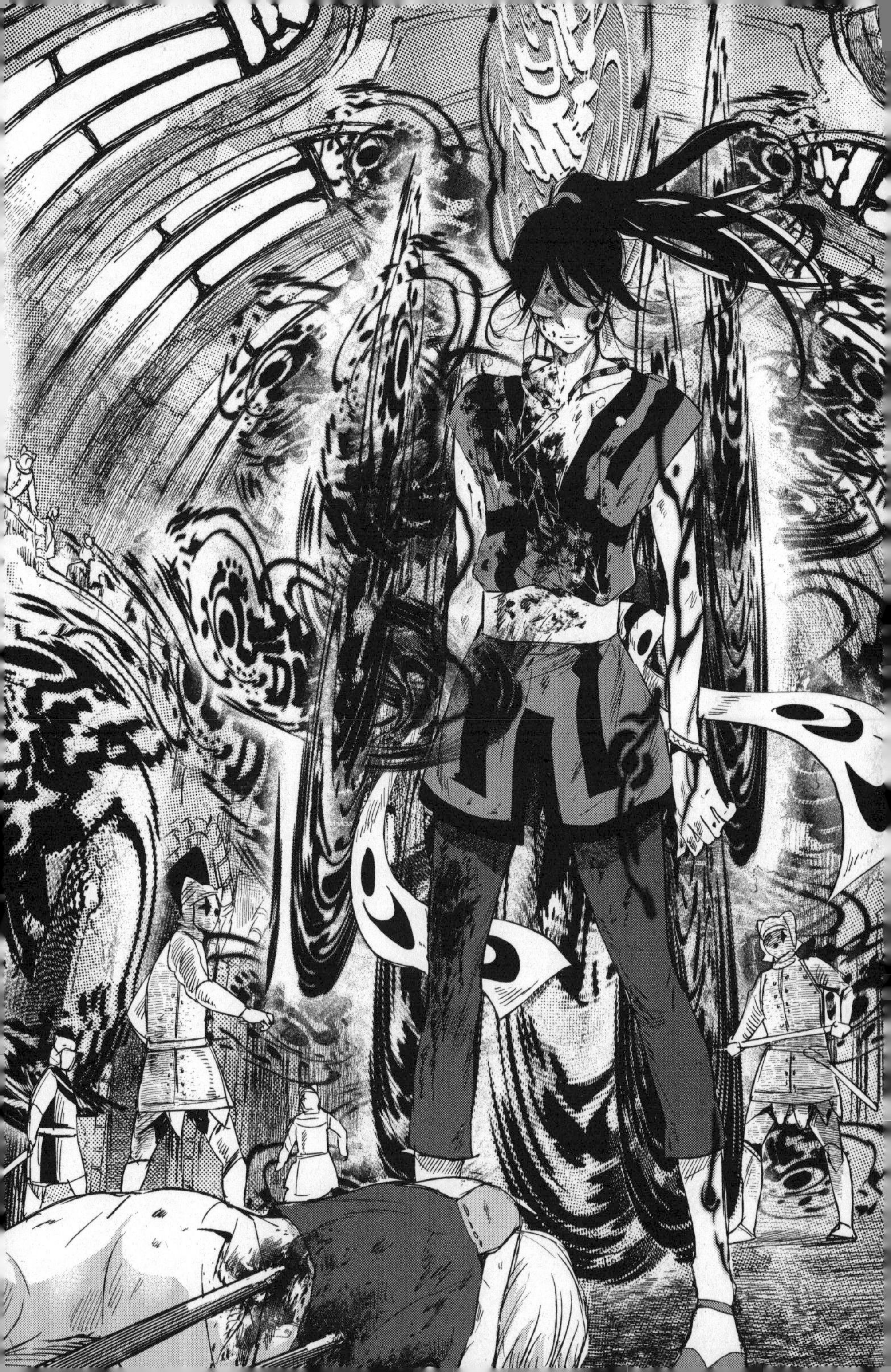

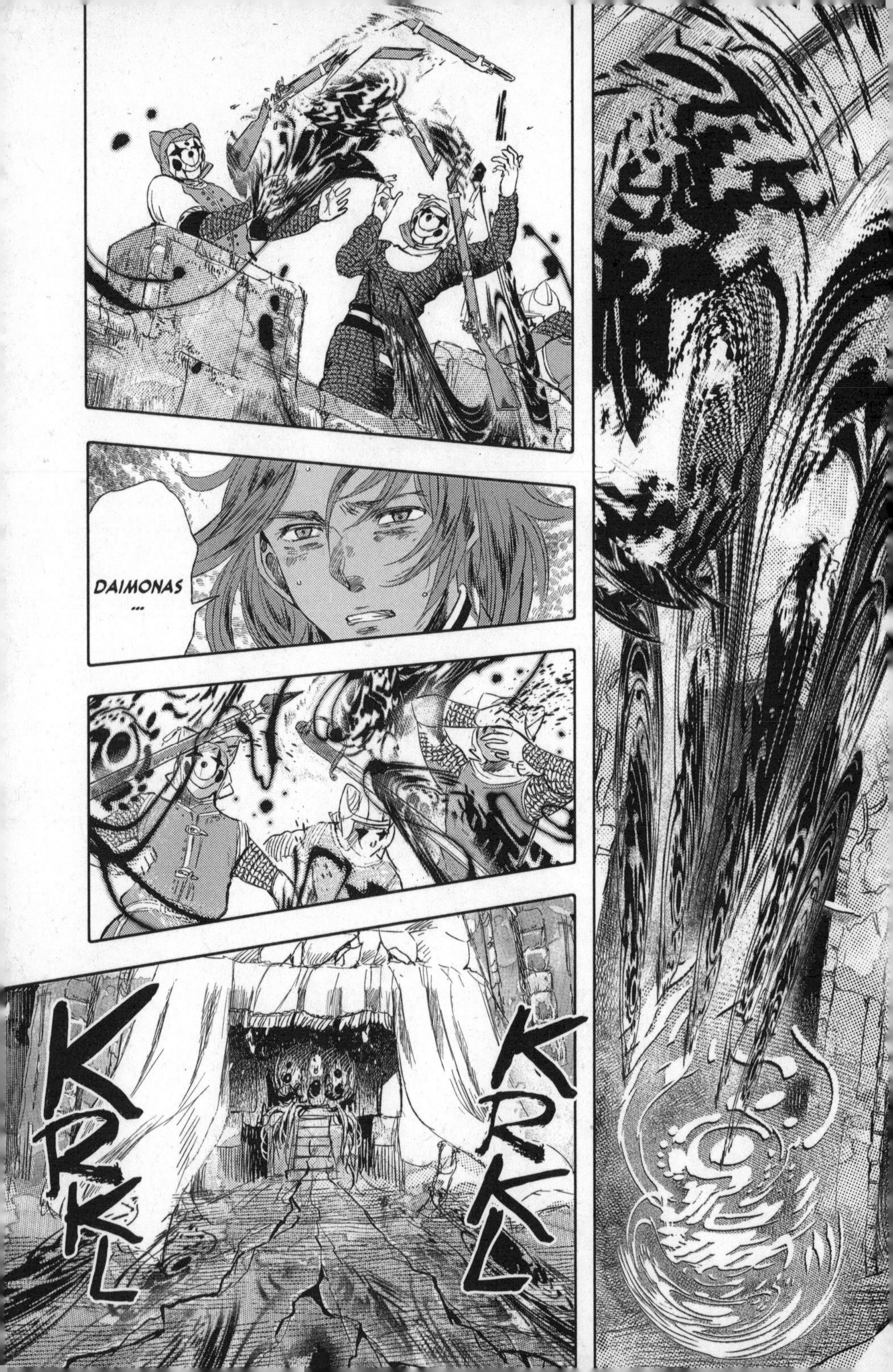
DAIMONAS
...
KRKL
KRKL

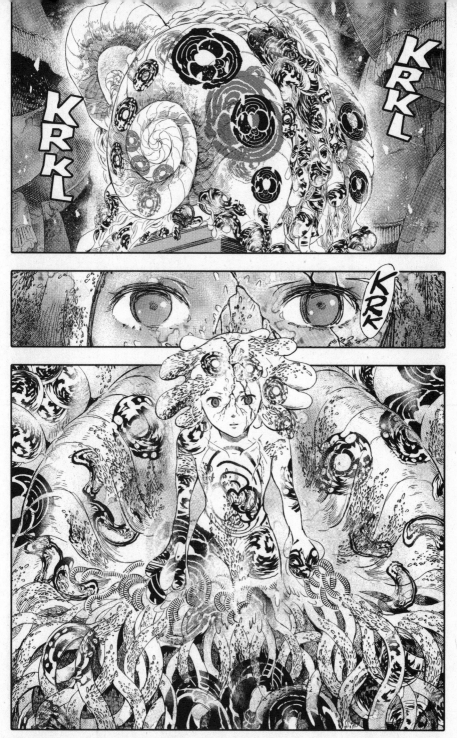

Your Memory, Our Fate -The End-

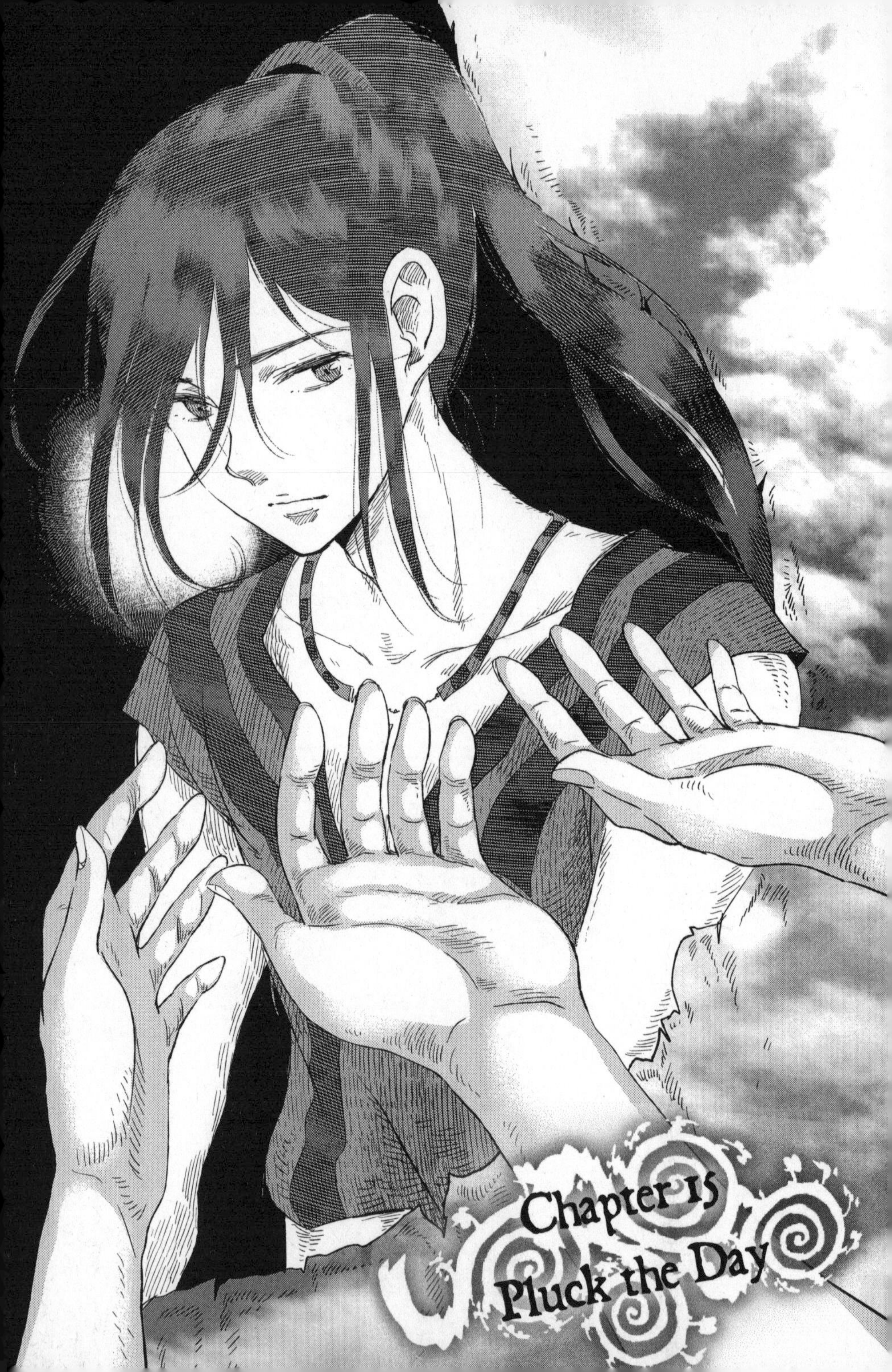
Chapter 15
Pluck the Day

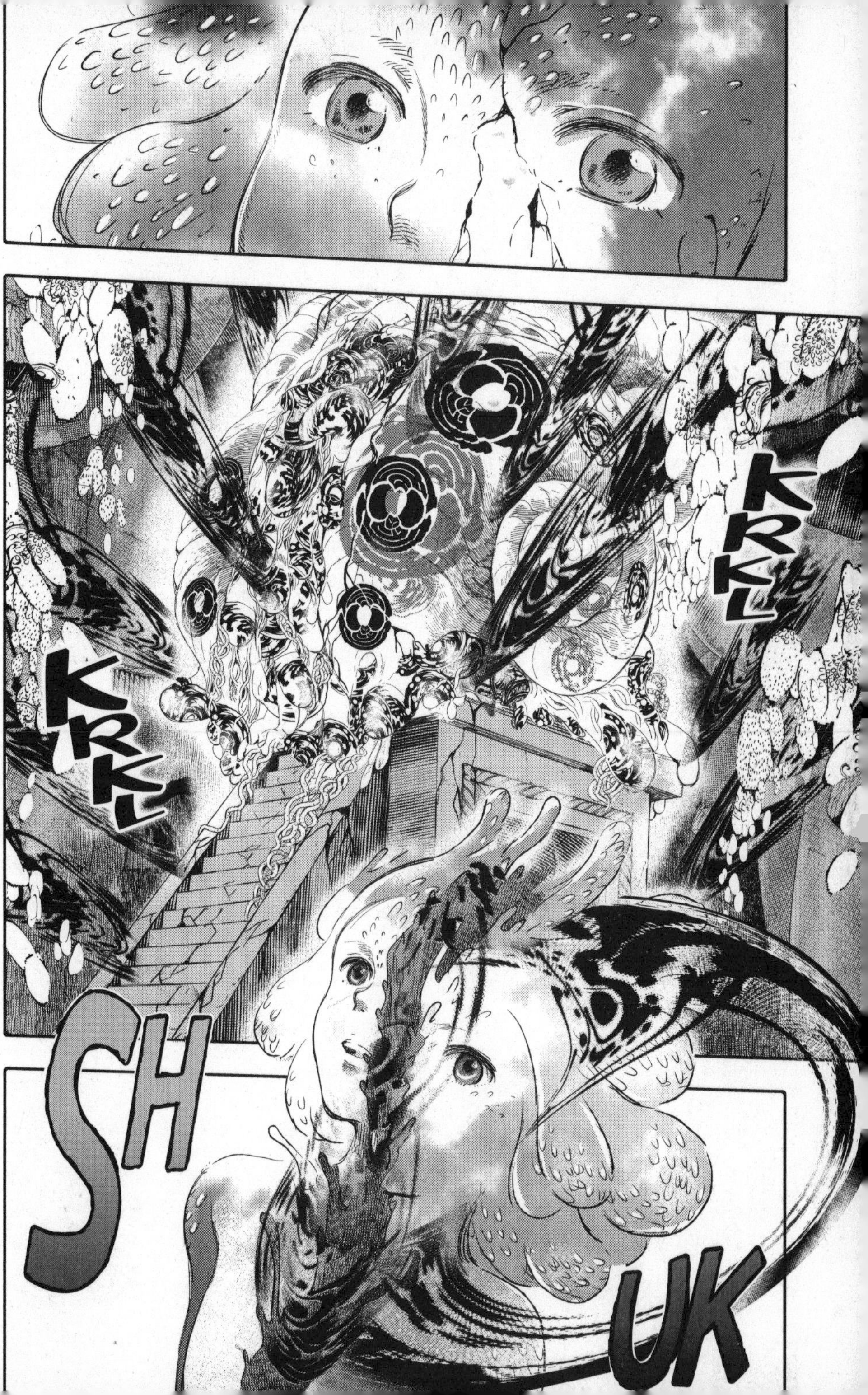
KRKL
KRKL
SHUK

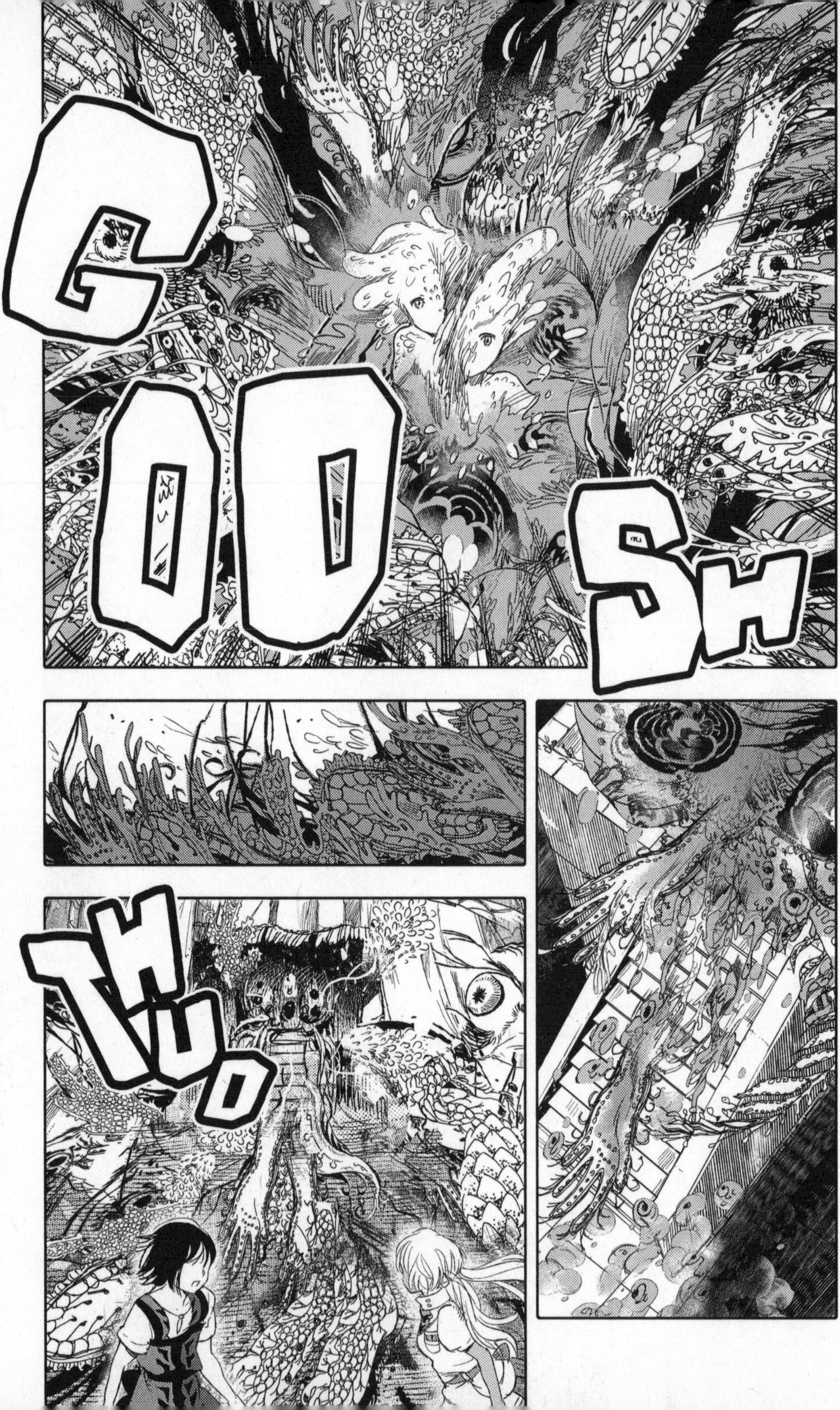
GOOSH
THUD

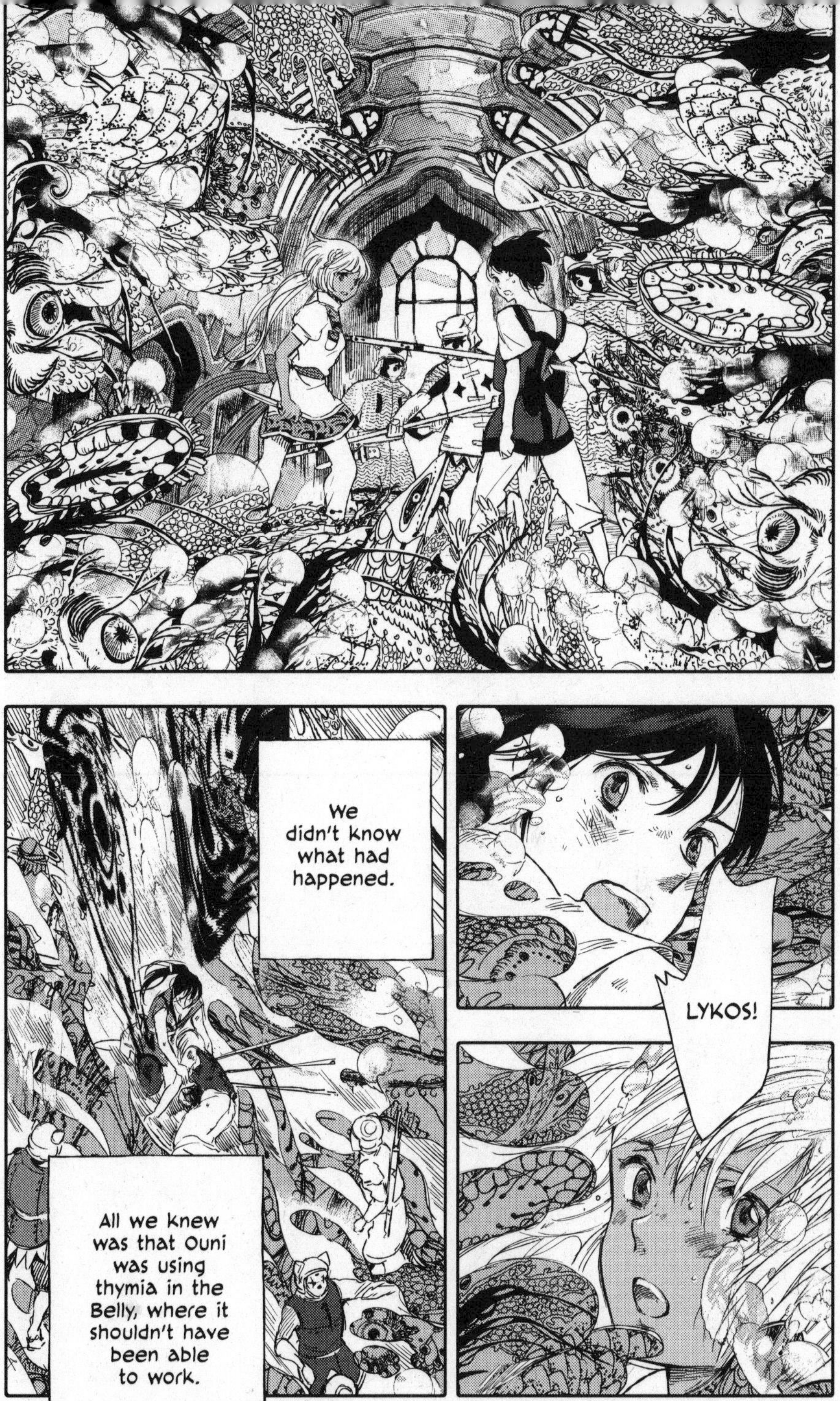
LYKOS!
We didn't know what had happened.
All we knew was that Ouni was using thymia in the Belly, where it shouldn't have been able to work.

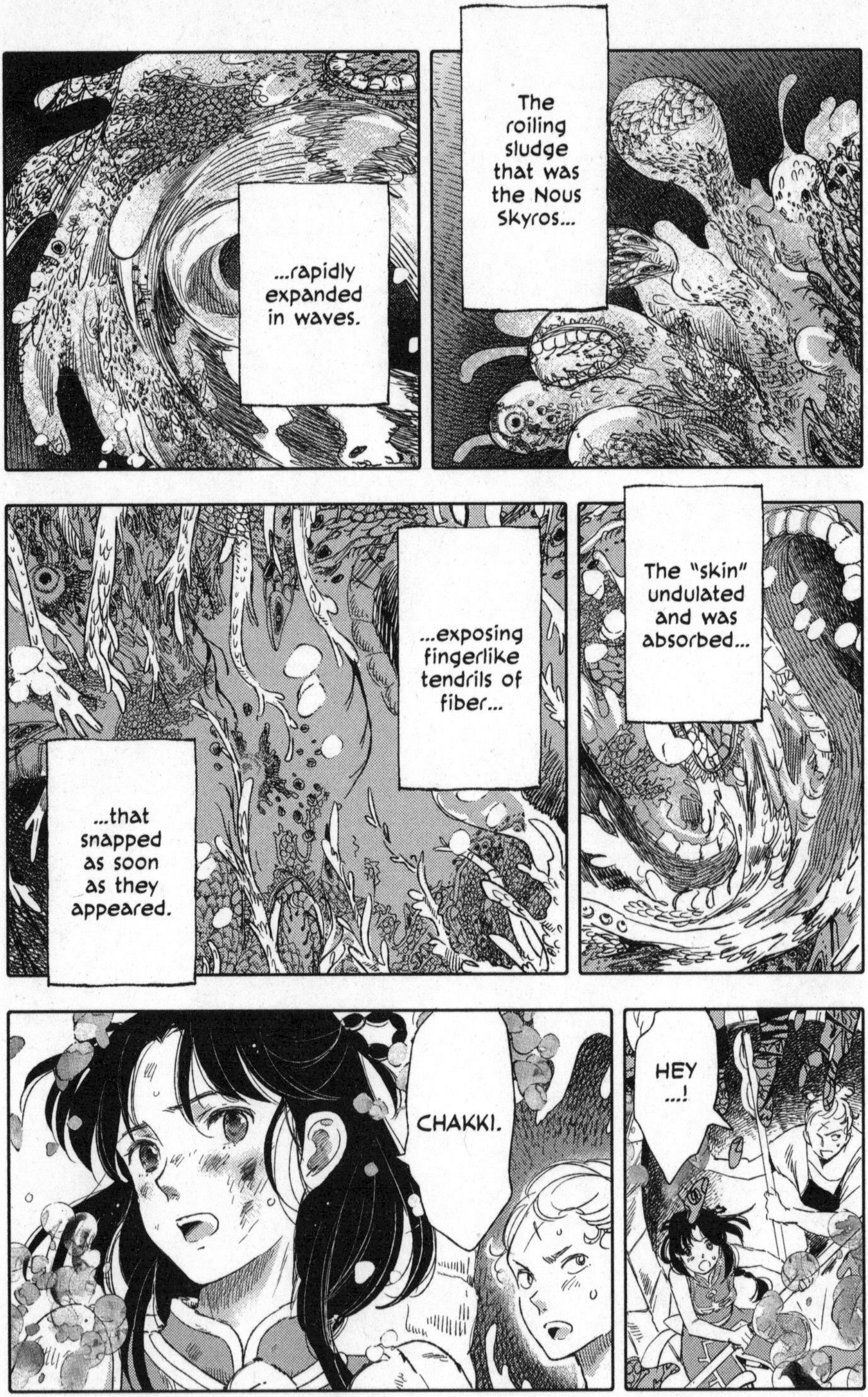
The roiling sludge that was the Nous Skyros...
...rapidly expanded in waves.
The "skin" undulated and was absorbed...
...exposing fingerlike tendrils of fiber...
...that snapped as soon as they appeared.
HEY ...!
CHAKKI.

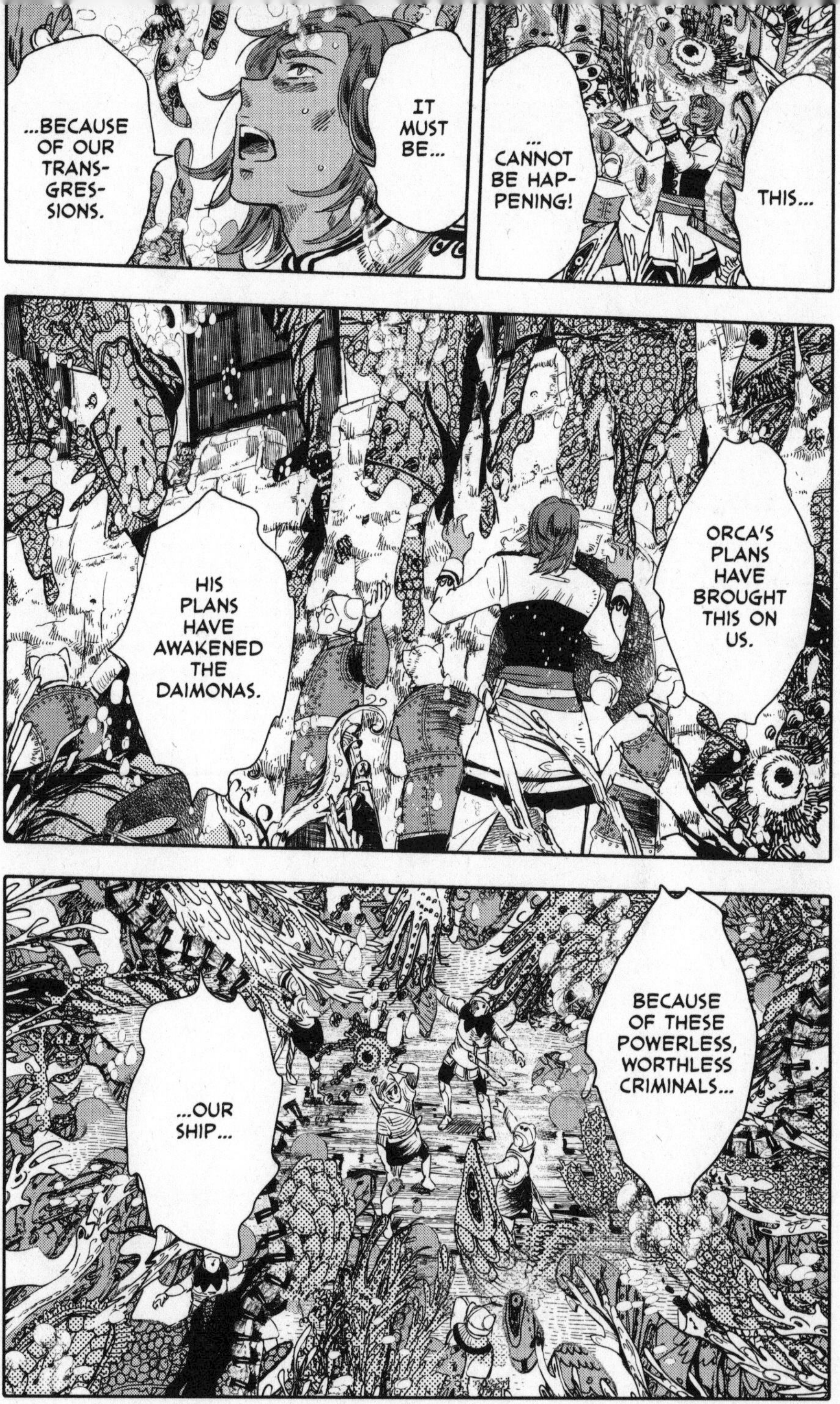
THIS...
...CANNOT BE HAP-PENING!
IT MUST BE...
...BECAUSE OF OUR TRANS-GRES-SIONS.
ORCA'S PLANS HAVE BROUGHT THIS ON US.
HIS PLANS HAVE AWAKENED THE DAIMONAS.
BECAUSE OF THESE POWERLESS, WORTHLESS CRIMINALS...
...OUR SHIP...

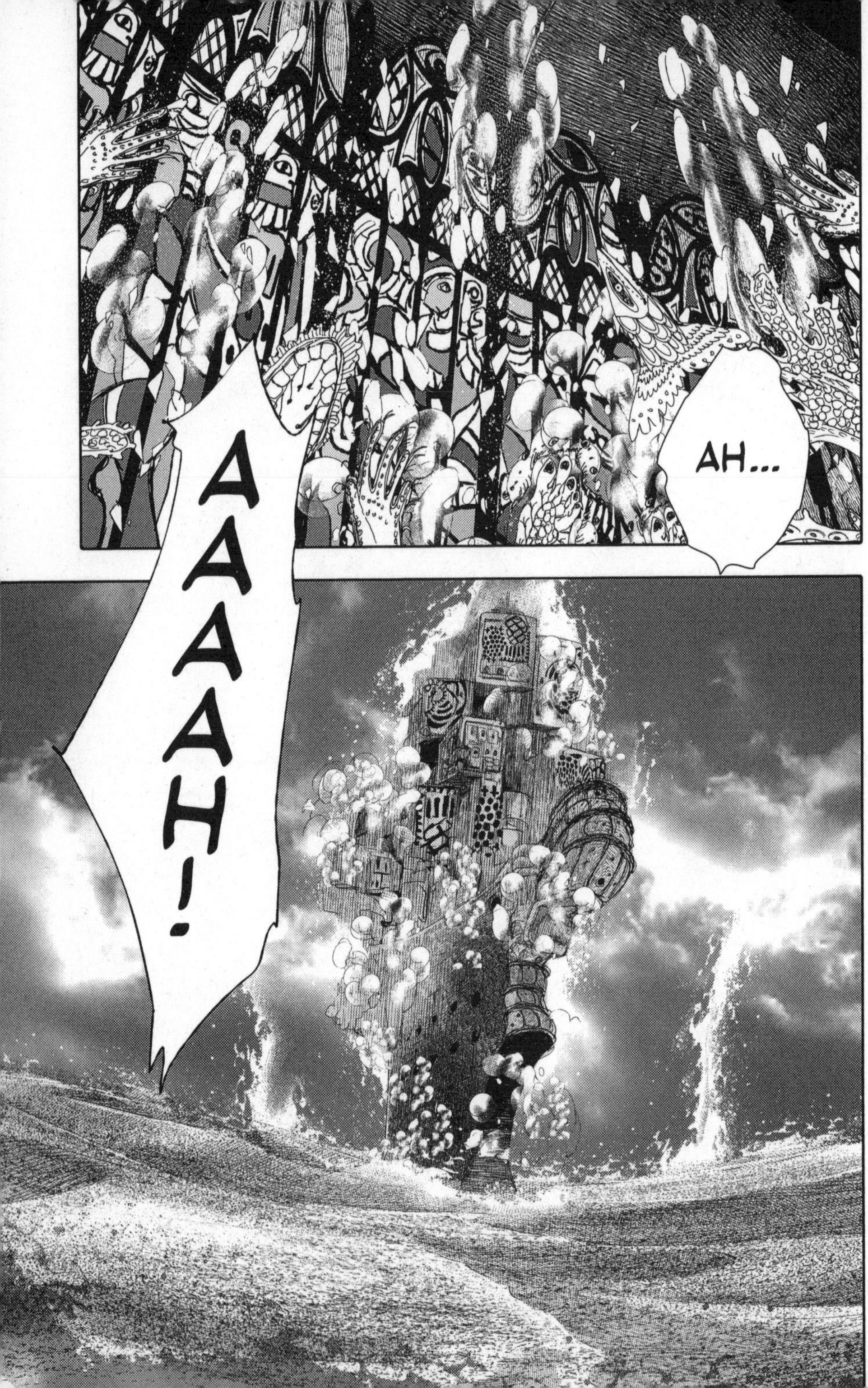
AH...
AAAAH!

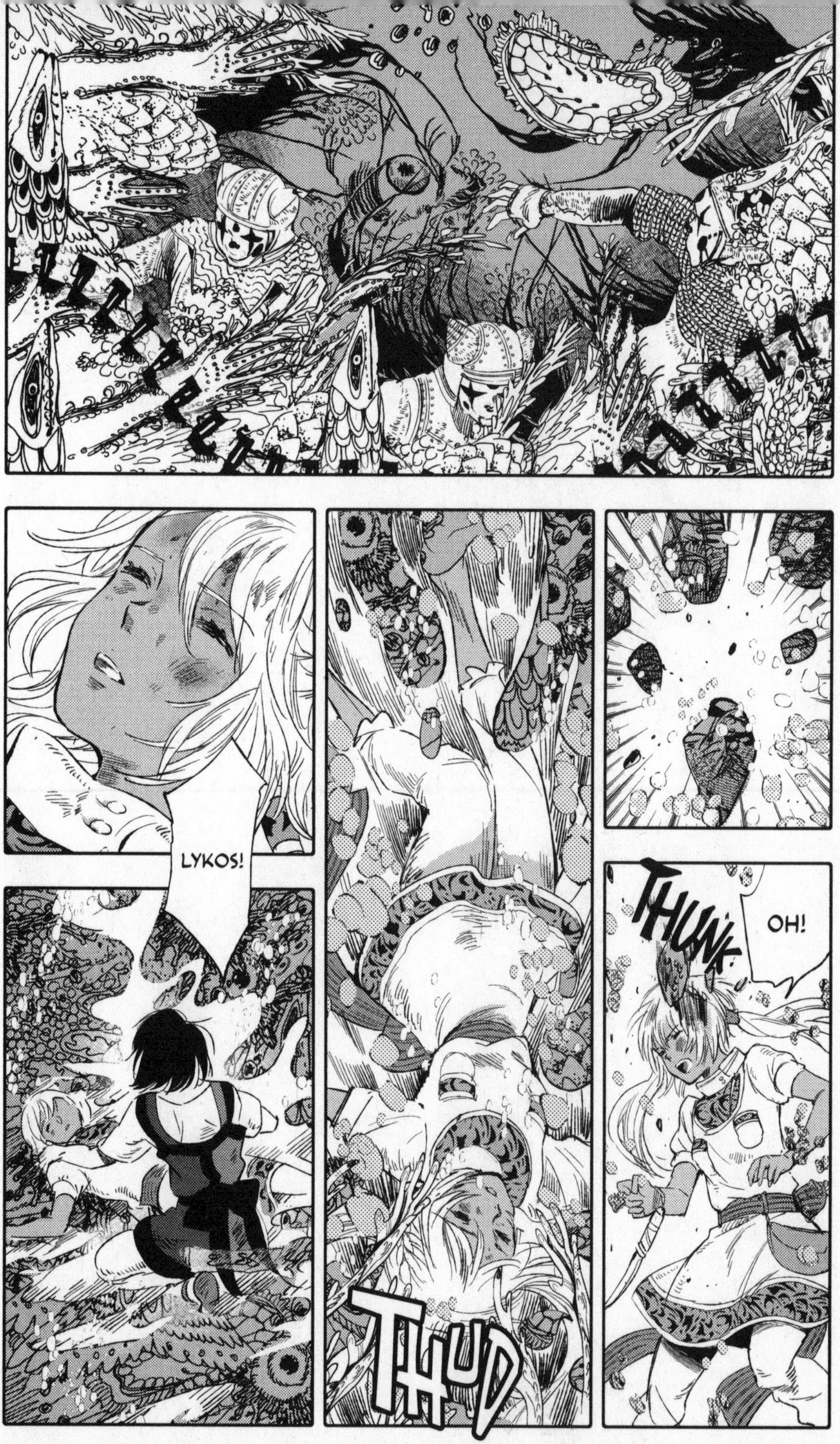
THUNK
OH!
THUD
LYKOS!

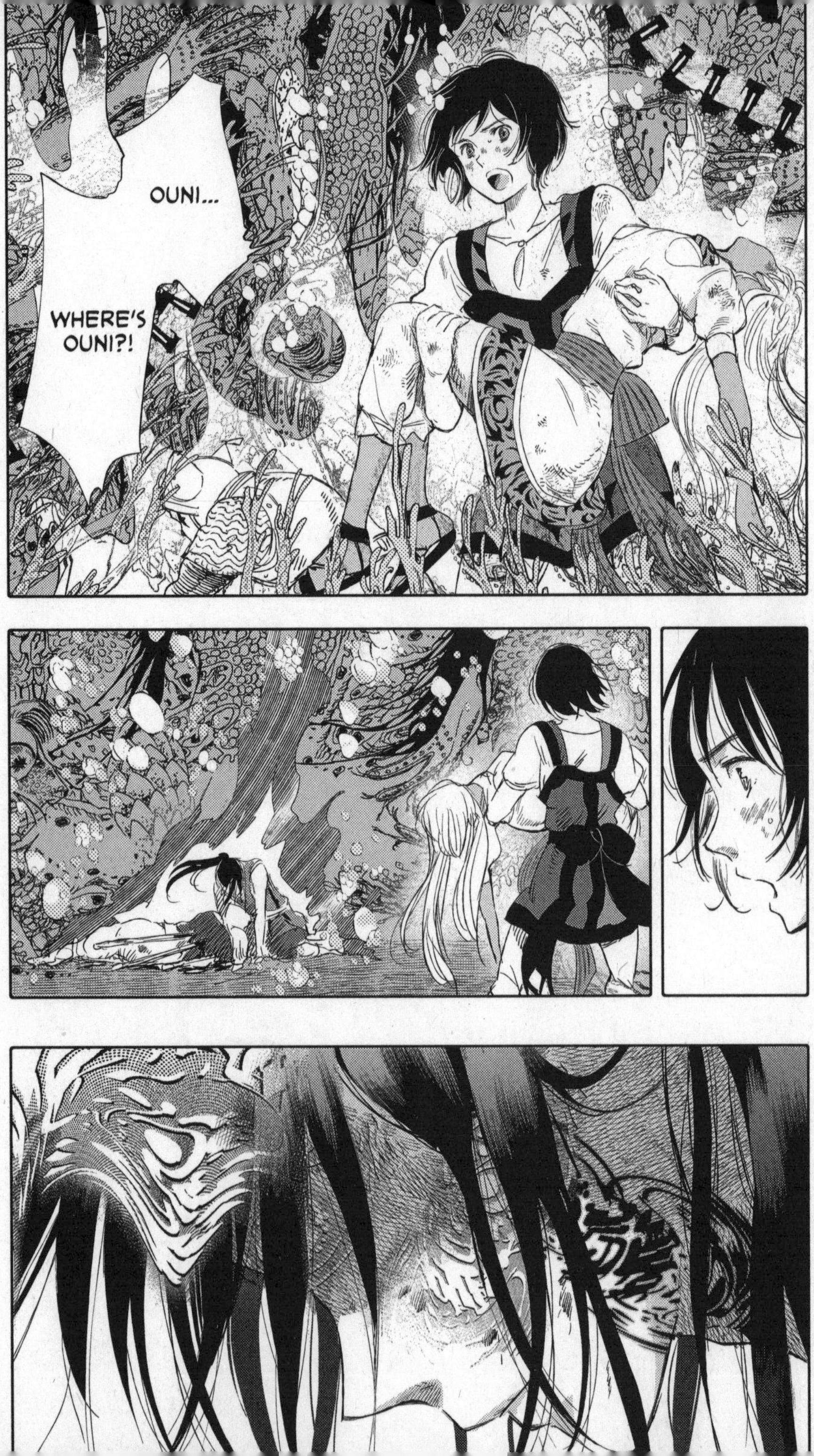
OUNI...
WHERE'S OUNI?!

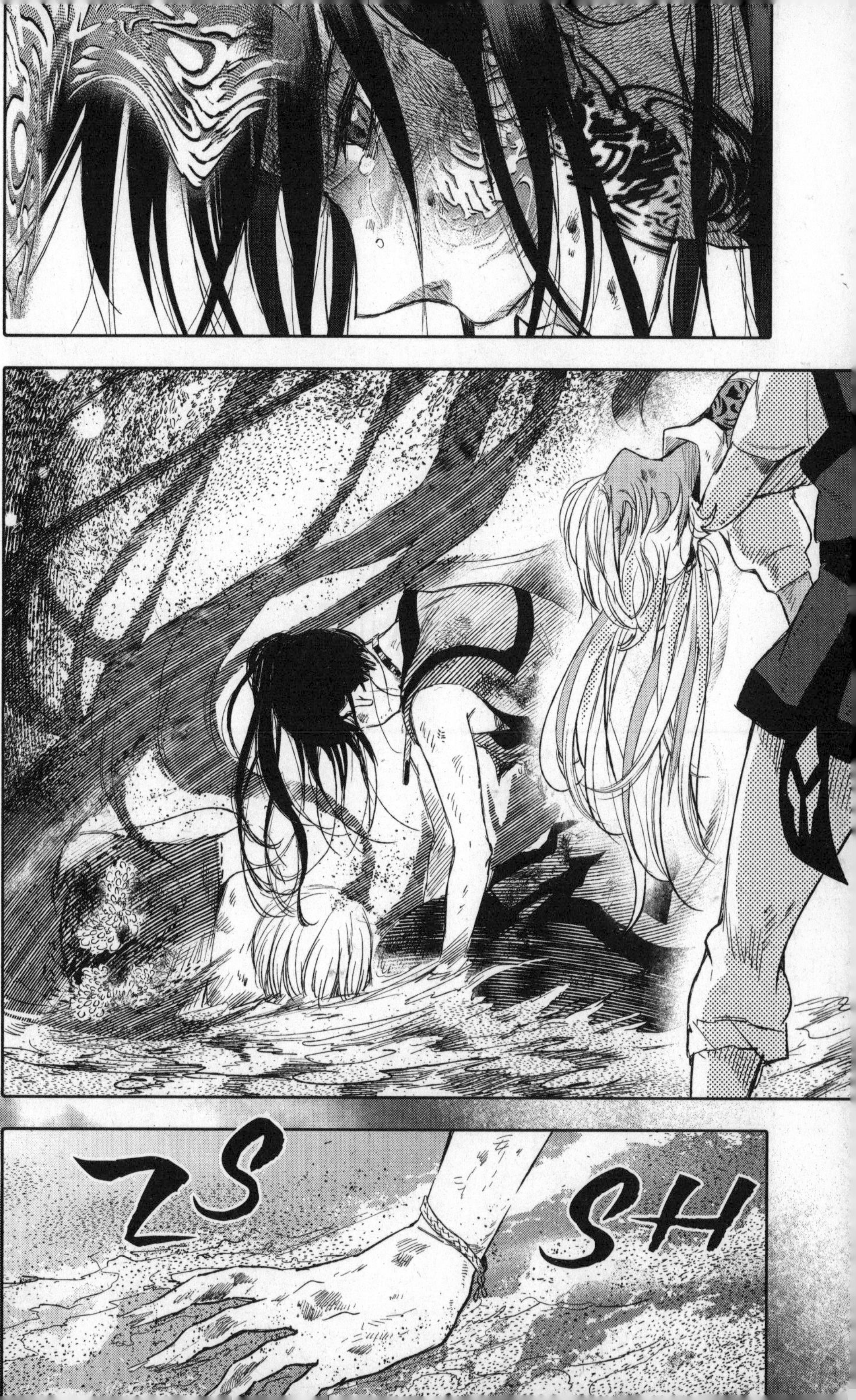
ZS
SH

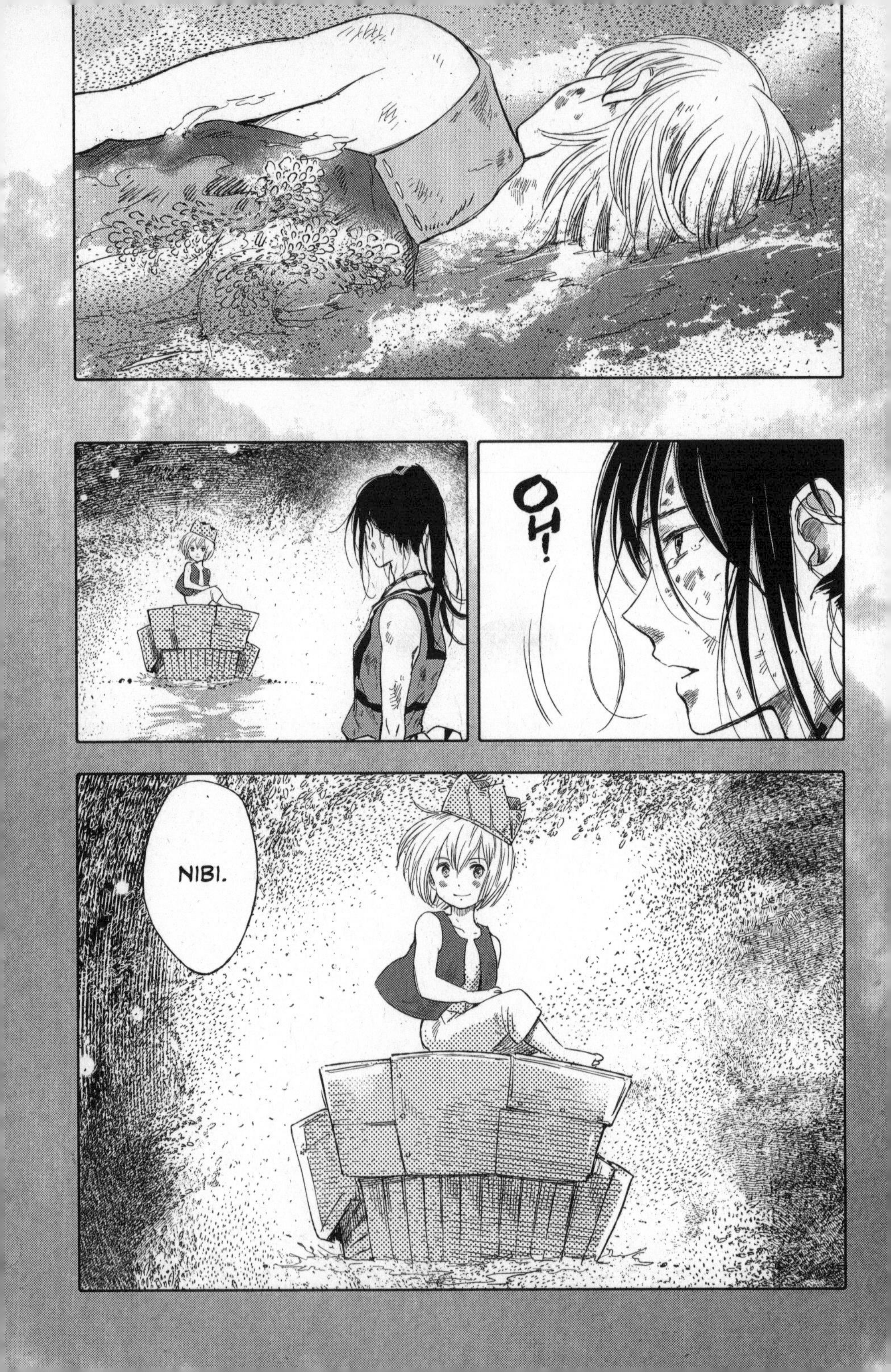
OH!
NIBI.

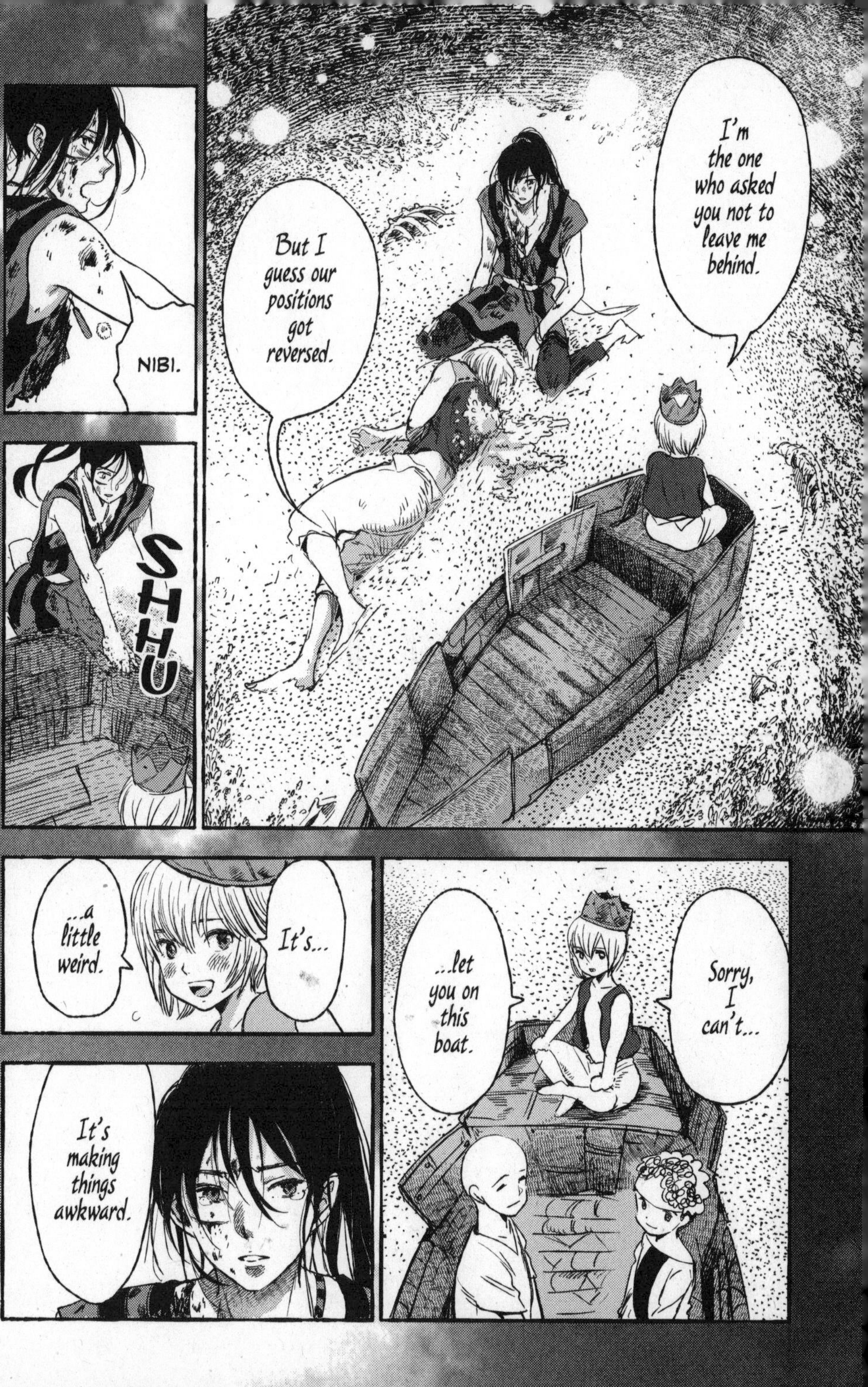
I'm the one who asked you not to leave me behind.
But I guess our positions got reversed.
NIBI.
SHHU
Sorry, I can't...
...let you on this boat.
It's...
...a little weird.
It's making things awkward.

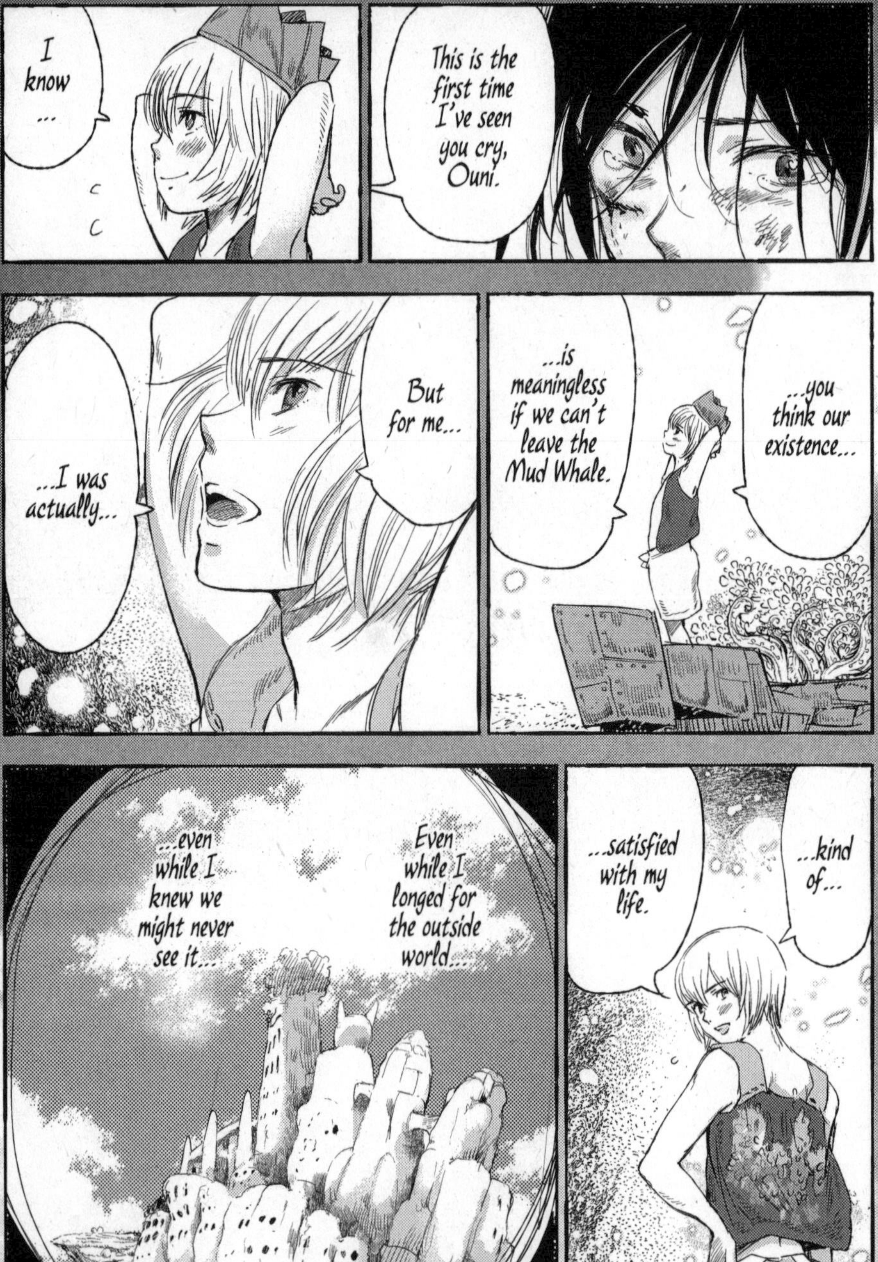
This is the first time I've seen you cry, Ouni.
I know ...
...you think our existence...
...is meaningless if we can't leave the Mud Whale.
But for me...
...I was actually...
...kind of...
...satisfied with my life.
Even while I longed for the outside world...
...even while I knew we might never see it...

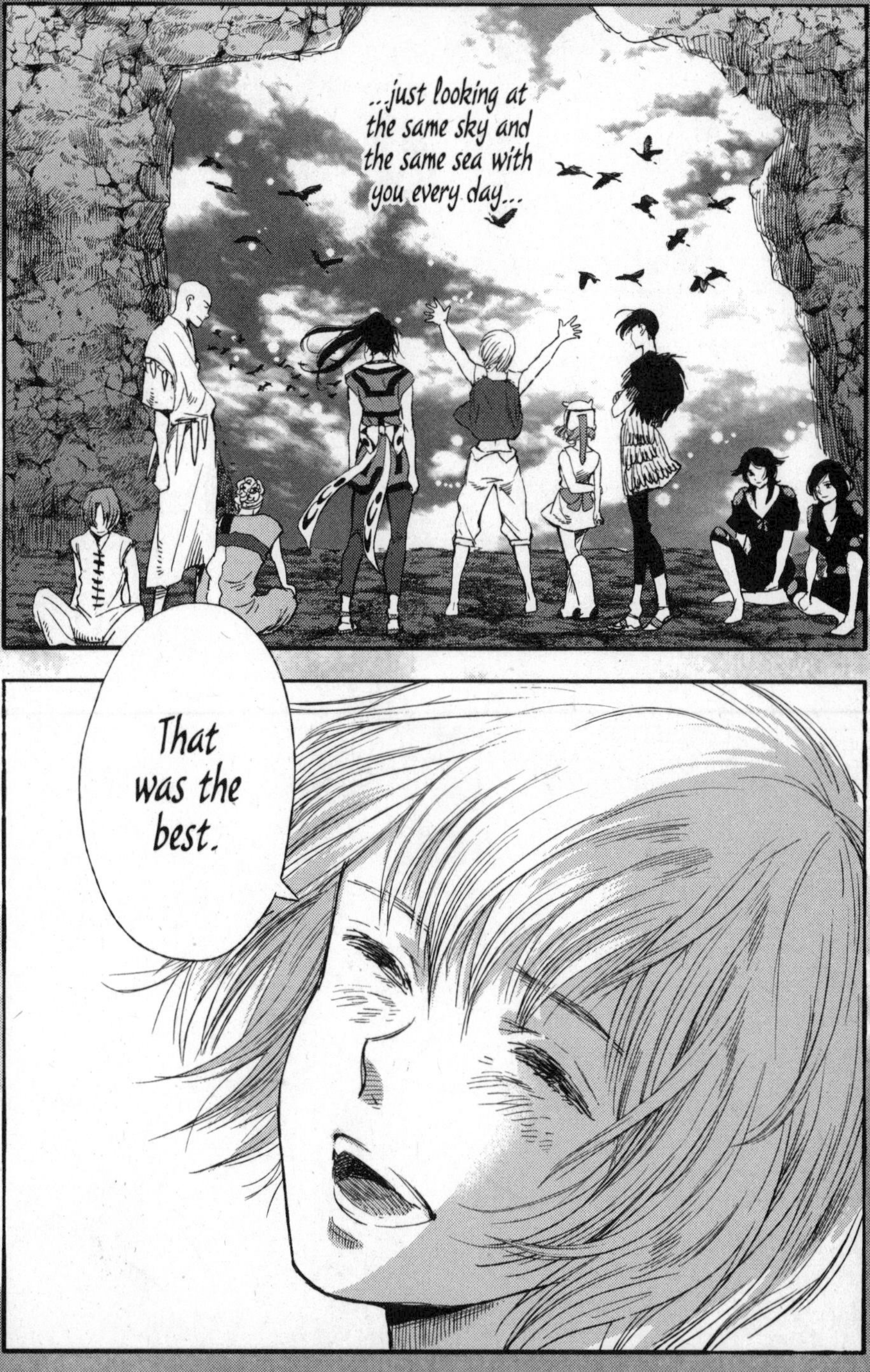
...just looking at the same sky and the same sea with you every day...
That was the best.

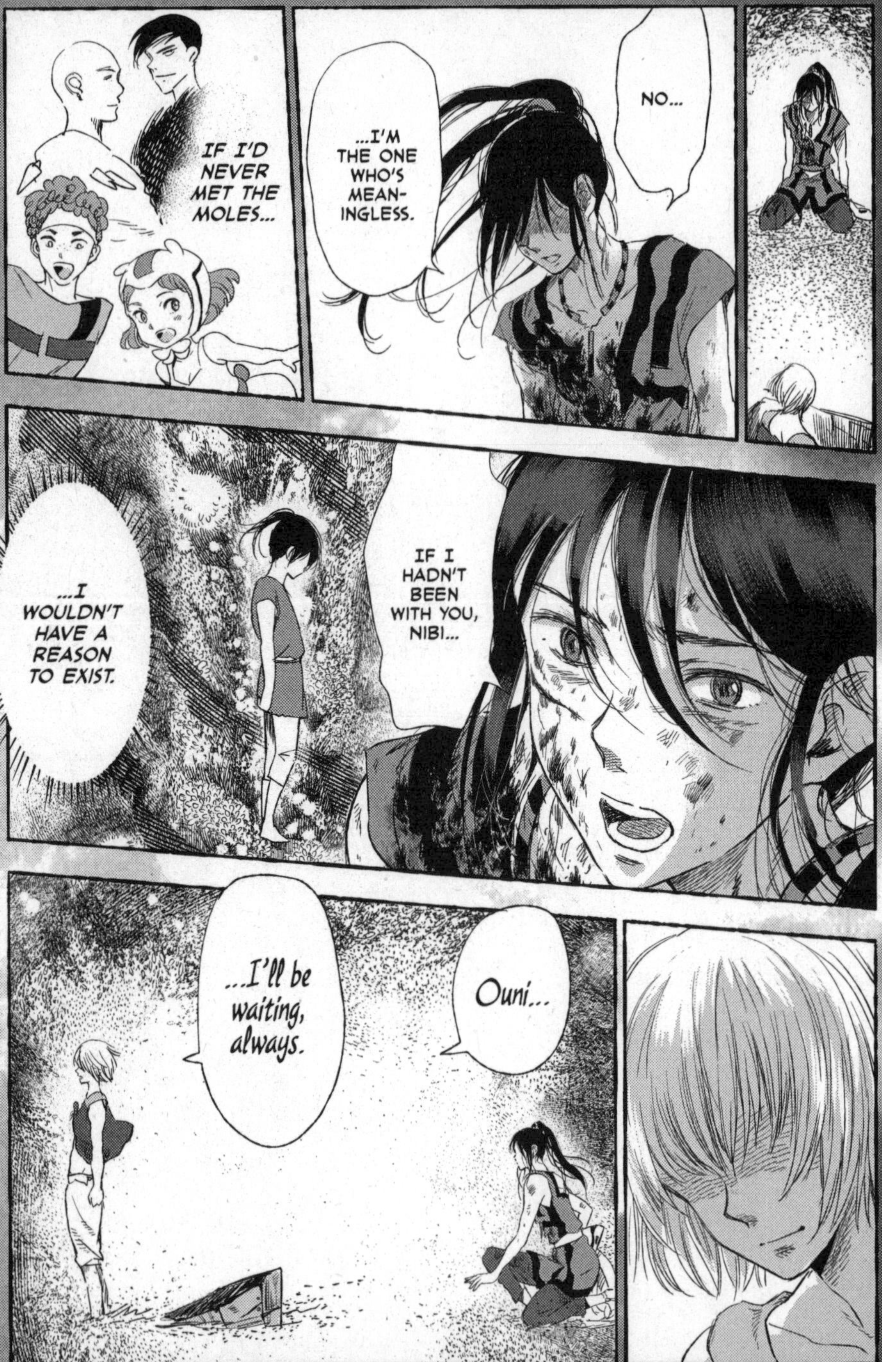
NO...
...I'M THE ONE WHO'S MEAN-INGLESS.
IF I'D NEVER MET THE MOLES...
IF I HADN'T BEEN WITH YOU, NIBI...
...I WOULDN'T HAVE A REASON TO EXIST.
Ouni...
...I'll be waiting, always.

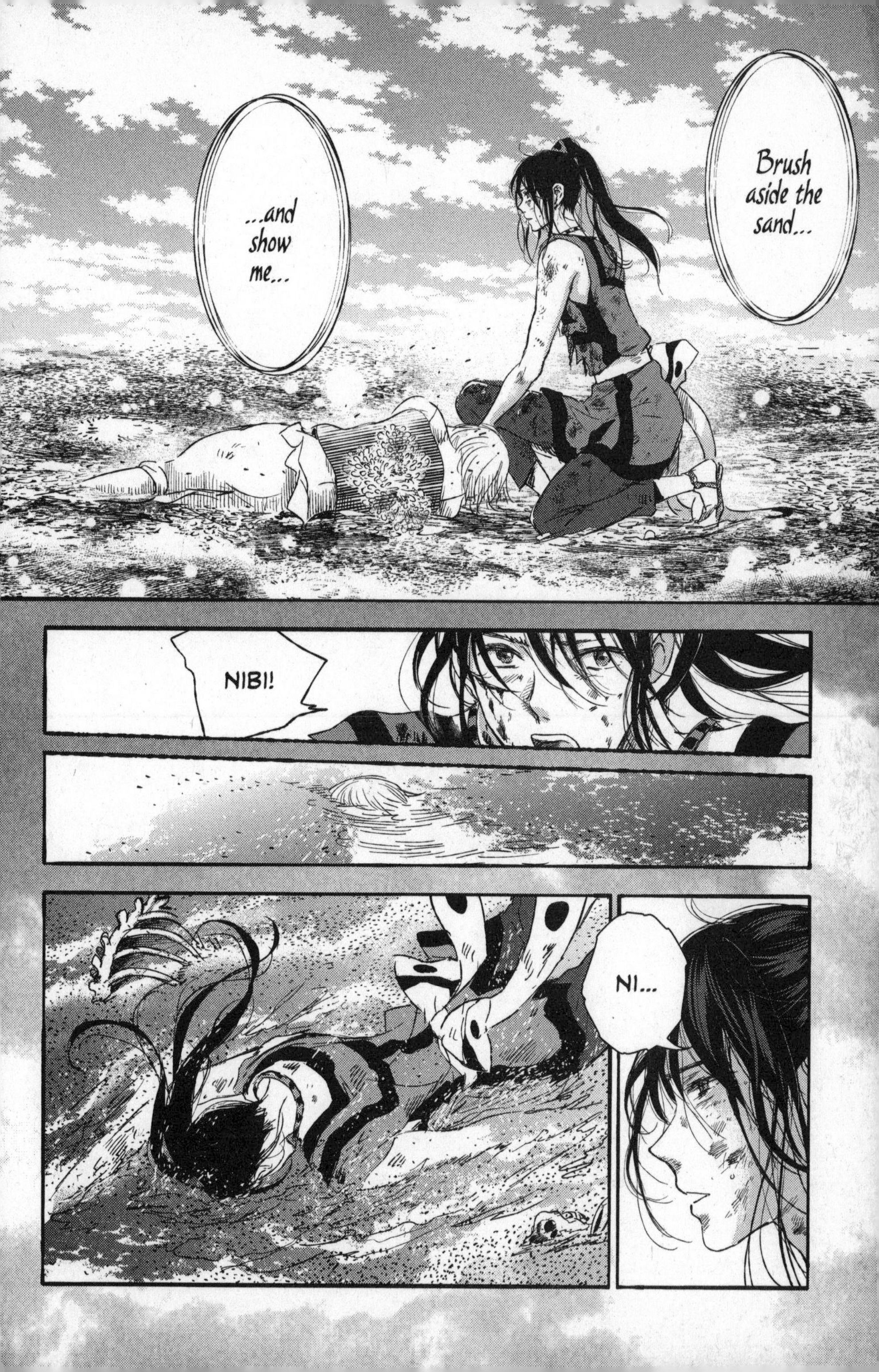
Brush aside the sand...
...and show me...
NIBI!
NI...

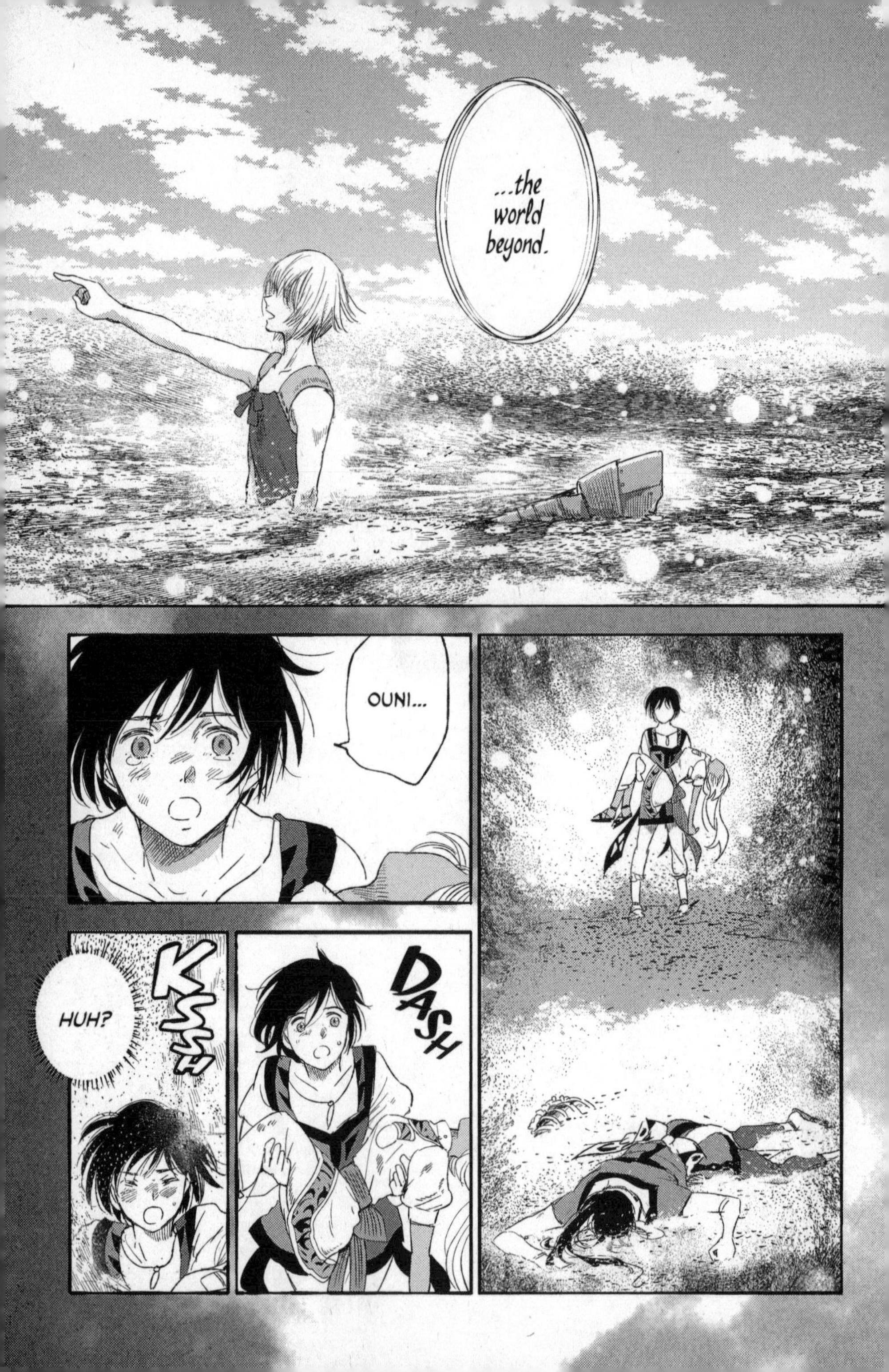
...the world beyond.
OUNI...
DASH
KSSH
HUH?

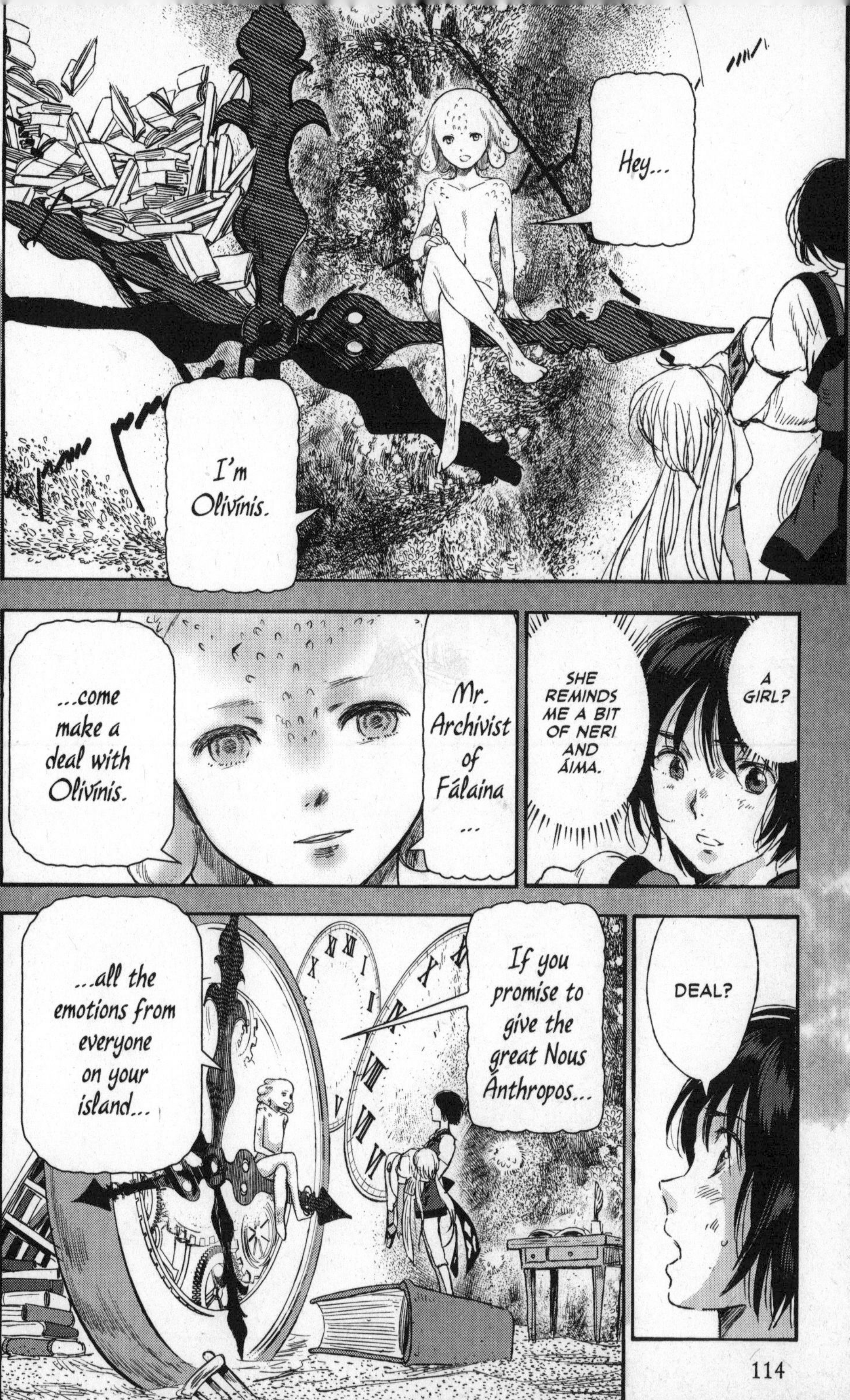
Hey...
I'm Olivínis.
A GIRL?
SHE REMINDS ME A BIT OF NERI AND ÁIMA.
Mr. Archivist of Fálaina...
...come make a deal with Olivínis.
DEAL?
If you promise to give the great Nous Ánthropos...
...all the emotions from everyone on your island...

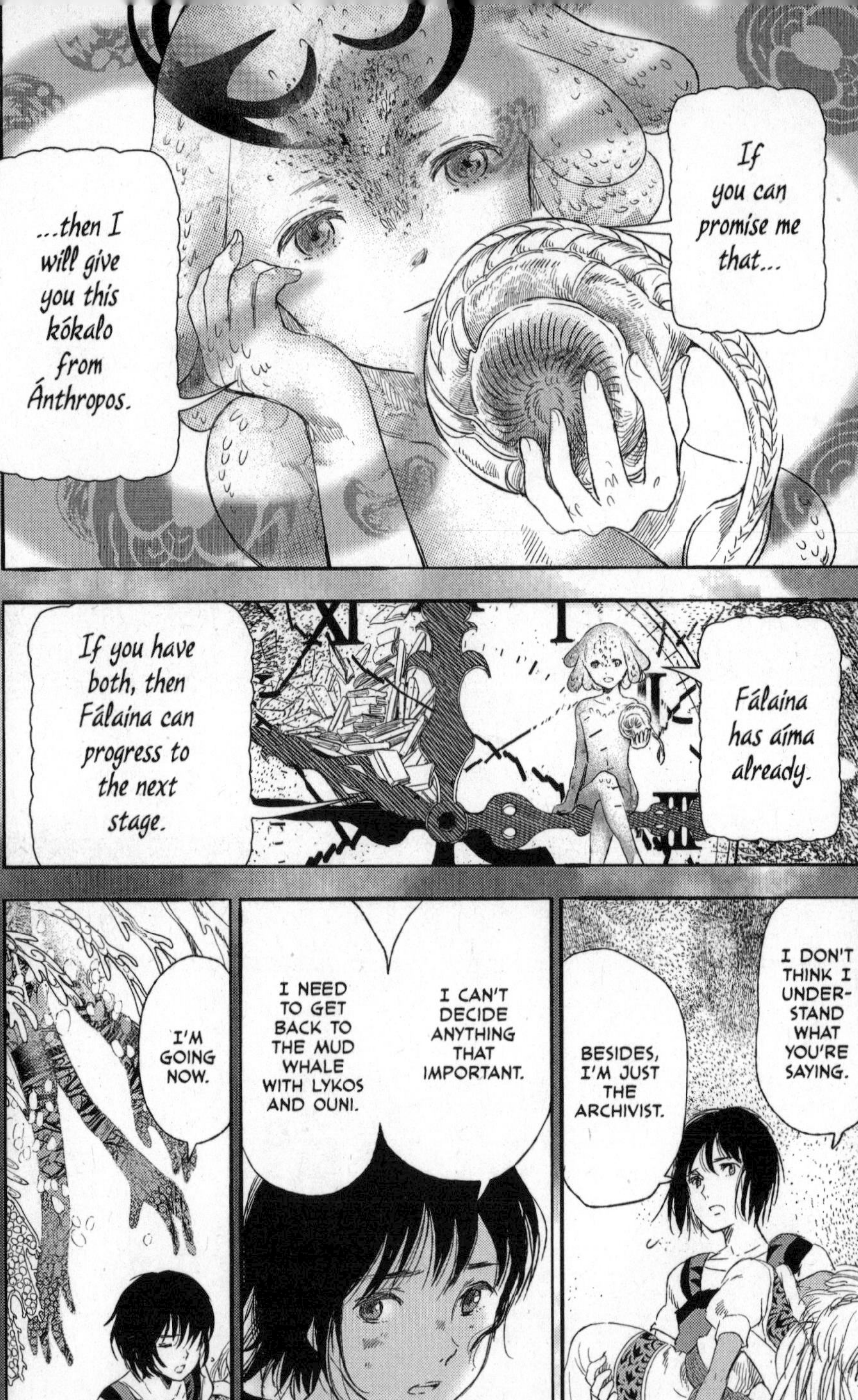
If you can promise me that...
...then I will give you this kókalo from Ánthropos.
Fálaina has aíma already.
If you have both, then Fálaina can progress to the next stage.
I DON'T THINK I UNDER-STAND WHAT YOU'RE SAYING.
BESIDES, I'M JUST THE ARCHIVIST.
I CAN'T DECIDE ANYTHING THAT IMPORTANT.
I NEED TO GET BACK TO THE MUD WHALE WITH LYKOS AND OUNI.
I'M GOING NOW.

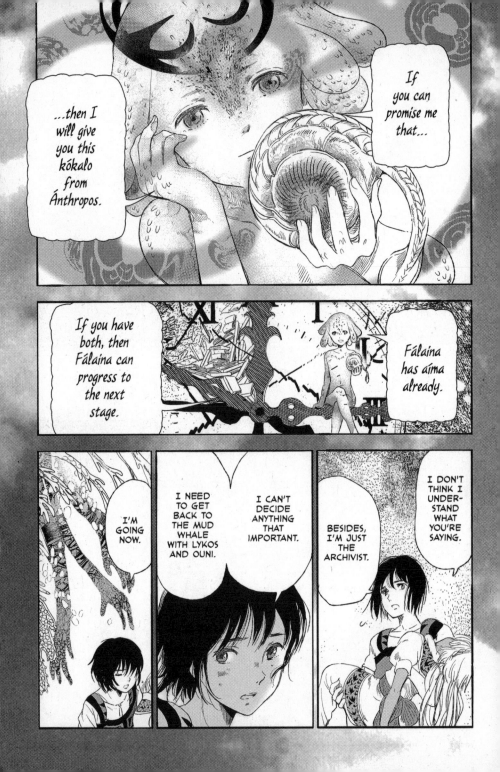

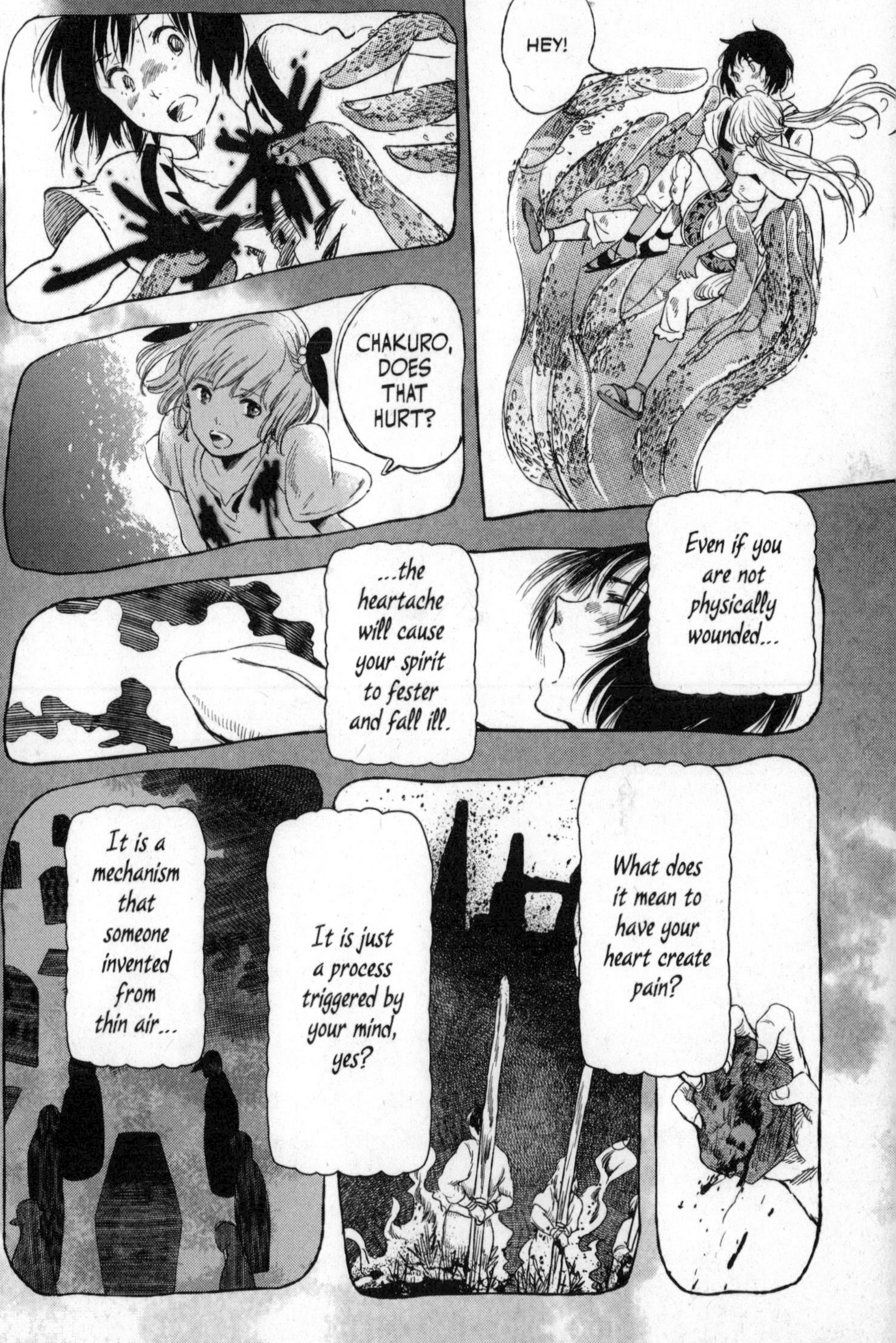
HEY!
CHAKURO, DOES THAT HURT?
Even if you are not physically wounded...
...the heartache will cause your spirit to fester and fall ill.
What does it mean to have your heart create pain?
It is just a process triggered by your mind, yes?
It is a mechanism that someone invented from thin air...

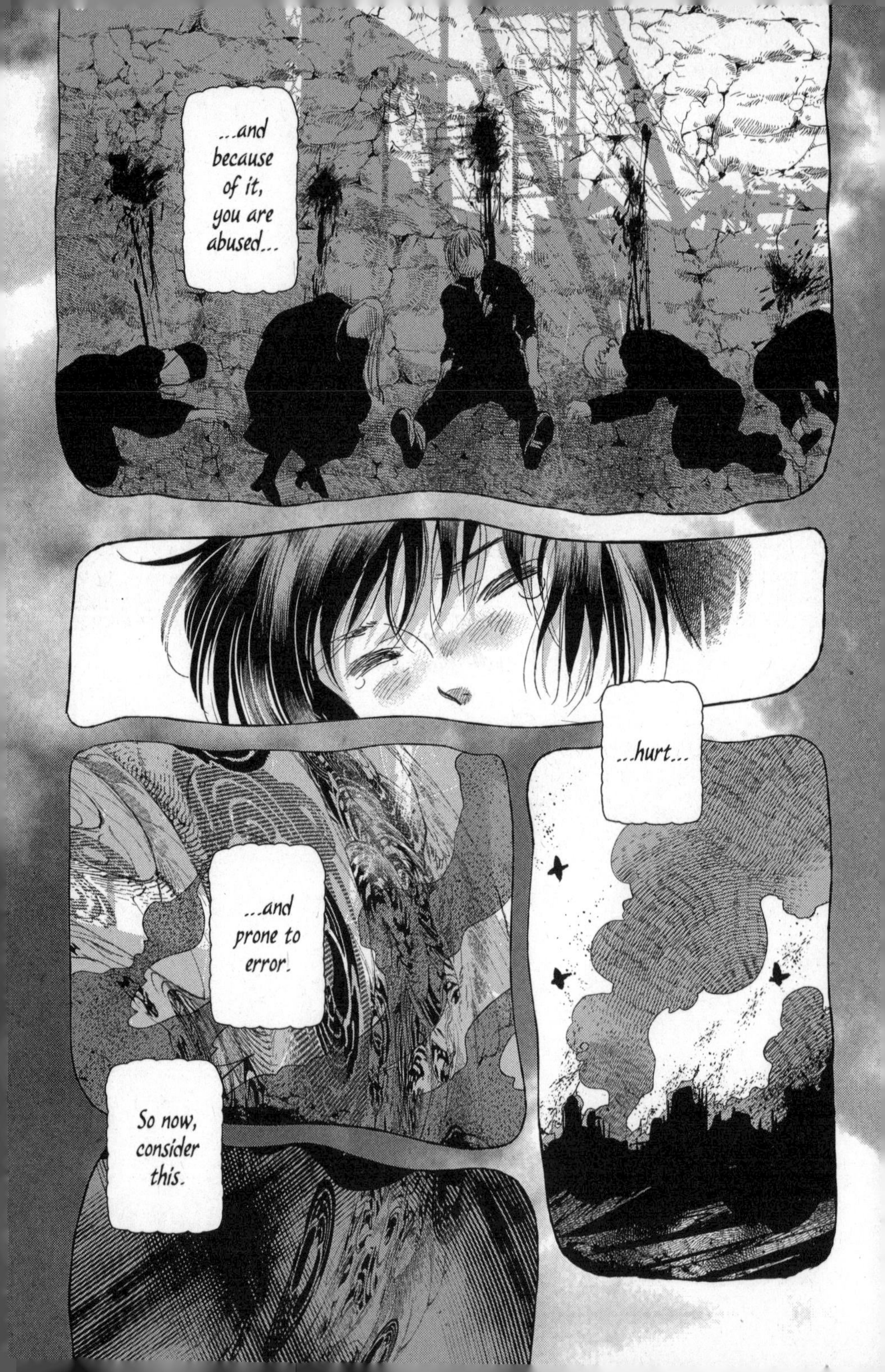
...and because of it, you are abused...
...hurt...
...and prone to error.
So now, consider this.

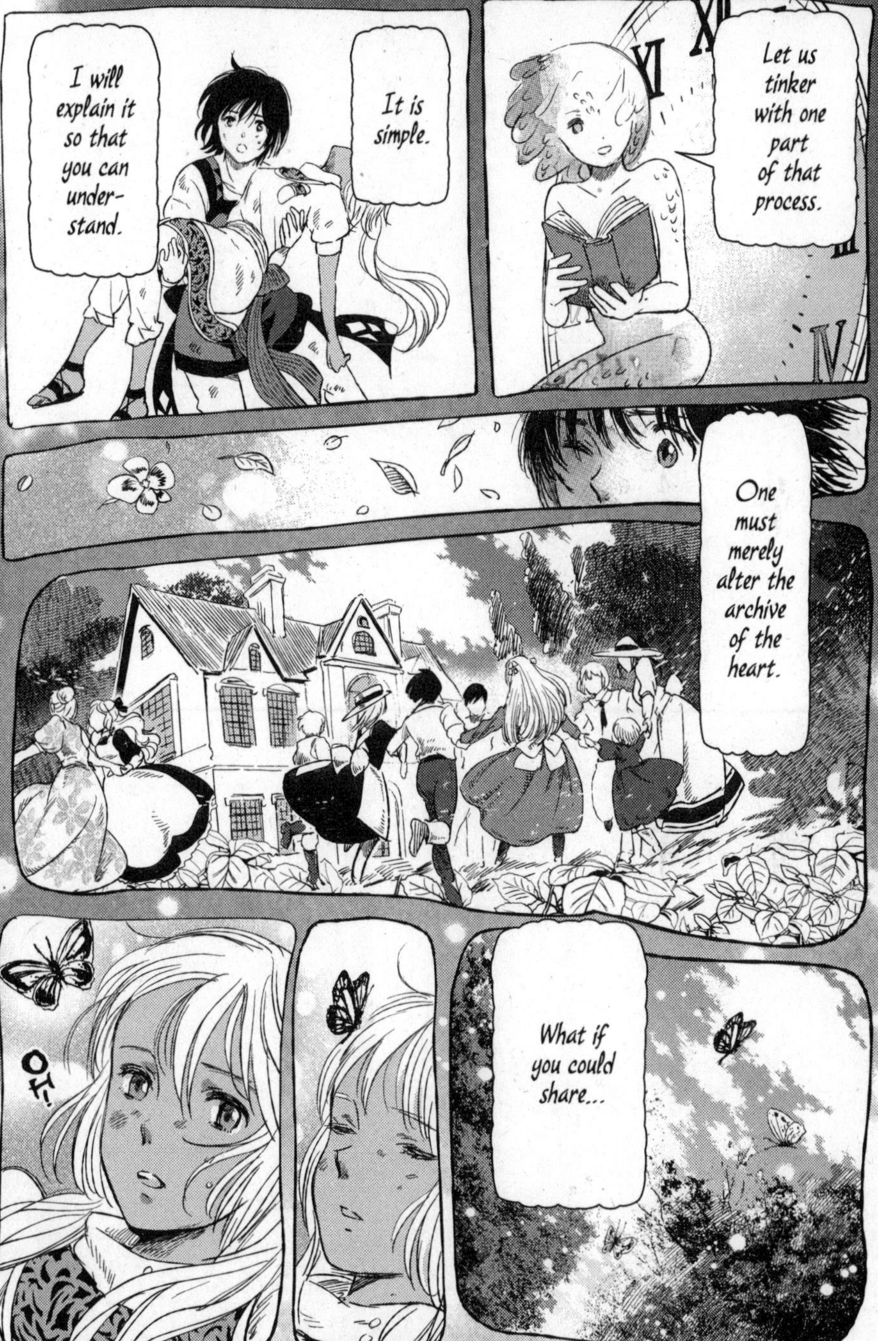
Let us tinker with one part of that process.
It is simple.
I will explain it so that you can under-stand.
One must merely alter the archive of the heart.
What if you could share...
OH!

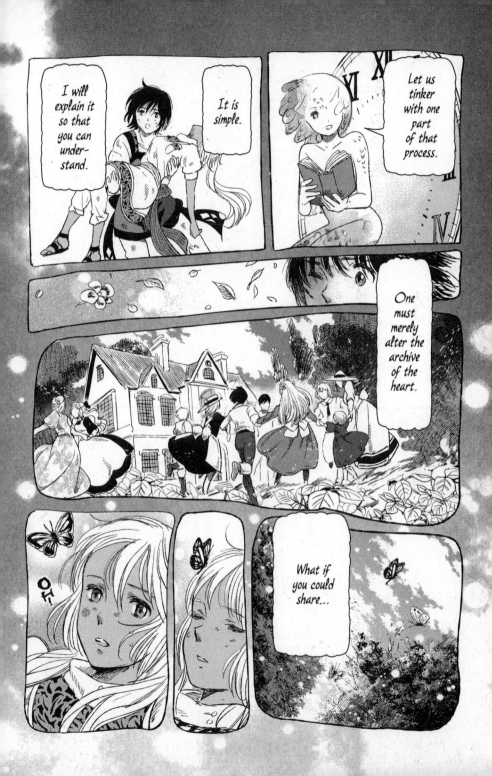

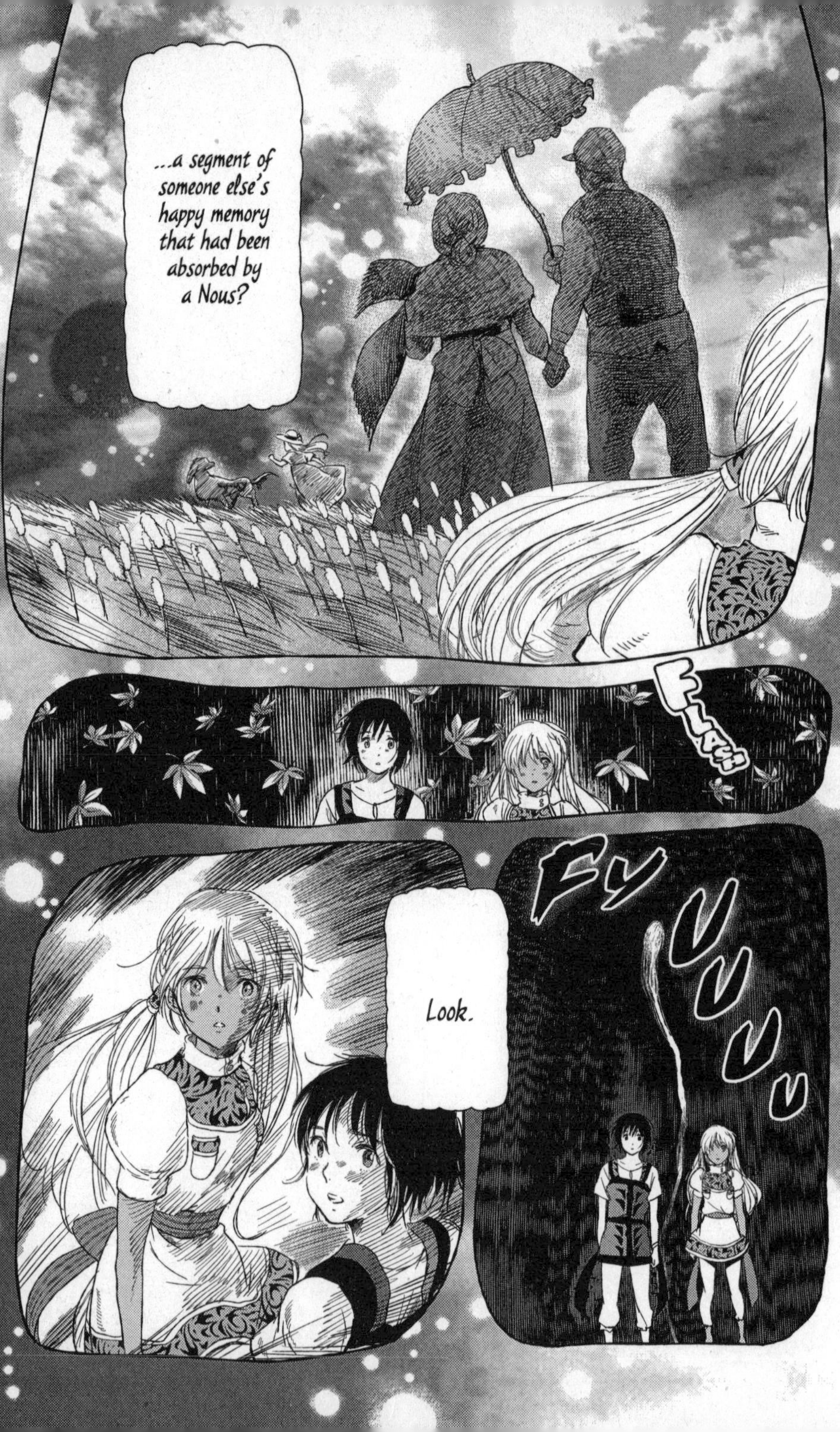
...a segment of someone else's happy memory that had been absorbed by a Nous?
FLASH
FYUUUUUU
Look.

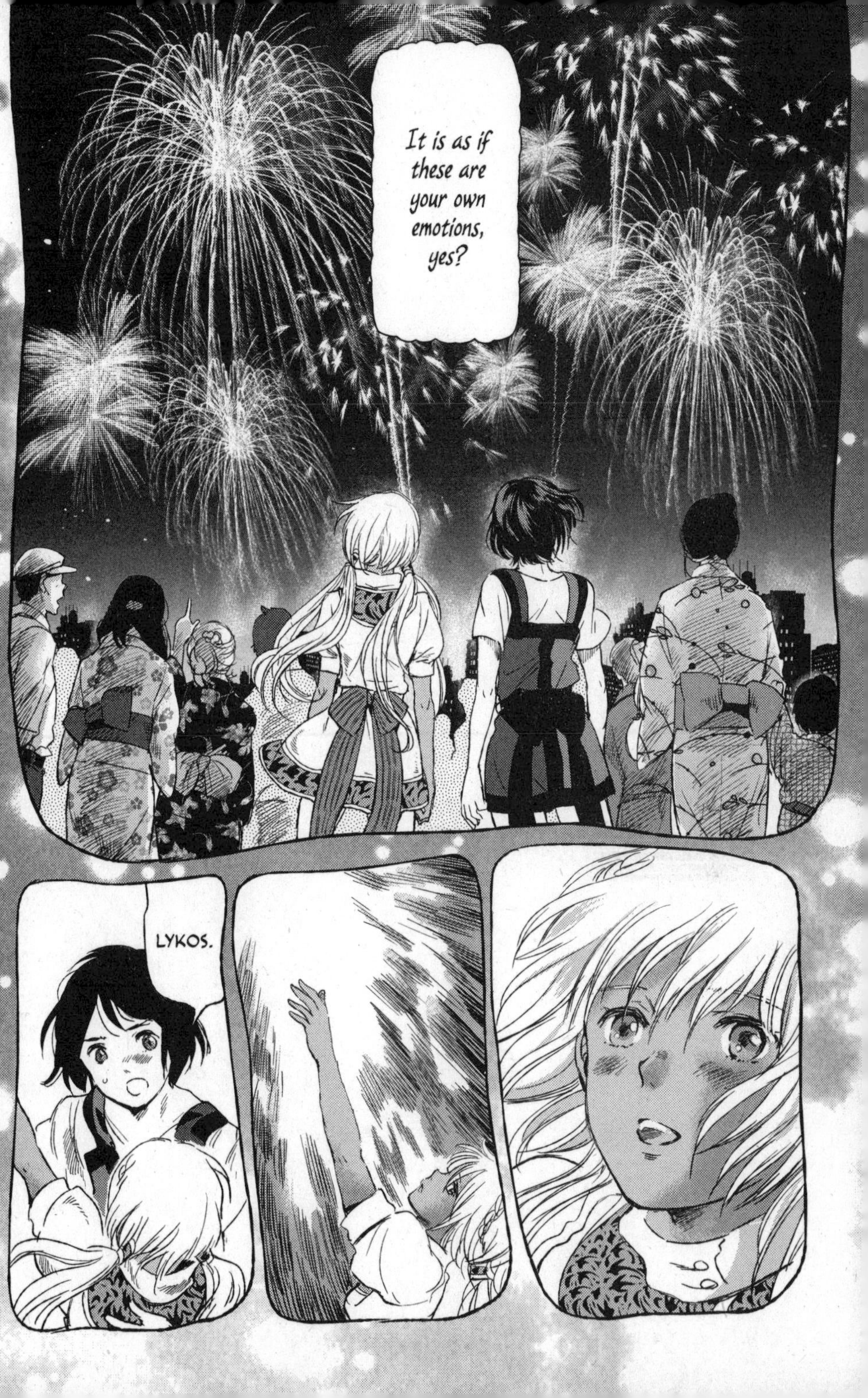
It is as if these are your own emotions, yes?
LYKOS.

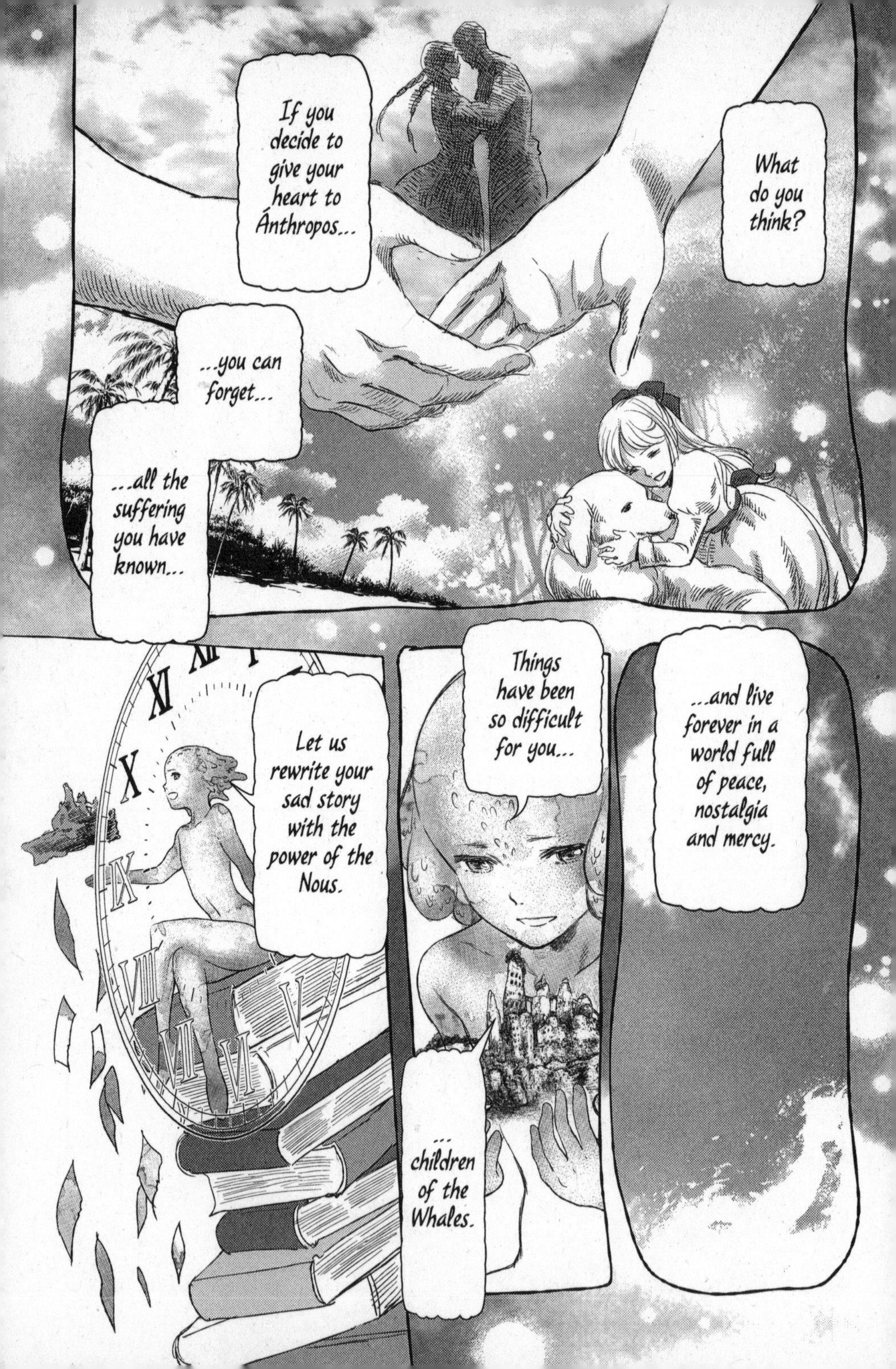
What do you think?
If you decide to give your heart to Ánthropos...
...you can forget...
...all the suffering you have known...
...and live forever in a world full of peace, nostalgia and mercy.
Things have been so difficult for you...
...children of the Whales.
Let us rewrite your sad story with the power of the Nous.

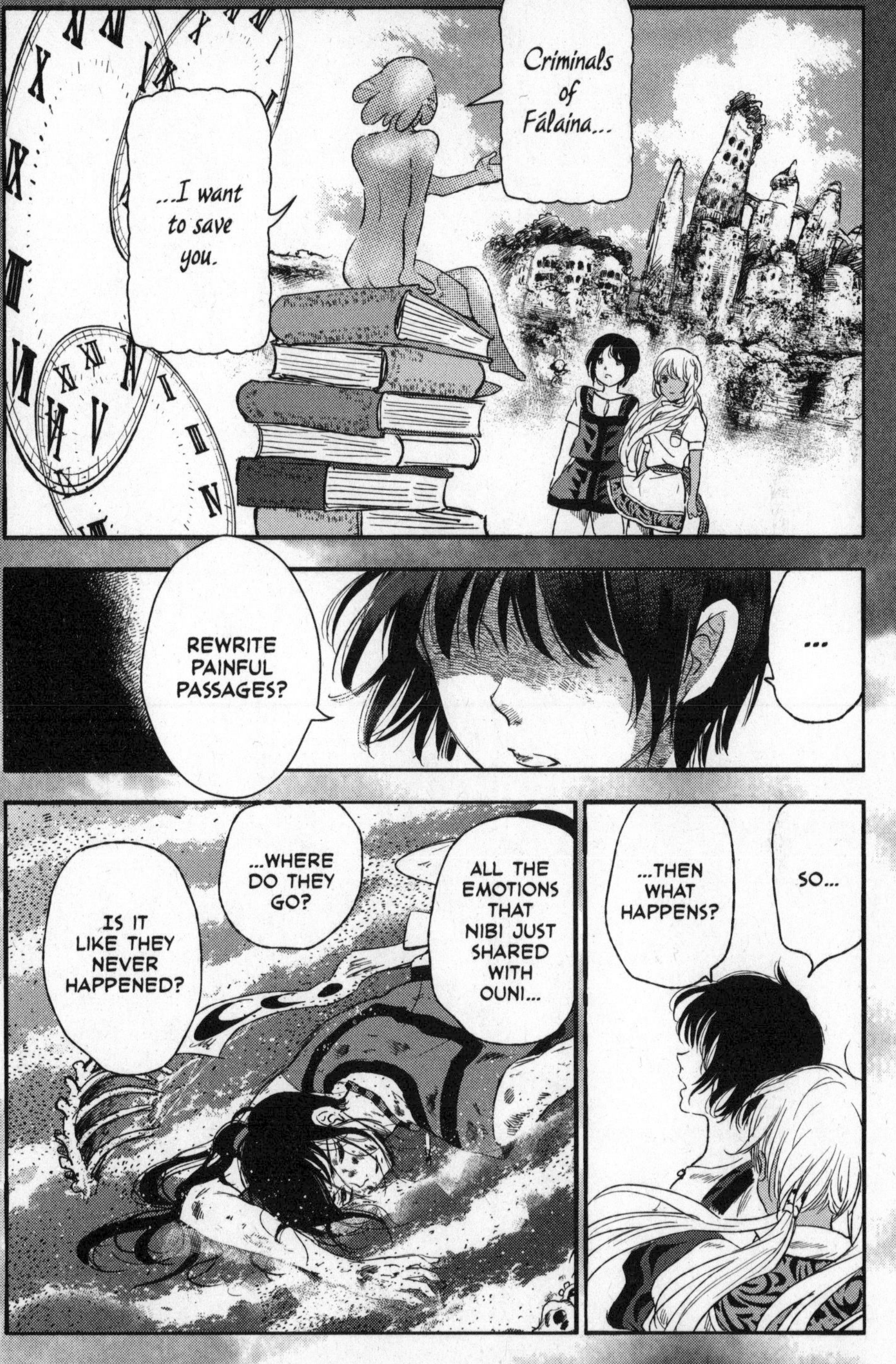
Criminals of Fálaina...
...I want to save you.
...
REWRITE PAINFUL PASSAGES?
SO...
...THEN WHAT HAPPENS?
ALL THE EMOTIONS THAT NIBI JUST SHARED WITH OUNI...
...WHERE DO THEY GO?
IS IT LIKE THEY NEVER HAPPENED?

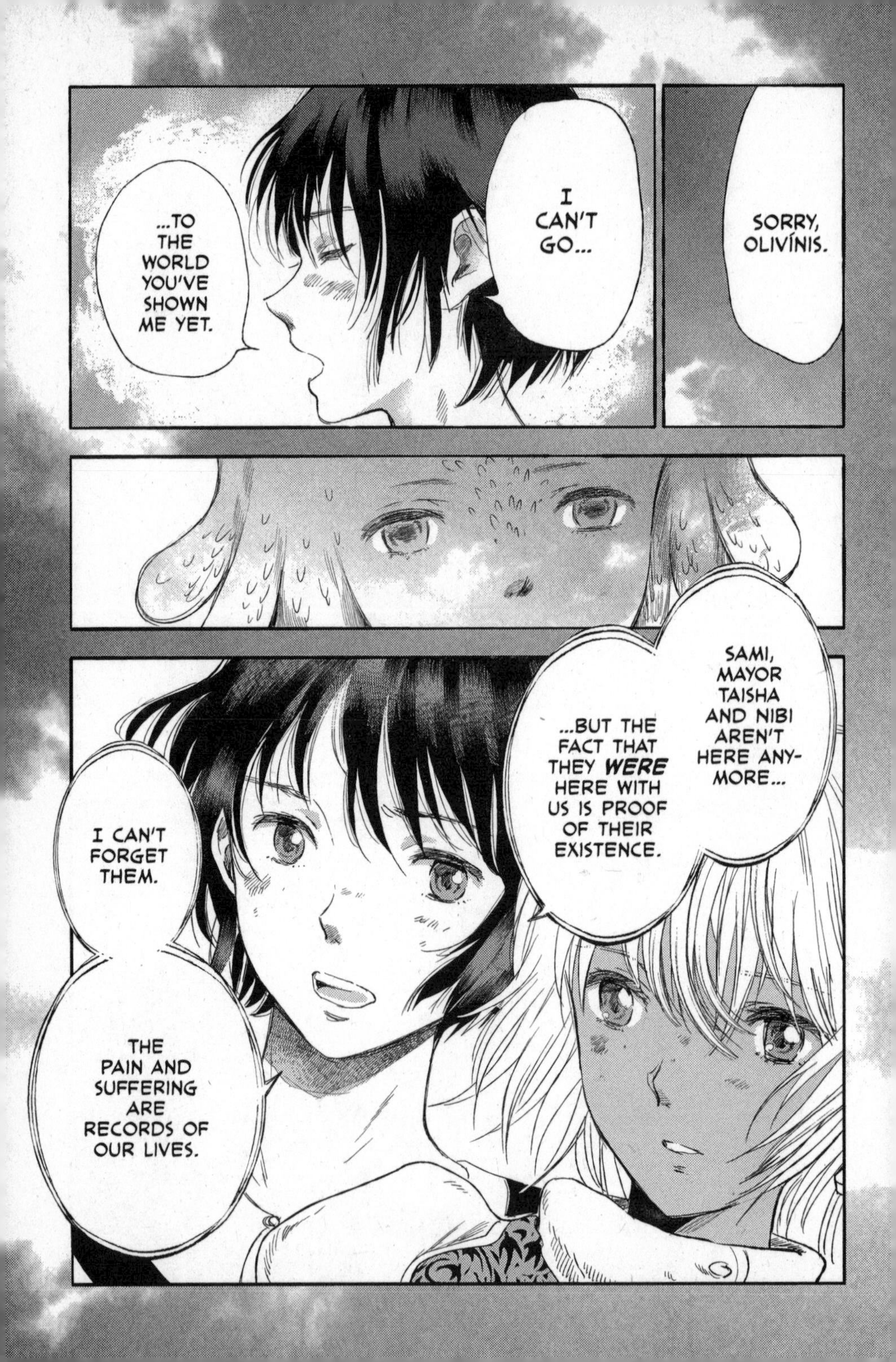
SORRY, OLIVÍNIS.
I CAN'T GO...
...TO THE WORLD YOU'VE SHOWN ME YET.
SAMI, MAYOR TAISHA AND NIBI AREN'T HERE ANYMORE...
...BUT THE FACT THAT THEY *WERE* HERE WITH US IS PROOF OF THEIR EXISTENCE.
I CAN'T FORGET THEM.
THE PAIN AND SUFFERING ARE RECORDS OF OUR LIVES.

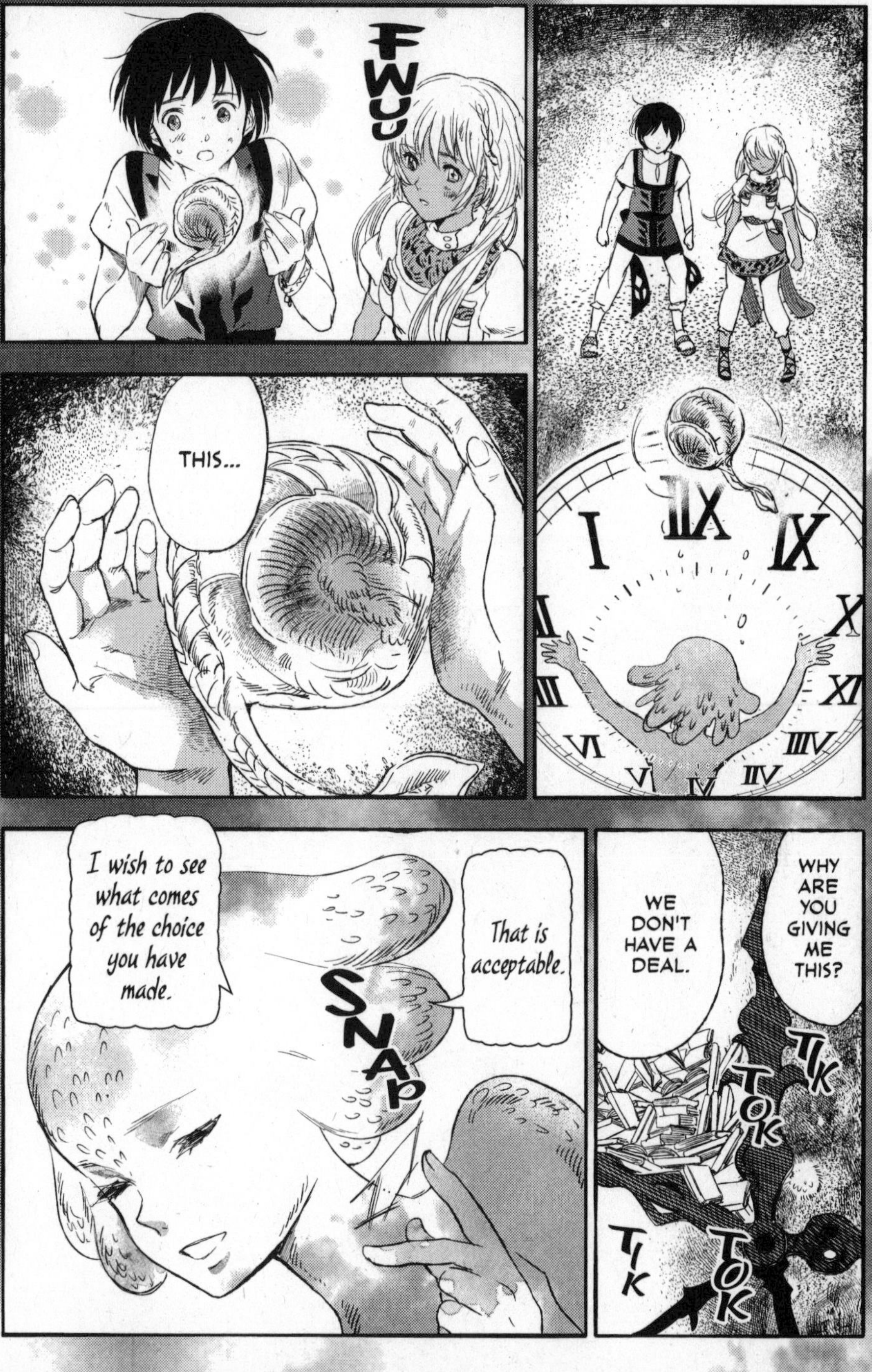
FWUU
THIS...
WHY ARE YOU GIVING ME THIS?
WE DON'T HAVE A DEAL.
TIK
TOK
TIK
TOK
That is acceptable.
I wish to see what comes of the choice you have made.
SNAP

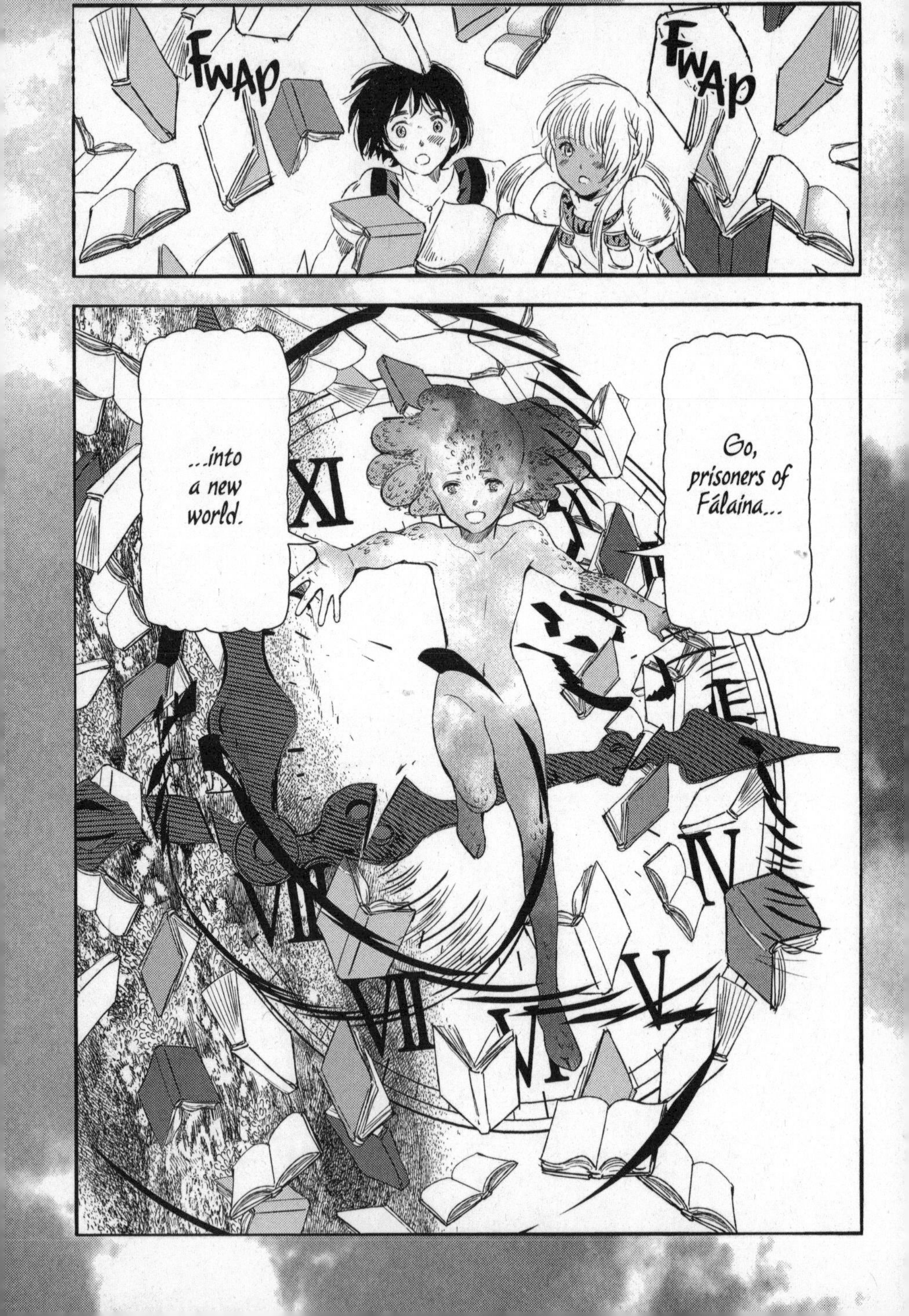
FWAP
FWAP
Go, prisoners of Fálaina...
...into a new world.

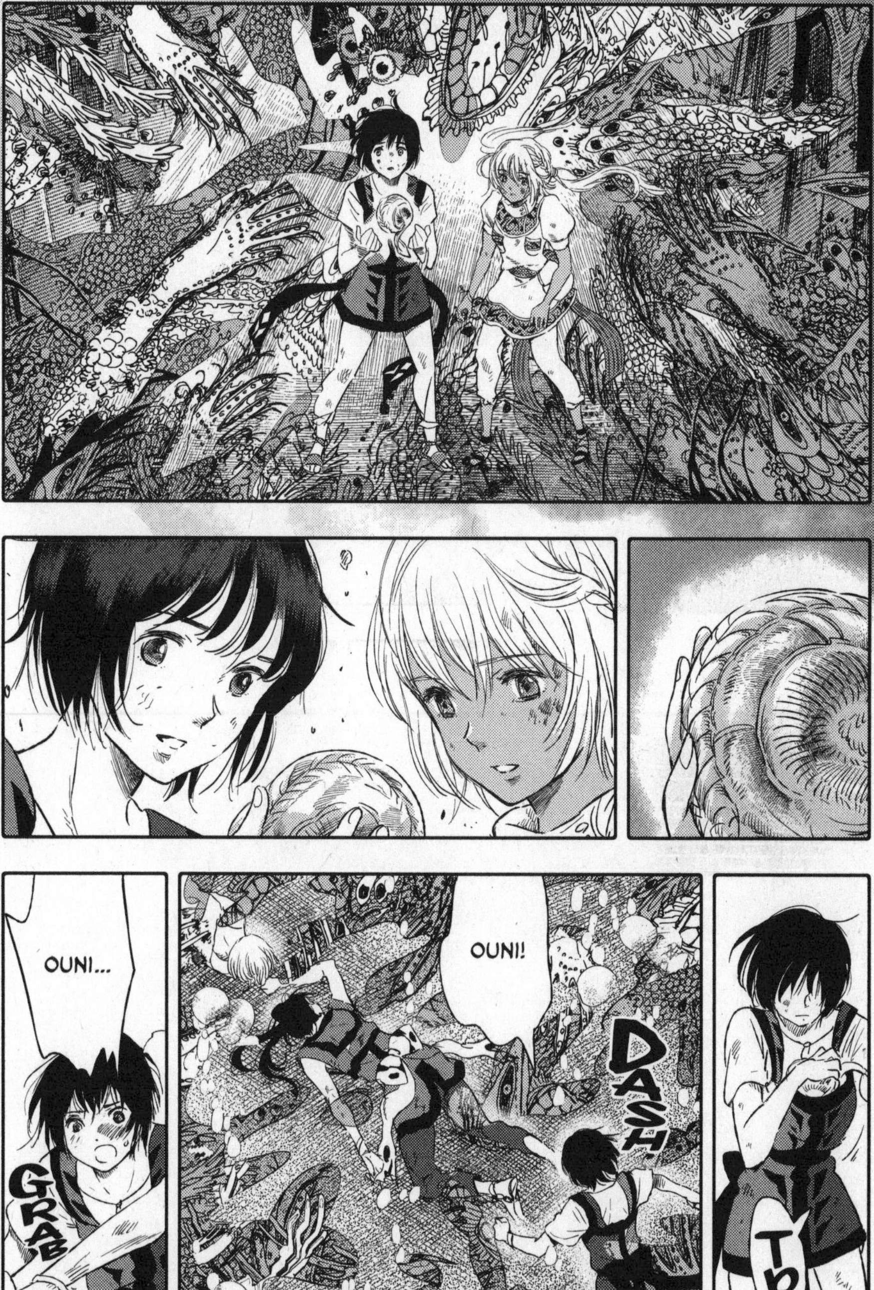
Tp
OUNI!
DASH
OUNI...
GRAB

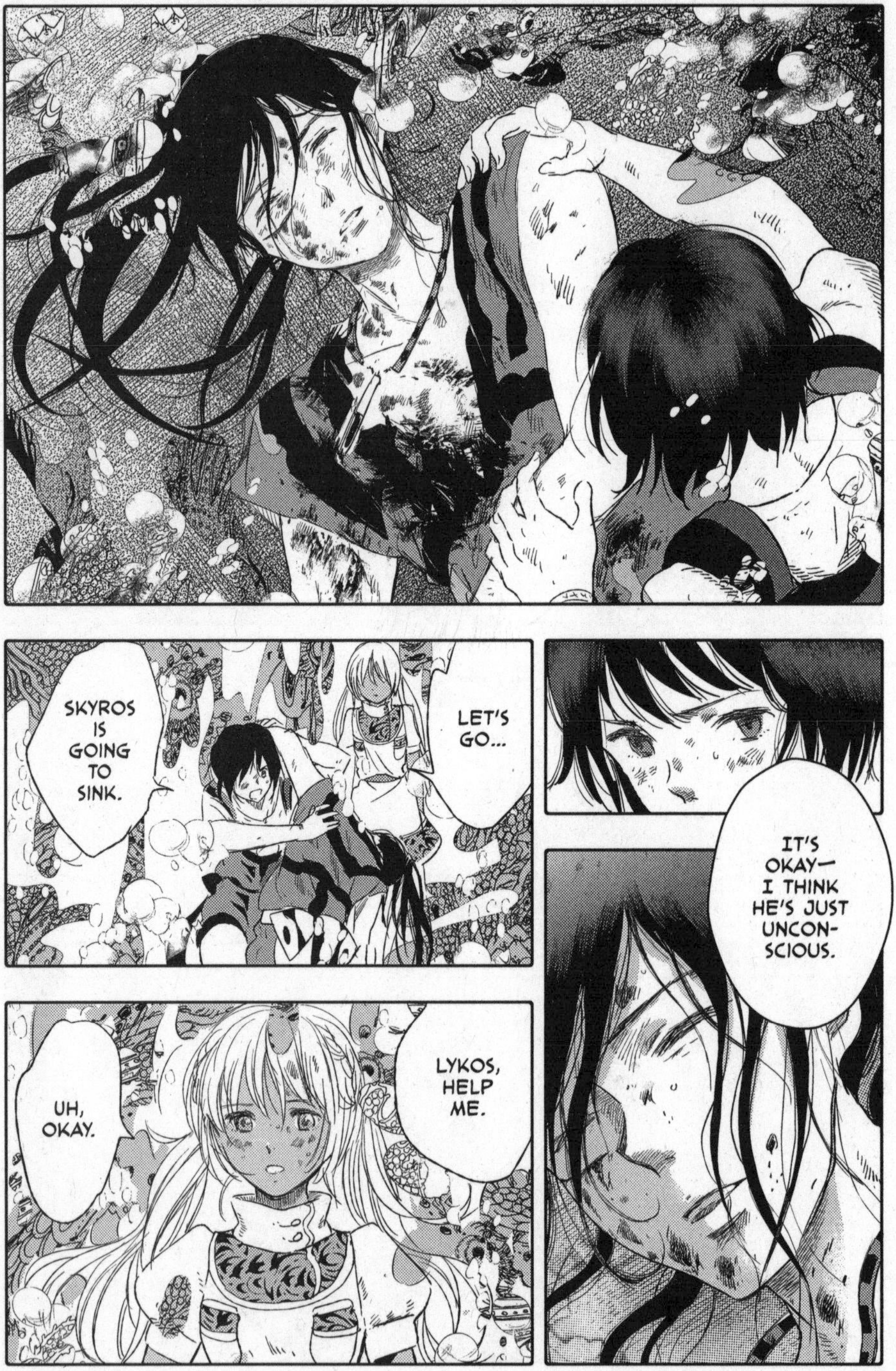
IT'S OKAY— I THINK HE'S JUST UNCON-SCIOUS.
LET'S GO...
SKYROS IS GOING TO SINK.
LYKOS, HELP ME.
UH, OKAY.

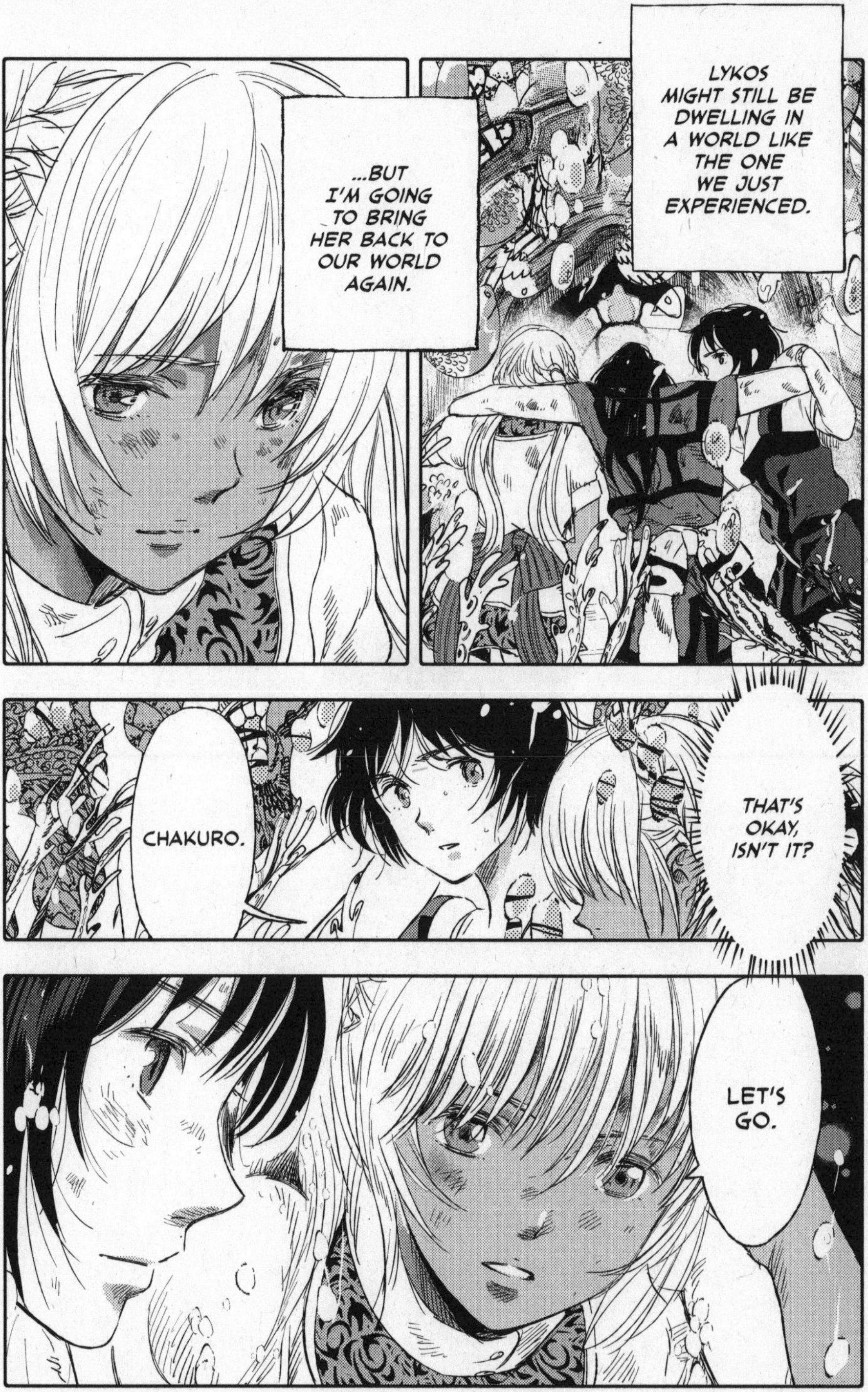
LYKOS MIGHT STILL BE DWELLING IN A WORLD LIKE THE ONE WE JUST EXPERIENCED.
...BUT I'M GOING TO BRING HER BACK TO OUR WORLD AGAIN.
THAT'S OKAY, ISN'T IT?
CHAKURO.
LET'S GO.

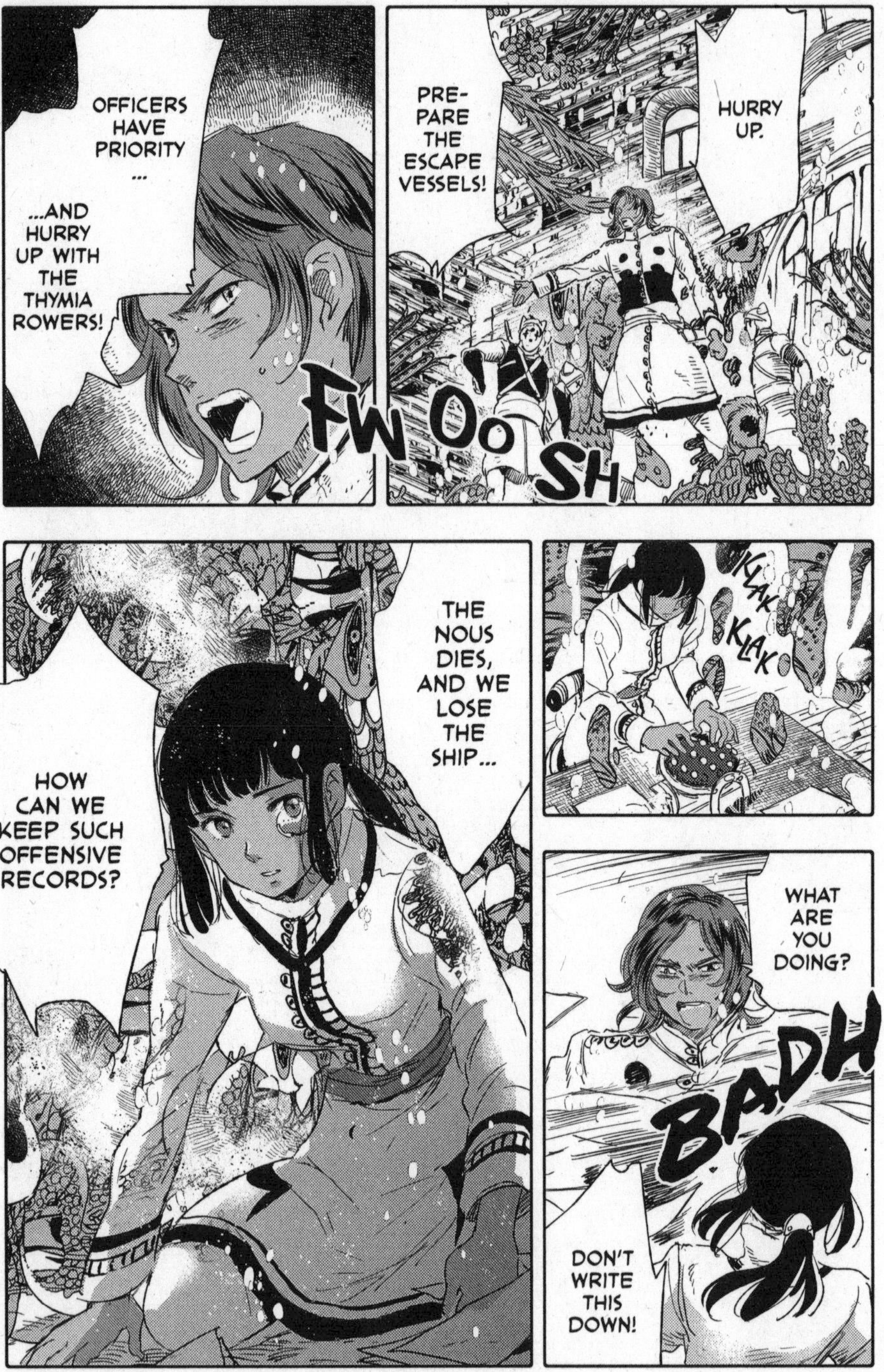
HURRY UP.
PRE-PARE THE ESCAPE VESSELS!
FWOOSH
OFFICERS HAVE PRIORITY ...
...AND HURRY UP WITH THE THYMIA ROWERS!
KLAK KLAK
WHAT ARE YOU DOING?
BADH
DON'T WRITE THIS DOWN!
THE NOUS DIES, AND WE LOSE THE SHIP...
HOW CAN WE KEEP SUCH OFFENSIVE RECORDS?

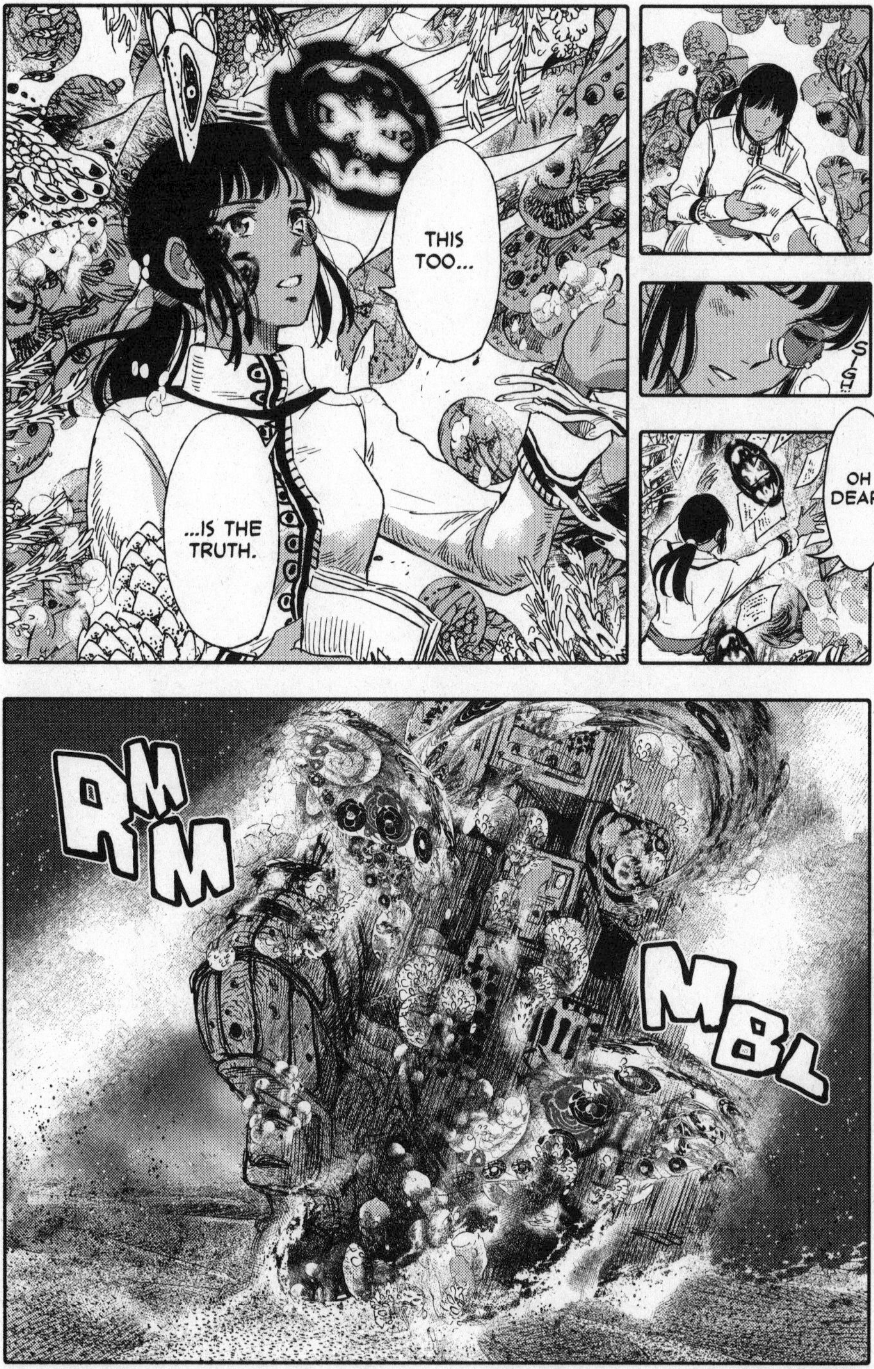
SIGH
OH DEAR.
THIS TOO...
...IS THE TRUTH.
RMMMBL

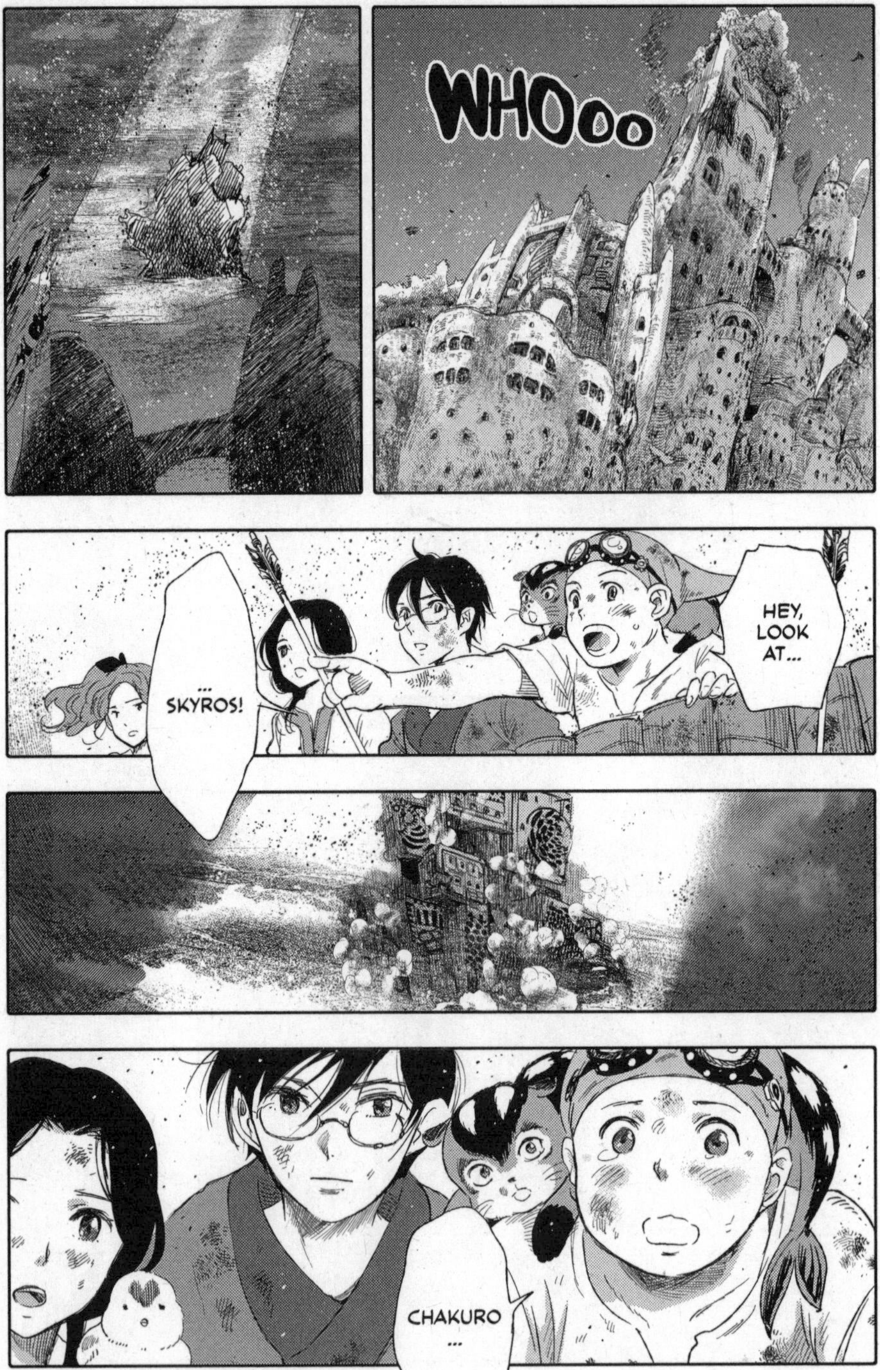
WHOOO
HEY, LOOK AT...
...SKYROS!
CHAKURO ...

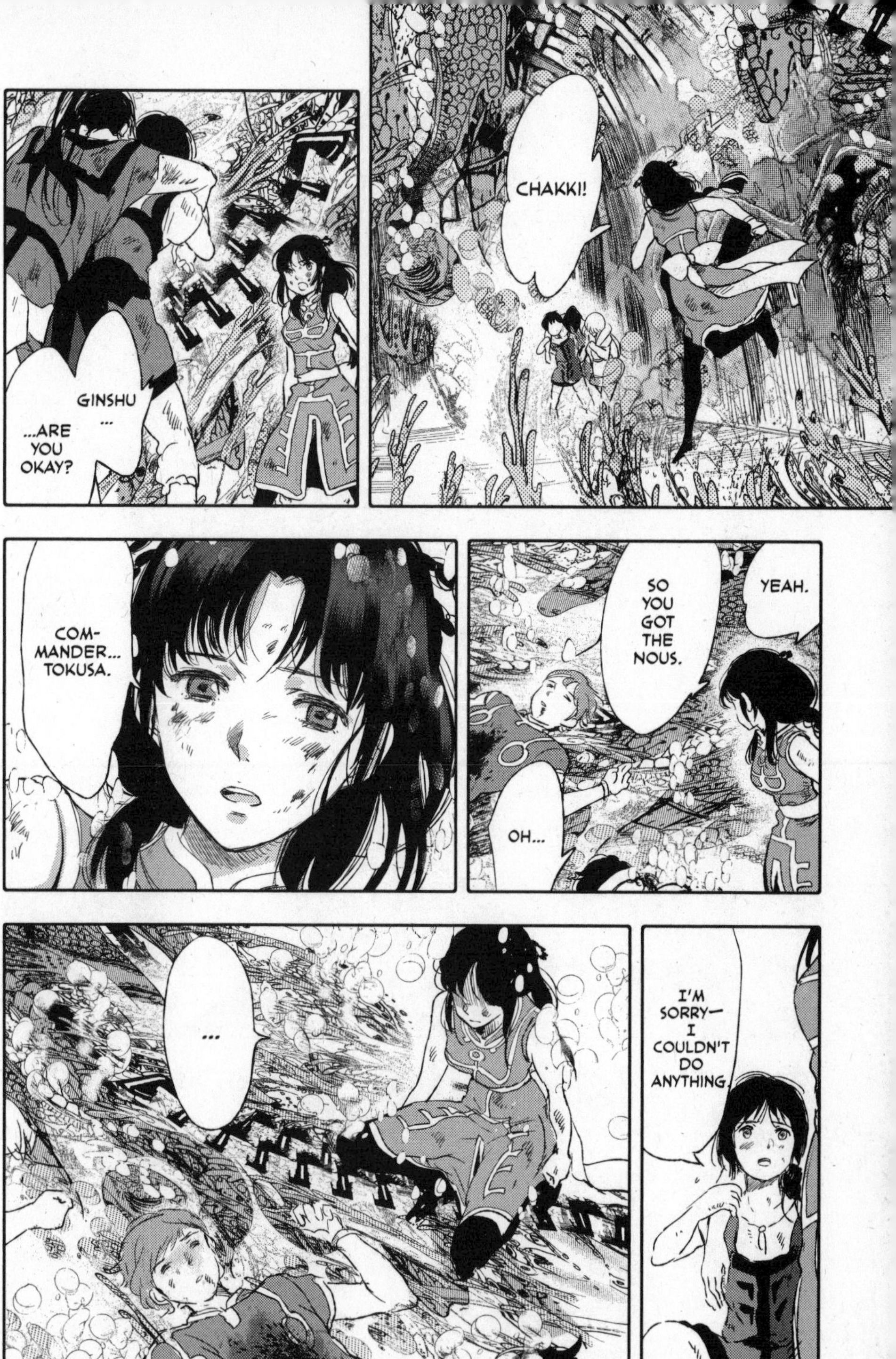
CHAKKI!
GINSHU ... ...ARE YOU OKAY?
YEAH.
SO YOU GOT THE NOUS.
OH...
COM-MANDER... TOKUSA.
I'M SORRY— I COULDN'T DO ANYTHING.
...

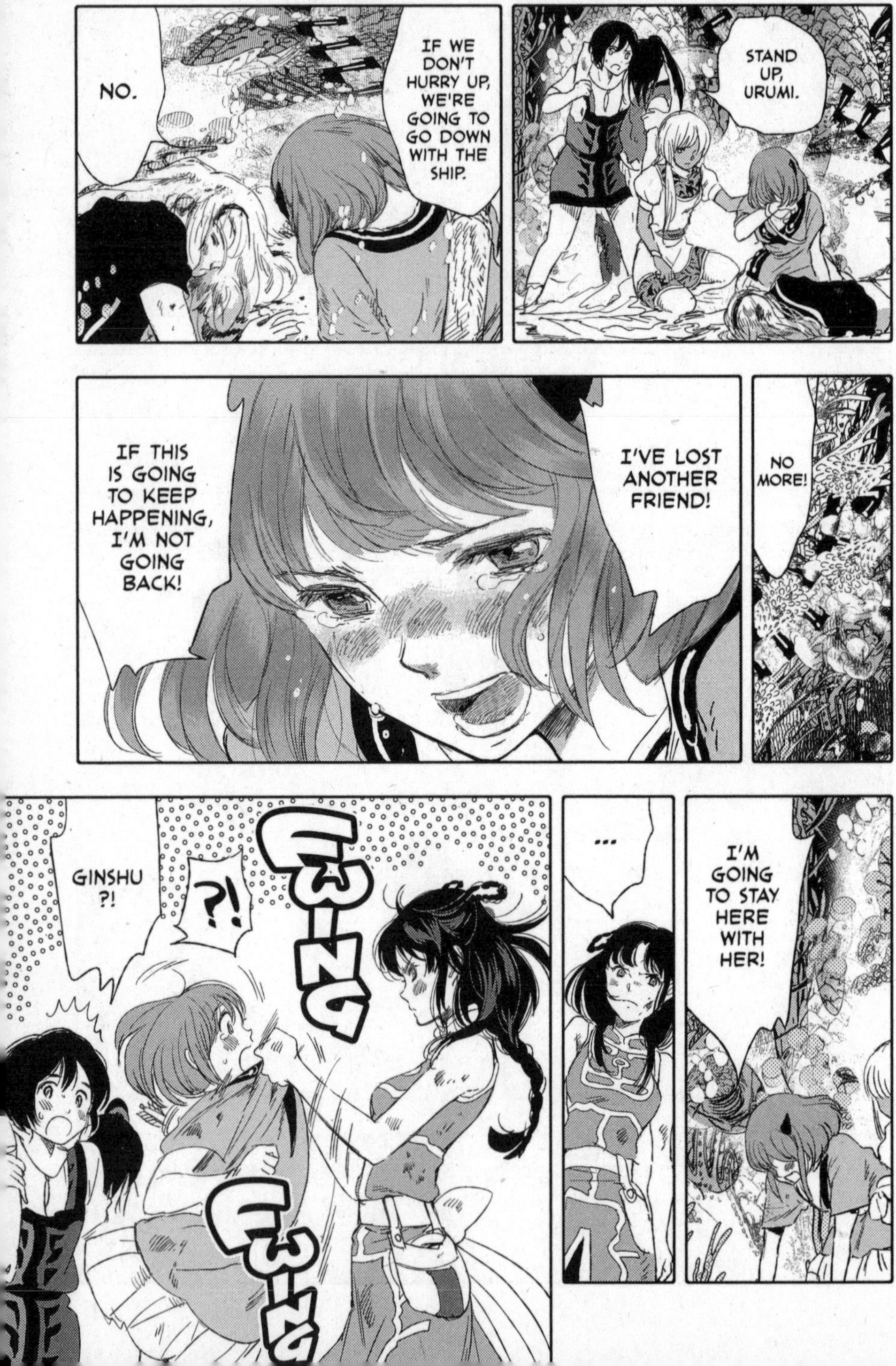
STAND UP, URUMI.
IF WE DON'T HURRY UP, WE'RE GOING TO GO DOWN WITH THE SHIP.
NO.
NO MORE!
I'VE LOST ANOTHER FRIEND!
IF THIS IS GOING TO KEEP HAPPENING, I'M NOT GOING BACK!
I'M GOING TO STAY HERE WITH HER!
...
FWING
?!
GINSHU ?!
FWING

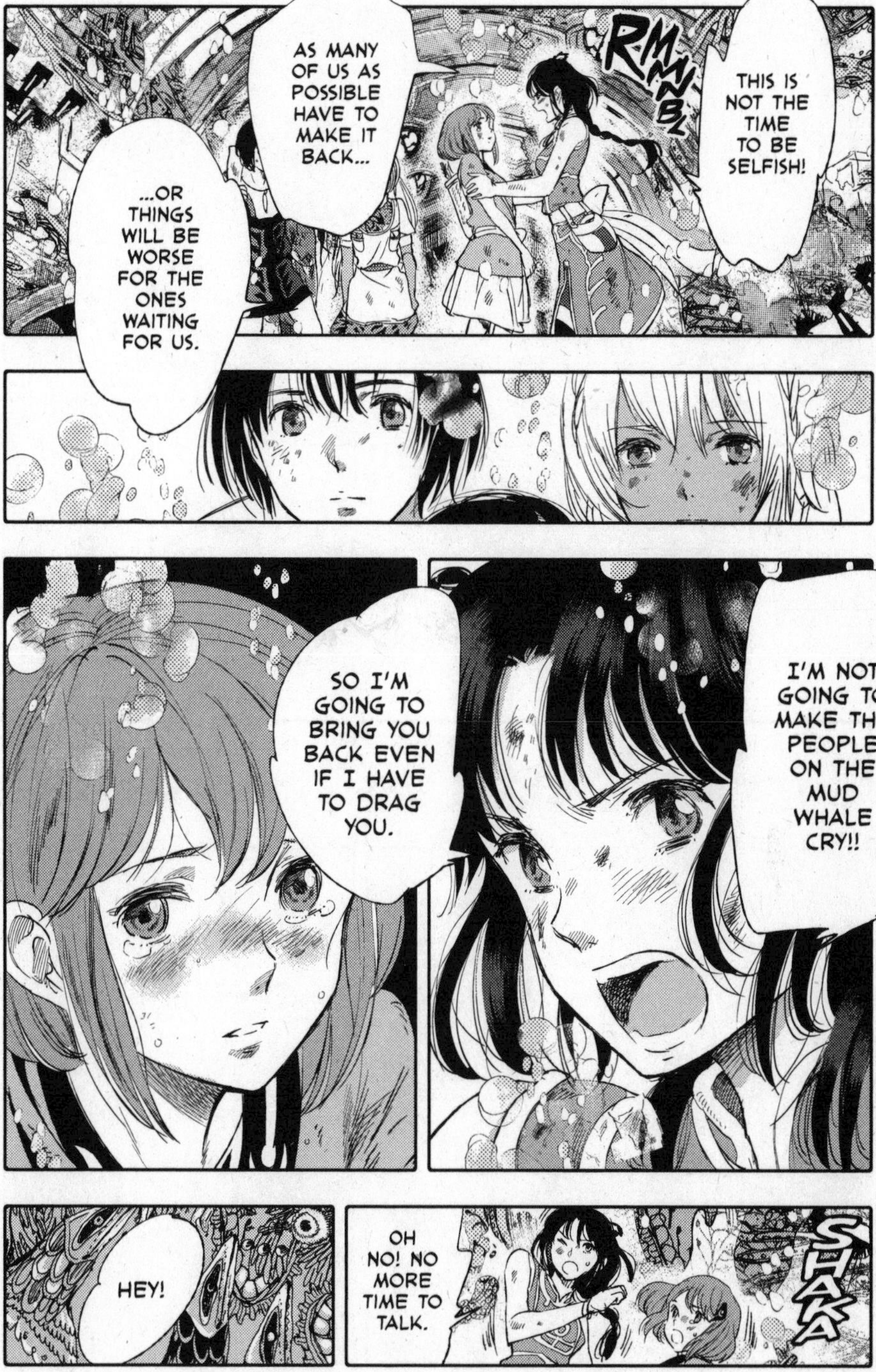
THIS IS NOT THE TIME TO BE SELFISH!
RMMMBL
AS MANY OF US AS POSSIBLE HAVE TO MAKE IT BACK...
...OR THINGS WILL BE WORSE FOR THE ONES WAITING FOR US.
I'M NOT GOING TO MAKE THE PEOPLE ON THE MUD WHALE CRY!!
SO I'M GOING TO BRING YOU BACK EVEN IF I HAVE TO DRAG YOU.
SHAKA
OH NO! NO MORE TIME TO TALK.
HEY!

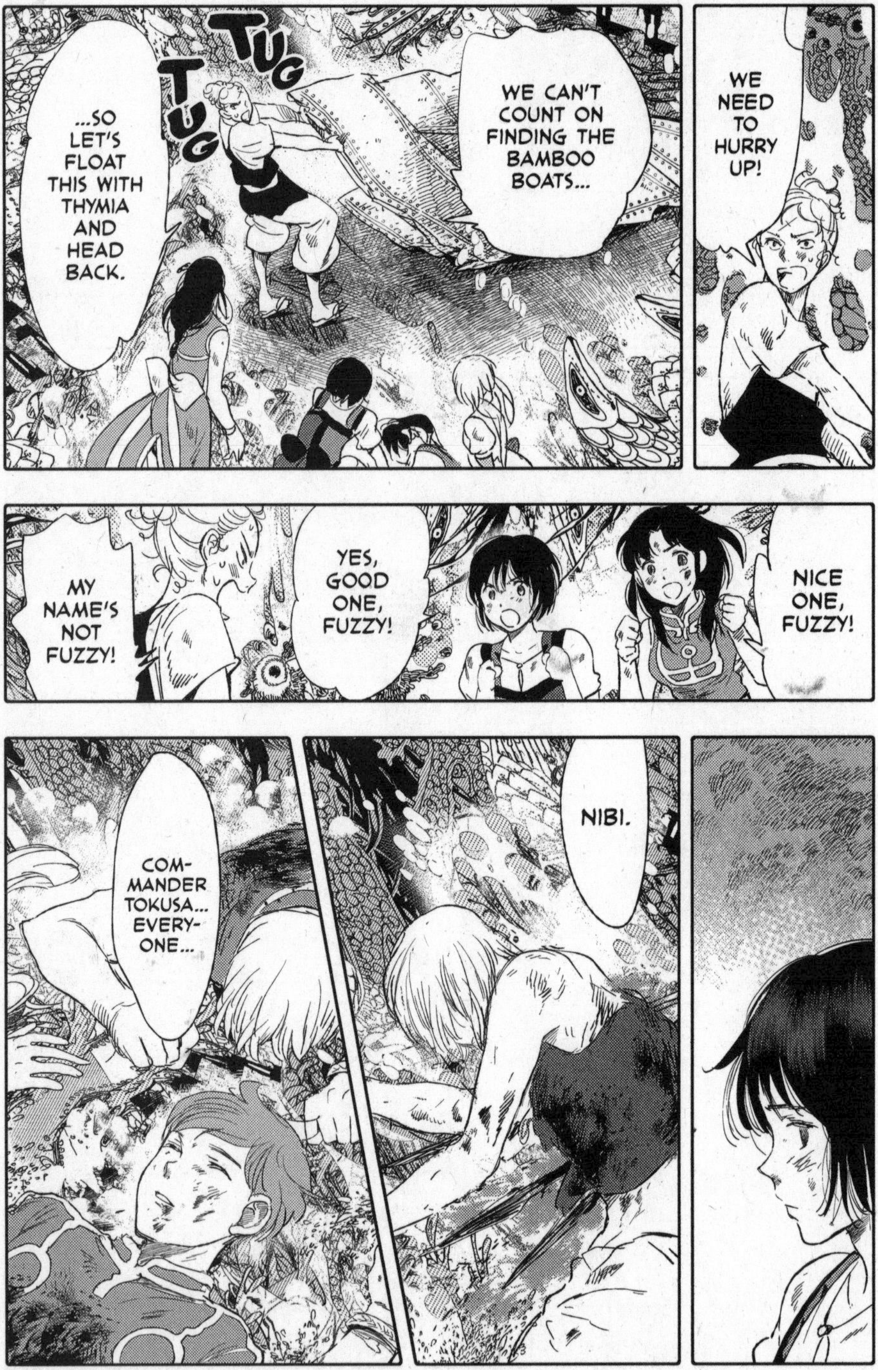
WE NEED TO HURRY UP!
WE CAN'T COUNT ON FINDING THE BAMBOO BOATS...
TUG
TUG
...SO LET'S FLOAT THIS WITH THYMIA AND HEAD BACK.
NICE ONE, FUZZY!
YES, GOOD ONE, FUZZY!
MY NAME'S NOT FUZZY!
NIBI.
COM-MANDER TOKUSA... EVERY-ONE...

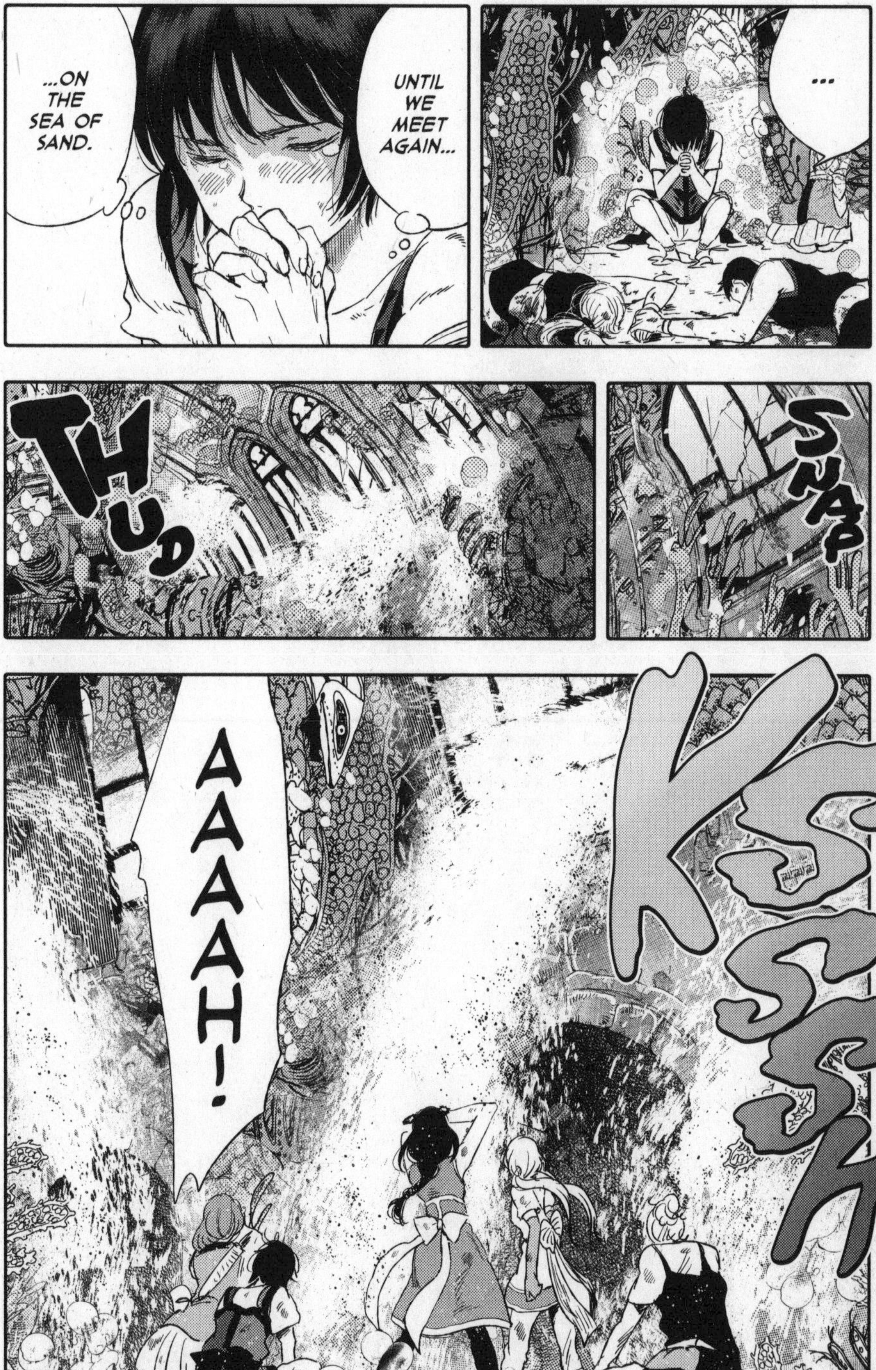
...
UNTIL WE MEET AGAIN...
...ON THE SEA OF SAND.
SNAP
THUD
KSSSH
AAAAH!

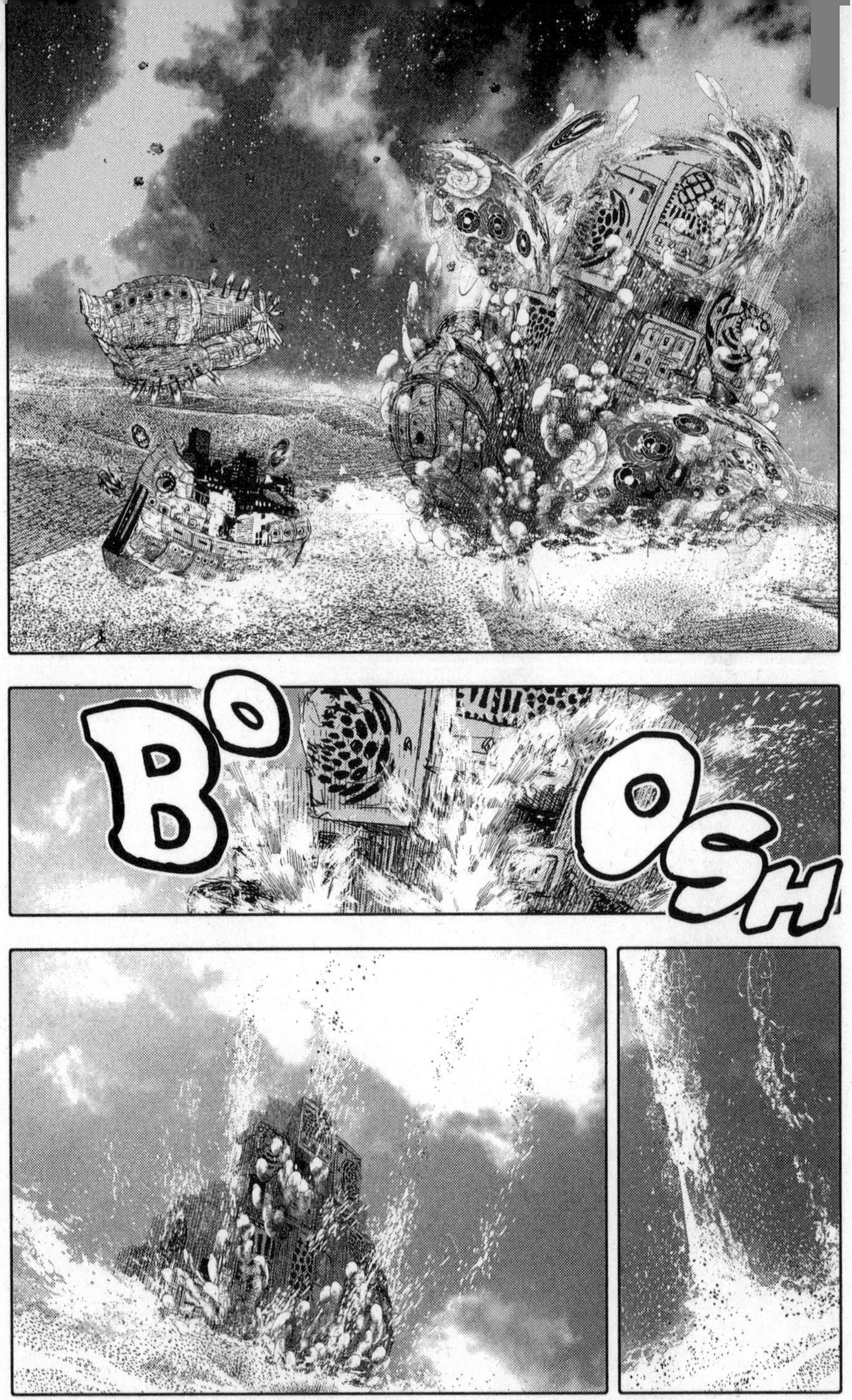
BOOSH

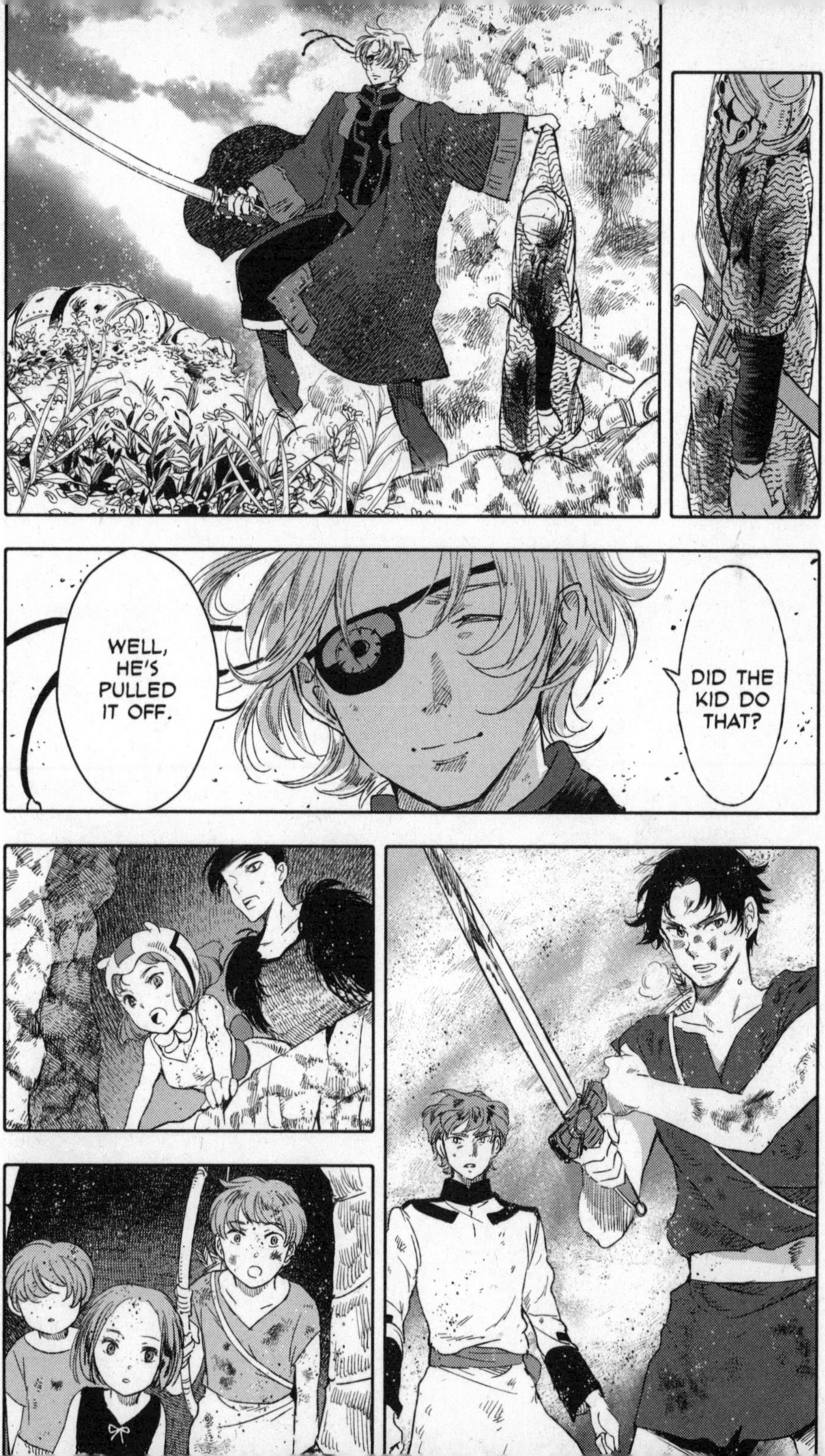
DID THE KID DO THAT?
WELL, HE'S PULLED IT OFF.

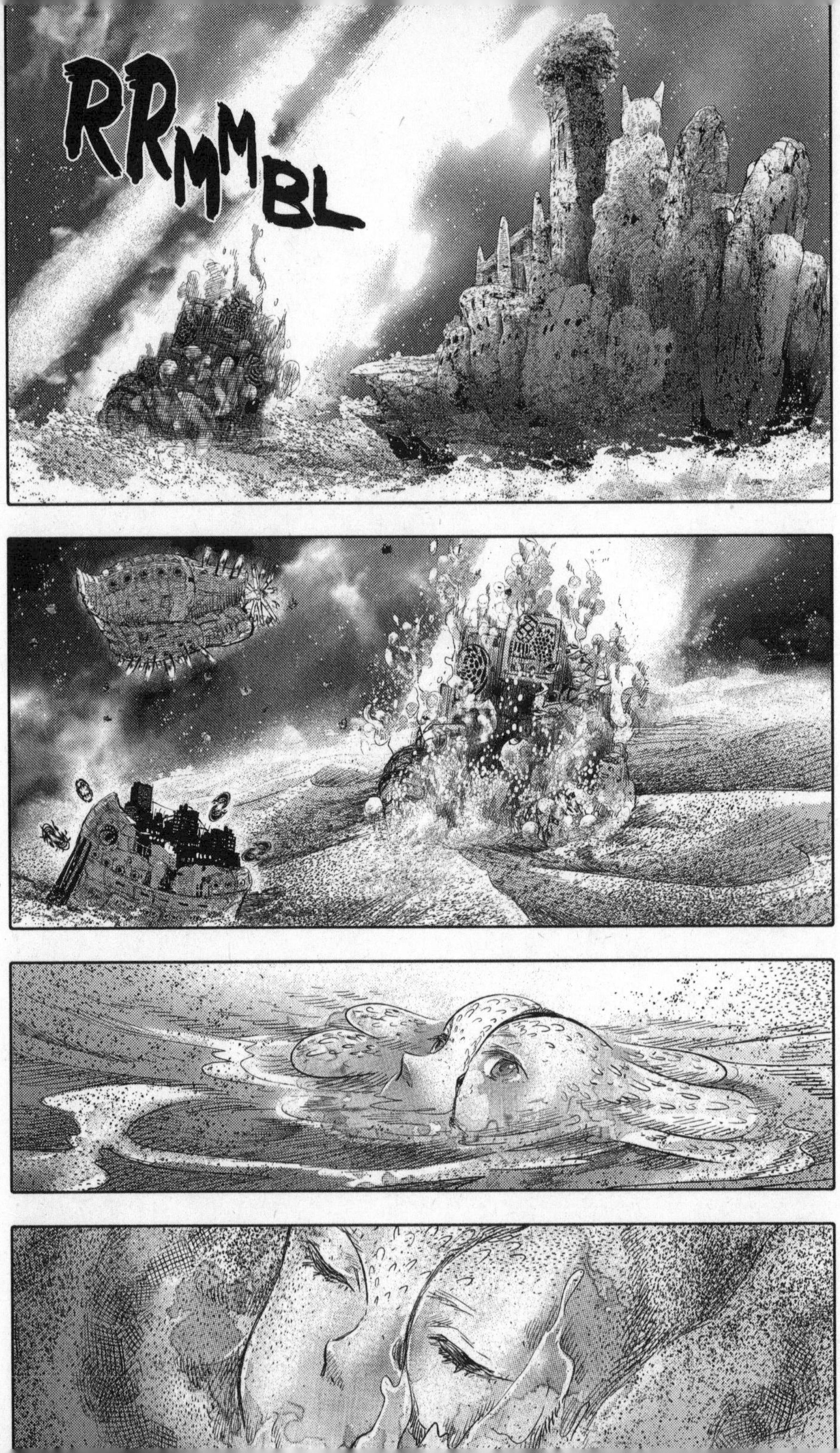
RRMMMBL

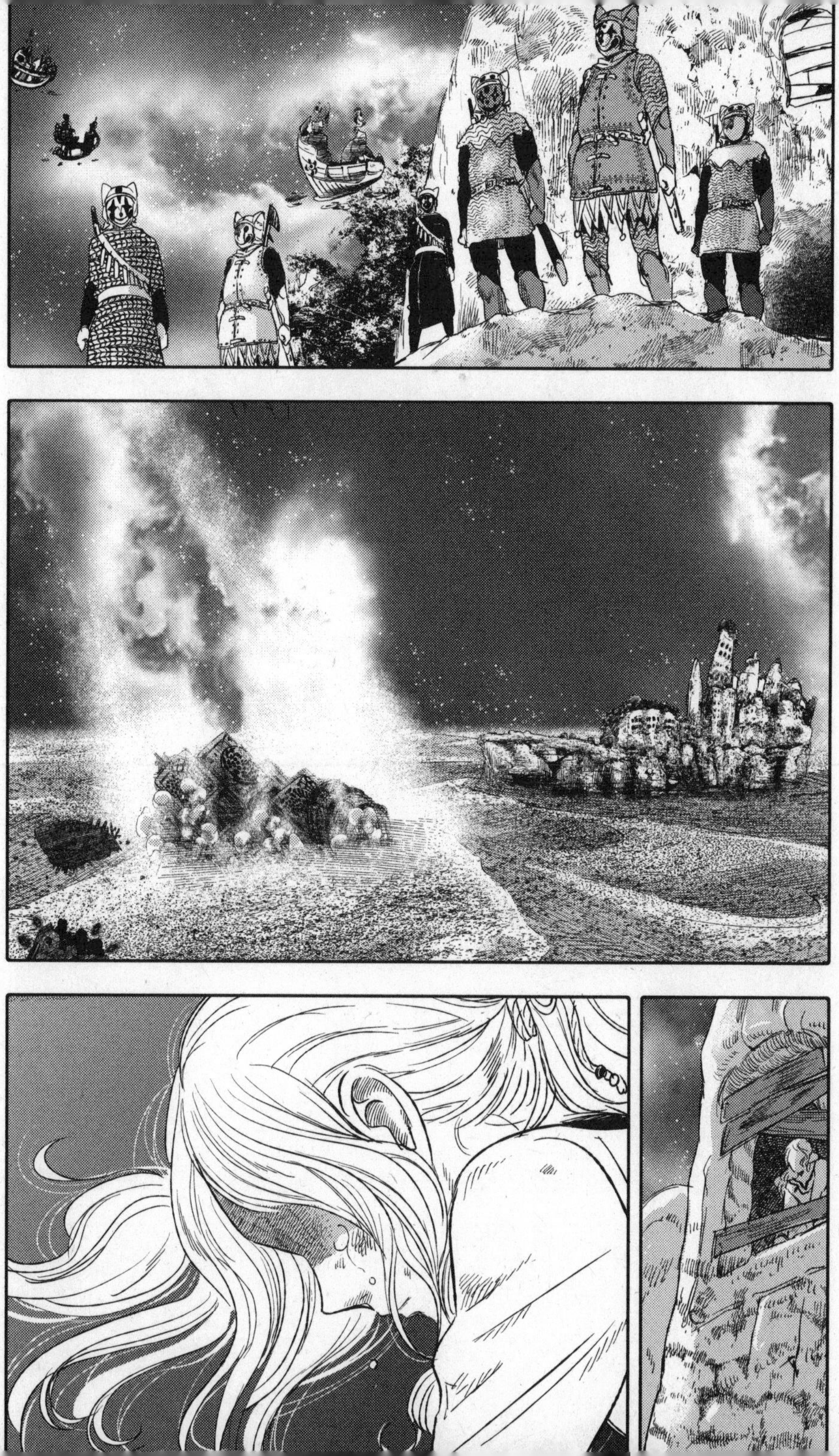

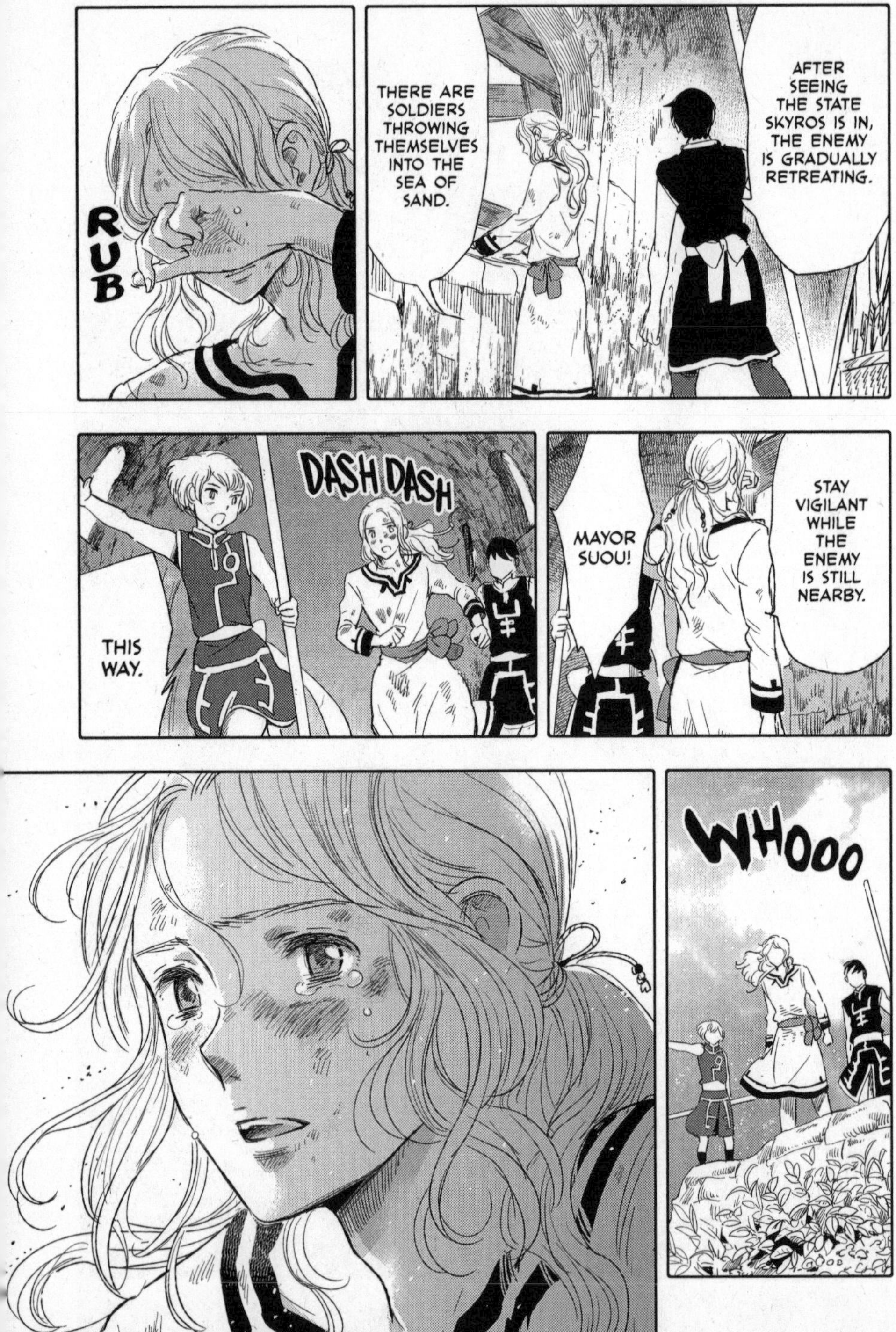
AFTER SEEING THE STATE SKYROS IS IN, THE ENEMY IS GRADUALLY RETREATING.
THERE ARE SOLDIERS THROWING THEMSELVES INTO THE SEA OF SAND.
RUB
STAY VIGILANT WHILE THE ENEMY IS STILL NEARBY.
MAYOR SUOU!
DASH DASH
THIS WAY.
WHOOO

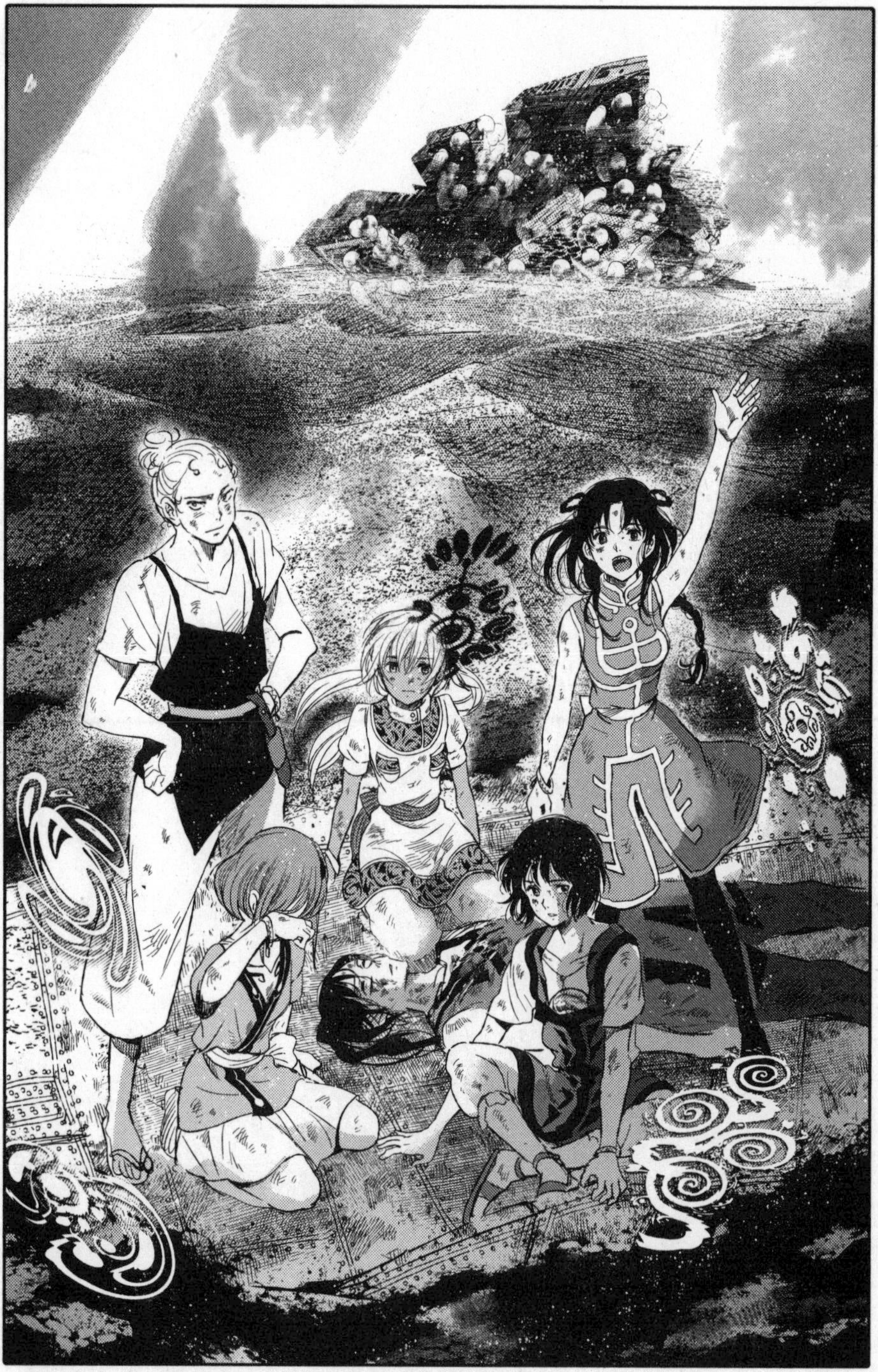

Pluck the Day -The End-

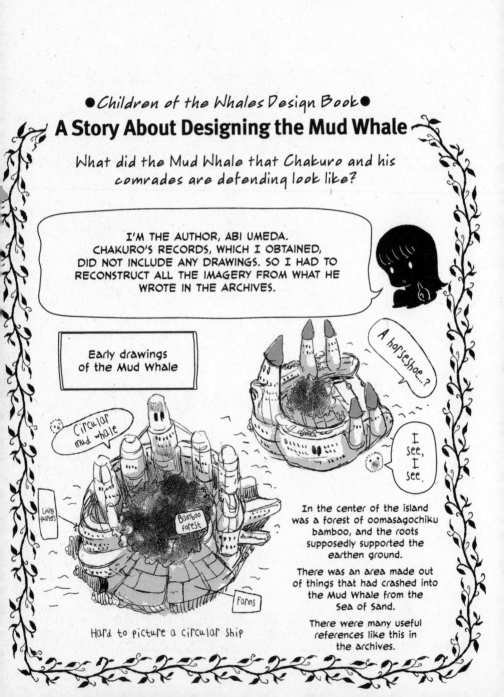

●Children of the Whales Design Book●

A Story About Designing the Mud Whale

What did the Mud Whale that Chakuro and his comrades are defending look like?

I'M THE AUTHOR, ABI UMEDA.
CHAKURO'S RECORDS, WHICH I OBTAINED,
DID NOT INCLUDE ANY DRAWINGS. SO I HAD TO
RECONSTRUCT ALL THE IMAGERY FROM WHAT HE
WROTE IN THE ARCHIVES.

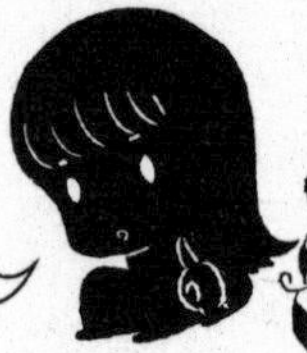

Early drawings of the Mud Whale

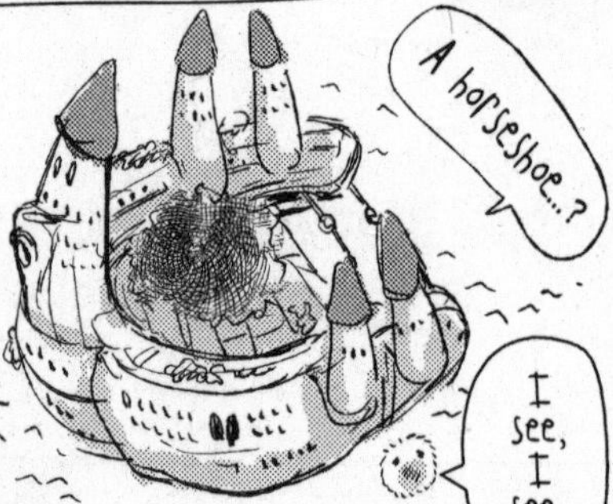
A horseshoe...?
I see, I see.

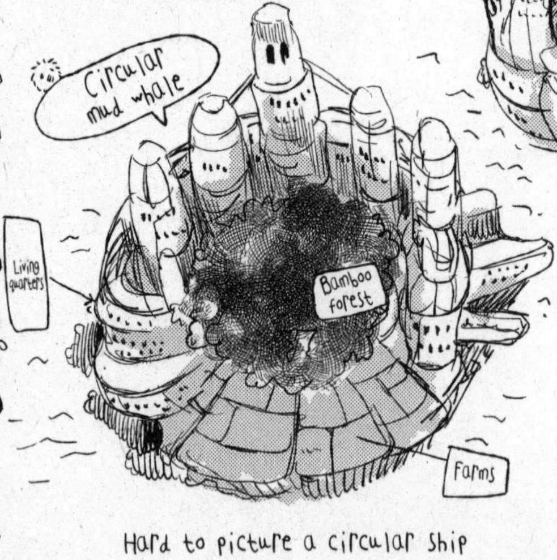
Circular mud whale
Living quarters
Bamboo forest
Farms

Hard to picture a circular ship

In the center of the island was a forest of oomasagochiku bamboo, and the roots supposedly supported the earthen ground.

There was an area made out of things that had crashed into the Mud Whale from the Sea of Sand.

There were many useful references like this in the archives.

●*Children of the Whales Design Book*●

A Story About Designing the Mud Whale (2)

The Mud Whale turned out the way it did because of the defense plan against the attack from Skyros. Chakuro recorded the teams and buildings in such detail that a clearer picture of the whole island emerged.

About the walls of the Mud Whale

A little rounded like this.
The Moles' secret hideaway, etc.
Areas with minimal damage are not repaired and have seams and cracks.

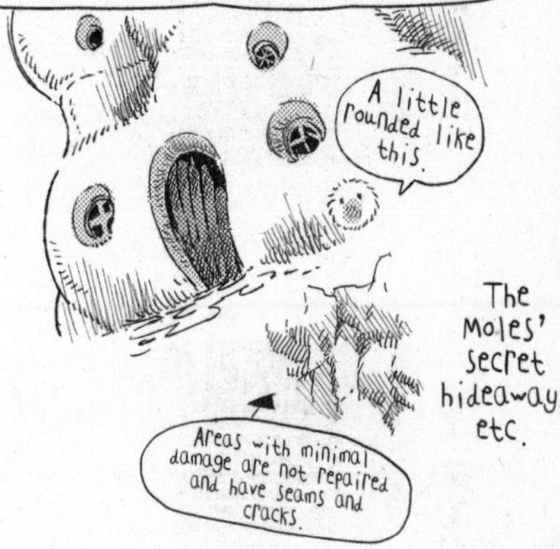

The walls of the buildings on the Mud Whale appear to be stacked mud bricks with mud plaster on top.

This kind of architecture doesn't have any joins (the seam where the different parts of the building meet). By piling more mud on damaged areas, I think the buildings become more rounded as time goes on.

Picture of the bathing ponds

This is a key detail too.

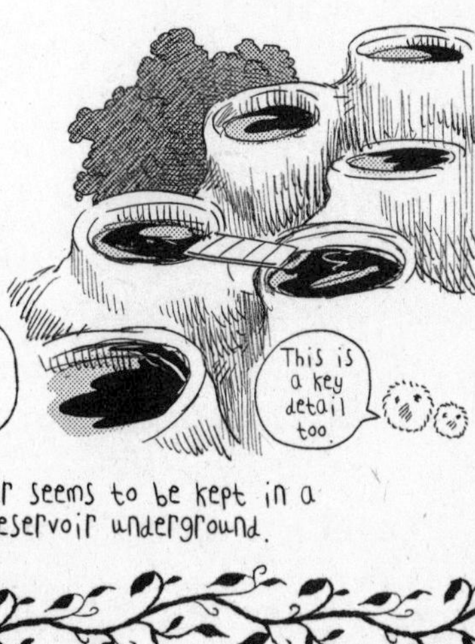

There are lots of little ponds made of mud??

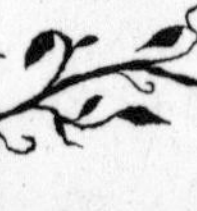

UMM, THEY'RE LIKE INDIVIDUAL BATHTUBS... I THINK THEY'RE BIGGER, LIKE POOLS...

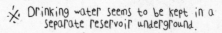

※ Drinking water seems to be kept in a separate reservoir underground.

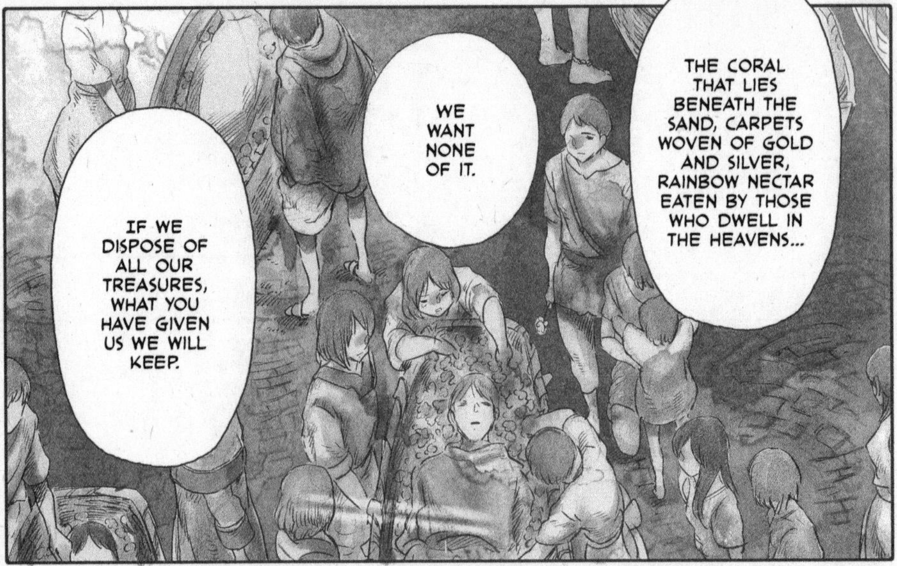
THE CORAL THAT LIES BENEATH THE SAND, CARPETS WOVEN OF GOLD AND SILVER, RAINBOW NECTAR EATEN BY THOSE WHO DWELL IN THE HEAVENS...
WE WANT NONE OF IT.
IF WE DISPOSE OF ALL OUR TREASURES, WHAT YOU HAVE GIVEN US WE WILL KEEP.
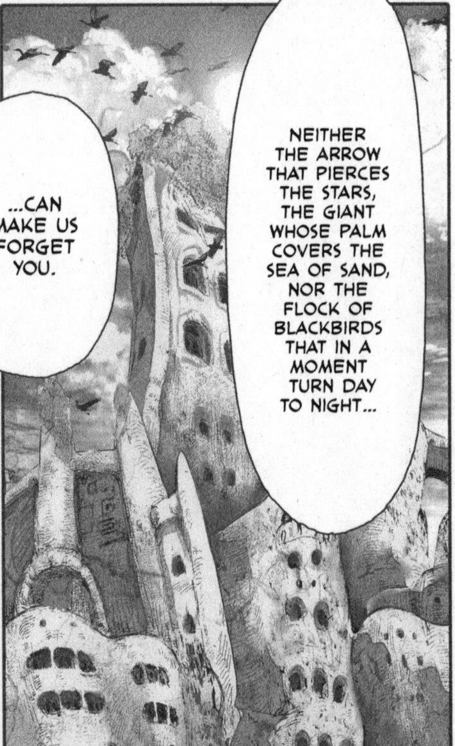
NEITHER THE ARROW THAT PIERCES THE STARS, THE GIANT WHOSE PALM COVERS THE SEA OF SAND, NOR THE FLOCK OF BLACKBIRDS THAT IN A MOMENT TURN DAY TO NIGHT...
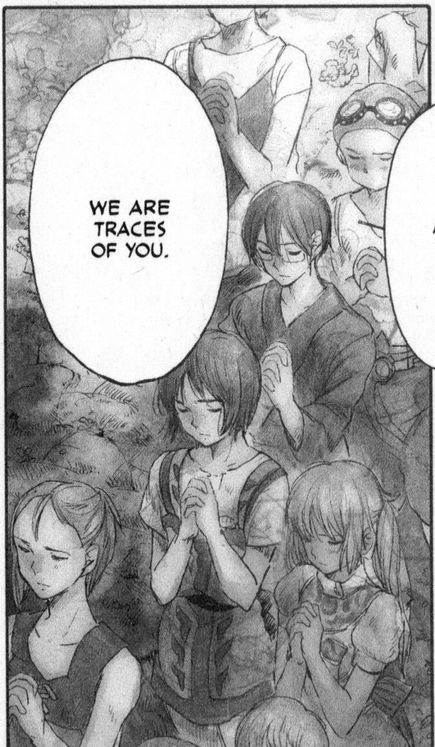
...CAN MAKE US FORGET YOU.
WE ARE TRACES OF YOU.

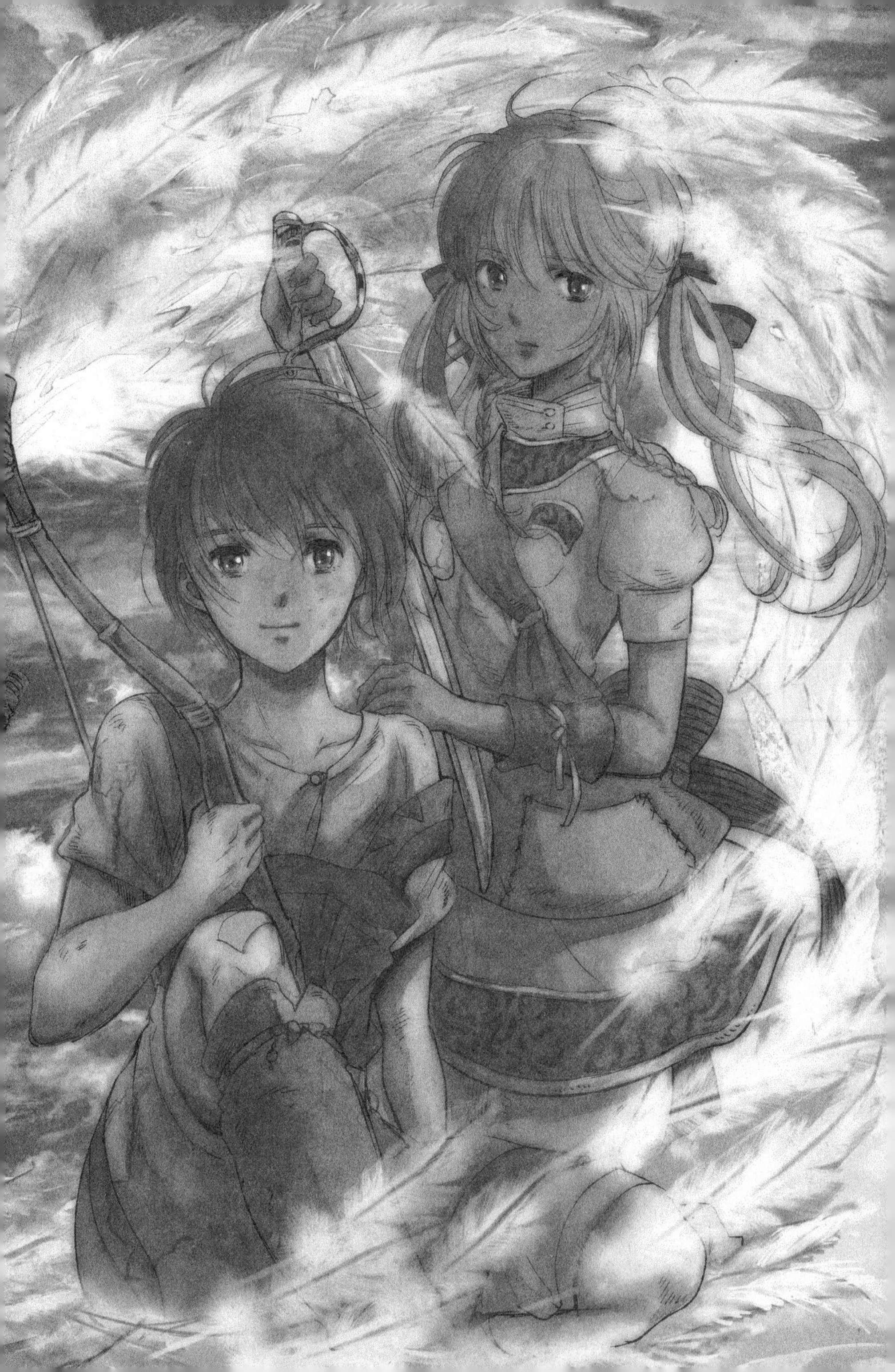

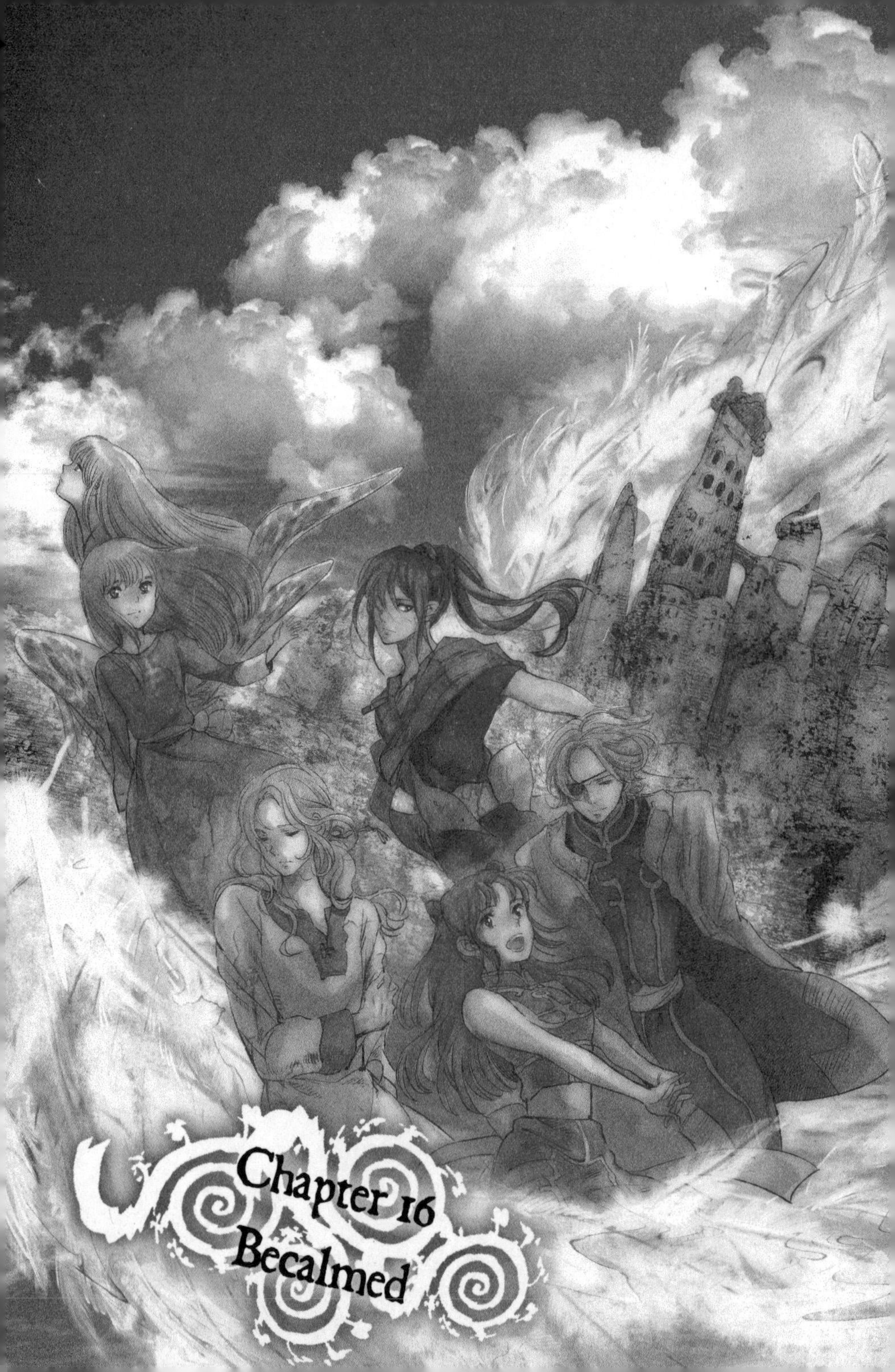
Chapter 16
Becalmed

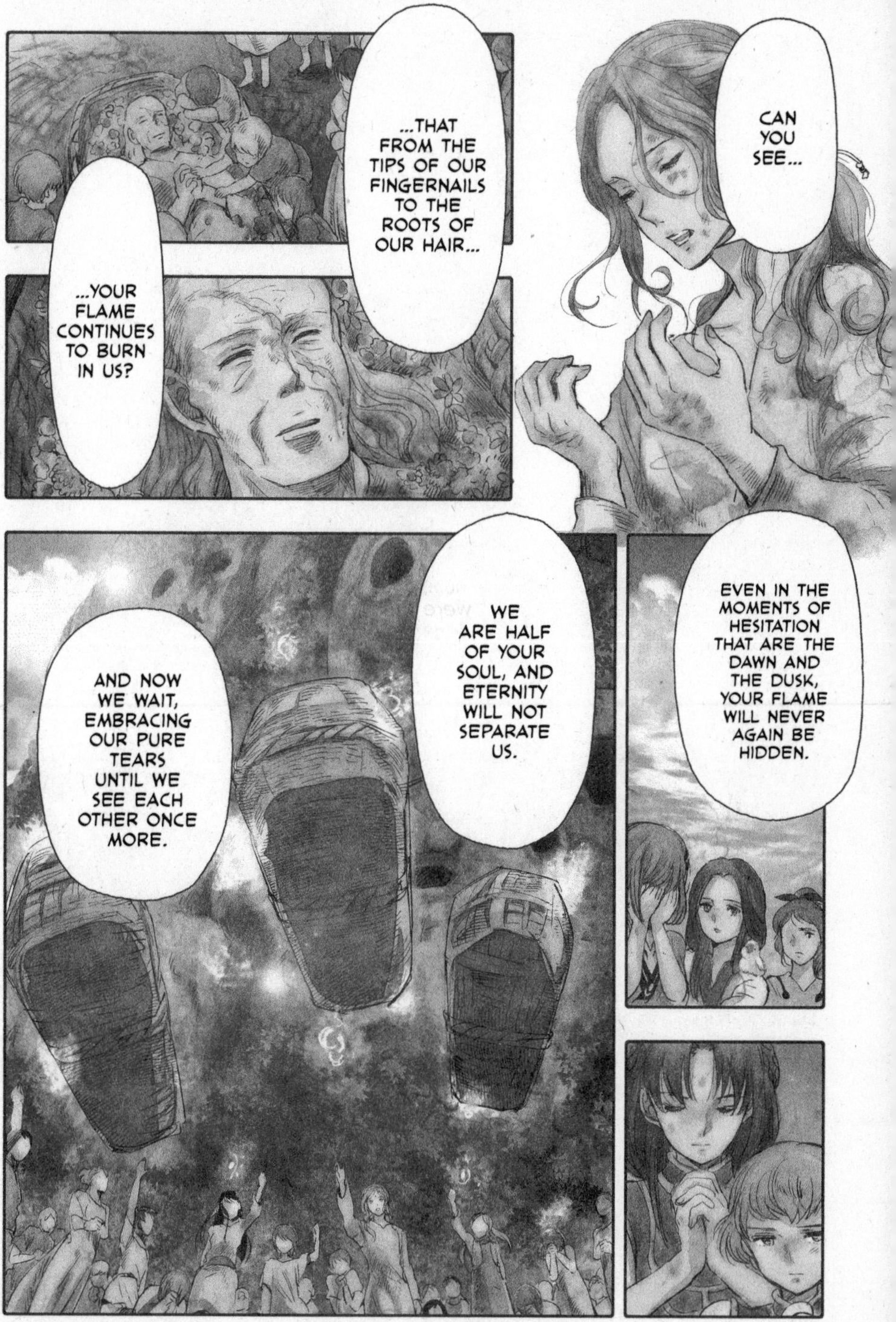
CAN YOU SEE...
...THAT FROM THE TIPS OF OUR FINGERNAILS TO THE ROOTS OF OUR HAIR...
...YOUR FLAME CONTINUES TO BURN IN US?
EVEN IN THE MOMENTS OF HESITATION THAT ARE THE DAWN AND THE DUSK, YOUR FLAME WILL NEVER AGAIN BE HIDDEN.
WE ARE HALF OF YOUR SOUL, AND ETERNITY WILL NOT SEPARATE US.
AND NOW WE WAIT, EMBRACING OUR PURE TEARS UNTIL WE SEE EACH OTHER ONCE MORE.

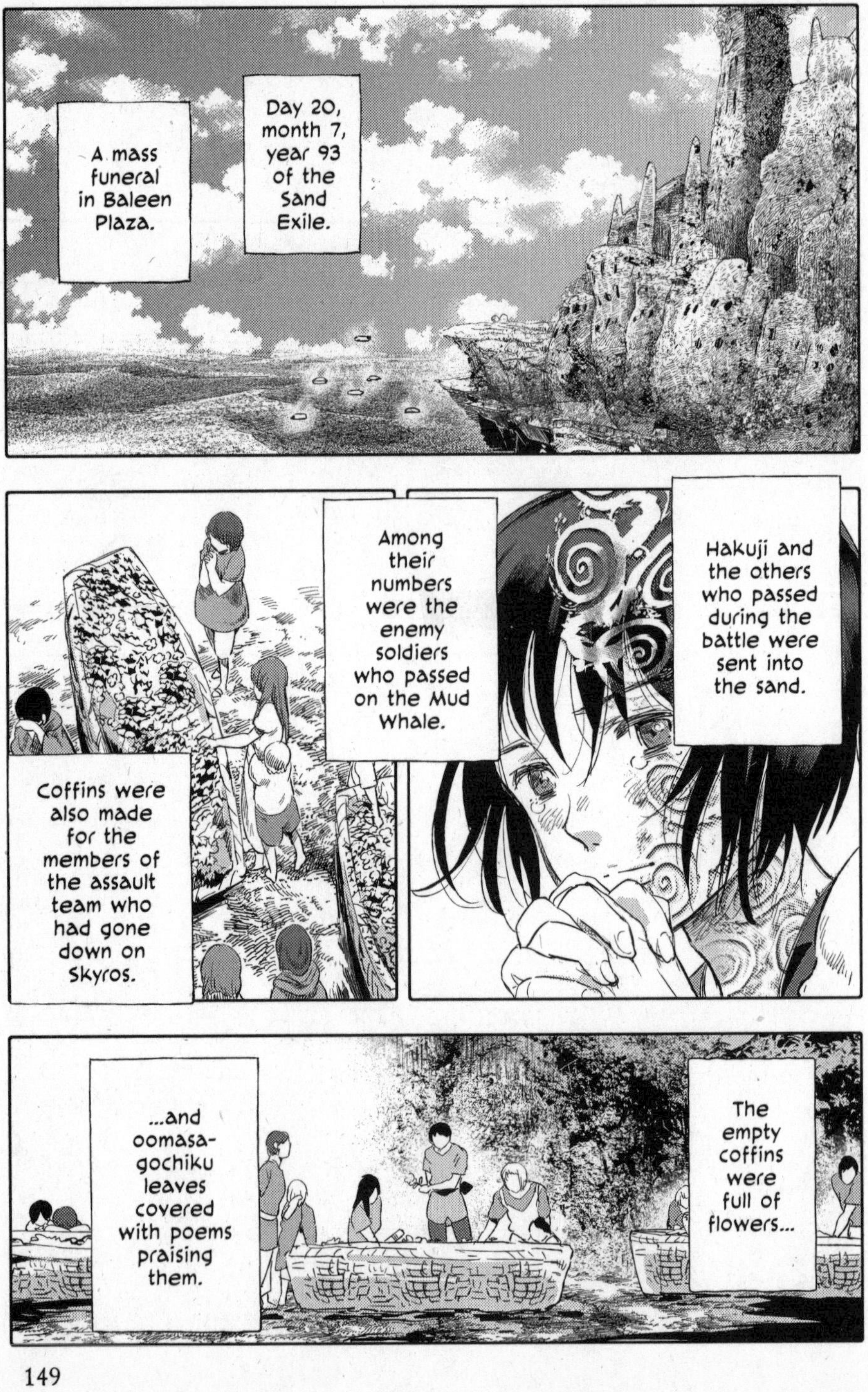
Day 20, month 7, year 93 of the Sand Exile.
A mass funeral in Baleen Plaza.
Hakuji and the others who passed during the battle were sent into the sand.
Among their numbers were the enemy soldiers who passed on the Mud Whale.
Coffins were also made for the members of the assault team who had gone down on Skyros.
The empty coffins were full of flowers...
...and oomasa-gochiku leaves covered with poems praising them.

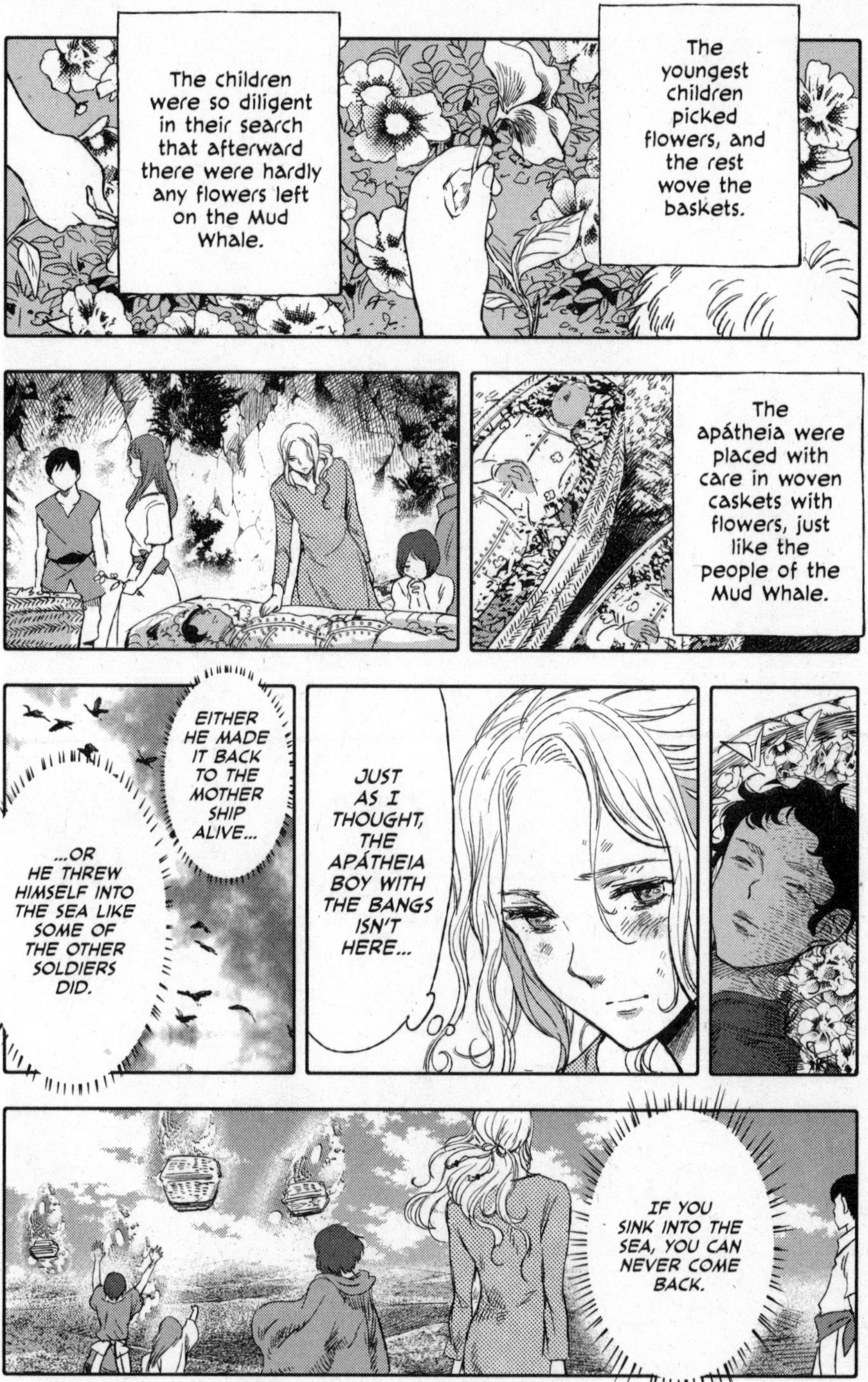
The youngest children picked flowers, and the rest wove the baskets.
The children were so diligent in their search that afterward there were hardly any flowers left on the Mud Whale.
The apátheia were placed with care in woven caskets with flowers, just like the people of the Mud Whale.
JUST AS I THOUGHT, THE APÁTHEIA BOY WITH THE BANGS ISN'T HERE...
EITHER HE MADE IT BACK TO THE MOTHER SHIP ALIVE...
...OR HE THREW HIMSELF INTO THE SEA LIKE SOME OF THE OTHER SOLDIERS DID.
IF YOU SINK INTO THE SEA, YOU CAN NEVER COME BACK.

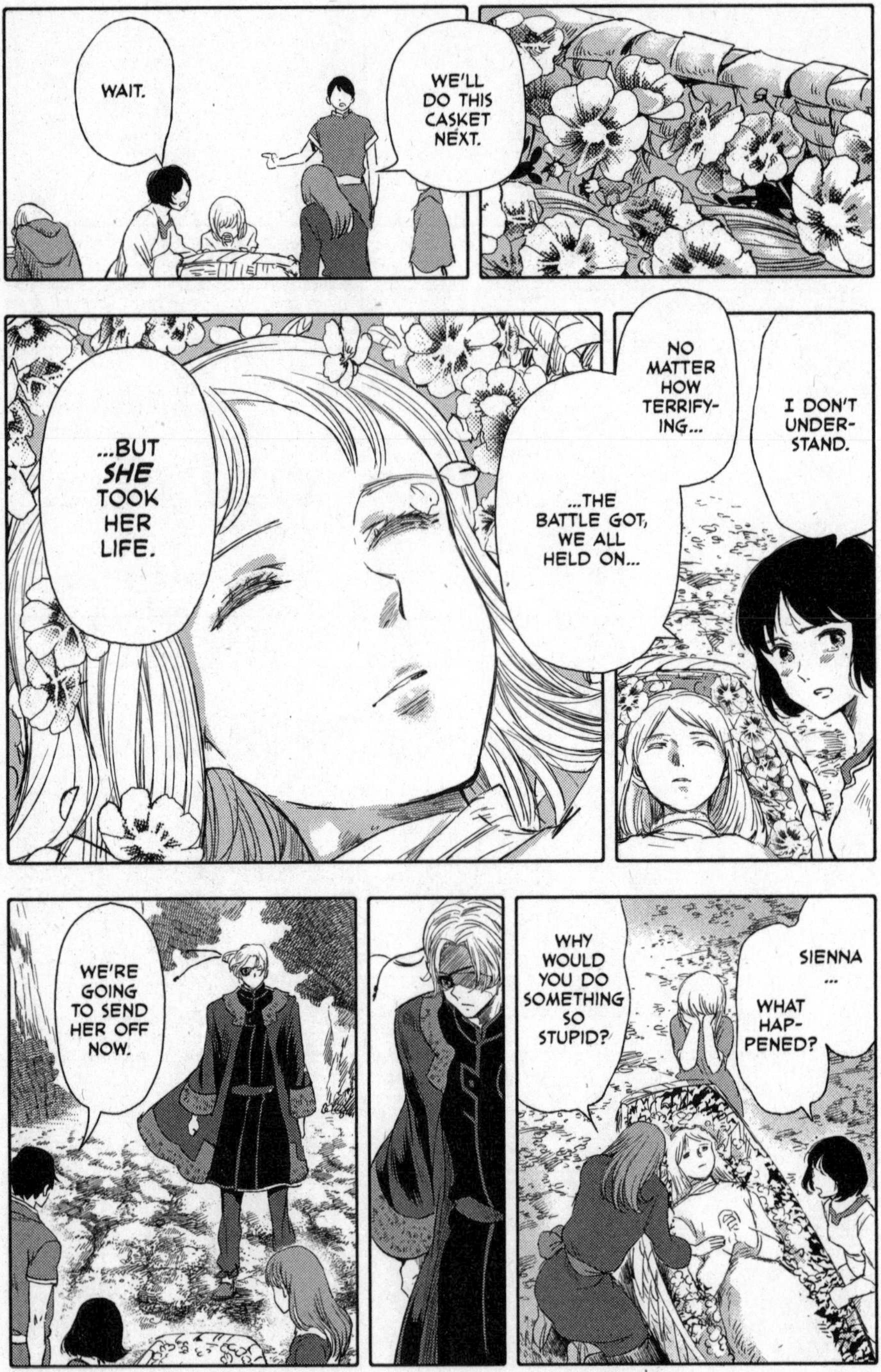
WE'LL DO THIS CASKET NEXT.
WAIT.
I DON'T UNDER-STAND.
NO MATTER HOW TERRIFY-ING...
...THE BATTLE GOT, WE ALL HELD ON...
...BUT *SHE* TOOK HER LIFE.
SIENNA ... WHAT HAP-PENED?
WHY WOULD YOU DO SOMETHING SO STUPID?
WE'RE GOING TO SEND HER OFF NOW.

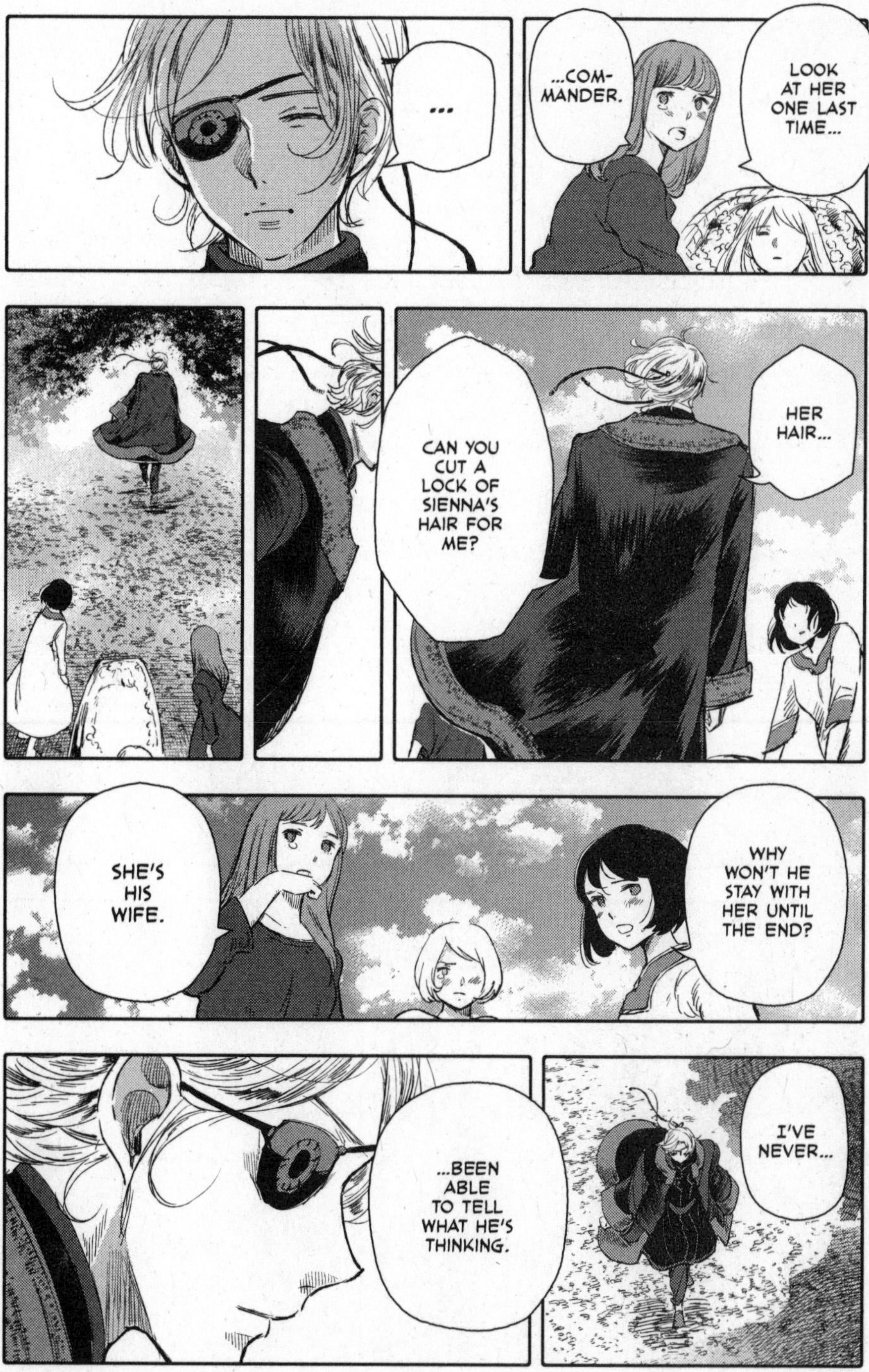
LOOK AT HER ONE LAST TIME...
...COM-MANDER.
...
HER HAIR...
CAN YOU CUT A LOCK OF SIENNA'S HAIR FOR ME?
WHY WON'T HE STAY WITH HER UNTIL THE END?
SHE'S HIS WIFE.
I'VE NEVER...
...BEEN ABLE TO TELL WHAT HE'S THINKING.

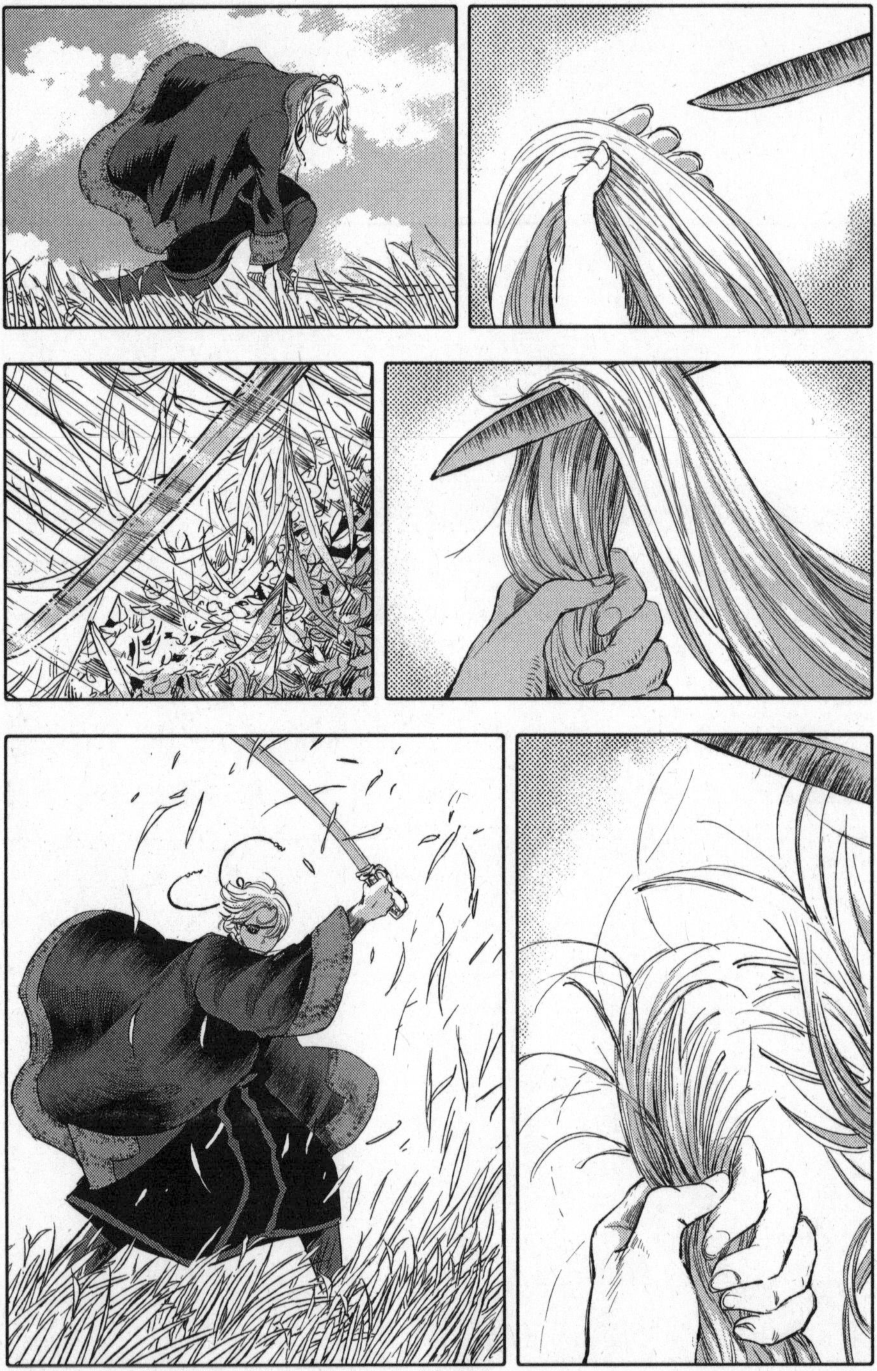

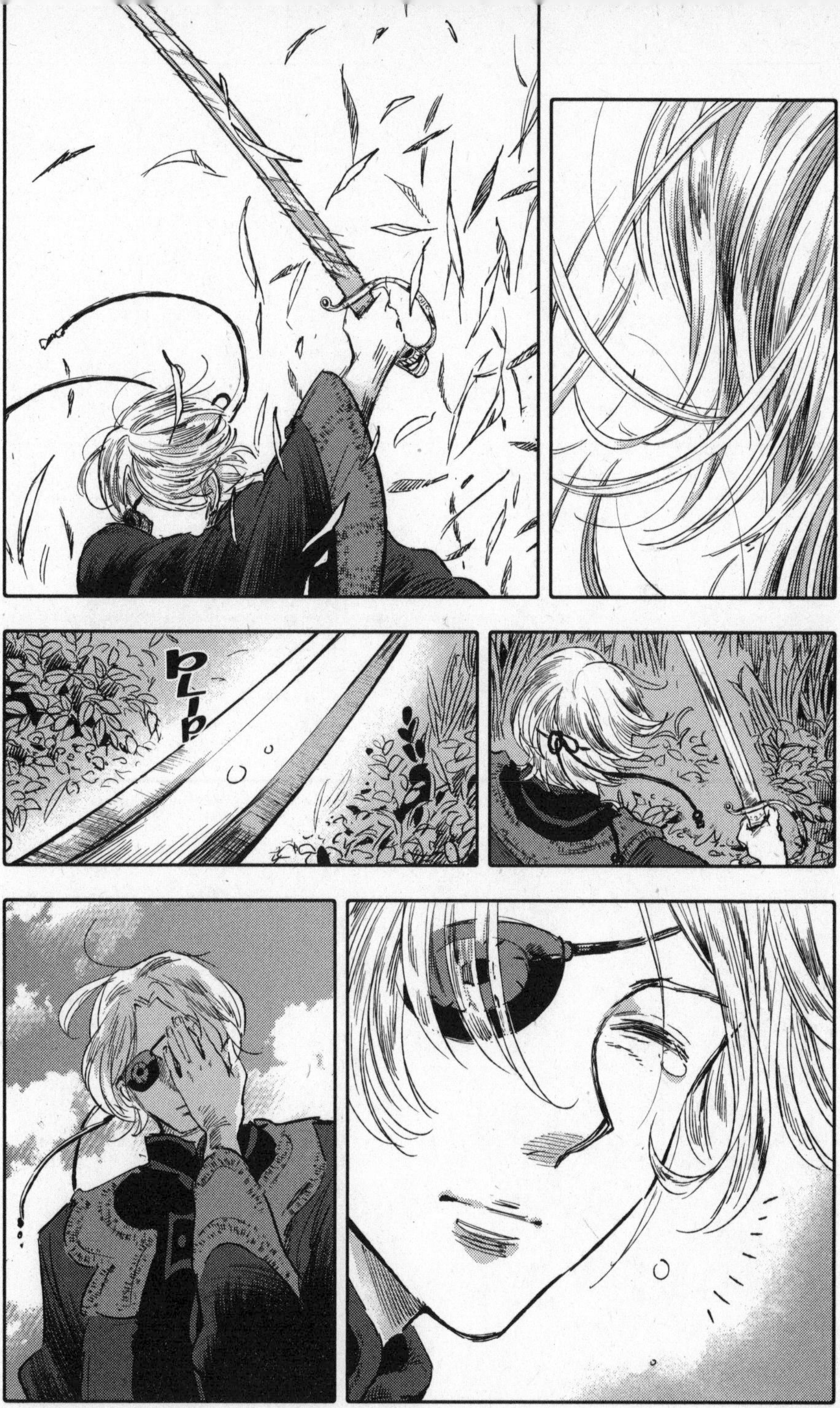
PLIP

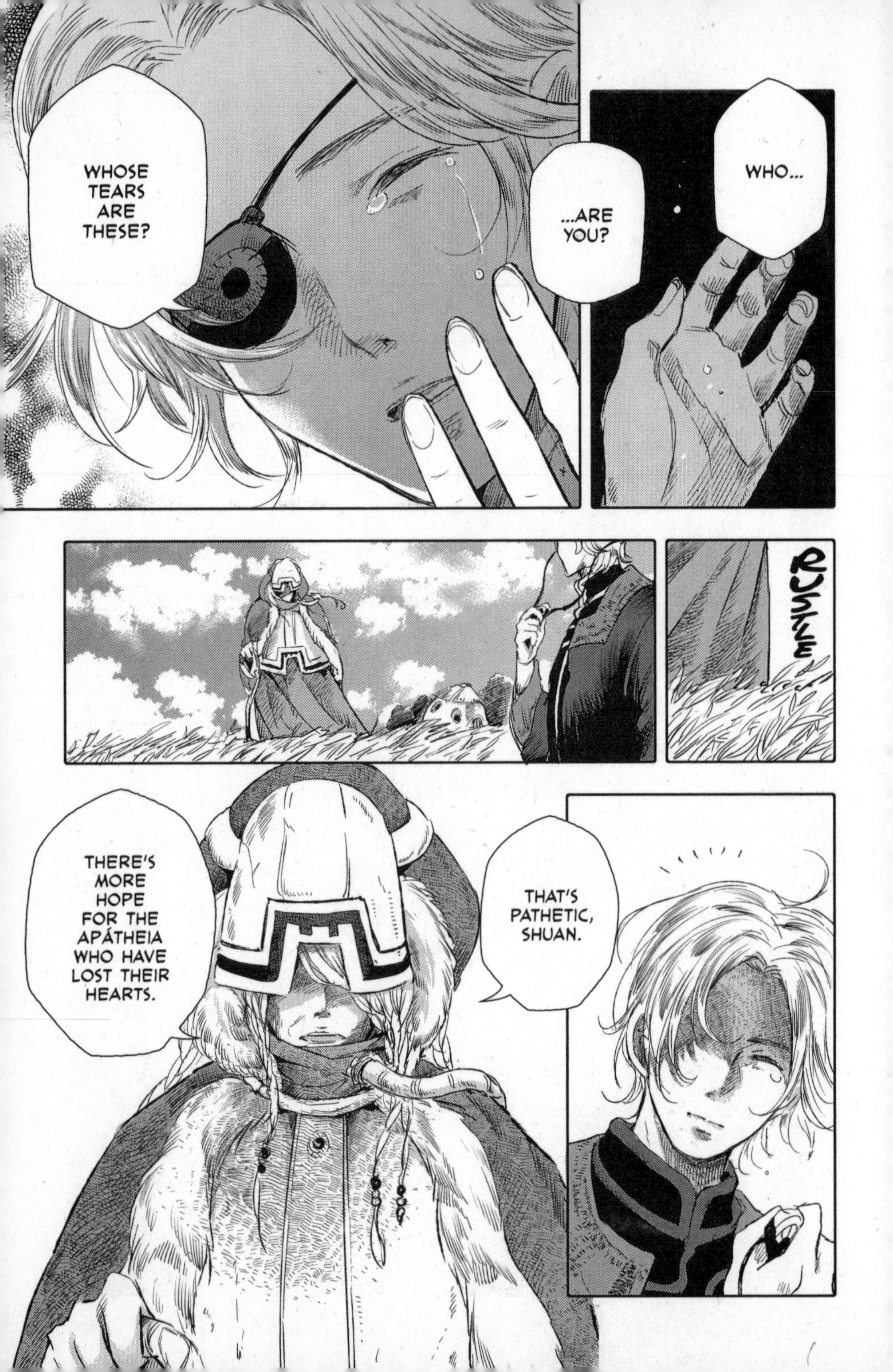
WHO...
...ARE YOU?
WHOSE TEARS ARE THESE?
RUSTLE
THAT'S PATHETIC, SHUAN.
THERE'S MORE HOPE FOR THE APÁTHEIA WHO HAVE LOST THEIR HEARTS.

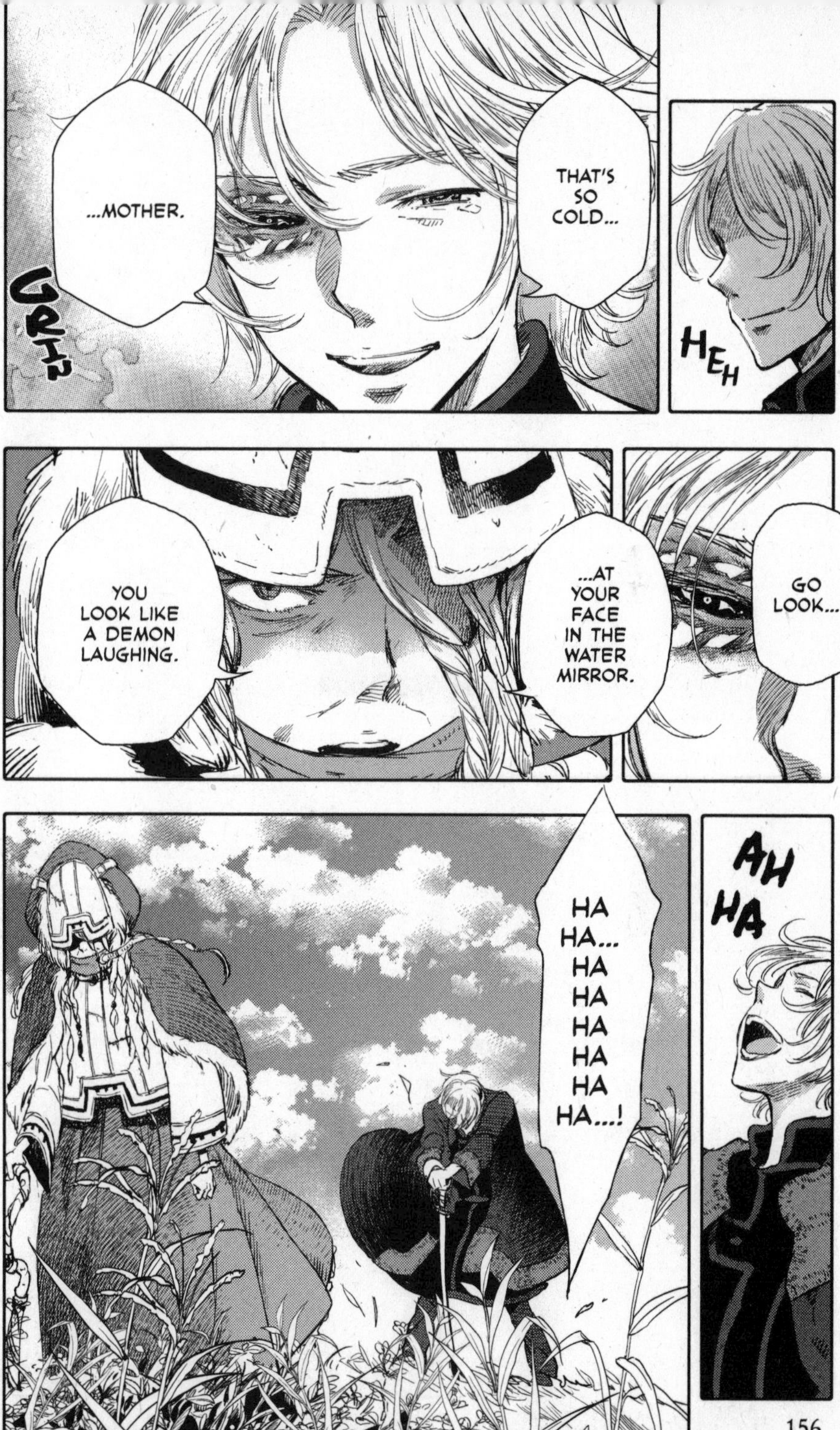
HEH
THAT'S SO COLD...
...MOTHER.
GRIN
GO LOOK...
...AT YOUR FACE IN THE WATER MIRROR.
YOU LOOK LIKE A DEMON LAUGHING.
AH HA
HA HA... HA HA HA HA HA HA...!

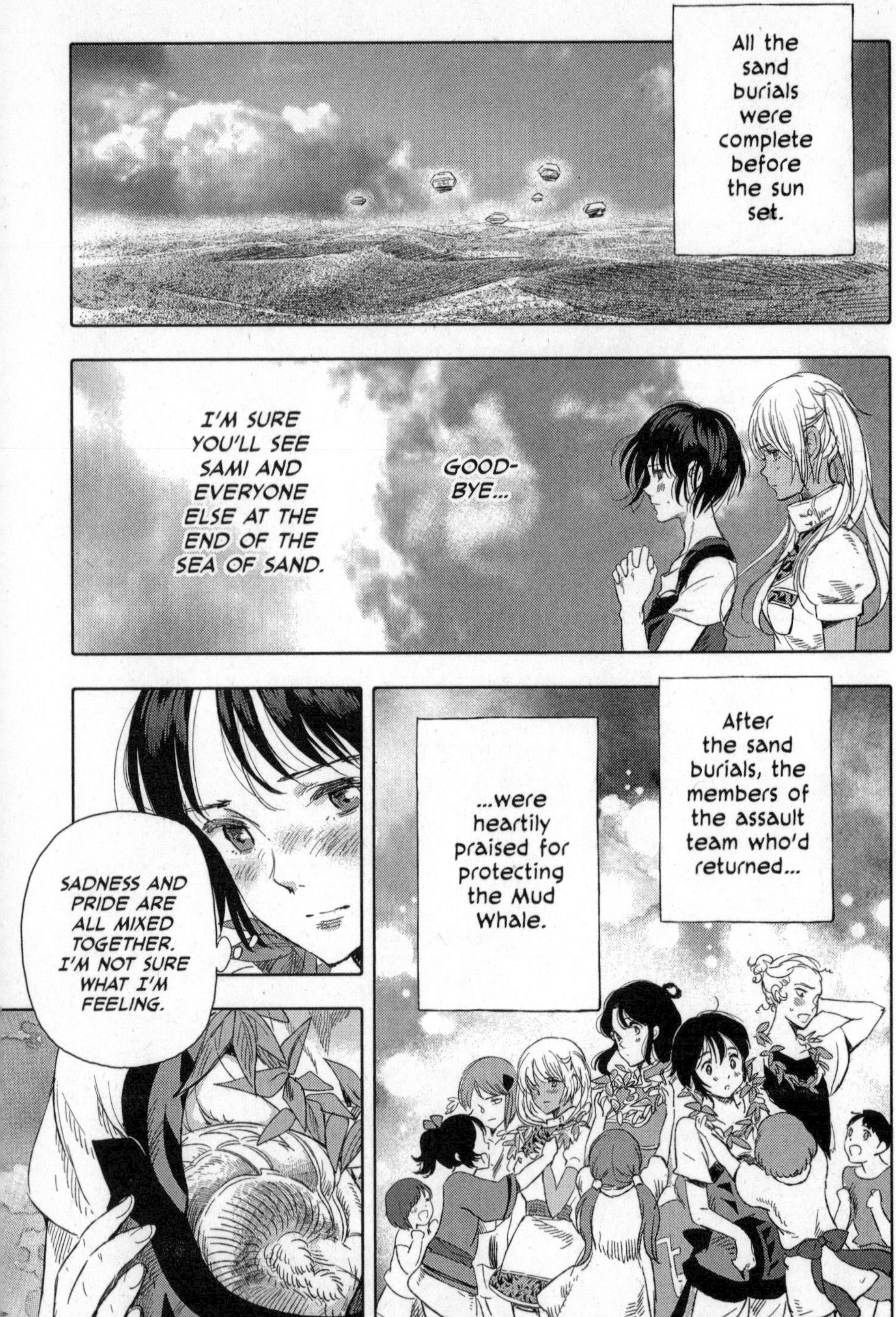
All the sand burials were complete before the sun set.
GOOD-BYE...
I'M SURE YOU'LL SEE SAMI AND EVERYONE ELSE AT THE END OF THE SEA OF SAND.
After the sand burials, the members of the assault team who'd returned...
...were heartily praised for protecting the Mud Whale.
SADNESS AND PRIDE ARE ALL MIXED TOGETHER. I'M NOT SURE WHAT I'M FEELING.

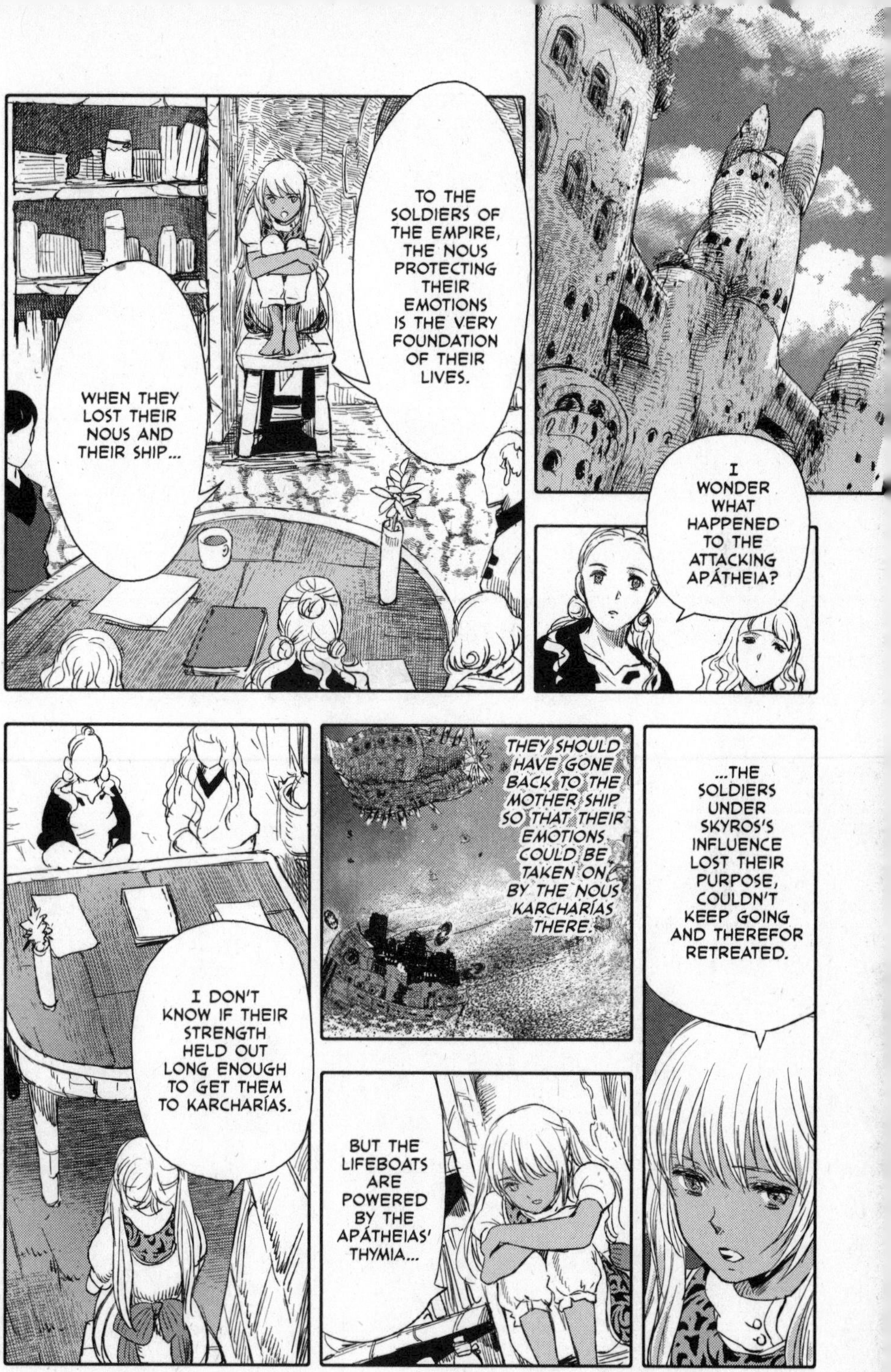
I WONDER WHAT HAPPENED TO THE ATTACKING APÁTHEIA?
TO THE SOLDIERS OF THE EMPIRE, THE NOUS PROTECTING THEIR EMOTIONS IS THE VERY FOUNDATION OF THEIR LIVES.
WHEN THEY LOST THEIR NOUS AND THEIR SHIP...
...THE SOLDIERS UNDER SKYROS'S INFLUENCE LOST THEIR PURPOSE, COULDN'T KEEP GOING AND THEREFOR RETREATED.
THEY SHOULD HAVE GONE BACK TO THE MOTHER SHIP SO THAT THEIR EMOTIONS COULD BE TAKEN ON BY THE NOUS KARCHARÍAS THERE.
BUT THE LIFEBOATS ARE POWERED BY THE APÁTHEIAS' THYMIA...
I DON'T KNOW IF THEIR STRENGTH HELD OUT LONG ENOUGH TO GET THEM TO KARCHARÍAS.

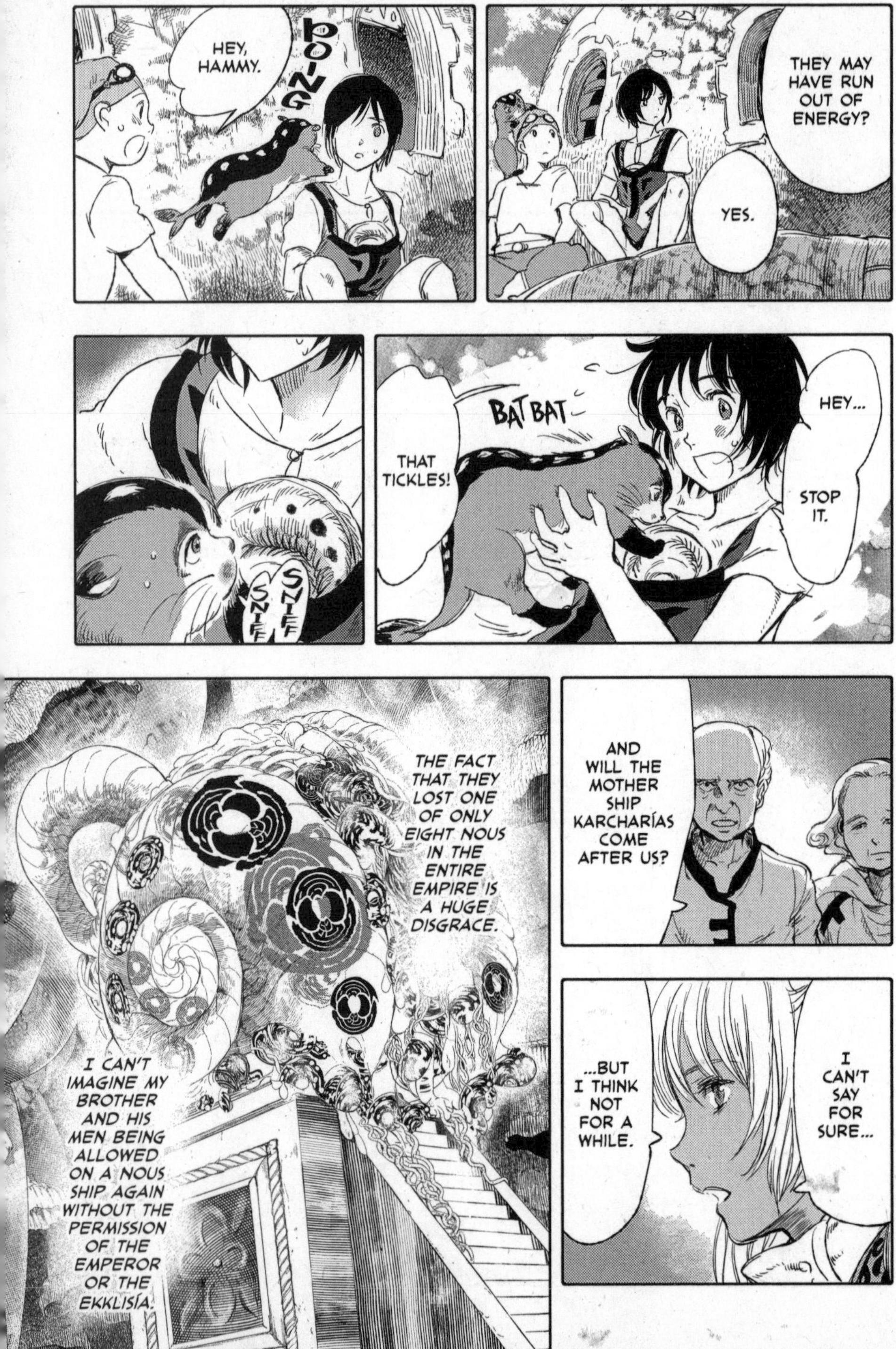
THEY MAY HAVE RUN OUT OF ENERGY?
YES.
HEY, HAMMY.
BOING
HEY...
STOP IT.
BAT BAT
THAT TICKLES!
SNIFF
SNIFF
AND WILL THE MOTHER SHIP KARCHARÍAS COME AFTER US?
I CAN'T SAY FOR SURE...
...BUT I THINK NOT FOR A WHILE.
THE FACT THAT THEY LOST ONE OF ONLY EIGHT NOUS IN THE ENTIRE EMPIRE IS A HUGE DISGRACE.
I CAN'T IMAGINE MY BROTHER AND HIS MEN BEING ALLOWED ON A NOUS SHIP AGAIN WITHOUT THE PERMISSION OF THE EMPEROR OR THE EKKLISÍA.

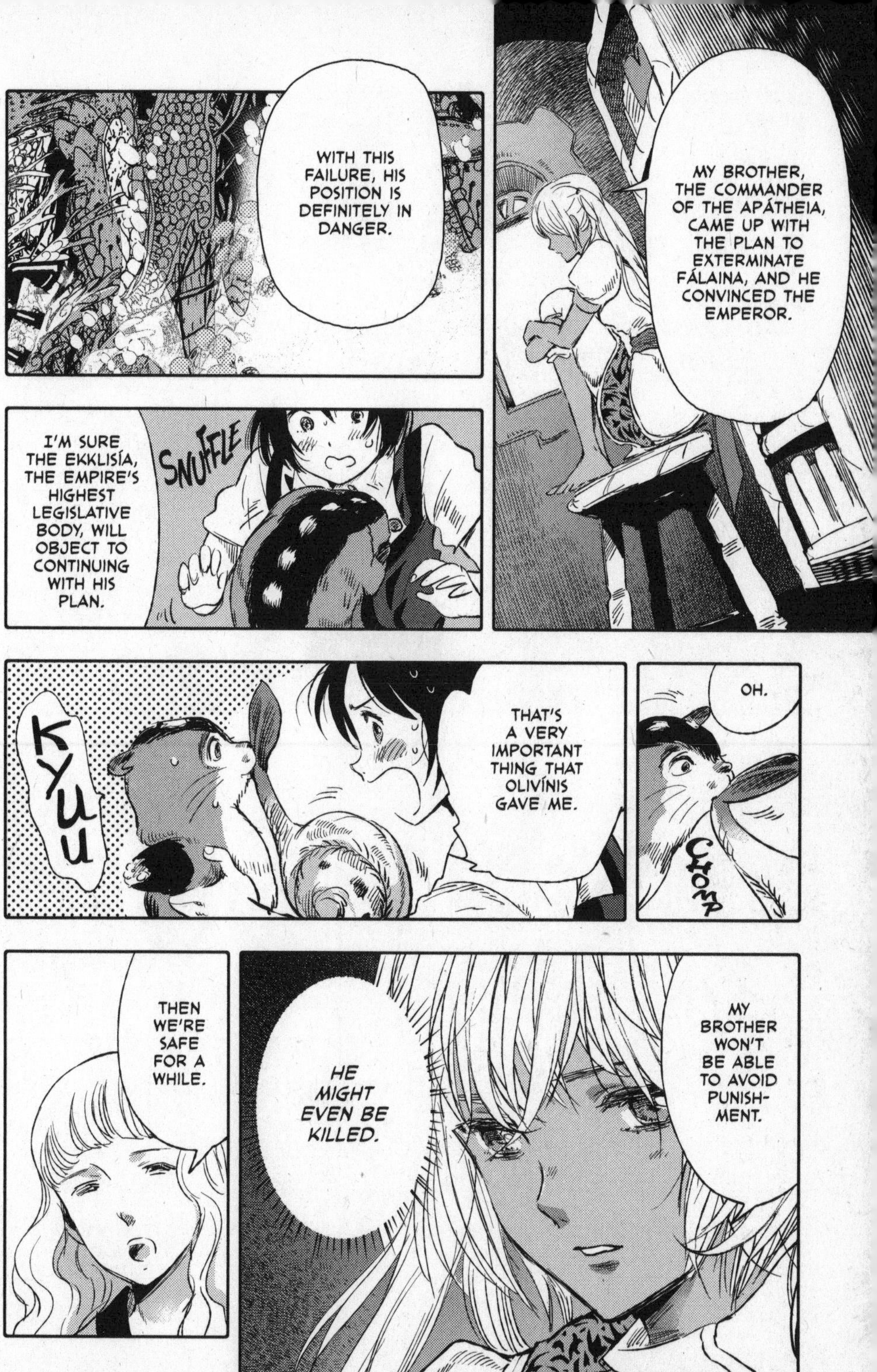
MY BROTHER, THE COMMANDER OF THE APÁTHEIA, CAME UP WITH THE PLAN TO EXTERMINATE FÁLAINA, AND HE CONVINCED THE EMPEROR.
WITH THIS FAILURE, HIS POSITION IS DEFINITELY IN DANGER.
SNUFFLE
I'M SURE THE EKKLISÍA, THE EMPIRE'S HIGHEST LEGISLATIVE BODY, WILL OBJECT TO CONTINUING WITH HIS PLAN.
OH.
CHOMP
THAT'S A VERY IMPORTANT THING THAT OLIVÍNIS GAVE ME.
KYUU
MY BROTHER WON'T BE ABLE TO AVOID PUNISHMENT.
HE MIGHT EVEN BE KILLED.
THEN WE'RE SAFE FOR A WHILE.

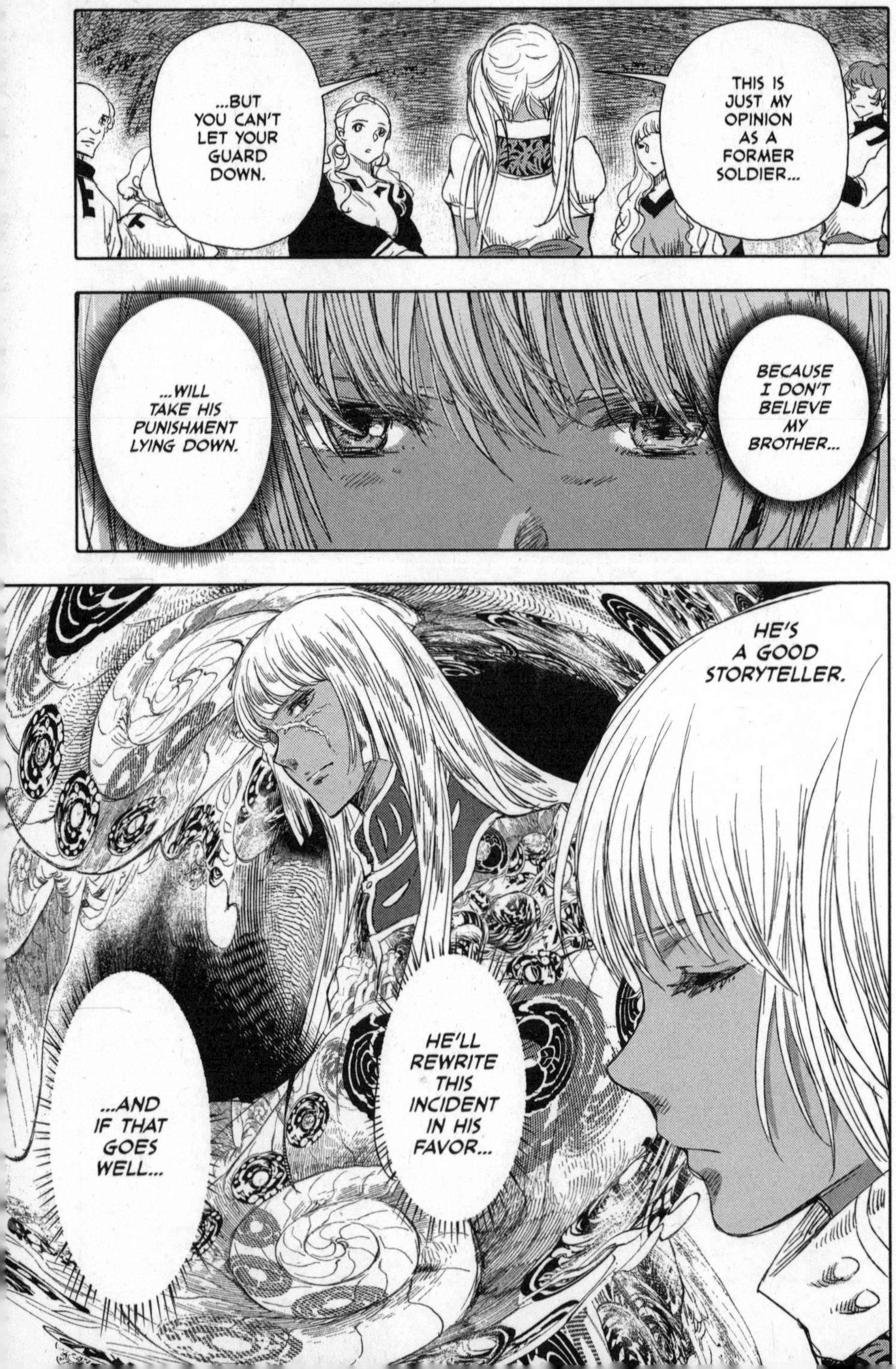
THIS IS JUST MY OPINION AS A FORMER SOLDIER...
...BUT YOU CAN'T LET YOUR GUARD DOWN.
BECAUSE I DON'T BELIEVE MY BROTHER...
...WILL TAKE HIS PUNISHMENT LYING DOWN.
HE'S A GOOD STORYTELLER.
HE'LL REWRITE THIS INCIDENT IN HIS FAVOR...
...AND IF THAT GOES WELL...

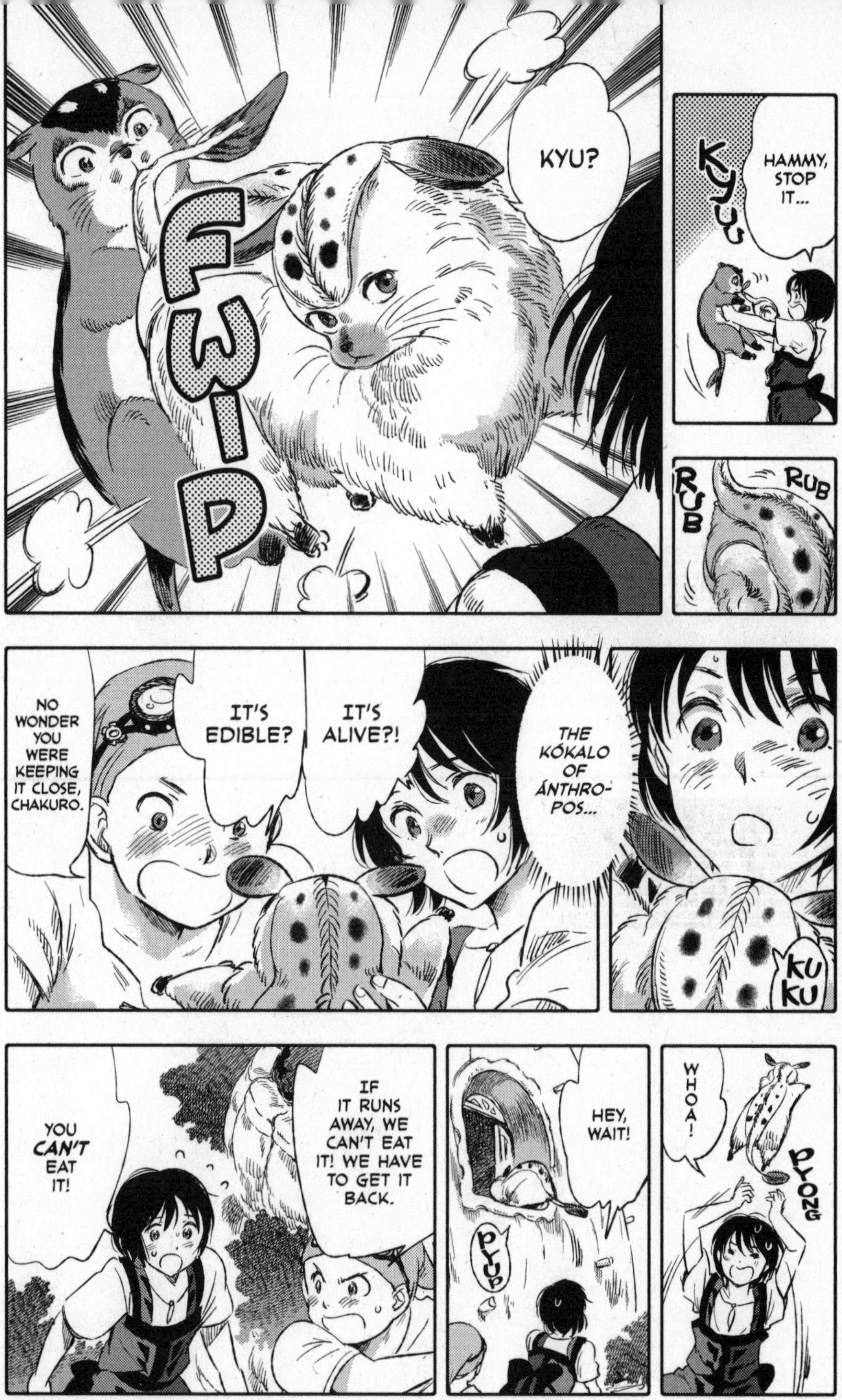
HAMMY, STOP IT...
KYUU
KYU?
FWIP
RUB
RUB
THE KÓKALO OF ÁNTHROPOS...
KU KU
IT'S ALIVE?!
IT'S EDIBLE?
NO WONDER YOU WERE KEEPING IT CLOSE, CHAKURO.
WHOA!
PYONG
HEY, WAIT!
PYUP
IF IT RUNS AWAY, WE CAN'T EAT IT! WE HAVE TO GET IT BACK.
YOU ***CAN'T*** EAT IT!

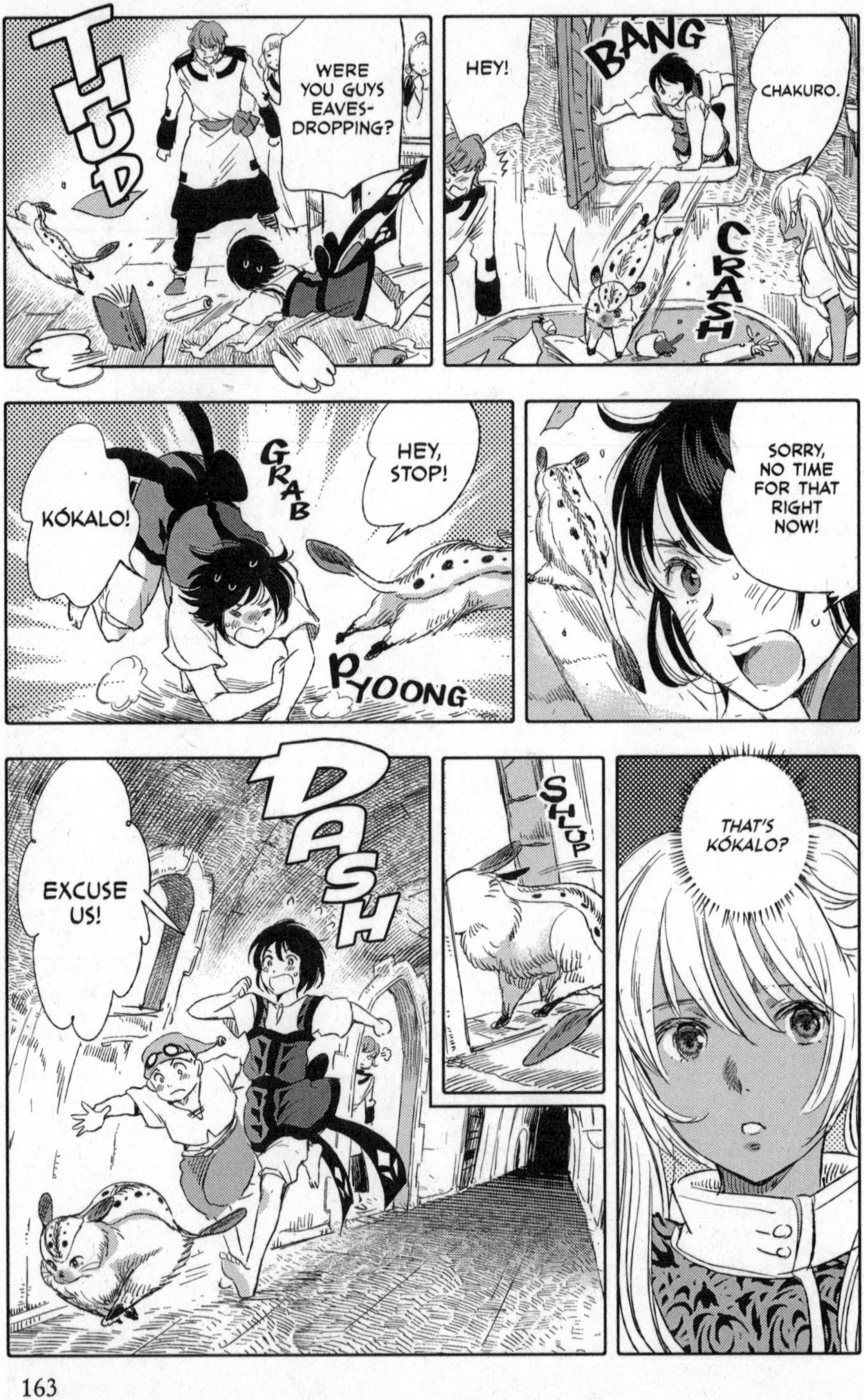
CHAKURO.
BANG
HEY!
CRASH
WERE YOU GUYS EAVES-DROPPING?
THUD
SORRY, NO TIME FOR THAT RIGHT NOW!
HEY, STOP!
GRAB
KÓKALO!
PYOONG
THAT'S KÓKALO?
SHLUP
DASH
EXCUSE US!

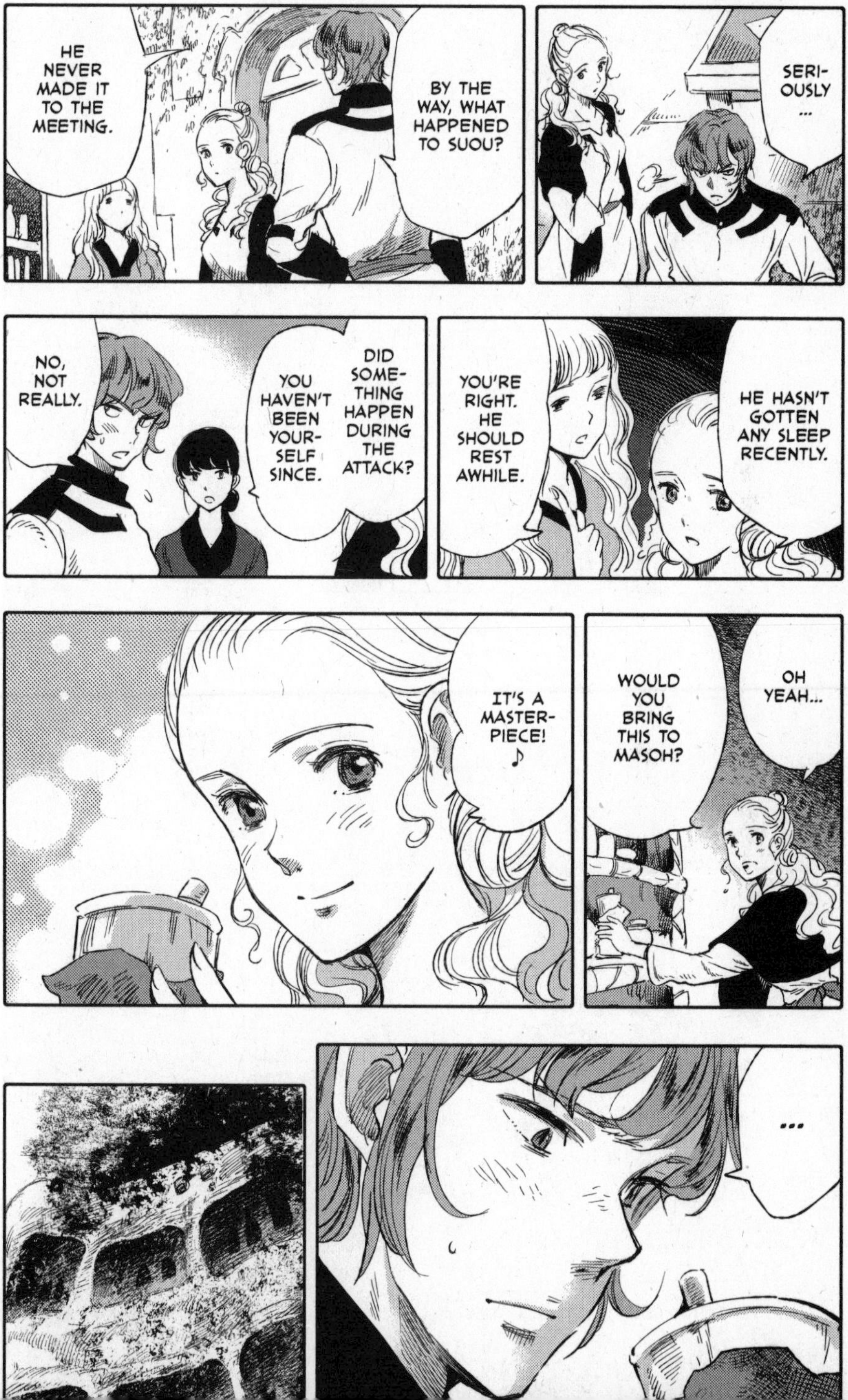
SERI-OUSLY ...
BY THE WAY, WHAT HAPPENED TO SUOU?
HE NEVER MADE IT TO THE MEETING.
HE HASN'T GOTTEN ANY SLEEP RECENTLY.
YOU'RE RIGHT. HE SHOULD REST AWHILE.
DID SOME-THING HAPPEN DURING THE ATTACK?
YOU HAVEN'T BEEN YOUR-SELF SINCE.
NO, NOT REALLY.
OH YEAH...
WOULD YOU BRING THIS TO MASOH?
IT'S A MASTER-PIECE! ♪
...

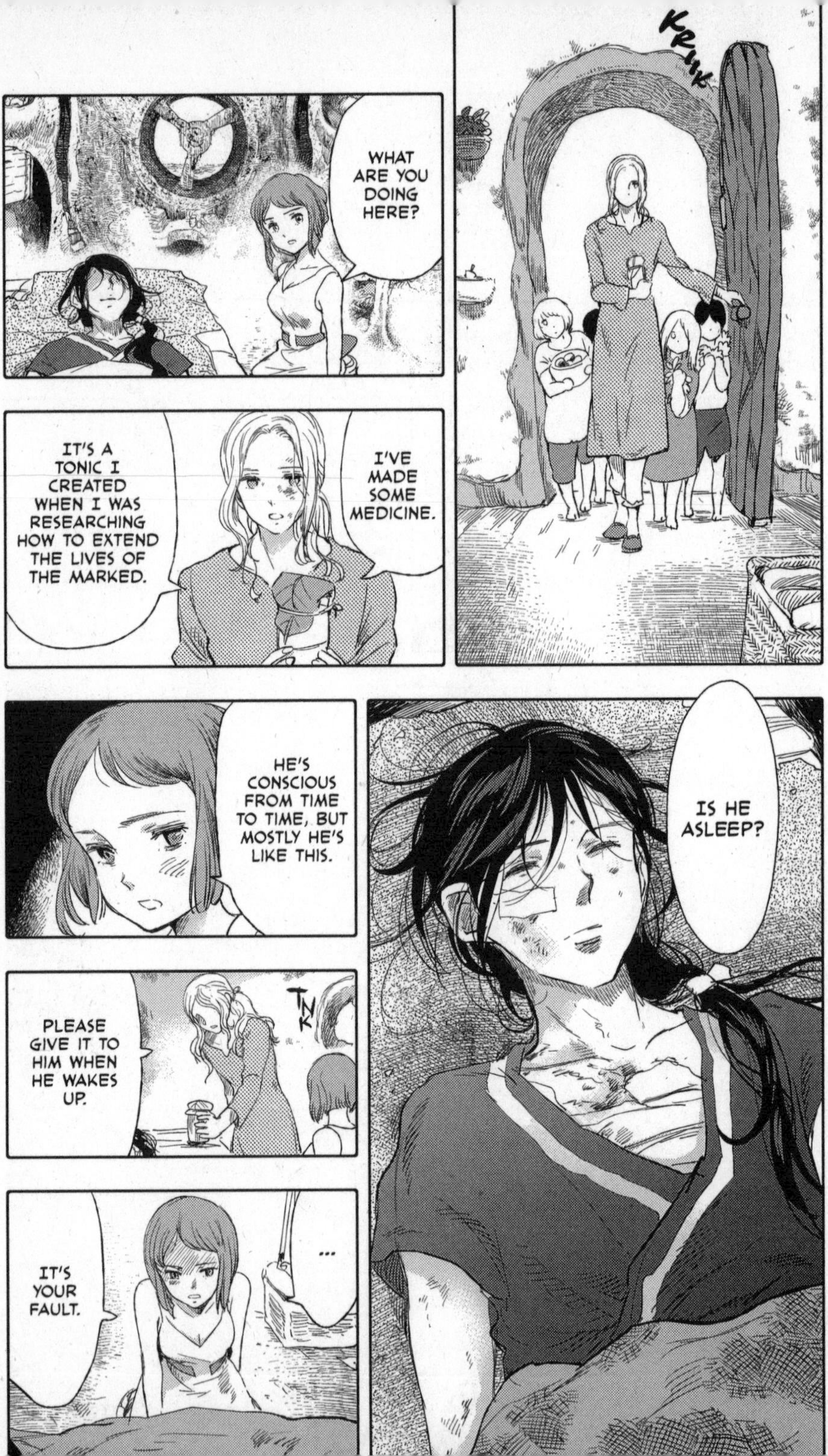
KRINK
WHAT ARE YOU DOING HERE?
I'VE MADE SOME MEDICINE.
IT'S A TONIC I CREATED WHEN I WAS RESEARCHING HOW TO EXTEND THE LIVES OF THE MARKED.
IS HE ASLEEP?
HE'S CONSCIOUS FROM TIME TO TIME, BUT MOSTLY HE'S LIKE THIS.
TNK
PLEASE GIVE IT TO HIM WHEN HE WAKES UP.
...
IT'S YOUR FAULT.

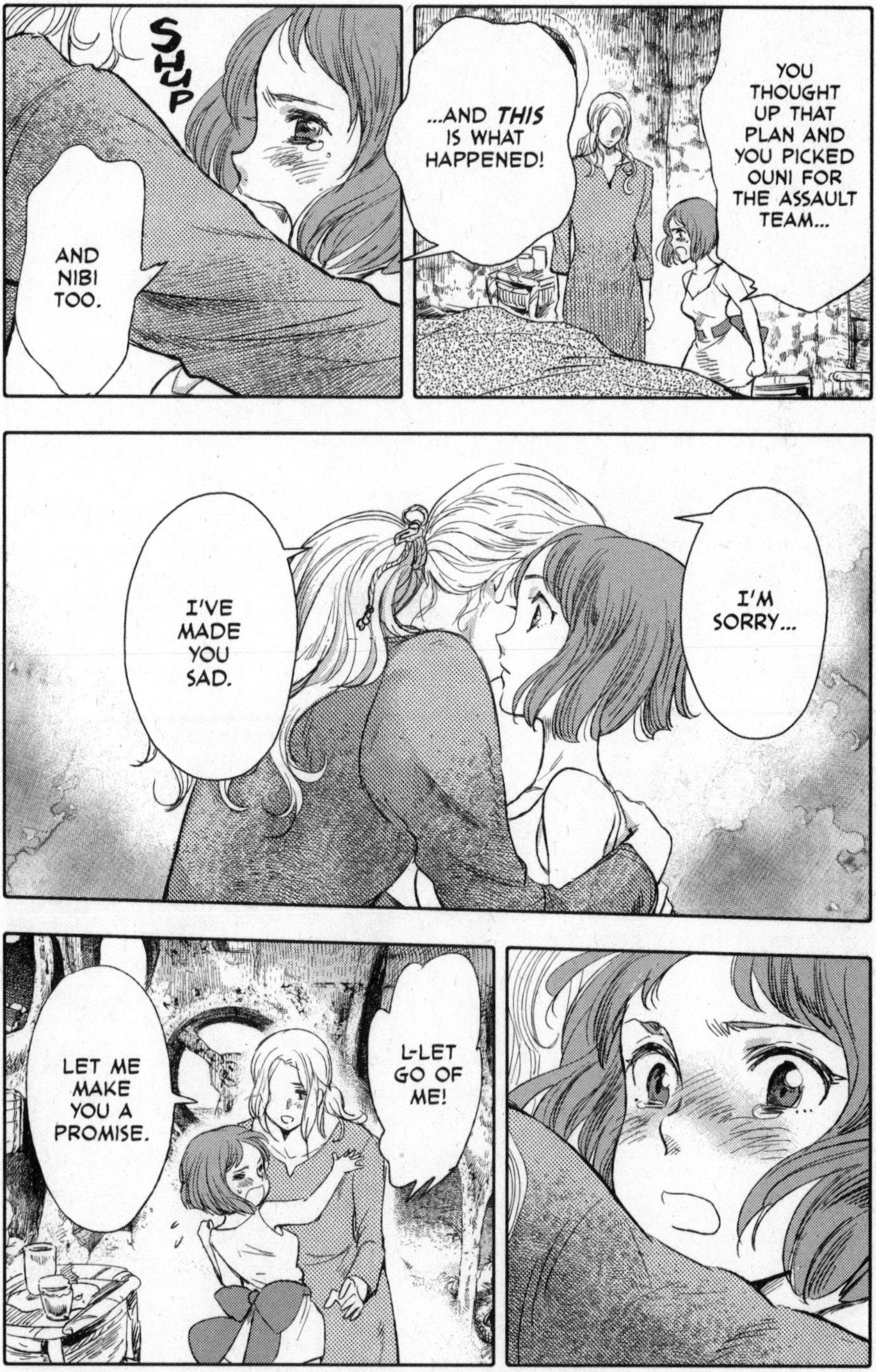
YOU THOUGHT UP THAT PLAN AND YOU PICKED OUNI FOR THE ASSAULT TEAM...
...AND THIS IS WHAT HAPPENED!
SHUP
AND NIBI TOO.
I'M SORRY...
I'VE MADE YOU SAD.
...
L-LET GO OF ME!
LET ME MAKE YOU A PROMISE.

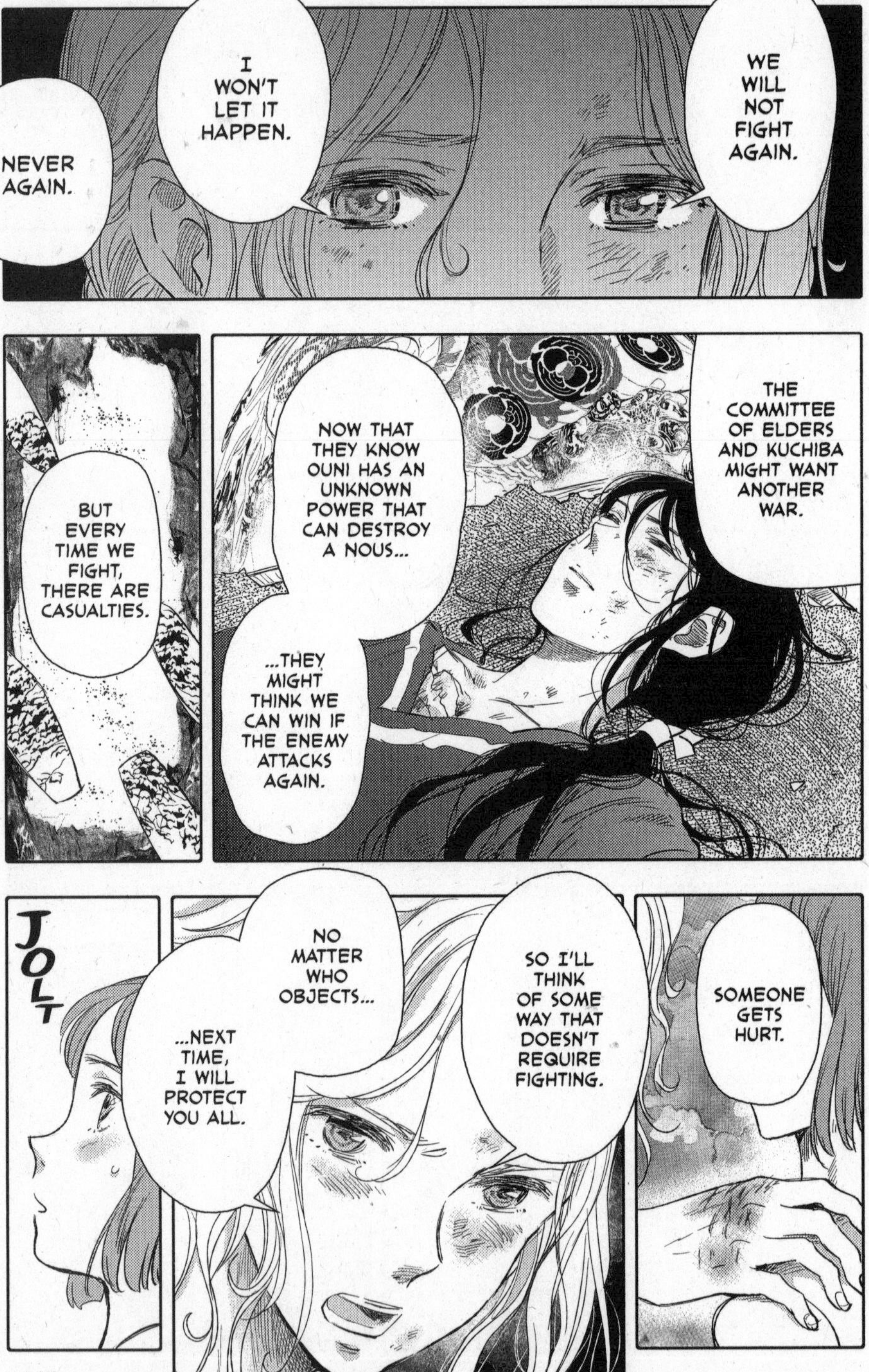
WE WILL NOT FIGHT AGAIN.
I WON'T LET IT HAPPEN.
NEVER AGAIN.
THE COMMITTEE OF ELDERS AND KUCHIBA MIGHT WANT ANOTHER WAR.
NOW THAT THEY KNOW OUNI HAS AN UNKNOWN POWER THAT CAN DESTROY A NOUS...
...THEY MIGHT THINK WE CAN WIN IF THE ENEMY ATTACKS AGAIN.
BUT EVERY TIME WE FIGHT, THERE ARE CASUALTIES.
SOMEONE GETS HURT.
SO I'LL THINK OF SOME WAY THAT DOESN'T REQUIRE FIGHTING.
NO MATTER WHO OBJECTS...
...NEXT TIME, I WILL PROTECT YOU ALL.
JOLT

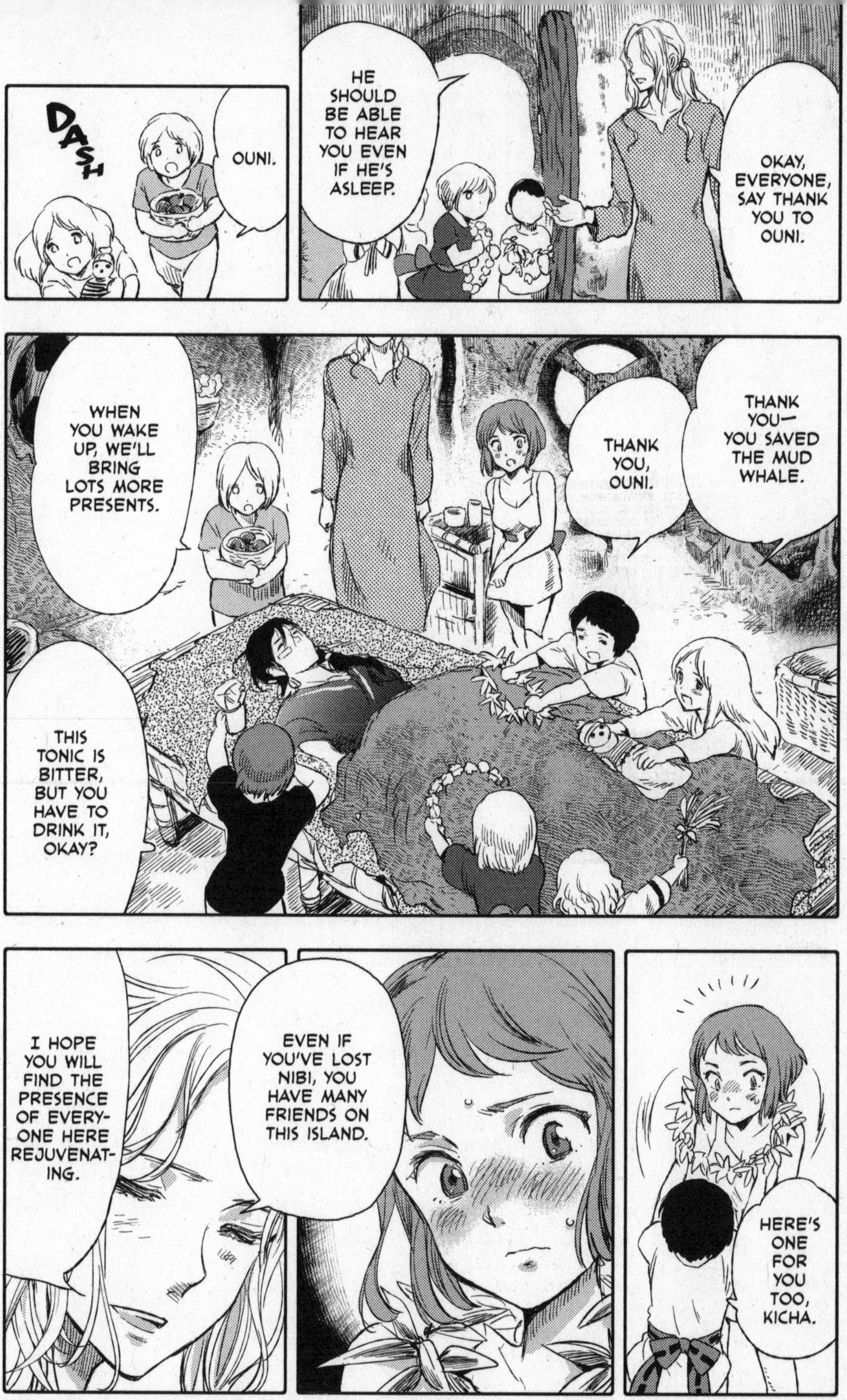
OKAY, EVERYONE, SAY THANK YOU TO OUNI.
HE SHOULD BE ABLE TO HEAR YOU EVEN IF HE'S ASLEEP.
DASH
OUNI.
THANK YOU— YOU SAVED THE MUD WHALE.
THANK YOU, OUNI.
WHEN YOU WAKE UP, WE'LL BRING LOTS MORE PRESENTS.
THIS TONIC IS BITTER, BUT YOU HAVE TO DRINK IT, OKAY?
HERE'S ONE FOR YOU TOO, KICHA.
EVEN IF YOU'VE LOST NIBI, YOU HAVE MANY FRIENDS ON THIS ISLAND.
I HOPE YOU WILL FIND THE PRESENCE OF EVERY-ONE HERE REJUVENAT-ING.

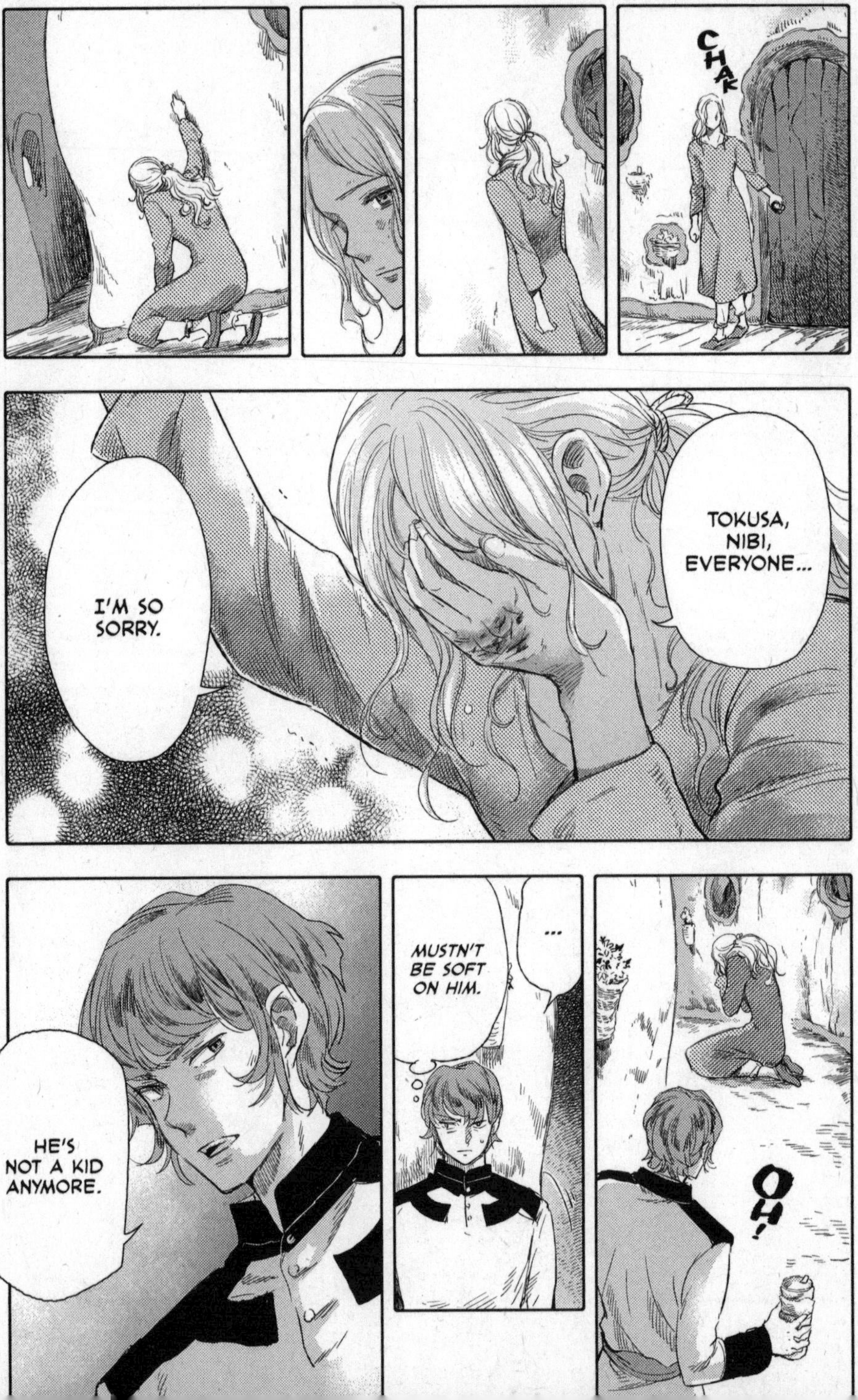
CHAK
TOKUSA, NIBI, EVERYONE...
I'M SO SORRY.
OH!
...
MUSTN'T BE SOFT ON HIM.
HE'S NOT A KID ANYMORE.

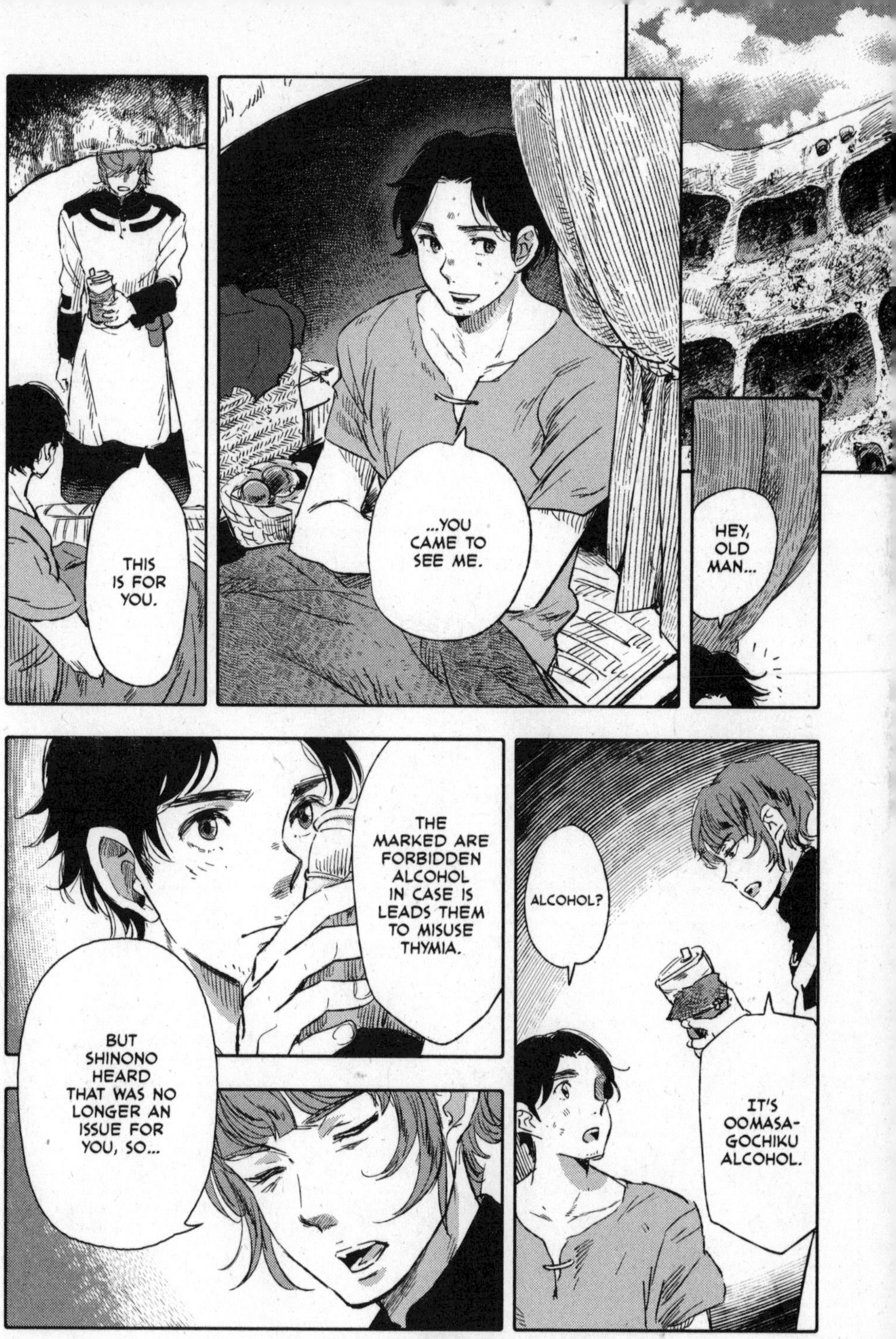
HEY, OLD MAN...
...YOU CAME TO SEE ME.
THIS IS FOR YOU.
ALCOHOL?
IT'S OOMASA-GOCHIKU ALCOHOL.
THE MARKED ARE FORBIDDEN ALCOHOL IN CASE IS LEADS THEM TO MISUSE THYMIA.
BUT SHINONO HEARD THAT WAS NO LONGER AN ISSUE FOR YOU, SO...

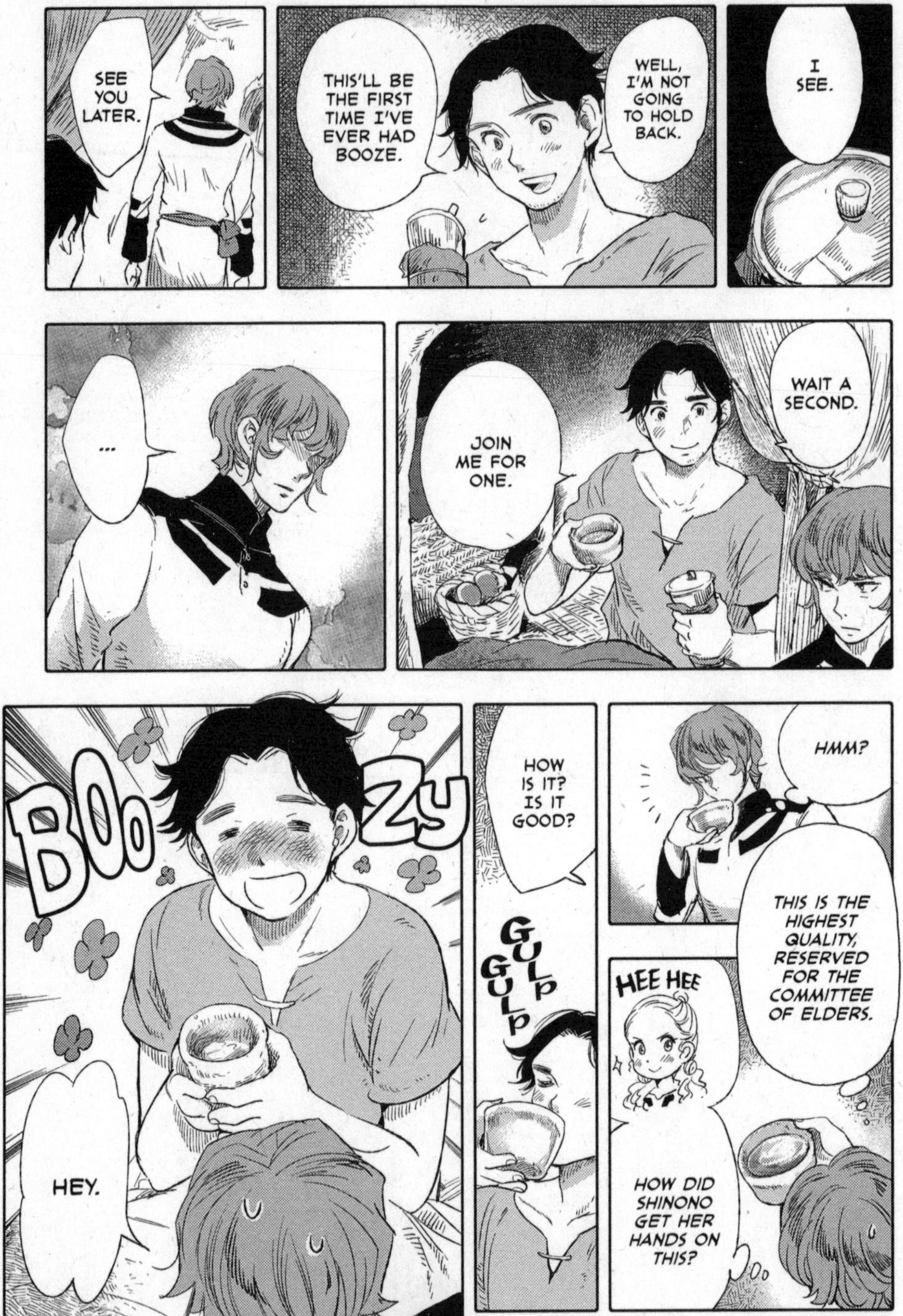

I SEE.
WELL, I'M NOT GOING TO HOLD BACK.
THIS'LL BE THE FIRST TIME I'VE EVER HAD BOOZE.
SEE YOU LATER.
WAIT A SECOND.
JOIN ME FOR ONE.
...
HMM?
THIS IS THE HIGHEST QUALITY, RESERVED FOR THE COMMITTEE OF ELDERS.
HEE HEE
HOW DID SHINONO GET HER HANDS ON THIS?
HOW IS IT? IS IT GOOD?
GULP GULP
BOOZY
HEY.

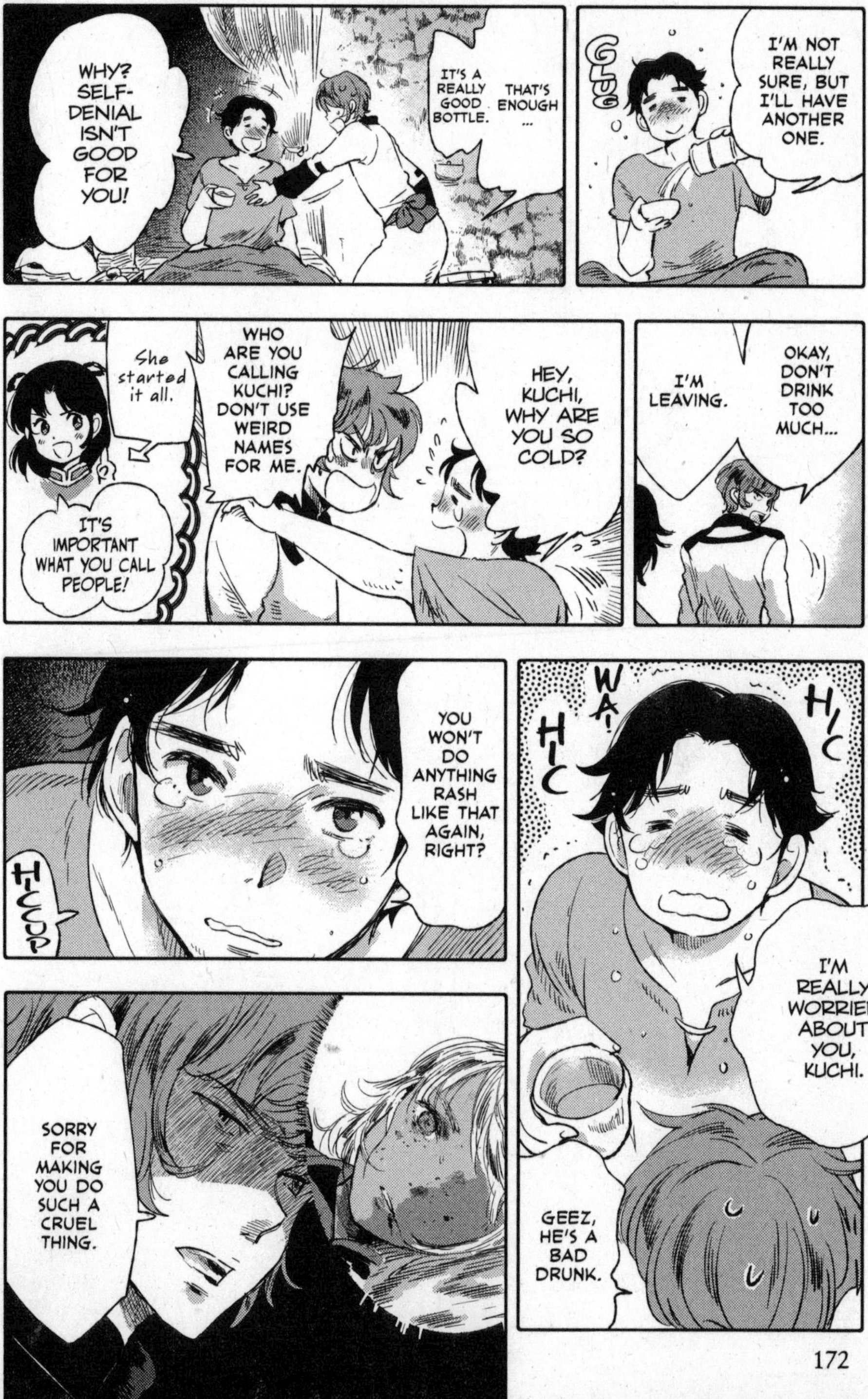
GLUG
I'M NOT REALLY SURE, BUT I'LL HAVE ANOTHER ONE.
THAT'S ENOUGH ...
IT'S A REALLY GOOD BOTTLE.
WHY? SELF-DENIAL ISN'T GOOD FOR YOU!
OKAY, DON'T DRINK TOO MUCH...
I'M LEAVING.
HEY, KUCHI, WHY ARE YOU SO COLD?
WHO ARE YOU CALLING KUCHI? DON'T USE WEIRD NAMES FOR ME.
She started it all.
IT'S IMPORTANT WHAT YOU CALL PEOPLE!
WA!
HIC
HIC
I'M REALLY WORRIED ABOUT YOU, KUCHI.
GEEZ, HE'S A BAD DRUNK.
YOU WON'T DO ANYTHING RASH LIKE THAT AGAIN, RIGHT?
HICCUP
SORRY FOR MAKING YOU DO SUCH A CRUEL THING.

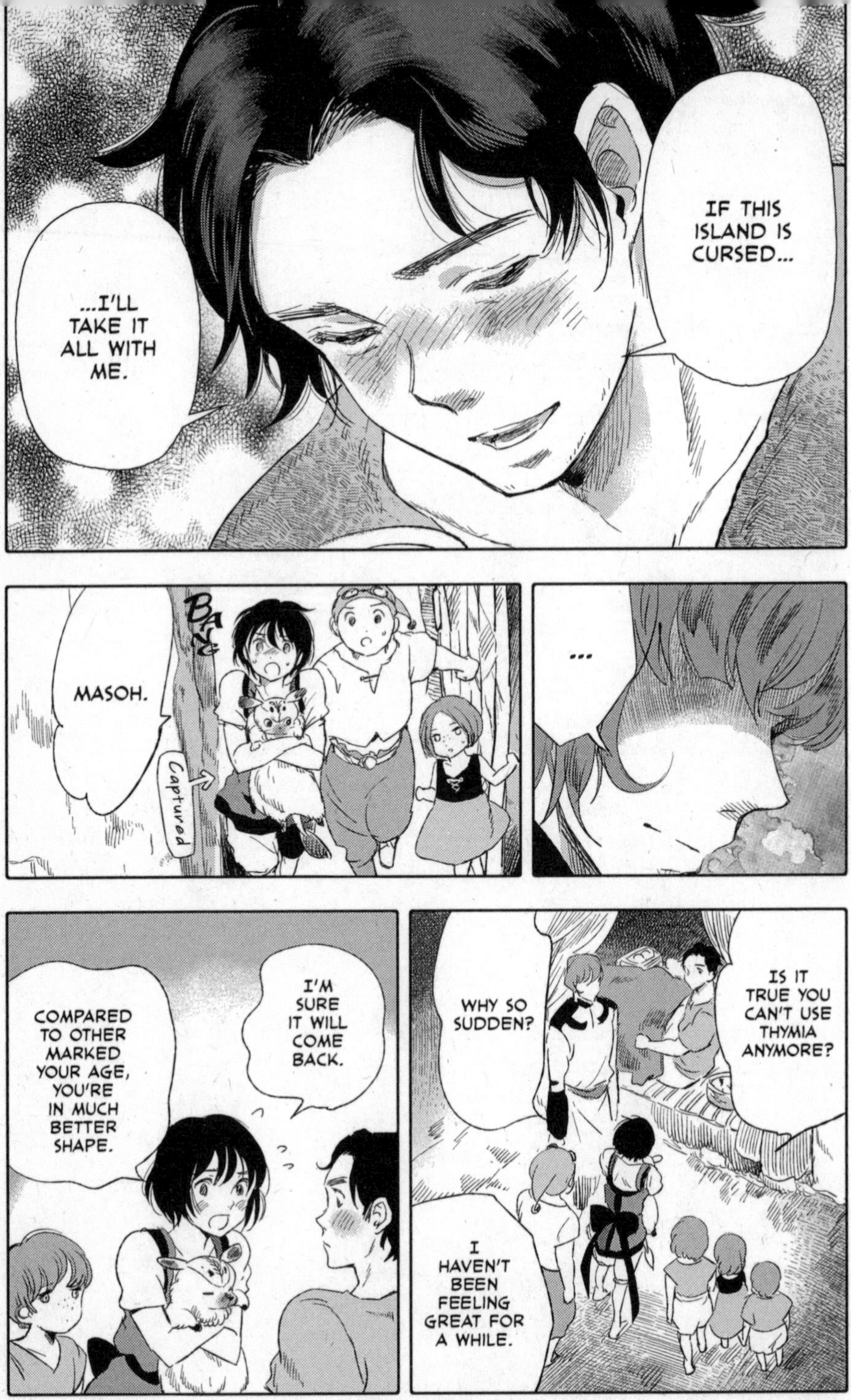
IF THIS ISLAND IS CURSED...
...I'LL TAKE IT ALL WITH ME.
...
BANG
MASOH.
Captured
IS IT TRUE YOU CAN'T USE THYMIA ANYMORE?
WHY SO SUDDEN?
I HAVEN'T BEEN FEELING GREAT FOR A WHILE.
I'M SURE IT WILL COME BACK.
COMPARED TO OTHER MARKED YOUR AGE, YOU'RE IN MUCH BETTER SHAPE.

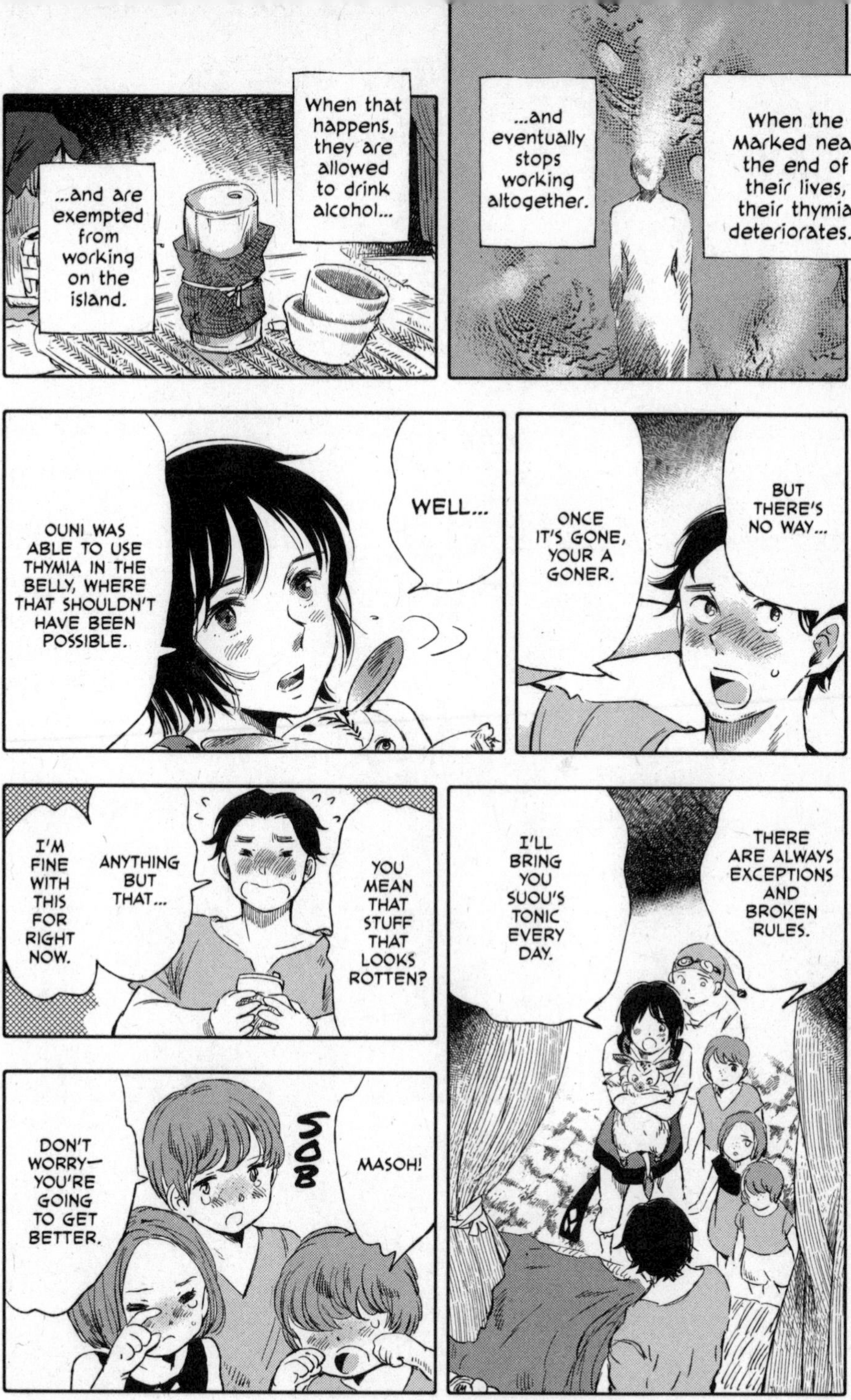

When the Marked near the end of their lives, their thymia deteriorates...
...and eventually stops working altogether.
When that happens, they are allowed to drink alcohol...
...and are exempted from working on the island.
BUT THERE'S NO WAY...
ONCE IT'S GONE, YOUR A GONER.
WELL...
OUNI WAS ABLE TO USE THYMIA IN THE BELLY, WHERE THAT SHOULDN'T HAVE BEEN POSSIBLE.
THERE ARE ALWAYS EXCEPTIONS AND BROKEN RULES.
I'LL BRING YOU SUOU'S TONIC EVERY DAY.
YOU MEAN THAT STUFF THAT LOOKS ROTTEN?
ANYTHING BUT THAT...
I'M FINE WITH THIS FOR RIGHT NOW.
MASOH!
SOB
DON'T WORRY— YOU'RE GOING TO GET BETTER.

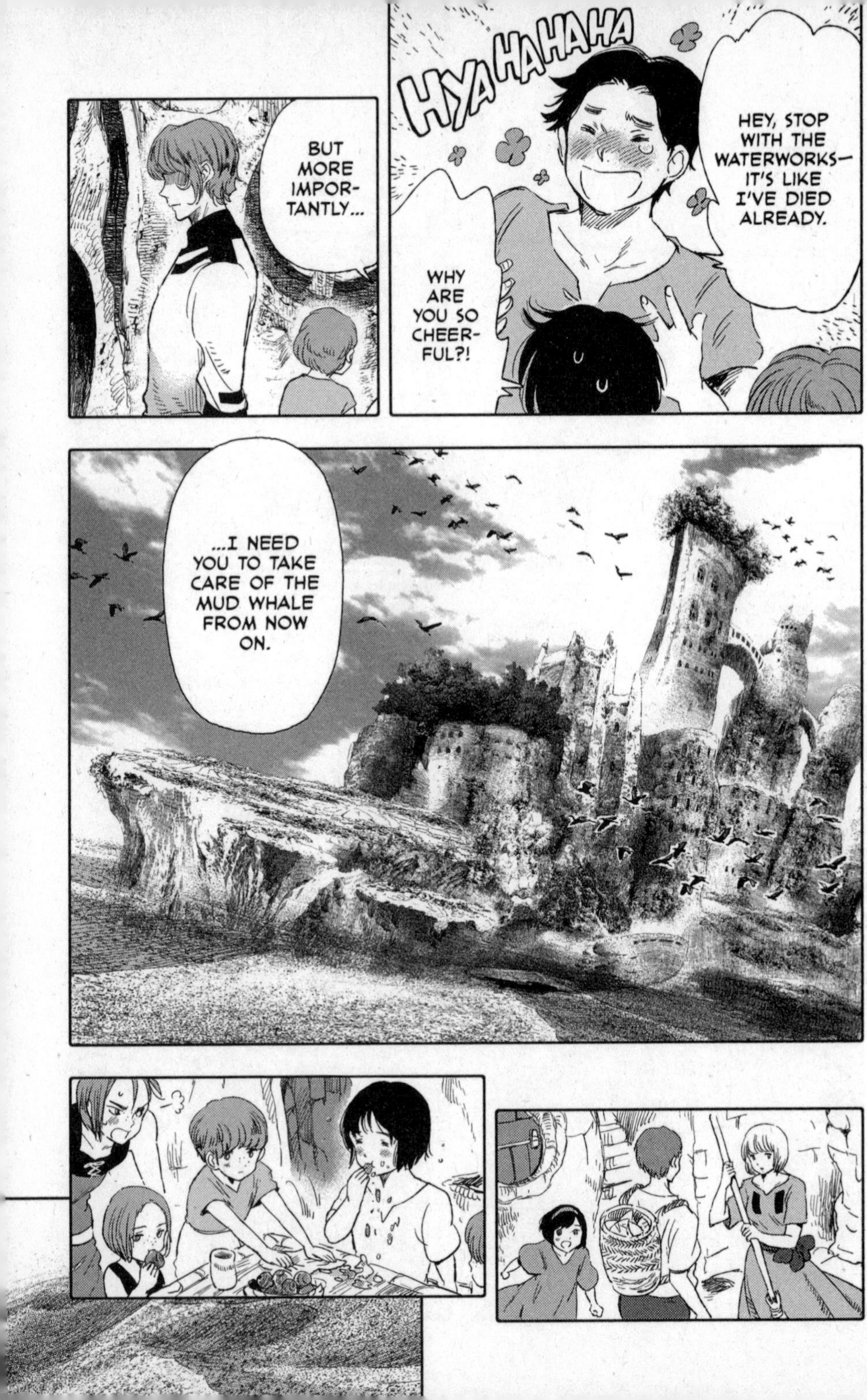
HEY, STOP WITH THE WATERWORKS—IT'S LIKE I'VE DIED ALREADY.
HYAHAHAHA
WHY ARE YOU SO CHEERFUL?!
BUT MORE IMPORTANTLY...
...I NEED YOU TO TAKE CARE OF THE MUD WHALE FROM NOW ON.

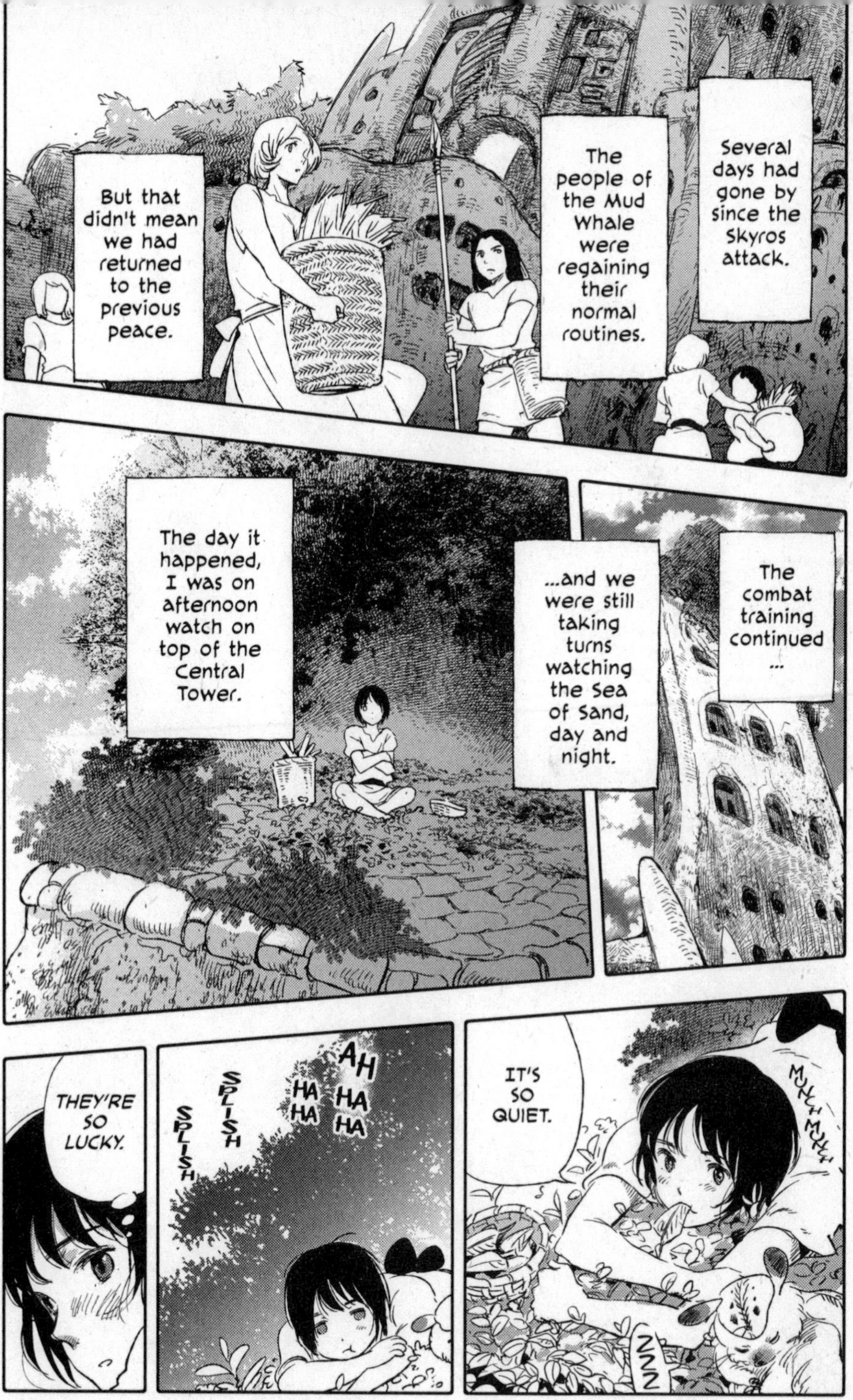
Several days had gone by since the Skyros attack.
The people of the Mud Whale were regaining their normal routines.
But that didn't mean we had returned to the previous peace.
The combat training continued ...
...and we were still taking turns watching the Sea of Sand, day and night.
The day it happened, I was on afternoon watch on top of the Central Tower.
IT'S SO QUIET.
MUNCH MUNCH
ZZZ
AH HA HA
HA HA
SPLISH
SPLISH
THEY'RE SO LUCKY.

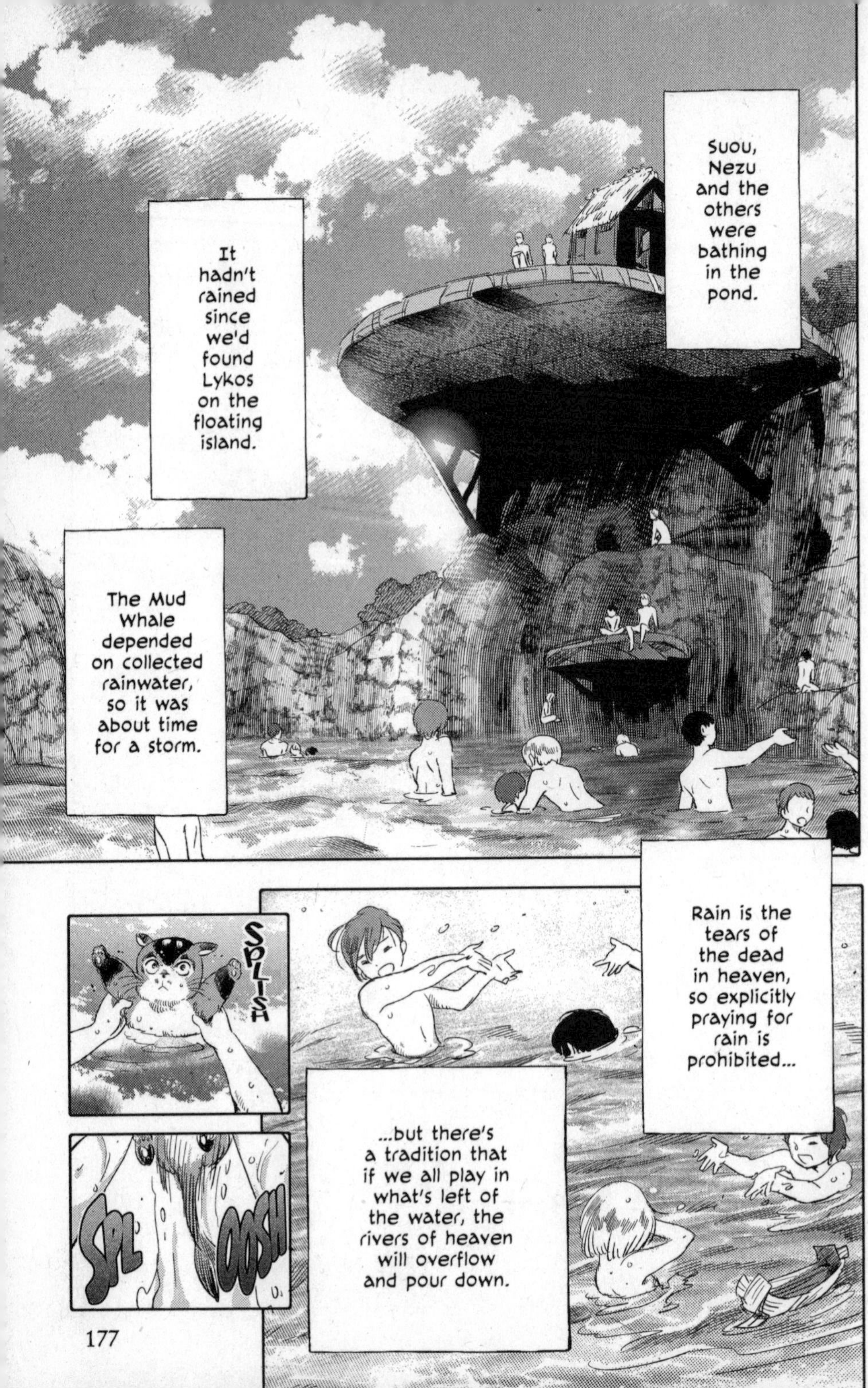
Suou, Nezu and the others were bathing in the pond.
It hadn't rained since we'd found Lykos on the floating island.
The Mud Whale depended on collected rainwater, so it was about time for a storm.
Rain is the tears of the dead in heaven, so explicitly praying for rain is prohibited...
...but there's a tradition that if we all play in what's left of the water, the rivers of heaven will overflow and pour down.
SPLISH
SPL OOSH

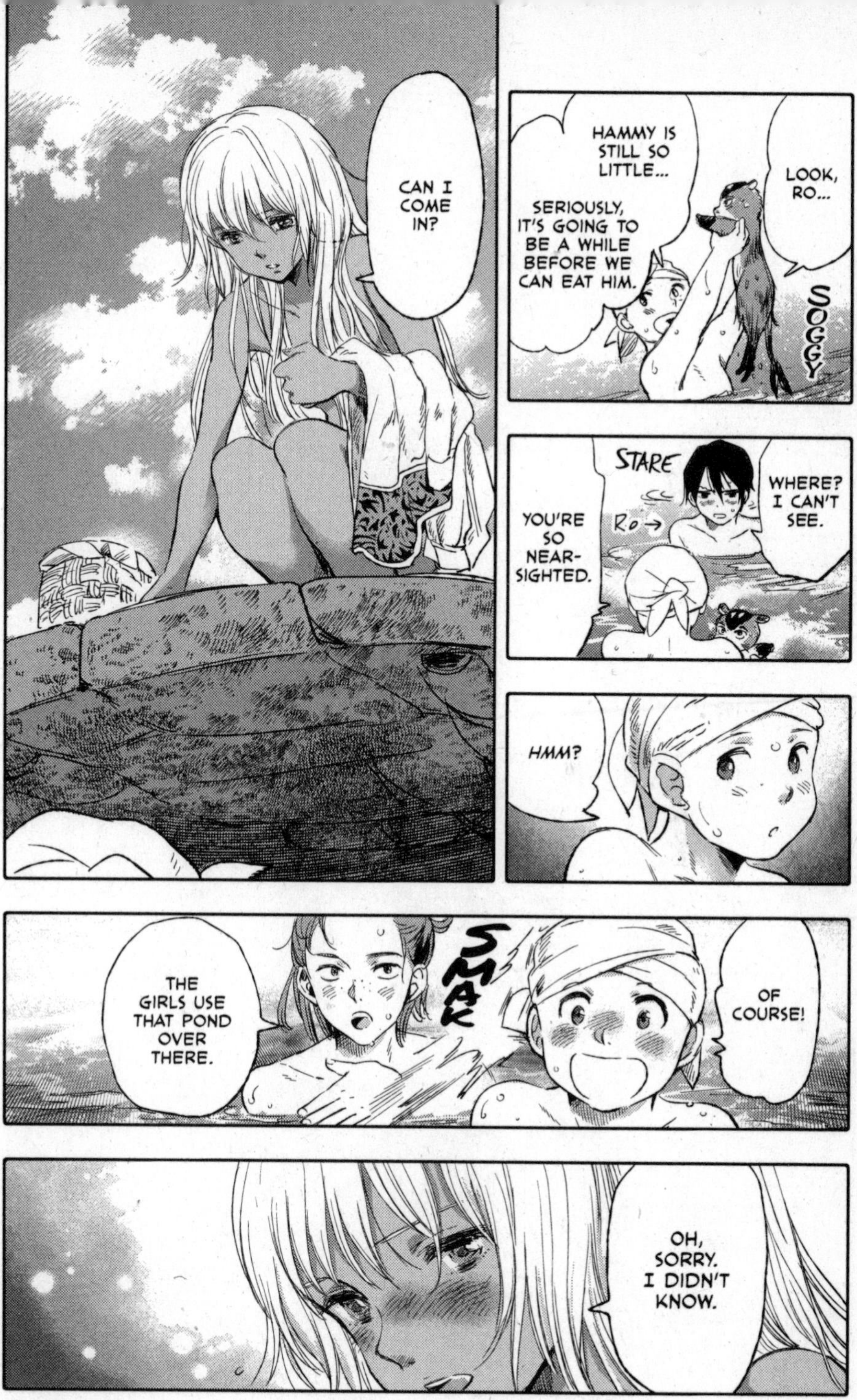
LOOK, RO...
HAMMY IS STILL SO LITTLE...
SERIOUSLY, IT'S GOING TO BE A WHILE BEFORE WE CAN EAT HIM.
SOGGY
WHERE? I CAN'T SEE.
STARE
Ro →
YOU'RE SO NEAR-SIGHTED.
HMM?
CAN I COME IN?
OF COURSE!
SMAK
THE GIRLS USE THAT POND OVER THERE.
OH, SORRY. I DIDN'T KNOW.

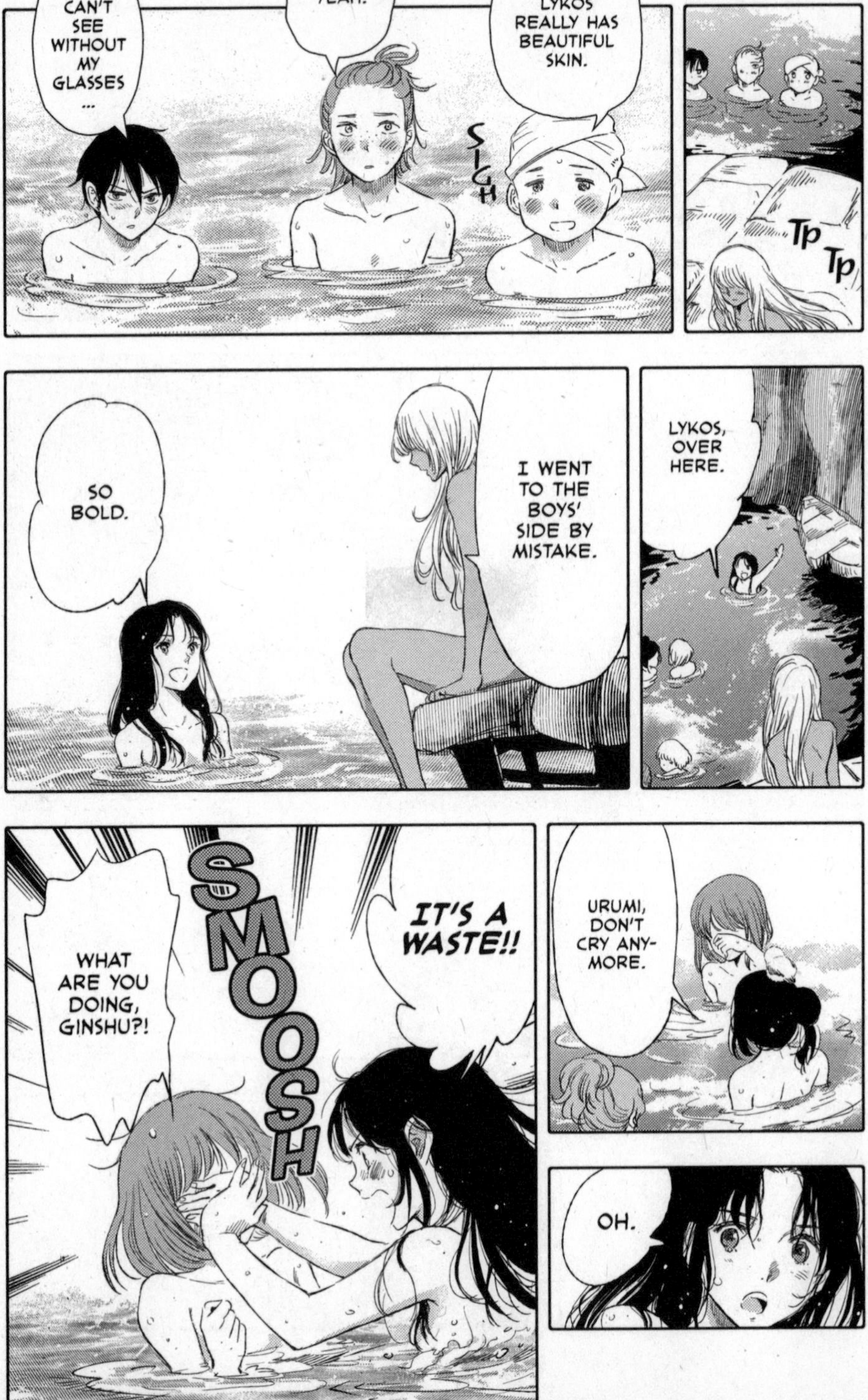
Tp Tp
LYKOS REALLY HAS BEAUTIFUL SKIN.
SIGH
YEAH.
I CAN'T SEE WITHOUT MY GLASSES ...
LYKOS, OVER HERE.
I WENT TO THE BOYS' SIDE BY MISTAKE.
SO BOLD.
URUMI, DON'T CRY ANY-MORE.
OH.
IT'S A WASTE!!
SMOOSH
WHAT ARE YOU DOING, GINSHU?!

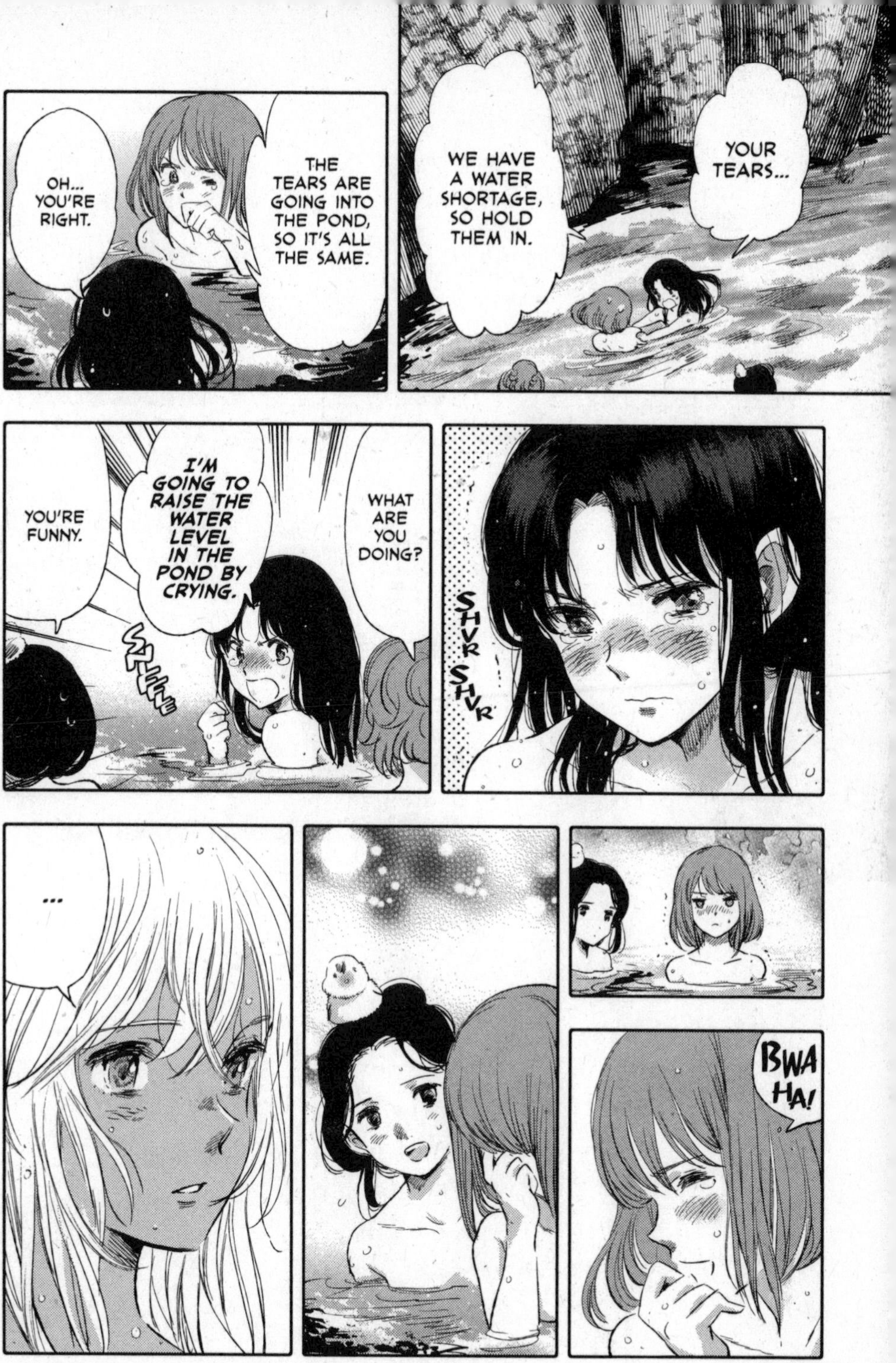
YOUR TEARS...
WE HAVE A WATER SHORTAGE, SO HOLD THEM IN.
THE TEARS ARE GOING INTO THE POND, SO IT'S ALL THE SAME.
OH... YOU'RE RIGHT.
SHVR SHVR
WHAT ARE YOU DOING?
I'M GOING TO RAISE THE WATER LEVEL IN THE POND BY CRYING.
SNIFFLE
YOU'RE FUNNY.
BWA HA!
...

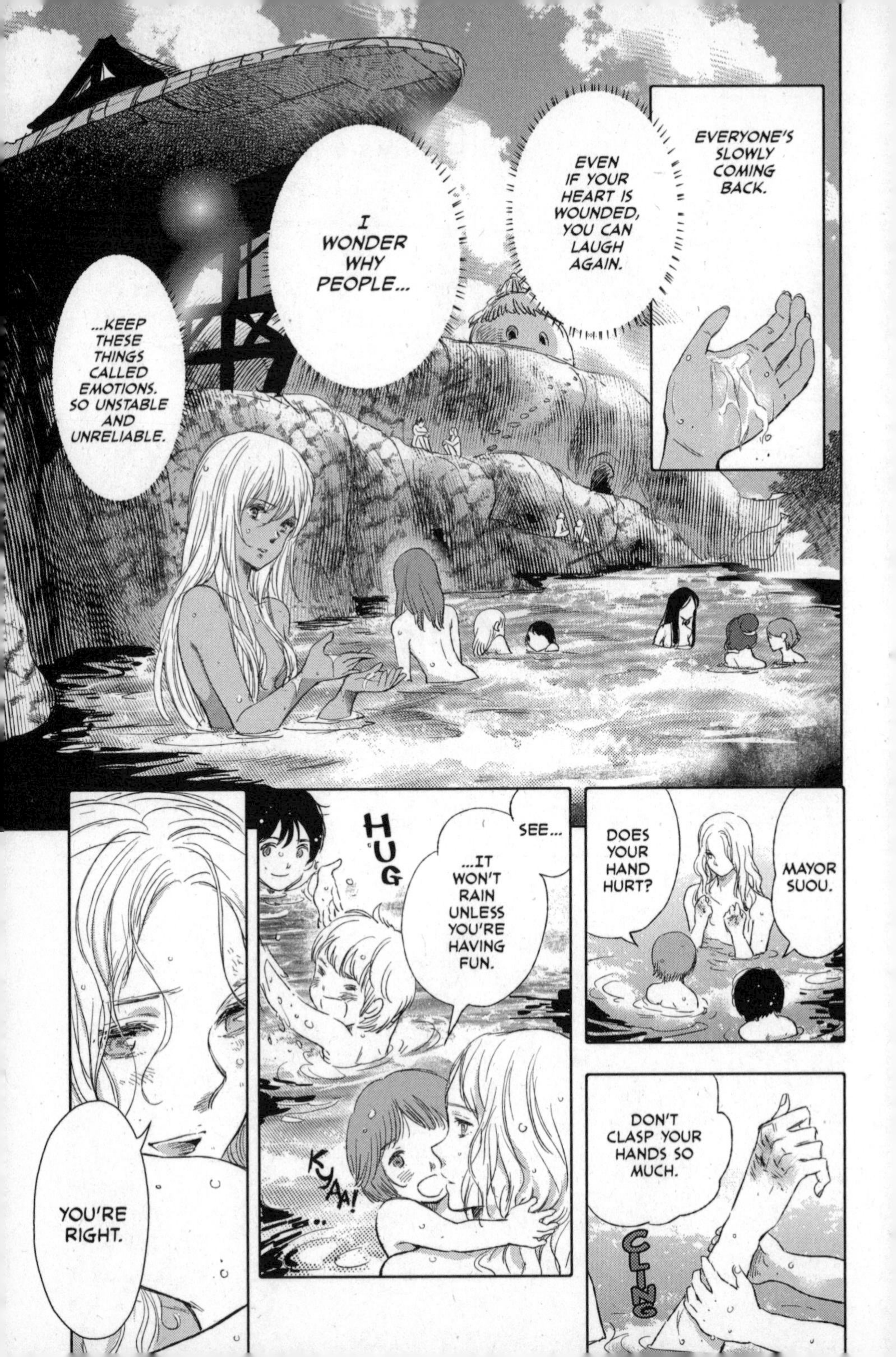
EVERYONE'S SLOWLY COMING BACK.
EVEN IF YOUR HEART IS WOUNDED, YOU CAN LAUGH AGAIN.
I WONDER WHY PEOPLE...
...KEEP THESE THINGS CALLED EMOTIONS. SO UNSTABLE AND UNRELIABLE.
MAYOR SUOU.
DOES YOUR HAND HURT?
DON'T CLASP YOUR HANDS SO MUCH.
CLING
SEE...
...IT WON'T RAIN UNLESS YOU'RE HAVING FUN.
HUG
KYAA!
YOU'RE RIGHT.

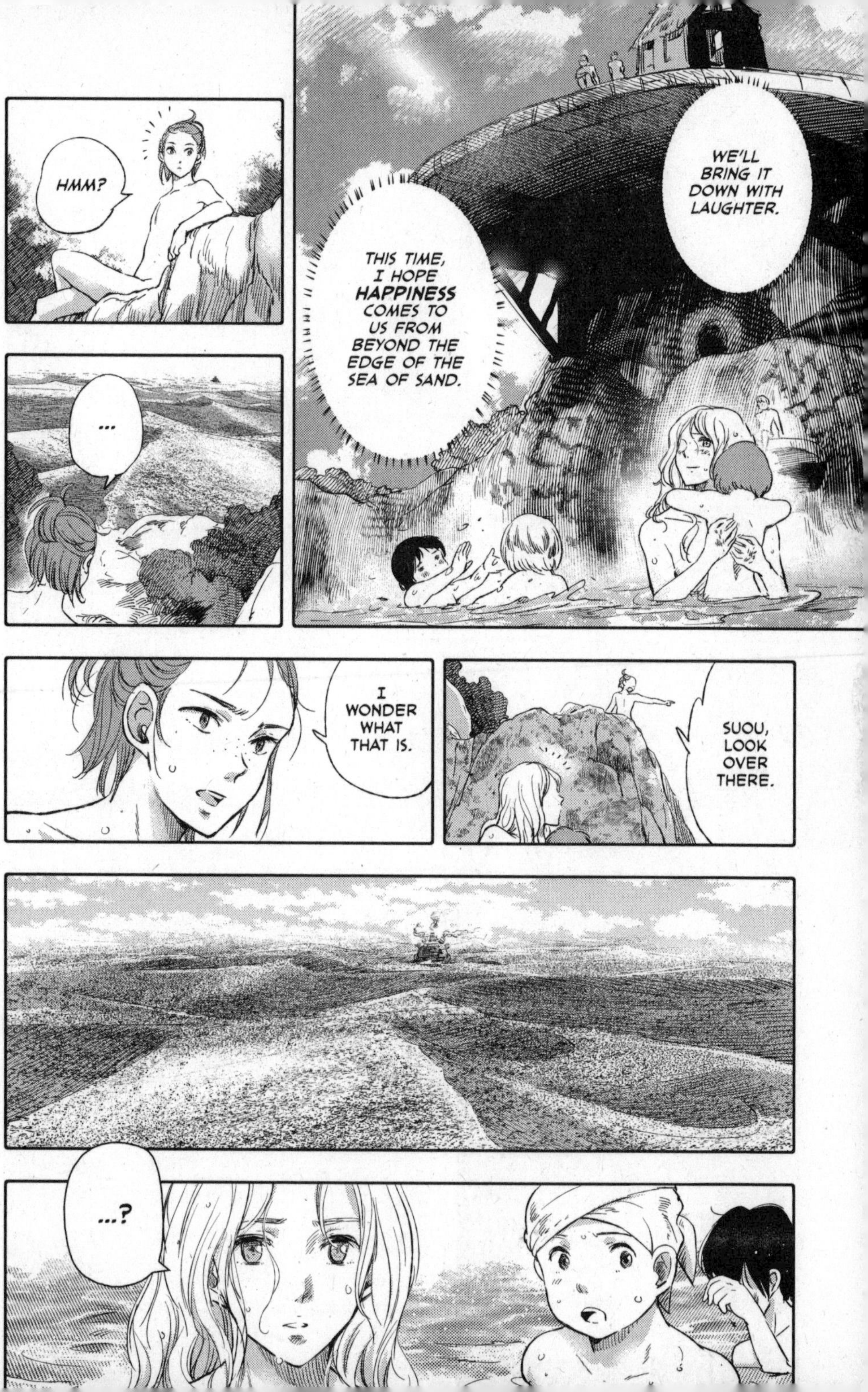
WE'LL BRING IT DOWN WITH LAUGHTER.
THIS TIME, I HOPE **HAPPINESS** COMES TO US FROM BEYOND THE EDGE OF THE SEA OF SAND.
HMM?
...
SUOU, LOOK OVER THERE.
I WONDER WHAT THAT IS.
...?

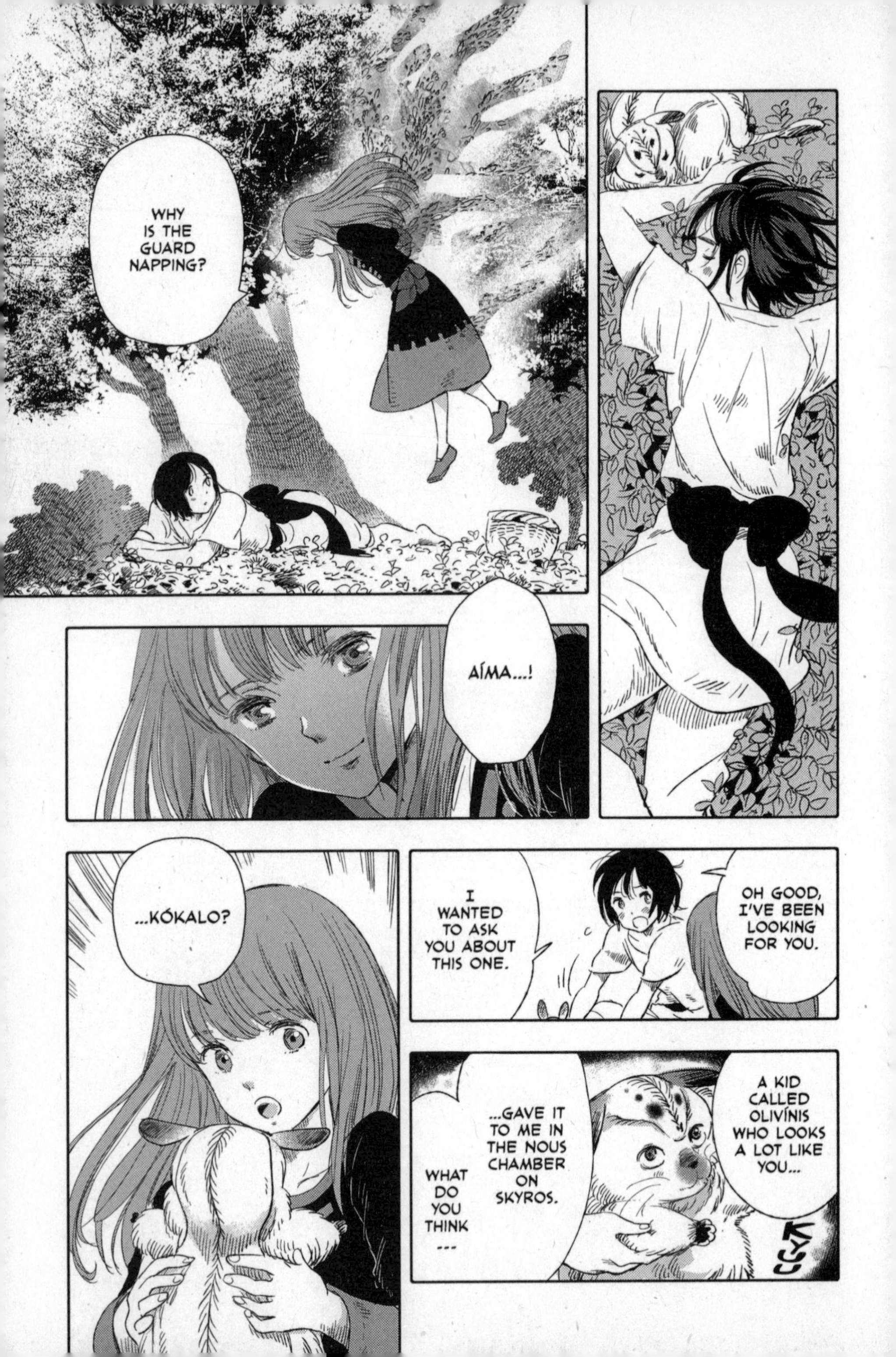
WHY IS THE GUARD NAPPING?
AÍMA...!
OH GOOD, I'VE BEEN LOOKING FOR YOU.
I WANTED TO ASK YOU ABOUT THIS ONE.
A KID CALLED OLIVÍNIS WHO LOOKS A LOT LIKE YOU...
KYUU
...GAVE IT TO ME IN THE NOUS CHAMBER ON SKYROS.
WHAT DO YOU THINK ...
...KÓKALO?

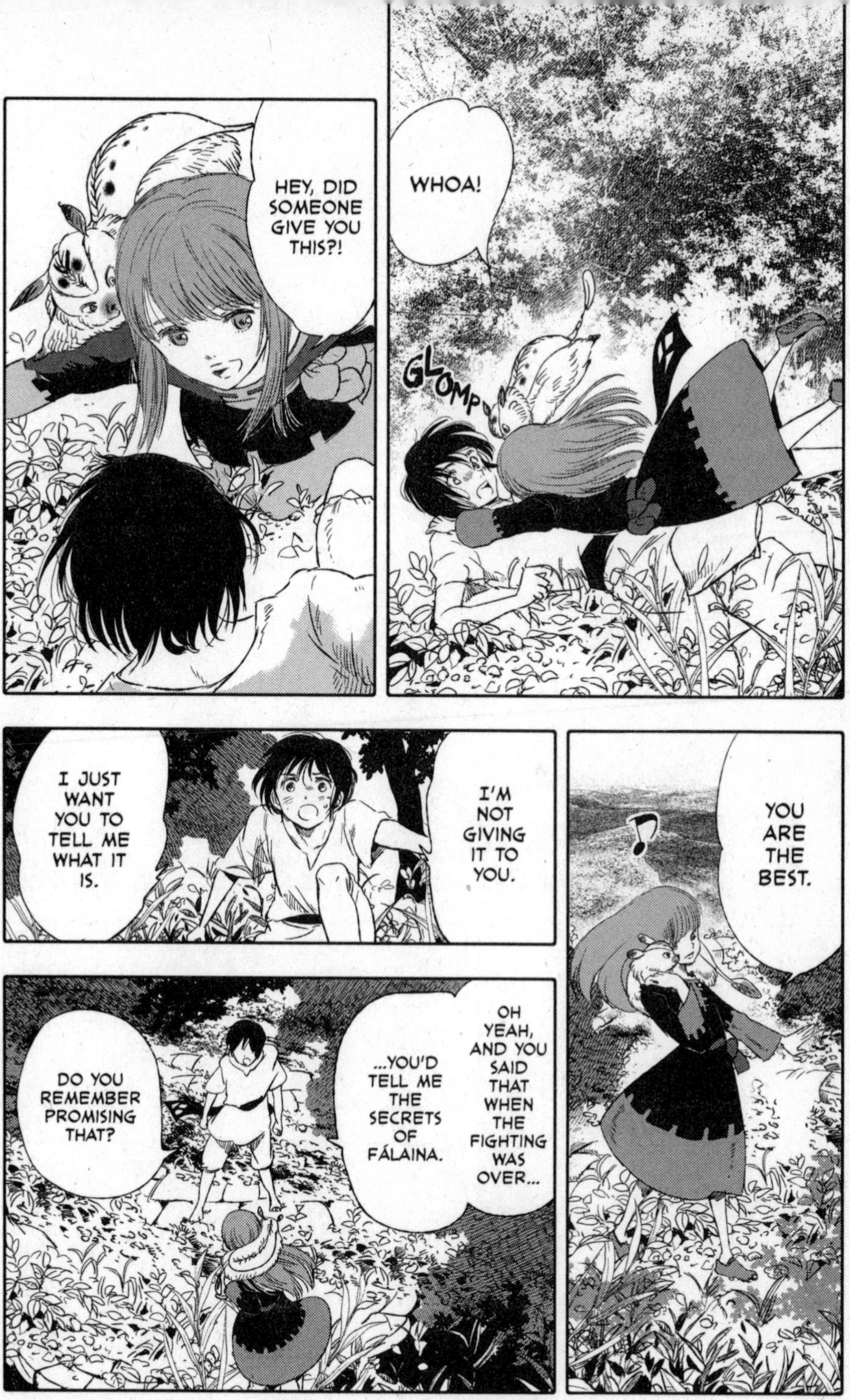
WHOA!
GLOMP
HEY, DID SOMEONE GIVE YOU THIS?!
YOU ARE THE BEST.
I'M NOT GIVING IT TO YOU.
I JUST WANT YOU TO TELL ME WHAT IT IS.
OH YEAH, AND YOU SAID THAT WHEN THE FIGHTING WAS OVER...
...YOU'D TELL ME THE SECRETS OF FÁLAINA.
DO YOU REMEMBER PROMISING THAT?

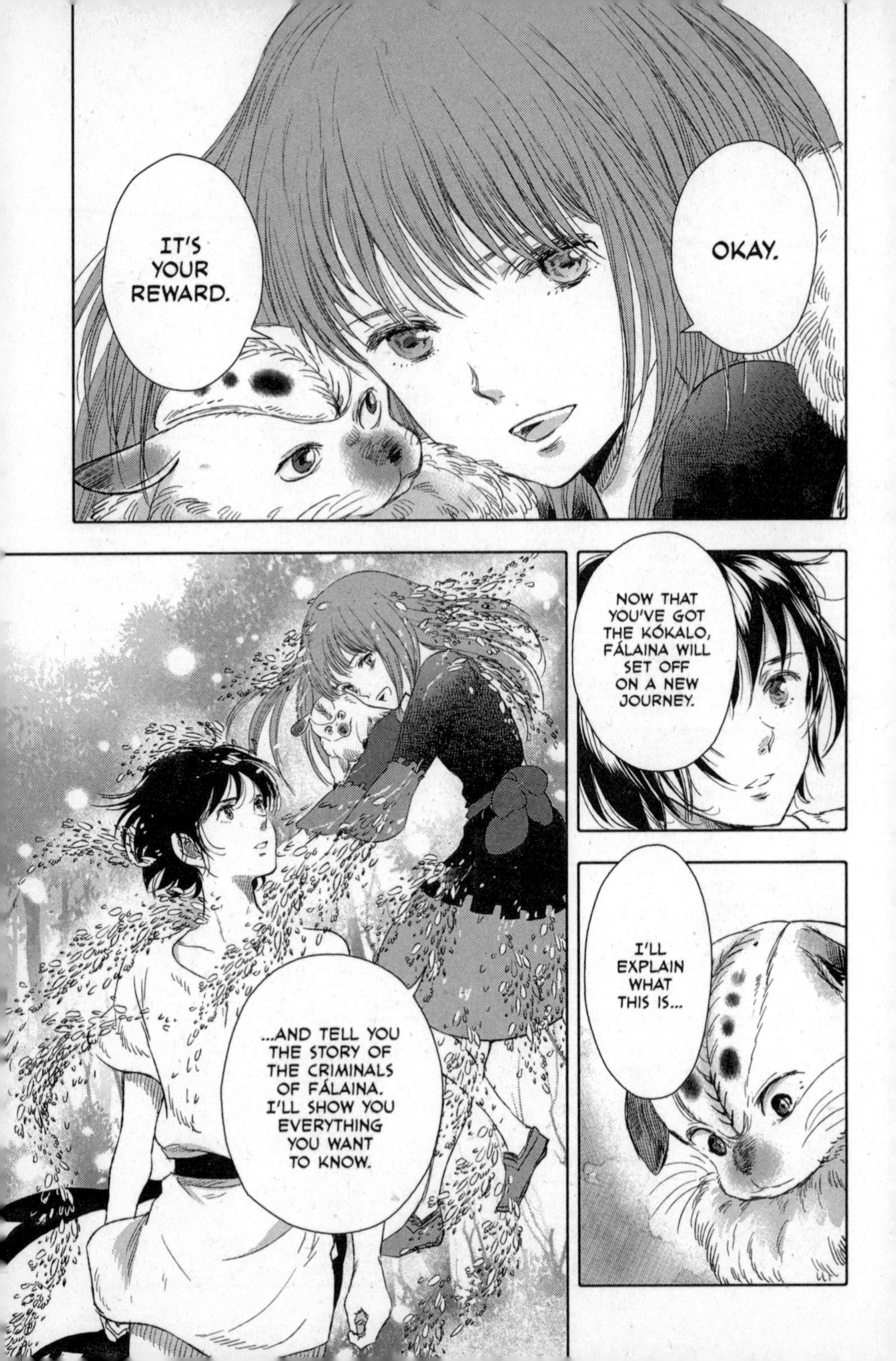
OKAY.
IT'S YOUR REWARD.
NOW THAT YOU'VE GOT THE KÓKALO, FÁLAINA WILL SET OFF ON A NEW JOURNEY.
I'LL EXPLAIN WHAT THIS IS...
...AND TELL YOU THE STORY OF THE CRIMINALS OF FÁLAINA. I'LL SHOW YOU EVERYTHING YOU WANT TO KNOW.

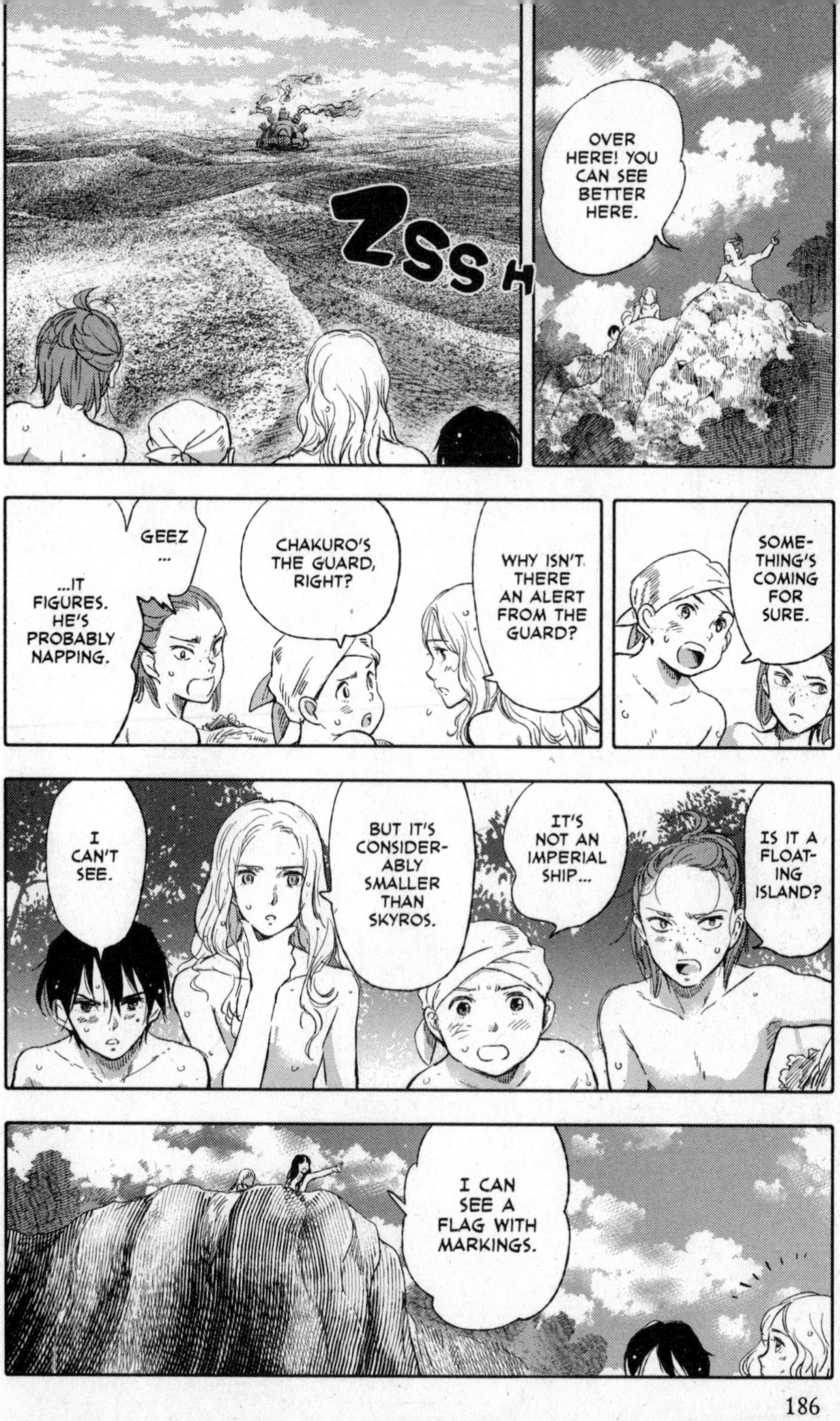
OVER HERE! YOU CAN SEE BETTER HERE.
ZSSH
SOMETHING'S COMING FOR SURE.
WHY ISN'T THERE AN ALERT FROM THE GUARD?
CHAKURO'S THE GUARD, RIGHT?
GEEZ...
...IT FIGURES. HE'S PROBABLY NAPPING.
IS IT A FLOATING ISLAND?
IT'S NOT AN IMPERIAL SHIP...
BUT IT'S CONSIDERABLY SMALLER THAN SKYROS.
I CAN'T SEE.
I CAN SEE A FLAG WITH MARKINGS.

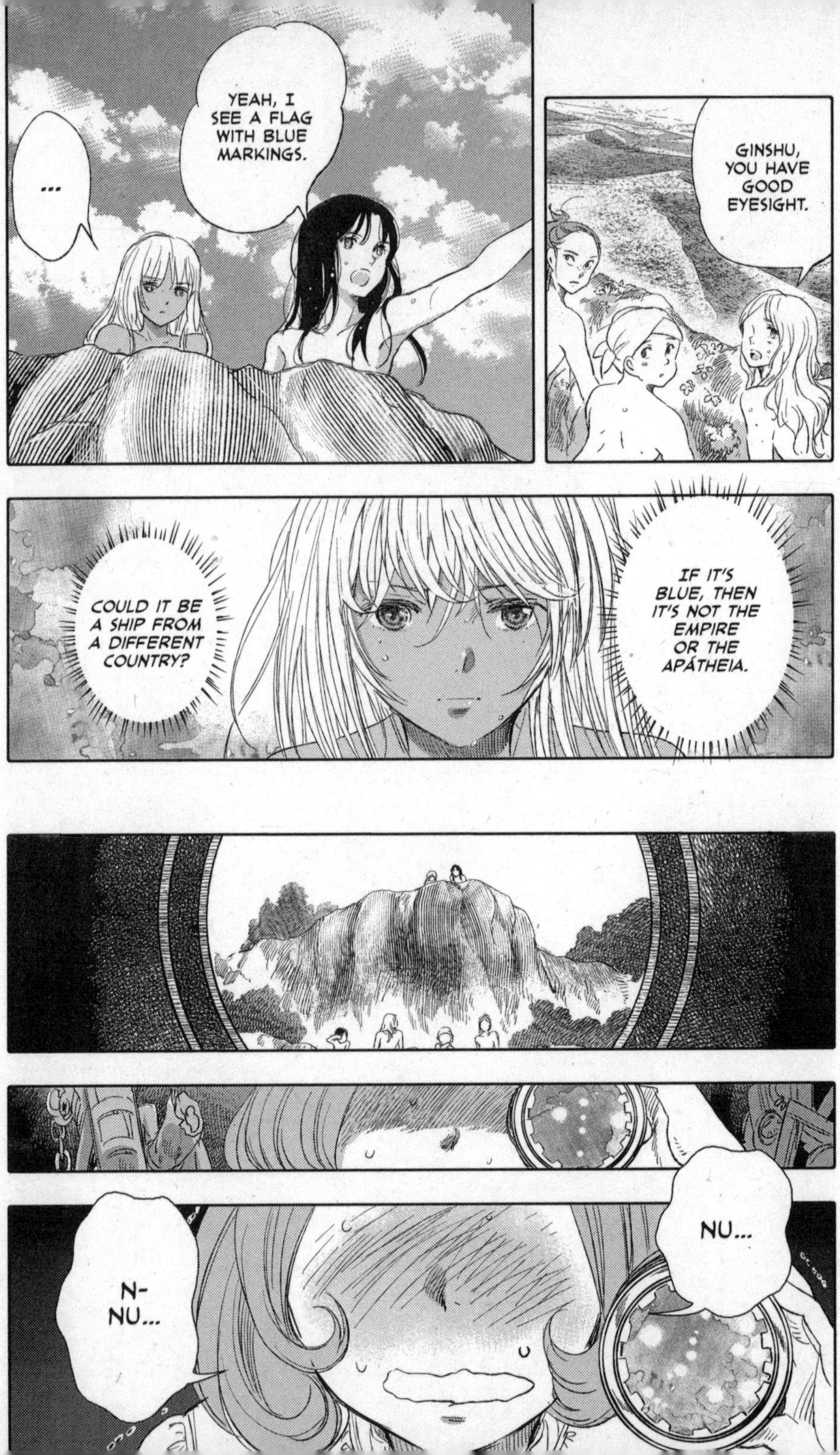
GINSHU, YOU HAVE GOOD EYESIGHT.
YEAH, I SEE A FLAG WITH BLUE MARKINGS.
...
IF IT'S BLUE, THEN IT'S NOT THE EMPIRE OR THE APÁTHEIA.
COULD IT BE A SHIP FROM A DIFFERENT COUNTRY?
NU...
N-NU...

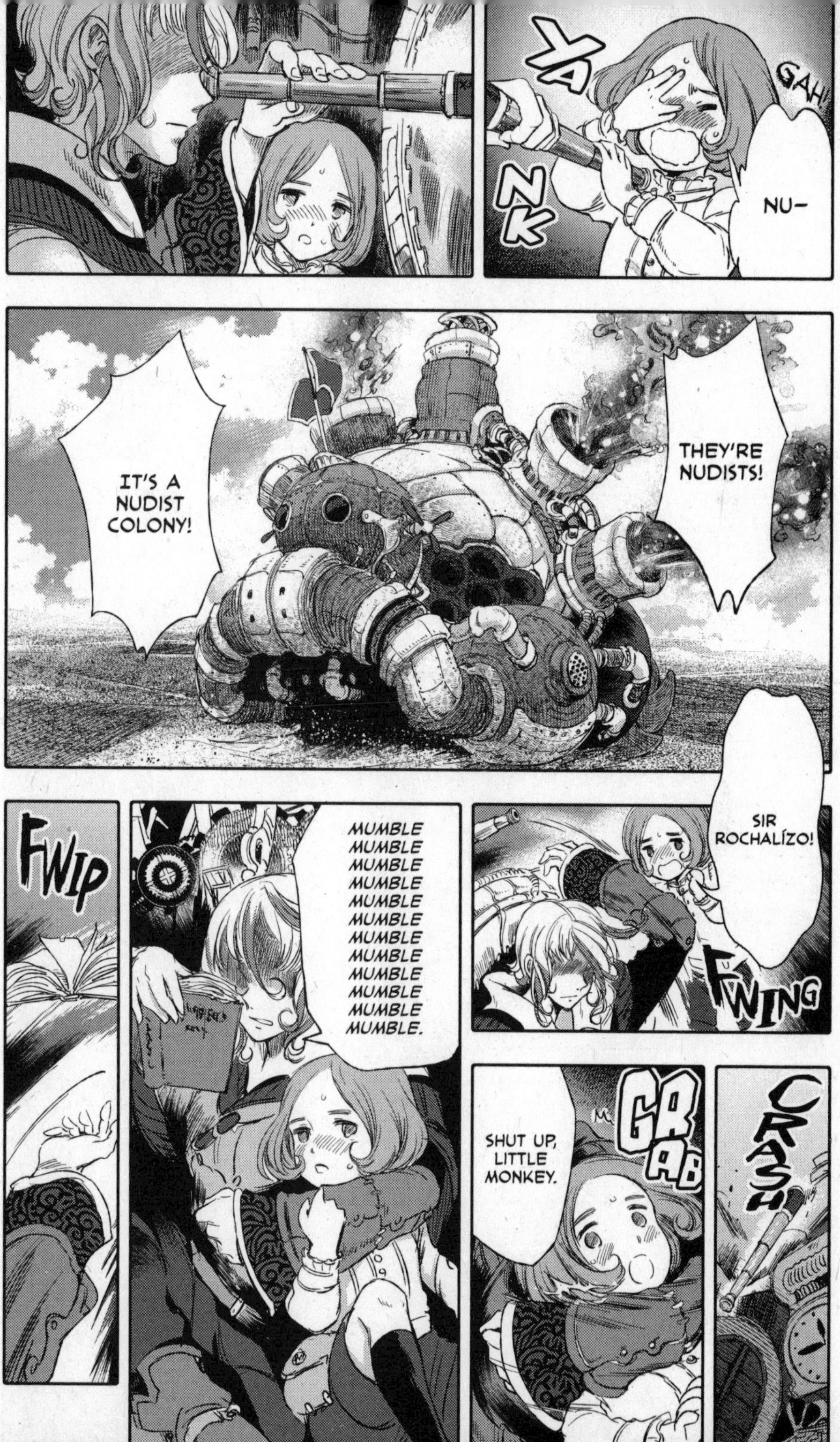

YANK
GAH!
NU–
THEY'RE NUDISTS!
IT'S A NUDIST COLONY!
SIR ROCHALÍZO!
FWING
MUMBLE MUMBLE MUMBLE MUMBLE MUMBLE MUMBLE MUMBLE MUMBLE MUMBLE MUMBLE MUMBLE MUMBLE.
FWIP
CRASH
GRAB
SHUT UP, LITTLE MONKEY.

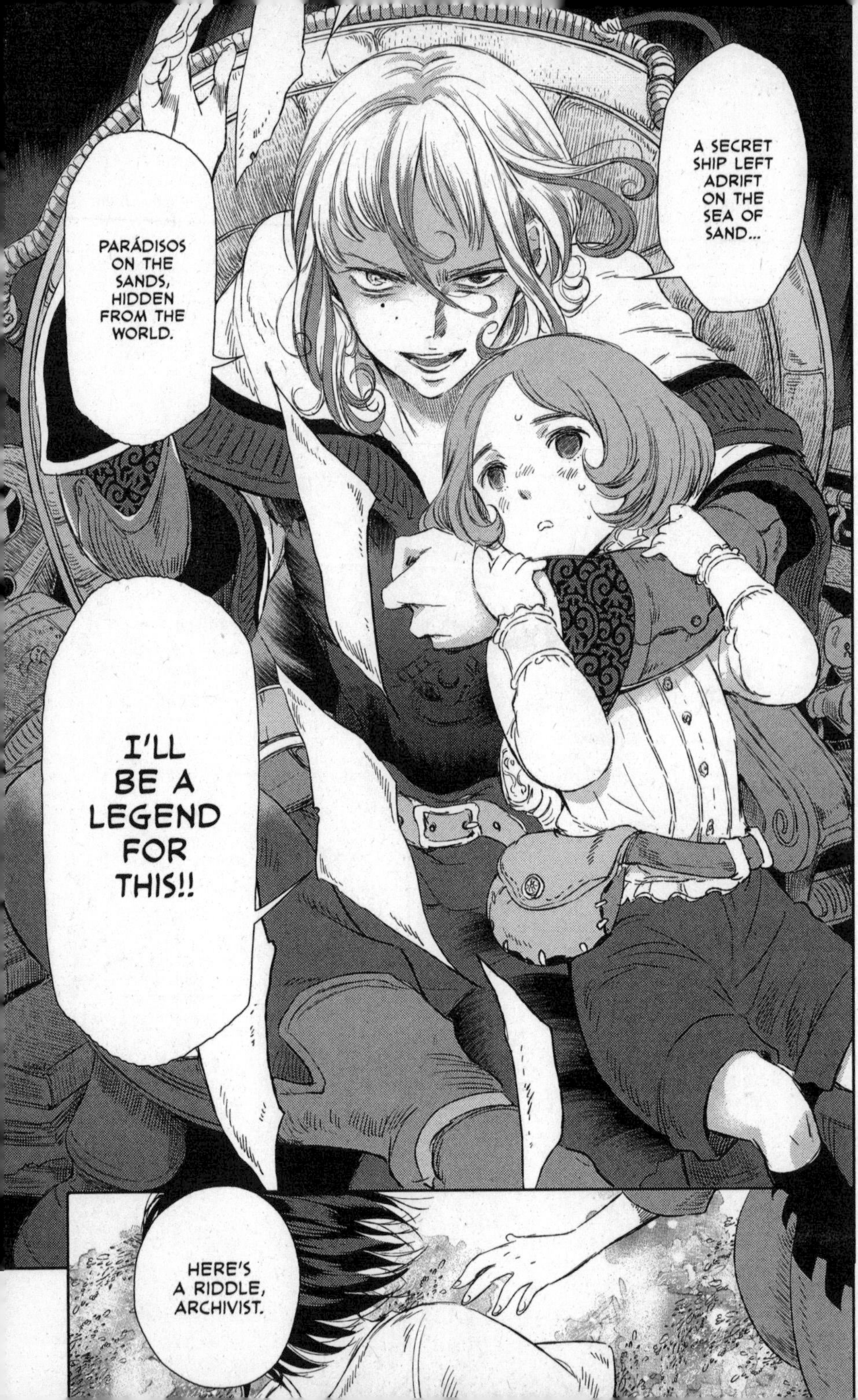
A SECRET SHIP LEFT ADRIFT ON THE SEA OF SAND...
PARÁDISOS ON THE SANDS, HIDDEN FROM THE WORLD.
I'LL BE A LEGEND FOR THIS!!
HERE'S A RIDDLE, ARCHIVIST.

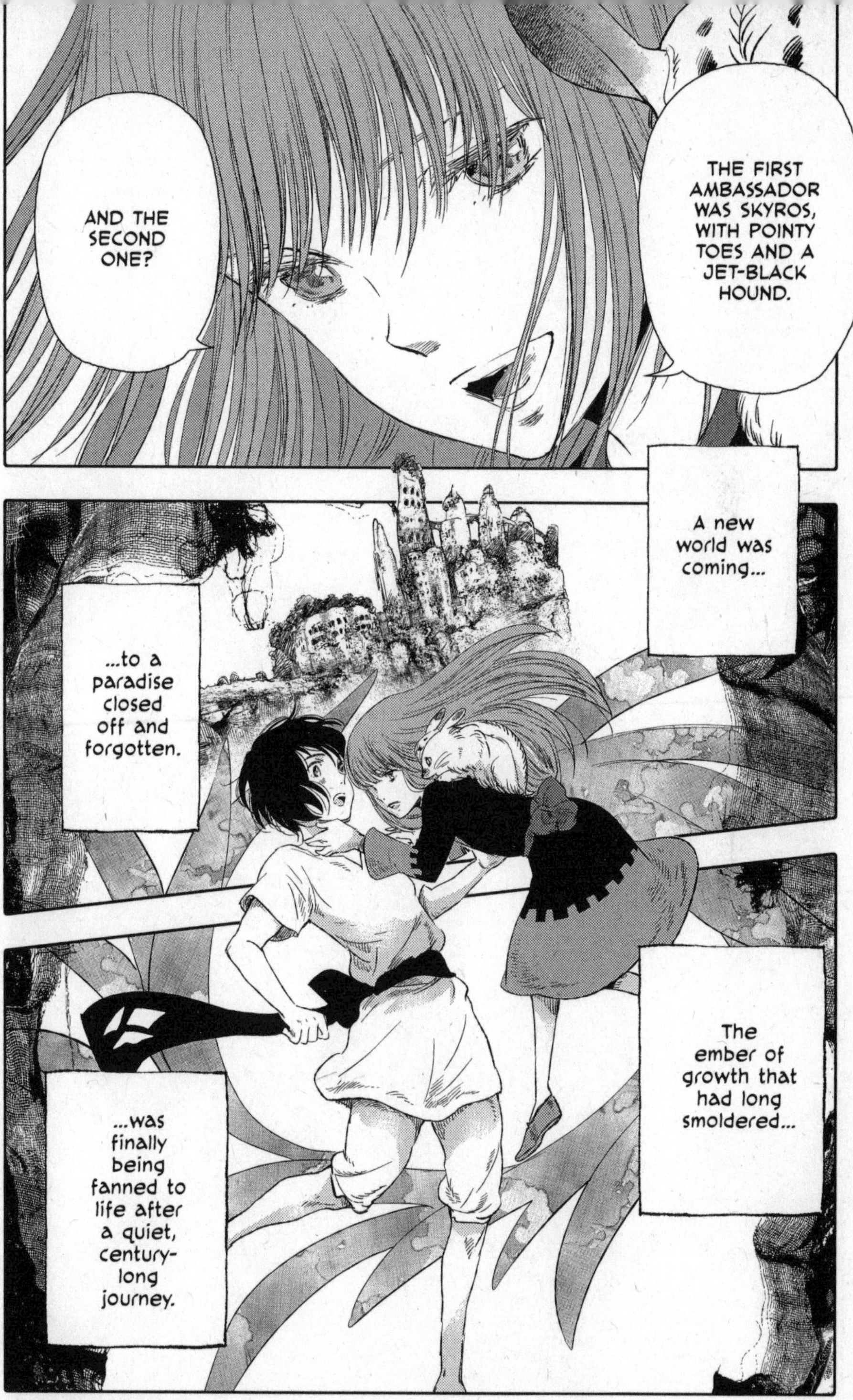
THE FIRST AMBASSADOR WAS SKYROS, WITH POINTY TOES AND A JET-BLACK HOUND.
AND THE SECOND ONE?
A new world was coming...
...to a paradise closed off and forgotten.
The ember of growth that had long smoldered...
...was finally being fanned to life after a quiet, century-long journey.

Becalmed -The End-

Children of the Whales volume 4 -The End-

A Note on Names

Those who live on the Mud Whale are named after colors in a language unknown. Abi Umeda uses Japanese translations of the names, which we have maintained. Here is a list of the English equivalents for the curious.

Aijiro	pale blue
Benihi	scarlet
Buki	kerria flower (*yamabuki*)
Chakuro	blackish brown (*cha* = brown, *kuro* = black)
Ginshu	vermillion
Hakuji	porcelain white
Jiki	golden
Kicha	yellowish brown
Kuchiba	decayed-leaf brown
Masoh	cinnabar
Neri	silk white
Nezu	mouse gray
Nibi	dark gray
Ouni	safflower red
Rasha	darkest blue, nearly black
Ro	lacquer black
Sami	light green (*asa* = light, *midori* = green)
Shinono	the color of dawn (*shinonome*)
Sienna	reddish brown
Suou	raspberry red
Taisha	red ocher
Tobi	reddish brown like a kite's feather
Tokusa	scouring rush green
Urumi	muddy gray

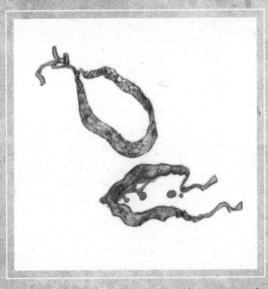

I feel like the same imaginary town always appears in my dreams. I often wake up while I'm leaving signs and symbols around town to confirm whether it's a dream or reality.

—Abi Umeda

ABI UMEDA debuted as a manga creator with the one-shot "Yukokugendan" in *Weekly Shonen Champion*. *Children of the Whales* is her eighth manga work.

CHILDREN OF THE WHALES

VOLUME 4
VIZ Signature Edition

Story and Art by Abi Umeda

Translation / JN Productions
Touch-Up Art & Lettering / Annaliese Christman
Design / Julian (JR) Robinson
Editor / Pancha Diaz

KUJIRANOKORAHA SAJOUNIUTAU Volume 4
© 2015 ABI UMEDA
First published in Japan in 2015 by AKITA PUBLISHING CO., LTD., Tokyo
English translation rights arranged with AKITA PUBLISHING CO., LTD. through
Tuttle-Mori Agency, Inc., Tokyo

Printed in the U.S.A.

Published by VIZ Media, LLC
P.O. Box 77010
San Francisco, CA 94107

10 9 8 7 6 5 4 3 2 1
First printing, May 2018

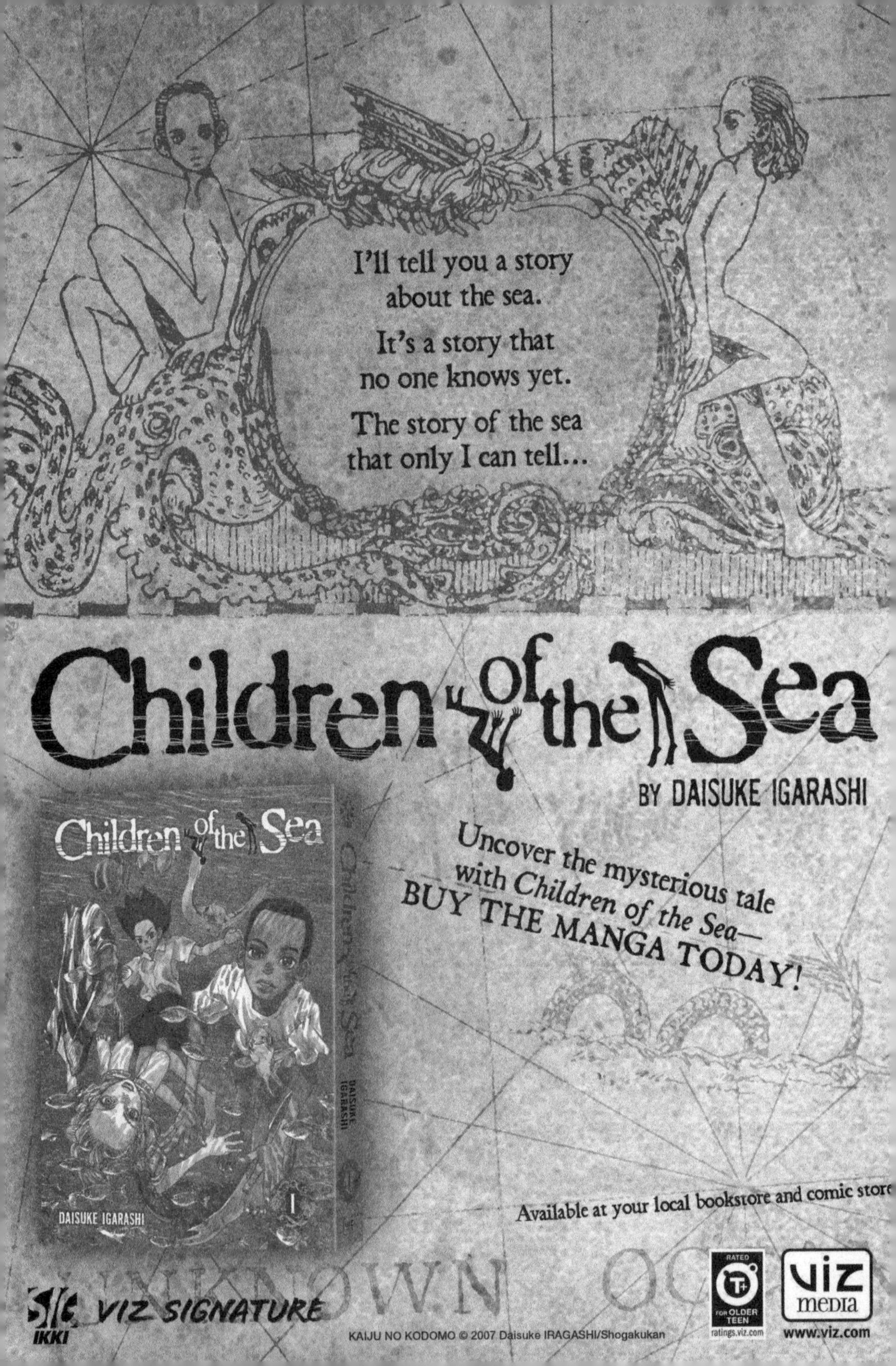

I'll tell you a story about the sea.
It's a story that no one knows yet.
The story of the sea that only I can tell...
Children of the Sea
BY DAISUKE IGARASHI
Children of the Sea
DAISUKE IGARASHI
1
Uncover the mysterious tale with Children of the Sea—
BUY THE MANGA TODAY!
Available at your local bookstore and comic store
VIZ SIGNATURE
IKKI
KAIJU NO KODOMO © 2007 Daisuke IRAGASHI/Shogakukan
RATED T+ FOR OLDER TEEN
ratings.viz.com
viz media
www.viz.com

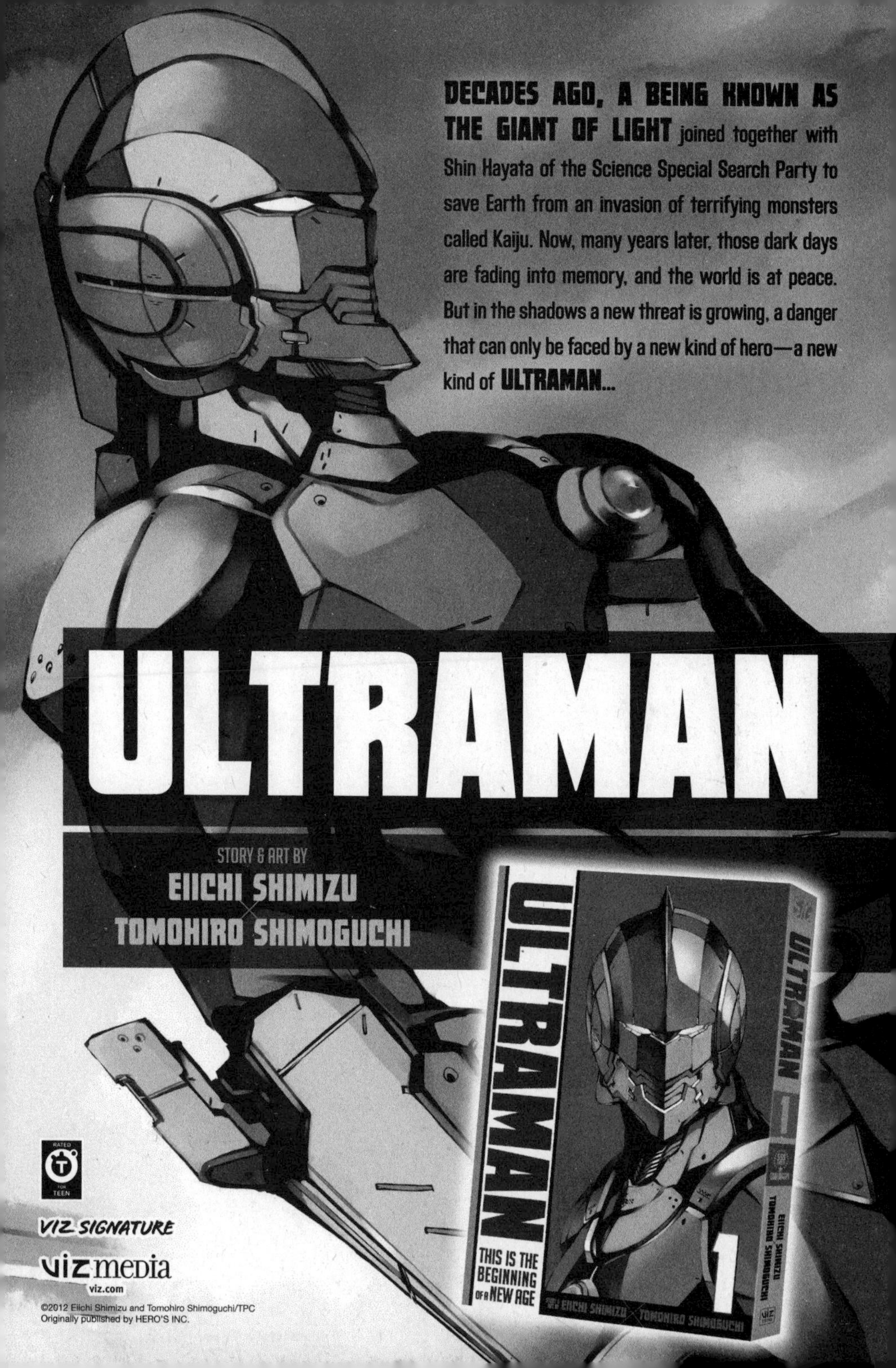
DECADES AGO, A BEING KNOWN AS THE GIANT OF LIGHT joined together with Shin Hayata of the Science Special Search Party to save Earth from an invasion of terrifying monsters called Kaiju. Now, many years later, those dark days are fading into memory, and the world is at peace. But in the shadows a new threat is growing, a danger that can only be faced by a new kind of hero—a new kind of **ULTRAMAN...**
ULTRAMAN
STORY & ART BY
EIICHI SHIMIZU
TOMOHIRO SHIMOGUCHI
ULTRAMAN
THIS IS THE BEGINNING OF A NEW AGE
1
RATED T FOR TEEN
VIZ SIGNATURE
viz media
viz.com
©2012 Eiichi Shimizu and Tomohiro Shimoguchi/TPC
Originally published by HERO'S INC.

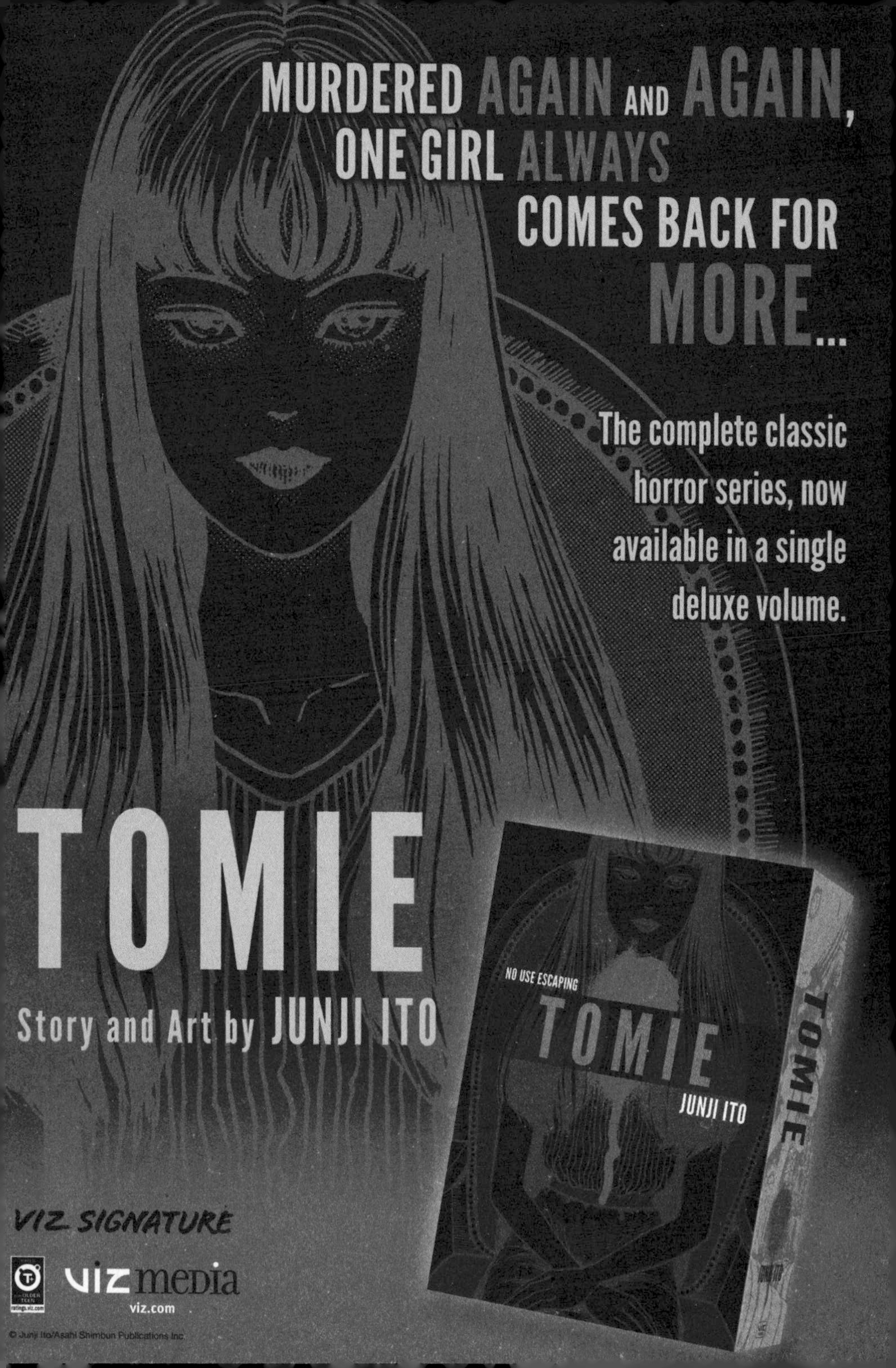
MURDERED AGAIN AND AGAIN,
ONE GIRL ALWAYS
COMES BACK FOR
MORE...
The complete classic horror series, now available in a single deluxe volume.
TOMIE
Story and Art by JUNJI ITO
NO USE ESCAPING
TOMIE
JUNJI ITO
TOMIE
VIZ SIGNATURE
OLDER TEEN
ratings.viz.com
VIZ media
viz.com
© Junji Ito/Asahi Shimbun Publications Inc.

MOBILE SUIT GUNDAM THUNDERBOLT

In the Universal Century year 0079, the space colony known as Side 3 proclaims independence as the Principality of Zeon and declares war on the Earth Federation. One year later, they are locked in a fierce battle for the Thunderbolt Sector, an area of space scarred by the wreckage of destroyed colonies. Into this maelstrom of destruction go two veteran Mobile Suit pilots: the deadly Zeon sniper Daryl Lorenz, and Federation ace Io Fleming. It's the beginning of a rivalry that can end only when one of them is destroyed.

STORY AND ART
YASUO OHTAGAKI
ORIGINAL CONCEPT BY
HAJIME YATATE
AND **YOSHIYUKI TOMINO**

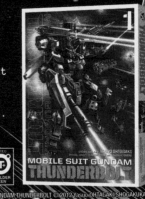

RATED
T+
FOR OLDER
TEEN

MOBILE SUIT GUNDAM
THUNDERBOLT

viz media
viz.com

MOBILE SUIT GUNDAM THUNDERBOLT ©2012 Yasuo OHTAGAKI/SHOGAKUKAN
©SOTSU · SUNRISE

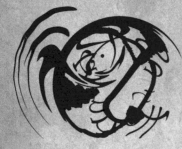

THIS IS THE LAST PAGE!

Children of the Whales has been printed in the original Japanese format to preserve the orientation of the original artwork.

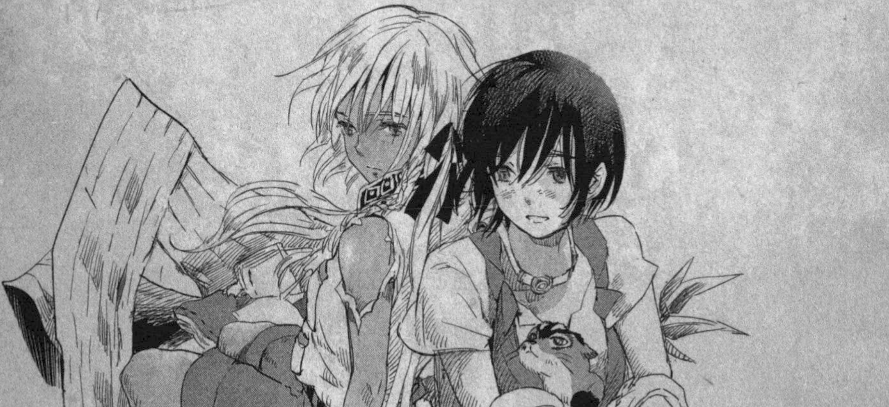